Ann Dwyer's
Easy Waters of California
• NORTH •

Ann Dwyer's
Easy Waters of California
• NORTH •

A GUIDE BOOK FOR NEW & NOVICE
• CANOEISTS & KAYAKERS •

Ann Dwyer

Disclaimer

This book is only a guide. It is not exact in any manner. The subject matter is fluid and capable of creating changes in its surroundings. Please use good judgment in interpreting the contents making wise and safe decisions.

River maps by Gail Kreuzberger and Ann Dwyer
Cartoons by Ann Dwyer and William Ribar, artist
Photos by Ann Dwyer unless otherwise credited
Cover design by Randi at Studio M

First Edition printed in July 2000

ISBN 0-9672880-0-2
Library of Congress Catalog Card Number: 00-092170

GBH Press
P.O. Box 1140
Windsor, CA 95492

This book is dedicated to my grandchildren
who often join me paddling.

Grace and Scott Hollingsworth
Erica and Jennifer Dwyer
Lauren and Evelyn Dwyer
Aaron, Kevin, Nathan, and Heather
Thoelecke

PREFACE

It was eighteen years ago when I said I would rewrite my book, *Canoeing Waters of California* but not reprint it. What a long and venturesome eighteen years it has been. I have created and sold two retail paddlesport stores, Canoe Trips West in Marin County and California Rivers in Sonoma County, designed and manufactured Class II kayaks as CEO of Kiwi Kayak Company, lead many canoe and kayak trips, taught canoe and kayak classes, and lead several month-long foreign trips. I also sold Kiwi Kayak Trips and Classes and Kiwi Kayak Company. During the years I was actively researching for the new book and in the "off season" busy writing it. The book was never forgotten but most often put "on hold" as my time was consumed by my business activities.

After the sale in 1998 of Kiwi Kayak Company the book has been my primary project. The name of the book has changed several times, but the format was finally established, with the state of California divided into North and South, the north section of it being this, the first book. I had the most fun doing the research, a.k.a. paddling. There were many waterways to explore and favorites to rerun, information to seek from other paddlers and agencies with knowledge about flows and access locations. Property owners proved interesting, as some would allow me (with my wrinkles and white hair) access, but when I mentioned I was writing a book said sorry, but "Please don't put it in your book." We found the Scott River with double barriers at the bridges. A local rancher rushing to us in his four-wheeler said that the bird watchers wanted cattle fanced away from the river. My friend's binoculars created his wheeled activity. And then there was the woman who had sold land to the state for a freeway and was keeping paddlers off this land thinking it was still hers. A phone call to CalTrans and a search of the tax records brought about a cease to her intrusions and an opening of a parking area (I'm sure others besides me were involved). Rancheria Creek access had a new property owner and let trespassers know with a sign. Some very nice paddlers or fishermen cleared the steep bank by the road and cut some steps for river access. Thank you from all of us. And so it goes. Fishermen do "blaze" some trails for paddlers as both activities share the same waterways.

With this book, *Easy Waters of California*, finished what will I do? Go paddling! I have yet to explore about five hundred miles of the waterways mentioned in the book, especially the rivers in western Nevada and the San Joaquin area. There are also about five hundred miles of rivers and sloughs that belong in the book yet to be "researched". Can you believe that there are probably three thousand miles of Class I and II waters north of Fresno for canoeing and kayaking?

Who is going exploring with me? The last time I tried a new run on the upper Russian River in Redwood Valley, the four of us all capsized, crawled through blackberry vines and poison oak, crept over a teetery log jam, and lowered our kayaks down the vertical face of a dam on this small benign creek. Then there was the run on Sonoma Creek, one with Randy Hodges that was tricky and technical, flowing through Kenwood and Boyes Springs. The second year of Randy's railroad-Noyo River outing had us arriving at the take-out just at dark, tired and shivering (though I had not capsized and was wearing a wet suit). But the upper Napa River with Andrea Wolf was a real challenge as we kept being ensnared by willow trees across the river, finally gave up at the back end of a winery, one where Andrea used to work. Running Putah Creek with Jerry Hetzer was cooling on a 107 degree day near Winters as we were trapped and capsized a time or two.

Now readers, we, the explorers, have made river running easier and safer for you. Do heed our warnings. If you are also an explorer and have discovered a new run, please let me know. Thank you to all the explorers, Randy Hodges, Terry Sauter-Haag and Gary Haag, Dick Schwind, Charlie Martin, Bob Foote, and so many more.

And that's not all. I have a long list "when the book is finished" of things to do, the top one being to learn how to "roll." Gail Jonas assured me she has had great success in teaching the maneuver. And there is the new Class II kayak I will be getting on the market. Not to mention, Southern California has already asked for their book.

Sounds like more research, the best part. Dragonfly Designs and Kayak Paddle Pool are waiting in the wings for my time and energy.

Happy paddling,

Ann Dwyer   June 2000
addragonfly@pon.net

HAVE A HAPPY DAY....

William Ribar, Artist

ACKNOWLEDGEMENTS

My name should not be in the title of this book, I was just the one who made the promise eighteen years ago, "I will not republish (meaning Canoeing Waters of California) but will rewrite. The knowledge incorporated in this new effort is from all those who paddled with me, even the ones willing to go exploring on a run that started as a skinny blue line on a map. Those who gave me information about runs I was curious about and wanted to try. The copious notes of the volunteers who edited the chapters as I completed them were invaluable in correcting copy and updating my memory. Thank you to my paddling buddies of the Kopapa Kayak Club (formerly Kiwi Kayak Club) who joined me at all times of the year on unscouted waters and in a variety of situations to assist in my waterway knowledge. We had some great times and experiences. But first there were those who returned the river run information request sheets I mailed and handed out in 1983. Yes, these were updated, especially the thick pile from Charles Albright. He and I spent one Tuesday night in Reno as he made changes on each run over pizza then continuing after the pool session was underway outside on a bench. Then more corrections by phone at ten at night (he had to go paddling after work first) when the chapter was finished.

The last push happened May 26, 2000 on the John Day River in Oregon at three am sitting up in my sleeping bag staring at the stars. Myy mind was spinning likebeing in a swirling eddy realizing "the book" was close to finished. If I hired help and organized well, I could have it off to the printer by the end of June.

Form "filler-outers and returners":
Jean Starkweather, Sue Beittel, Keith Miller, John Dunlap, Elizabeth Terwilliger, Steve Hart, Eileen Simard, Sharon C. Cupp, John T. Hawthorne, Bob Foote, Carl Sawyer, Jim Kirwan, Bill Tuthill, Bob Hanson, Herb & Mary Fitz, Charles A. Beazell, Bob York, Bob & Jean Hackamack, Wini Heppler, Bill Hitchings, Jim Sughrue, L.G. Hope, Joe & Elsie Handy, Eric Erickson, Shiela Junge, Leon J. Dura, and Charles Albright.

My kayaking buddies:

Andrea Wolf, Edy Sorensen, Richard D. Arendt, Janis M. Arendt, Marta Anatra, Evan Anatra, Steve Kreuper, Connie Diernisse, Ron Rumney, Susan Watson, Robin Hoegerman, Marc Alexander,Timothy I. Aoki, Jan Aoki, Ann Klug, Hannah Klug, Rick Klug, Nate Klug, Robert L. Nelson, Don Davis, Holly Callaghan, Kay Brady, Mark Woodworth, Wendy Page, Lauren Kateley, Kim Arfsten, Marti Wagner, Don George, Katherine Spivy, Myfanwy Plank, Lenora Thoelecke, Jennifer Dwyer, Erica Dwyer, Pen Dwyer, Lowell Dwyer, Paul thoelecke, Heather Thoelecke, Nathan Thoelecke, Arlene Wasserman, Jon Solter, Rob Nelson, Pat Solter, Simone Wilson, Betty Verse, Gray Gallogly, Gloria Linder, Suzy Gebhardt-Clark, Rosemarie Bowler, Pat Duclos, Linda Selover, Stephen Rauch, Pam Cook, Doris Golden, Steve Wilkie, Lois Phillips, Bill Cutts, Mary Ann Cutts, Gerald Hetzer, Tyson Wolf, Rachael Krugman, Barbara Pritchard, Mike Vorysowicz, Barry Lipsky, Tom Baumgras, Dan Phy, Pat Stie, A.J. Pike, Wilson B. Goddard, Kelly Ingle, Ralph Daniels, Stanley Searles, Louisa Arndt, Marge Kamb, Anne Toschi, Chris Caul, Theresa Wistrom, Jon Akre, Deanne Endobran, larry Deckard, Rob Pack, Vivian Clayton, Bijili Abbey, Lois Frantz, Lindy Frantz, Maruice Robbon, Dennis Lewon, Stuart Daren, Miles Everett, Ron Allgood, Matt Bradle, Robert Bradle, Ginny Anderson, Kathy Haimsen, Kevin Thoelecke, Aaron Thoelecke, Joanne Mattison, Jim Mattison, Randy Hodges, Carolyn Hodges, Amy Hodges, Ella Hodges, and William Hodges. This is an incomplete list, please add your name if you belong here! Thank you for joining me.

And then there were all the canoe trips on the Russian, Eel, Klamath, and Trinity Rivers, the paddle around San Francisco Bay with friends, and those who joined me on the three hundred mile paddle down the Sacramento River, the trips of other clubs I went on, the races at Elk Horn Slough put on by Mark Pastick and Margaret Collins at Kayak Connection, the Angel Island Races put on by Sea Trek, the canoe classes at Laguna Grande in Seaside organized by Dawn Cope followed by a trip on the Carmel River, Marin Canoe Club trips, and more, and more....

Many agencies were contacted in my search for information, they have been very helpful; the various Forest Service Districts, National Parks, State Parks, Chambers of Commerce, Fish and Game Department, Recreation and Park Dept. local waterway organizations, even the Fresno Police Department as they would know where the river access locations would be downstream of US-99. Wherever I thought I could get information, I phoned. (My thoughtful children gifted me with a cell phone to help cut my phone costs.)

River access property owners were asked if they would agree to having their access location listed in a book. The answer was generally ,"No" quickly followed by, "but you are welcome to cross my property to go paddling." Their requests have been honored.

The on-going encouragment from Randy Hodges, Bill Hitchings, Wini Heppler, Andrea Wolf, Jerry Hetzer, Terry Sauter Haag, Gary Haag, Miles Everett, Ralph Daniels, Louisa Arndt and my very positive children: Lowell, Louise, Larry, and Lenora definitely helped. Many others kept the positive words coming.

Very special thanks to the chapter editors for their corrections and suggestions: Terry Sauter Haag, Gary Haag, Neil Rucker, Wini Heppler, Bill Griffith, Nancy Dagle, Leon Dura, Charles Albright and Don Garrell. More welcome suggestions from: Penny Wells, Sharon Schumaker, Bruce Schumaker, Joanne Olson, Eric Olson, Miles Everett, and many more.

The June 2000 "wrapup — off to the printer select group," who I literally "couldn't have done it without you" included: Ella Hodges, Amy Hodges, Kevin Thoelecke, Lenora Thoelecke, and Aaron Thoelecke. All these were assisted by the professional expertise of computer installer, Pagemaker, and proof reading experts: Jean Vi Lenthe and Rick Klug.

EASY WATERS OF CALIFORNIA
NORTH

CONTENTS

CHAPTER

CHAPTER 1 - READ AND HEED

California waterways in this long lovely state of such varying topography, rainfall and climate gives canoeists and kayakers an endless variety of paddling locations year round. The winter rains supply the smaller creeks with water deep enough for a pleasant day run and late spring snow-melt fills the rivers on both sides of the Sierra for whitewater excitement. Tidewaters are available year round generally better in the fall and winter when the climate is cooler and not as subject to strong afternoon winds. In the writing of this book I added up the number of miles mentioned, not including lakes, totals over 2,600 of mostly Class I and II waters for new and novice paddlers. By paddling twenty miles each weekend on a different run, it would take two and a half years to explore every mile in this book. But be aware, there are more than 500 eligible miles not yet included.

Let's go, lets have some fun paddling...

First, rent a canoe or kayak and give it a try, go on a guided trip, take classes on how to paddle and especially safety skills, then buy a canoe or kayak and the necessary equipment, join a club so you have paddling buddies and enjoy!

This can be a couple activity, family or solo, any way works. In the Kopapa Kayak Club there are many paddlers without their spouses, both men and women. In contrast the Marin Canoe Club is mostly couples and families though the trips generally consist of equal numbers of canoes and kayaks.

About this book...

Now that you have this book you should know that it is out of date and the information incorrect BECAUSE a tree fell down! It fell across a river written about in this book! There is no way that this book can be absolutely correct, although I and others tried to be as accurate as possible. But I'm writing about moving waterways that have constant pressures on them caused by natural forces like running water, wind, beaver, and us. Man with his tractors, bulldozers, and mammoth shovels scooping up tons of gravel for building more freeways for us to drive on to get to the rivers we wish to paddle. "We have found the enemy and it is us."

The geographic reorganization of California

California has been divided in half, sort of, folded and snipped across, starting at Carmel then east to and north of Fresno, east some more then northeast to Lake Crowley and into Nevada and north to Oregon. This north California area has been divided into eight chapters. The chapters are geographic to include the terminal location of waterways. The Pacific Ocean is the terminus for North Coast, Eureka to Oregon and South Coast chapters. Sacramento River carries into San Francisco Bay waters from the central valley, northeast corner of the state by way of the Delta. Then it becomes part of The Delta Chapter, where rivers from the east and west join including the San Joaquin. The San Joaquin is its own chapter flowing north through its valley and having several large rivers enter from the Sierra Nevada in the east. The San Francisco Bay is also a chapter by itself though the Sacramento River flows into it after collecting the waters of the Delta and San Joaquin. Several rivers flowing down the east slope of the Sierra Nevada terminate in desert lakes in western Nevada, they have been included in the East Slope chapter.

Of course, there are exceptions; the middle and north forks of the Feather River originate close to Nevada then flow west north of the sierra.. The Feather River flowing from Lake Oroville has been included in the Sacramento Valley chapter. A few lakes and lagoons have been mentioned. Humboldt and Arcata Bays have been included. Many sloughs, great paddling locations when the river flows slow, are included.

How to read the write-ups...

The write-ups are composed so that the most important and critical information is first. The first line is the main waterway, followed by the specific location of the run, the distance, and finally the river classification. Consult the abbreviations and glossary for explanations. Classifications can change very quickly as flows are affected by rain and dam releases. In the last three years there have been many more changes with the internet becoming widely available and government agencies becoming a part of the new technology. River flows are now available on web sites and newspapers are also now publishing flow information. There are more paddlers and others are seeking flow information.

The "SEASON" information is approximate and should be used as a guide but not an absolute! An "All Year" classification means when the flow is gentle which it would not be after a severe storm or hot weather causing a heavy snow nelt. Use common sense and be safe!

River miles are approximate. They vary according to the flow. At lower flows, paddlers frequently cross rivers in search of the deep channel. Higher flows go over bushes and rocks that lower flows necessitated going around.

Reading the confusing maps...

The organization of the waterways of California - North was decided according to where the river terminated. Did it flow into the ocean, San Francisco Bay, Sacramento River or into a lake in western Nevada or some other location. The termination of the river determined which chapter of the state would "claim it. ' The Sacramento River has 2 terminal locations, the river itself or in The Delta area before it flows into San Pablo Bay, the north portion of San Francisco Bay. One exception is the north and middle forks of the Feather River that originate close to Nevada and flow through a slit between Sierra Nevada and Cascades so they have been added to the East Slope rivers. However the Feather river flowing from Lake Oroville ends in the Sacramento river so it is part of that chapter. Cache Creek is pumped almost dry in the summer but with a winter flow

Road maps are oriented north but not all rivers flow north. The river maps are drawn to flow up the map as the river itself flows when being paddled. If this is confusing at first turn the river map to face north to relate it to a road map. When on the river have it face from page bottom to top. There are directional flow arrows on the rivers unless they are also affected by tidal action. Only primary roads are on the maps. The maps used to aid in the book maps are referred to in the write-ups. Bridges are marked with two dots and a curve in the flow of the water. Hand-drawn maps were used as they were quicker to execute than computer generated maps. (Haste has been of extreme importance in completing this book.) Be warned, roads change names often, sometimes more than twice. Roads also are changed by similar conditions that change rivers, though maybe not beavers.

"BEWARE:"...

As a new or novice paddler it is your duty to learn how to paddle safely in the craft you choose, how to know what is safe paddling, and how to be prepared to help fellow paddlers when needed.

As the saying goes "It is better to be safe than sorry." This is a very true statement for paddlesports. Read the warnings, wear a Coast Guard sproved lifevest (PFD) of the correct size (NO! Don't buy one for Mike that he will "grow into".) and snuggly fastened. The vest is pushed by the water and can be pushed right over the head if it is too large, not snuggly fastened and the wearer is on the skinny side. Be safe, NOT SORRY! In running a river, be cautious, make sure the bottom and entire rapid can be "read" before going. When in doubt get out and scout. Strainers trap paddleboats and paddlers, hold them and drown them. Snags can catch open boats and hold them, even kayak cockpits. Footwear should protect the feet from broken glass and stay on when swimming. Use sun protection for skin and eyes. Eyeglasses often come off backwards. Duck down and bring paddle parallel to the boat when going through bushes. Better yet stay out of bushes.

International Scale of River Classifications

CLASS I • Moving water with a few riffles and small waves. Few or no obstructions.

CLASS II • Easy rapids with waves up to 3 feet, and wide, clear easy channels that are obvious without scouting. Some maneuvering is required.

CLASS III • Rapids with high, irregular waves often capable of swamping an open canoe. Narrow passages that often require complex maneuvering. May require scouting from shore,

iV
CLASS VI • Long, difficult rapids with constricted passages that often require precise maneuvering in very turbulent waters. Scouting from shore is often necessary, and conditions make rescue difficult. Generally not possible for open canoes. Boaters in deck canoes or canoes with airbags, and kayakers should be able to Eskimo roll.

CLASS V • Extremely difficult, long, and very violent rapids with highly congested routed which nearly always must be scouted from shore. Rescue conditions are difficult, and there is significant hazard to life in event of a mishap. Ability to Eskimo roll is essential for kayaks and canoes.

CLASS VI • **SUICIDE!**

Flows and how to find them...

We want our sport to be as safe as possible so trial lawyers will use the river for enjoyment and not for law suits. We do not want to be legislated off of our rivers BECAUSE they are considered too dangerous. Prevent accidents and know how to help when needed. One accident "hurts" all paddlers.

Class I and II rivers vary much more than whitewater runs. Often large rocks that are firmly positioned cause the rapids and change very little. A rainstorm can quickly result in the opening of one gravel channel and the closing of another on a Class I waterway. Class I and II boaters should be skilled at "reading" the flows that they are running.

Where to find cfs flows

California Data Exchange	http://cdec.water.ca.gov
Dream Flows	http://www.dreamflows.com/flows..html
USGS	http://water.wr.usgs.gov
California Creekin'	http://www.creekin.net/index.htm'
Hodges	http://sonic.net/kkct/whitewat.htm
K-Phone	916.368.8682

Women as kayakers

Women make great kayakers, as good as men. Wow! Here's a sport where females do as well as males and are respected by the male population for their kayaking skills. After all when in whitewater garb paddlers are identified by the color of their kayak or helmet or both. Change clothes or boat and no one would know who was paddling what kayak. My paddle jacket is identical to the jacket worn by one of our fellow male paddlers. The heavier female hips and lighter shoulders than males is definitely a plus when kayaking as the center of gravity is lower making their kayaks more stable. Women learn skills differently than men. Men tend to want to more quickly to the next level of paddling keeping the adrenaline flowing. Whereas women want to learn more thoroughly the skills they've just acquired before venturing to a higher level. After all men have to kill the mastodon to feed the tribe and women have to tend the children and keep the home fires burning so there is a tribe to feed. Each is just as important as the other. So as the males are daring their newly found skills on more exciting runs and capsizing in every rapid, women are slowing getting their confidence level secure before going up to the next level. After a while the males realize that they have to slow down and work on their technique to progress to the next level. With females having their skills in god command they are quickly moving up to the higher levels. The learning curves look like this as they both arrive at the higher level at the same time. The male curve is almost vertical then more horizontal, as the female curve slowly goes vertical after a long horizontal line followed by a steep vertical climb.

New waterways

Before venturing on a new waterway please read about it first to learn about the pluses and warnings. Check ous⁻<he p9,dling dA;tance, length of the shuttle, possible weather conditions, check on the flow, and warn fellow paddlers that it is an exploratory trip. Make sure the group paddling skill level is equal to the adventure, the includes safety training and expertise. Have emergency plans, just in case of an accident.

GLOSSARY

KAYAK:

Bow — front of the kayak (bow to the front)
Stern — back of the kayak (you are stern behind)
Deck — top of the kayak
Cockpit — opening for the paddler to enter and exit
Grabloops — handles of webbing, plastic pulls or handles molded in at each end of the
      kayak
Footbraces — adjustable foot pedals on the bow of the kayak
Float bag — added inflatable flotation in the bow or stern ends
Pillar — lateral stiff foam support inside kayak
Rudder — adjustable blade added at the stern of the kayak
Skeg — adjustable blade on the bottom stern end of the kayak
Release valve — small plastic button that unscrews to release pressure or water

KAYAK PADDLE:

Two-piece or break-down, separates in the center for feathering one blade
Blade — large sections at paddle ends that go in the water
Spoon — curved blades
Flat — no curve in the blade
Shaft — center pole section of the paddle
Drip ring — Plastic ring that fits on shaft near the blade to stop water drips

CANOE:

Bow — front end
(Fore — direction of bow).
Stern — rear end
(Aft — direction of stern).
Gunwale — added top to the open sides of the canoe.
Thwart — center supports going from gunwale to gunwale.
Decks — end caps on the bow and stern often having a handle.
Painter — rope attached to the decks, about 16' long.
Keel — longitudinal support at mid-center of the bottom.
Midships — center of the canoe.
Trim — balance of the canoe fore and aft.
Tumblehome — upper side of the canoe that curves in.

CANOE PADDLE:

Blade — the wide part that goes in the water
Shaft — the pole that is held by the lower hand
Grip — the cross section that is held by the upper hand

Flow — the movement of the water

Down-river "V" — a "V" pointing downriver caused by the flow

Up-river"V" — an up-river pointing "V" in the flow caused by an obstruction

Standing waves — constant wave action in one location

Pillow — stream flowing higher over a rock or other object ("Pillows are stuffed with rocks")

Eddy — side current flowing upstream or in a circle caused by the power of the downriver flow, also downriver below large rocks or obstructions

Safe haven — beach or eddy where a paddler can find quiet water out of the current

Snag — a tree part that creates a navigational hazard

Log jam — a pile up of logs and debris that could be in an eddy or across the entire stream.

Strainer — tree or tree branch that allows the water to flow through but not a paddle craft of paddler

Keeper, souse hole, reversal — Flow below a rock or rapid where the water drops down creating a vertical circular motion with the flow going upstream

ABBREVIATIONS

3 - SFB	San Francisco Bay
4 - NC	North Coast
5 - EO	Eureka to Oregon
6 - SV	Sacramento Valley
7 - TD	The Delta
8 - SJ	San Joaquin Area
9 - ES	East Slope
10 - SC	South Coast

In write-ups and maps:

riv.	river
cr.	creek
sl.	slough
St.	Street
Ave.	Avenue
Rd.	Road
Blvd.	Boulevard
I - 880	Interstate - 880
US - 101	United States
SR - 39	State Route
CR - 46	County Route
SP	State Park
*cpgr.	campground
pkg.	parking
*RRm.	restroom
C. of C.	Chamber of Commerce
FS	Forest Service
Hdq.	Headquarters
AAA	American Automobile Association

cfs	cubic feet per second
pfd	personal flotation device
mi.	miles
Cl.	Class
NACO	North American Camping Organization
L.	Lake
Bch.	Beach
KOA	Campgrounds of America
sta.	station
Vets.	Veterans
Mem.	Memorial
Co.	County
Pk.	Park
Pkng.	Parking
N	North
S	South
E	East
W	West

(Plus combinations like NW or SE, etc.)

R, rt.	Right
L.	Left
Rec.	Recreation
*SRA	State Recreation Area
Reg.	Region
*YMCA	Young Mens Christian Association
Cyn.	Canyon
*Mtn.	Mountain
*Pt.	Point
*Ft.	Fort
No. Fk.	North Fork
So. Fk.	South Fork
p.	Page
pp.	Pages
RV	Recreational Vehicle
Pk.	Peak
N. Fk.	North Fork
S. Fk.	South Fork
Info.	Information

Months of the year with 3 letter abbreviations.

No. CA	Northern California

Notes:

Chapter 2 - Equipment

You've become intrigued by paddlesports and have decided to "jump in with both feet," so to speak, and do it on your own. You've seen sea kayaks on San Francisco Bay, canoes paddling down the Russian River, and week-long canoe trips listed in the Sierra Club Outings program. So you're going to do it! This really isn't the best way to start paddling, but it is the route of more than one paddler, or ex-paddler. (It worked for Bob Foote, now a Class V open canoeist, who leads open canoe trips on the Grand Canyon and is also a canoe designer.) So with great expectations into the paddlecraft store you go. Three hours later your vehicle is topped with a shiny new paddlecraft, inside is an array of products you have no idea what to do with nor what they are, and your credit card has a new $2,000 entry. Waving good-bye from the store door is the salesperson with a happy smile.

STOP! There is a better way to begin paddling!

   Rent a canoe or kayak for an hour or a day.

   Better yet, **join a club** that welcomes beginning paddlers. Canoeists are often in search of a bow paddler, good spot for a beginner.

First time paddling

For that first outing here's what you will need to wear and bring if you are canoeing on a pleasant day on easy class I water:

   1. Paddle, plastic to reach your chin from the ground. (Often paddles come with the canoe.)

   2. Pfd (personal flotation device/life vest), preferably the jacket type. Wear it firmly fastened or the water could push it over your head just when you need it most.

   3. Clothing: read the labels! NO 100% cotton! Cotton kills! It wicks warmth away from the body as it drys. Wear polypropylene or a cotton-polypropylene mix or any one of the new materials designed to be worn on river trips that don't absorb water or are warm when wet. These could be costly but they could be very inexpensive at Goodwill or Salvation Army stores as cotton and polyester mixes were "in" a few years ago. NOTE: the wearing of a swim suit is not necessary as a capsize is usually done quickly without time to remove outer clothing. And underwear (Not 100% cotton) is suitable for swimming.

   4. Footwear: make sure it floats, will protect the feet when walking on sharp rocks or broken glass, is not heavy and bulky in the canoe, and is easily used for swimming, e.g. tennis shoes with holes in the toes, beach shoes with good soles or sandals that will stay on when swimming. Socks: firm in fit and no 100% cotton.

   5. Headgear: a lightweight hat that shades the face, floats, and will stay on in the wind (under the chin straps often result in the hat staying on but the sun-protective brim blows back from the face).

   6. Sunglasses & glasses strap. When paddling glasses often come off from front to back taking the back-of-the-head straps with them. If these straps float it aids in recovery but the water current may make this difficult. Glasses that do not float generally are lost, seldom recovered. There are many glasses straps and flotation devices on the market. I prefer to have a glasses strap attached to the shoulder of my pfd for my prescription glasses (tinted and darken in the sun) so

if my glasses come off they are still attached (maybe!). NOTE: On one trip, the rain made visibility difficult so my glasses were stowed and I still saw well enough to be lead kayak.

7. Also: Water; a day's supply, in easy to drink from container. In a watertight container that can be firmly attached to the canoe, bring: Lunch, sunscreen (some work best when put on several hours before going on the water), lip protection, Band-Aids, small knife, bandana. A change of clothes in the vehicle or in the canoe in a watertight bag.

WATERTIGHT CONTAINERS: Zip-lock bags, plastic jars with tight lids.

Canoeing or kayaking or both?

The best reasons to canoe:

Canoes:

> Are easy to get in
> Are good young family craft
> Can take camping gear
> Hold more gear (folding chairs)
> Are good beginner craft
> Are stable for standing and scouting rapids
> Are easy to access from docks
> On land serve as rain shelter, sort of.

Downside on canoeing:

> The canoe is heavy (or expensive if light)
> Often takes two people to carry it
> Paddling in a straight line takes longer to learn
> Trial and error canoeing works, sort of
> It must be car-topped
> Solo canoeing is slower than solo kayaking
> No back support, but can be added

Why the big growth in solo kayaking?

> No discussion on where & when to paddle
> Many kayaks can be transported in/on a vehicle
> Easier to one-person carry
> Ready to paddle, quicker on the water, maybe
> Basic strokes take less time to learn
> Quicker route to whitewater or sea kayaking
> Easier for children to paddle
> Can run whitewater with "old-age knees"
> Comfortable to sit in with back support

Downside on kayaking:

> Can't take as much gear
> Not as easy to get in and out

Difficult to access using docks
Difficult to carry a spare paddle

OK I heard you! those of you who know all about canoes and kayaks. These comments are just general statements to give a bit of knowledge to beginners and not specific to any special type of canoe or kayak. Yes, canoes come in a variety of sizes and shapes for a wide range of uses, likewise kayaks. My thoughts reflect the many miles I have paddled in the Blue Hole OCA., QStar and Kopapa kayaks. Both of these craft are well suited for Class I and II waters as are others.

What material is best for canoes?

Material:	Why?
Royalex,	RoyaliteCan take abuse, has a "memory", repairable, fairly light
Polyethylene	Has similar qualities to Royalex, costs less, heavier
Fiberglass and/or Kevlar	Best paddling canoe, easily damaged but easy to repair, light weight, especially Kevlar, expensive AluminumNoisy, easily "to talled", repair expensive, hot when its hot and cold when its cold, torn aluminum on a rock in a rapid can shred bodies and other craft that come in contact with it, large decks reflect sun

Class II canoes for novice paddlers

When tandem paddling Class II rivers the best materials that can take abuse are Royalex, Royalite and polyethylene. The recommended width is about 36" with a depth of 14" to 15" at midship and about 16' to 17' length.

Class II canoes should stay fairly dry when running Class II and II+ rapids. They should turn easily yet track well, have fairly good initial stability and good secondary stability. There should be sufficient gear space for extended camping trips when packing light. Remember the extra length is in the middle of the canoe, the ends remain the same.

General charactertics of a canoe for paddling Class I

It should be made of fiberglass, aluminum, polyethylene,
Royalex or something similar.
It is canoe shapped with two seats,
1 or 2 thwarts,
15 to 17 feet long,
35 to 36 inches wide, depth of 12 to 13 inches.

A canoe for running Class II + water should:

Be of Royalex or polyethylene or something similar.
Seats should be high enough for kneeling or use pedestals.

About kayaks...

Kayak beginners have many kayaks to choose from, they're short with large cockpits that a paddler can just get in and go. From this level most kayaks make a big jump into short, quick to respond, whitewater play boats or long skinny heavy(50 - 60 lbs.) expensive sea kayaks. There are very few Class II kayaks.

Class II kayaks for novice paddlers

What characteristics should a Class II kayak have?
> Short, about 9'
> Lightweight, about 28 - 34 lbs.
> Track, go fairly straight when paddled
> Turn quickly for technical Class II+ rapids
> Good performing boat in Class II+ rapids
> Hold gear, packing light for camping
> Knee braces for "rolling"
> Can be "Eskimo rolled"
> Comfortable, good back support
> Longer cockpit for ease of access
> Can bend knees for long paddling days

Additional gear for cold weather paddling...

Warm layered clothing that is warm when wet. Add a wool or synthetic cap or helmet, warm gloves of neoprene, or wool or synthetic, or use Pogie that provide a hand cover on the paddle, neoprene booties with a good slip-proof sole and warm when wet socks.

Be prepared to get wet

Wearing a paddle jacket generally does the job in warm weather. For cold and wet conditions add clothing under the paddle jacket. A rain hat in warm or cold weather unless a helmet is being worn is advisable. Rain pants or wet suit for the legs add polypro tights for added warmth. Neoprene zipper boots with good soles for wet cold weather will do the job. Be sure to bring a change of clothes in a dry-bag for changing on the river and another change in the car. Getting too chilled can be a miserable experience as well as life-threatening. Always remember that you have to be able to swim in whatever you wear and then possibly walk on sharp rocks.

Safety equipment

Safety equipment should be the most important part of your list.

> Life vest, PFD, Coast Guard approved. Should be the right size and worn firmly fastened.
> Painters on canoes.
> Throw rope.
> In waterproof container: lip guard, mirror, bandaids, bandana, paper & pencil, sun screen, flashlight (new batteries), (first aid kit.)
> Change of clothers in waterproof container.
> Clothes for rain and cold in a waterproof container.
> Tow rope.
> Extra paddle.

BROOKS ISLAND

TURTLE (ONCE A CHILD'S GIFT)

RICHARDSON BAY WILDLIFE

RICHARDSON BAY ARCHITECTURE

CHAPTER 3 - SAN FRANCISCO BAY

CONTENTS

Page:

SAN FRANCISCO BAY

SOUTH BAY

EAST BAY

NORTH BAY

PADDLING SAN FRANCISCO BAY

Paddling on San Francisco Bay can be like kayaking on a quiet pond or being pushed by wind and waves (following sea), wondering which of the swirling currents might be 'friendly", getting stuck in the gooey black bay mud or being pushed at a good speed by an out-going tide. The "Bay" means the entire 175+ miles of shoreline from the Golden Gate northeast to Vallejo and south to Alviso. Seven bridges span the Bay, two of note, the Golden Gate and the San Francisco-Oakland Bay Bridge which broke in the 1989 Loma Prieta Earthquake, dropping a car into the Bay. The changes since I circumnavigated the Bay in 1984-85 are mostly good; there is now more marsh in preserves and more public boat ramps.

A wide variety of boats criss-crossing the Bay make for a busy harbor. Water flowing from the Central Valley to the ocean passes through the Bay providing food for fish, crabs, clams, and shrimp. Jack London records an evening of shrimp fishing in one of his stories. Many other tales relate to the Bay. One of several children's book, *The Flying Ferryboat*, includes a kayaker.

The Bay is beautiful with its kaleidoscope of shoreline scenes that are both natural and man-made. Sea lions and birds are numerous, adding a sight and sound dimension to a paddling adventure. BEWARE! This great bay can be treacherous!

Before venturing on the bay:

1. Read and heed the tide tables (available at local dive shops, fishing and marine shops). They are full of information, including the date, time, and height of the tides. In addition to this they also contain moon and currents information as well as the adding and subtracting (from the Golden Gate) of the time and heights of the tides. (It takes a high tide 9 hours to reach Sacramento. At Alviso Slough the tide is about 2+ feet higher than at the "Gate.") Having just been stuck in the Bay mud...read and heed the tide tables.

2. Paddle a craft that is adequate for the location.

3. Wear appropriate gear that provides protection from the weather, including the wearing of a snugly-fitted pfd (life vest).

4. Be prepared for adversity with food, water, warm and rain clothes, flashlight, matches, small candle, compass, map, rope, and cell phone. (Put items that can be water-damaged in watertight containers.)

5. After deciding on the put-in and take-out locations:
    a. Calculate the time and height of high and low tides.
    b. Consult the currents in the area, especially Raccoon & Carquinez Straits, between Points San Pablo & Pedro & E. side of Alameda.
    c. Check the weather forecast for rain, wind, and fog.
    d. Calculate for larger groups; they're slower.
    f. Know the paddling skills of each participant, plan the day accordingly.
    g. In the winter, plan to be off the water one to two hours before sunset.

6. Know and obey the California Boating Laws. Paddlecraft should stay out of the way of larger boats and ships as the smaller craft cannot be easily seen and the larger craft cannot stop quickly or maneuver easily. Also the wakes of larger craft can present problems to small craft, face or quarter the waves and stay away from banks and walls that can rebound waves.

BEST TIDES: 3'-6'. When possible go in the direction of the flow of the tide, especially if the difference between high and low tide is more than 5', the power of the flow in either direction ebbing (out-going) or flooding (in-coming) will be strong. Use the flow of the tide to your advantage. If there is a goof and boats get stuck in the mud from a fast out-going tide, there are some options: wait for the next tide to come in to refloat your craft, about 3-4 hours, or somehow alert the authorities (call 911) for help which may be by helicopter (may cost about $500) or by airboat, which skim across the mudflats. DO NOT attempt to walk in the mudflats!

CURRENTS: The bay is a waterway, like a river, but connected to the ocean. Therefore it has two flows, one from the water flowing into the bay and the other, the tidal flow, coming in the Golden Gate from the ocean. A paddler has to know where these currents are and, if restricted by a land mass, how fast the water flows past in either direction.

WINDS: The bay is more apt to be calm in the morning with wind picking up as the sun rises and heats the air, hence causing a flow—wind. More of the paddlecraft is above water thereby creating a greater surface to be pushed by the wind. Boats that are more than 14 feet long should use a rudder, especially paddling with a cross-wind. When paddling in a windy situation, try to paddle near the wind protected shore, but be wary of passing boats that can send out waves to bounce off of banks and buildings.

FOG: A common Bay occurrence, especially in the summer. Don't, don't, don't paddle out in the shipping lanes in the fog. The big ships can't see you and you can't see them until, maybe, too late! An accident in a smallcraft hurts all smallcraft paddlers, so be very careful, please!

ACCESS: Beaches, boat ramps, and docks, better for canoes, are access areas. Be prepared to pay a launching fee, $5-$10, per boat. Some communities have public marinas with boat ramps, often with parking and rest rooms.

INFO: Maps: AAA — "San Francisco Bay Region." DE LORME — pp. 94, 104, & 115. A "Map Guide to California Boating Facilities," "North Area," and "Central Area." "Coastal and Inland Waterways," as well as "California Boating Laws," at the Dept. of Boating & Waterways, 1629 S Street, Sacramento, CA 95814: 916.445.2616.
"San Francisco Shoreline Guide," Univ. of CA Press, Berkeley, CA 94720.

SAN FRANCISCO BAY

GGNRA - Crissy Field to Oyster Point, 15 miles, Class I+

ACCESS: Put-in • Crissy Field. Go to Crissy Field (GGNRA) via Doyle Dr. or Marina Blvd. in San Francisco. From Mason St. going W., turn R. on Livingston St., L. on Marine Drive. There are other launch sites in the area. The bayside pipe organ sculpture emits sounds at the right tide.

2 miles to • Aquatic Park From US-101 turn east on Van Ness to the end, or go to the E. end of Hyde St. Limited parking & Rrm.

COMMENTS: The C. A. Thayer, and other historical ships, are interesting from the water view, followed by Fishermans Wharf, then barking seals at touristy Pier 39, complete with sight-seeing boats coming and going. Be very careful. The reactivated Ferry Building has piers on one side and a yacht harbor on the S. side near the S.F. - Oakland Bay Bridge.

STORY: I had a surprise when kayaking near Fisherman's Wharf seeing a familiar-looking turtle in the water with green, yellow, and red stripes. I'm sure it was a 7" version of the 2" turtles that were popular children's gifts in days past.

2 miles to • Ferry Bldg. (Agricultural Bldg.) tidal steps. Tidal steps are also at Rincon Park, pier 22.5, near the Fire Boat Dock. To the south of the Bay Bridge is the new (2000) Pac-Bell Park adding a new sight to the city.

2 miles to • Boat ramp at Pier 52, of China Basin St. .5 miles S. of China Basin.

1.5 miles to • Islais Creek Channel SW end of Third St. Bridge.

COMMENTS: Paddling south from Pier 52, the route goes past Central Basin, then take a short paddle up Islais creek for about a mile before continuing on past San Francisco's container terminal, then around Hunter's Point Naval Shipyard (inactive). If you want to feel small, really tiny, paddle too close to one of the ocean-going ships and look up. It's a long way"up" and that ship is a monster!

Next is Candlestick Point, site of 3-Com Park, former Giants field. The US-101 is parallel to the Bay for several miles before Sierra Point, followed by Oyster Point and two marinas named for these points.

8 miles to • Boat ramp at Oyster Point Marina. Exit off of US-101 on Oyster Point Blvd. turn right on Marina Blvd. to boat ramp..

• • • • • • • • • • • • • •

Lake Merced, San Francisco

ACCESS: Lake Merced is in the SW section of San Francisco near the ocean. Exit on Harding Rd. from Skyline Blvd. to Boat House. Parking & Rrm. Canoe rentals: 415.753.1101. Lake Merced is somewhat of a wilderness park, very pleasant, though it could be foggy. Call for hours and which section for paddling.

HISTORY: In days past, Lake Merced was canoeist "Pop" Linehan's "lake" for his canoeing activities. Here he taught Red Cross canoe classes and had a junior racing team workout. He had been a champion flat-water canoe racer on the East Coast and was interested in coaching his son and friends.

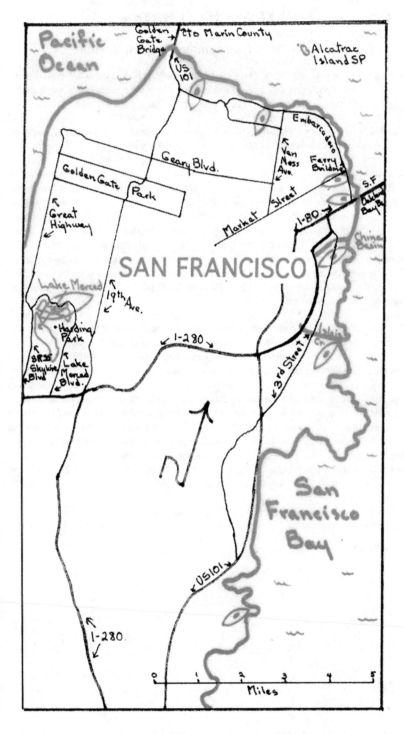

SAN FRANCISCO BAY (con't)

Alcatraz Island Circumnavigation, 3 miles

ACCESS: Put-in • Aquatic Park, at the foot of Hyde St. in San Francisco. Limited parking. Rrm. Beach launch. Good staging place with parking for loading and restrooms for changing. The breakwater calms the wave action.

COMMENTS: Alcatraz, THE ROCK, awaits a close inspection by paddlecraft (preferably kayak, well skirted) as it is only a mile away. But the island is near the Golden Gate, crossing a shipping lane, and with sight-seeing boats going in every direction—fast! So close and yet, with so many potential dangers in between. Early morning would be an ideal time, when the water is calmer, to make the crossing, unless the fog is low on the water. There are two rocky "islands"—really sea lion haul-out spots to paddle around at the west end of Alcatraz. The east side, where the passenger boats dock, is more protected. It is also where island information is widely broadcast. We sat comfortably in our kayaks eating lunch and listening to the National Park Service tell much about Alcatraz and its infamous history of famous felons. From "jail breaks," or "swims," to the take-over by Native Americans when it was terminated as a prison and not yet part of the National Park System, it has a fascinating history. It is one of the most popular tourist attractions in San Francisco and the National Park system.

Be wary of the wake from the sight-seeing boats. The the 3 to 4 foot tail waves can really churn up the water. The container ship swells are over 5', another big hazard for paddlecraft. Five of us, experienced paddlers, did this trip on 4-15-98 with ideal weather conditions. It was great. But another kayak excursion using the same route, although this time to Treasure Island, resulted in our paddling "upriver" against a fast out-going tide on the return trip. The whole time we were carefully watching a large ship just entering under the Golden Gate bridge. It turned, heading in our direction. Our group had split up, with the faster paddlers about to enter the shipping lane, when the ship blasted a warning, not once but twice! We regrouped as a pod and waited for our turn to cross to Aquatic Park. During the "wait" though, we had drifted fairly close to Alcatraz; before the ship blasted us out of its path, we had been much closer to the Oakland Bay Bridge. WARNING! The water can move your kayak very quickly with a fast out-going tide.

BEWARE: To protect endangered birds, it is illegal to approach within 100 yards of Alcatraz during bird nesting season.

RETIRED FERRYBOAT

ALCATRAZ

DOWNTOWN SAN FRANCISCO

SOUTH BAY

Oyster Pt. Marina to Redwood City (incl. Foster City & Coyote Point), 18 miles, Class I+

ACCESS: Put-in • Boat ramp at Oyster Point Marina. From US-101, go E. to the Marina on Oyster Pt. Blvd., and L. on Marine Blvd. to boat ramp.

COMMENTS: The paddle to Coyote Point is past SFO, a very busy airport. When I was going around the bay, I was going north on this leg on a late Sunday afternoon in the winter. I could see airplane lights all around the horizon as planes were slowly coming in to take their turns landing. I watched a plane touch-down every 2.5 minutes and this was 15 years ago.

6 miles to • Coyote Point public boat ramp. From US-101 near Burlingame exit at Coyote Point Dr., go east to the marina. Coyote Point Co. Rec. Area is a large environmental and recreational facility. A public beach with nearby parking is available for launching paddlecraft.

4 miles to • Foster City boat ramp at Leo J. Ryan Park. From US-101 exit on E. Hillsdale Blvd., 1.5 miles to Shell, turn right to Foster City Rec. Center: 650.286.3380. Or Boat Park. Boat ramp, parking & Rrm. On Foster City Blvd. Or Gull Park. Beach launch. Gull Ave. off of E. Hillsdale Blvd. Or Marlin Park, beach launch. Going S. on Foster City Blvd., turn east on Marlin Ave. to park.

COMMENTS: Foster City is built around a lagoon that has several access parks and about 5 miles of curving waterways and islands to paddle around. No powerboats allowed, ideal for paddlecraft.

4 miles to • Redwood City boat ramp, 2 miles W. of the Bay on Redwood Creek. From US-101 exit at SR 84 Woodside Rd., go east to Seaport Blvd. then north on Chesapeake Dr. to the water and public boat ramp. There are boat ramps at 675 Seaport Blvd., 451 Seaport Blvd., and 1548 Maple St. off of Bloomquist via Seaport Blvd.

COMMENTS: More slough exploring in preserved or built-on waterways. Redwood Shores Lagoon is a smaller version of Foster City. Natural Bair Island has about 10 miles of paddling waters, including Steinberger Slough bordering on Redwood Shores, connected to Redwood Creek with Corkscrew Slough going through the marsh. Or paddle west on Redwood Creek under US-101.

●●●●●●●●●●●●●●●●

San Mateo Marina Lagoon, Parkside Aquatic Park

ACCESS: Seal St. & Roberta Dr. off of S. Norfolk just NE of where US-101 and SR-92 cross. Boat ramp, parking & Rrm.: 650.522.7463. This is a 4-mile curved protected waterway west of Foster City offering a day of paddling. Power boats.

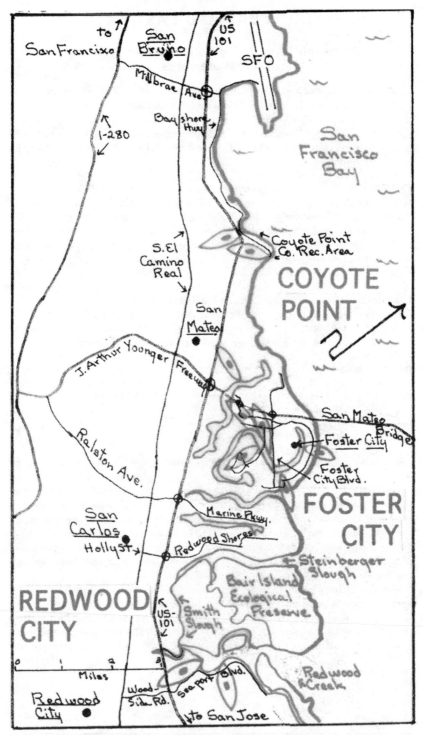

SOUTH BAY AND EAST BAY

Redwood City, Palo Alto, across to Fremont, 24 shore miles

ACCESS: Put-in • Redwood City boat ramp, 2 miles W. of the Bay on Redwood Creek. From US-101, exit at SR-84 Woodside Rd., go east to Seaport Blvd. then N. on Chesapeake Drive to the water and public boat ramp.

8 miles to • Lucy Evans Baylands Nature and Interpretive Center boat dock. From the US-101 exit at Embarcadero Rd., go east to end. Pkng. & Rrm. (Near Palo Alto Airport.)

COMMENTS: The natural sloughs in the south bay are filled with birdlife—gulls, ducks, wading birds. This is especially true at low tide when birds feed in the mudflats day and night. At an exceptionally high tide, the small black rails may be glimpsed as they escape their homes in the marsh grass when the high water floods them out. The Alviso area needs a fairly high tide to access it without being stuck in the mud. The high tide is often followed by a lower than normal low tide. We know; we goofed and ended up stuck in the mud.

(10 miles from Alviso Marina to L. Evans Baylands dock, Palo Alto.)

7 miles to • Coyote Hills Regional Park across the Bay (3 mi) plus up the slough.

Across to East Bay and Coyote Hills Sloughs

SEASON: All year BEST TIDE: 4'-6'

ACCESS: Put-in • for paddle craft off of Thornton Ave. (exit from I-880) and Hickory Street. Limited parking.

BEWARE: Getting stuck in the mud due to low tide.

COMMENTS: The Coyote Hills Regional Park (510.795.9385) near Newark has developed several miles of land and water trails. Some of these trails are along the bay near Dumbarton Bridge and the water trails in the sloughs are great for birding. In the summer they offer guided canoe trips. There are just a few miles of slough to paddle, so for a day's outing add Plummer Creek (Mowry Slough is closed to boating due to its large harbor seal colony). The waterway at the far southeast end of the bay is Coyote Creek, just west of Mowry Slough and on one side of Drawbridge. When the railroad was built to San Jose in 1884 the town of Drawbridge (el. 2') came into being. Ranger-lead tours during the summer are the only access to this very interesting "town."

Paddling in the south end of the bay is very different, many water paths have been straightened. The route is along miles of salt ponds and some natural marsh area. Salt ponds have been an important part of the bay for over 100 years. Leslie (now Cargill) is the prime producer of salt in the area. The sea water goes through an interesting process before ending up in small round boxes.

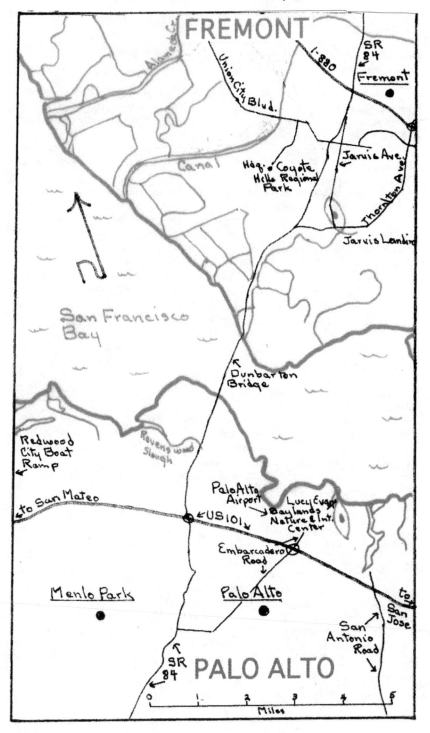

"STUCK IN THE BLACK BAY MUD"

Four women stuck in the mud as night fell report their experiences:

Arlene Wasserman's Adventure:

"We were stuck in the mud, the four of us: Ann Dwyer, Andrea Wolf, my 19 year old daughter, Rachael Krugman, and me. We had set out to kayak from the Alviso slough to the Palo Alto Yacht Harbor on a day that threatened rain but brought (mostly) a muted and peaceful gray....

"I felt my paddle hit a hard surface dismissed this...then saw mud on the tip of my paddle. A little while later I felt like I wasn't moving and...dismissed the feeling as an illusion until I realized that I was stuck in the mud.

"Ann and Andrea were maybe a football field away from me and Rachael was ahead of them. I yelled for them to wait for me, then realized that (a) they couldn't hear me and (b) they were also stuck in the mud. I caught fragments of what they were saying. I blew my whistle, but the wind took most of its high pitched sound. I tried to move the kayak forward by putting the paddle in the mud and pushing off from it.... I tried various techniques....

"As the skies darkened, my fears began to bunch up around me. Having seen *Titanic* a few days earlier, I sang bits of hymns and popular tunes and made up some songs to fit the occasion. I listened to the cries of the feeding birds, gazed at the lights in the distance, and found my place in the cold muddy darkness. The feeling was, raw, pure, and exhilarating.

"The others knew, as I did not, that we were never in any real danger. They decided that Andrea would join Rachael while Ann would stay where she was so that I wouldn't be left alone. Ann shouted encouragements for me to edge forward. I scooted inch by inch...this was exhausting work, but at least it kept me warm. Eventually I got close enough for Ann to hear me.

"Eventually the tide came in. I managed to get my kayak over to Ann. 'Follow me,' she said. I flopped around some...Ann attributed my clumsy efforts to exhaustion and said she was going to tow me. As we moved through the water I noticed bright lights on shore....I realized that we were going to get rescued. An airboat, with Rachael on board, came out to get us. One rescuer helped me into the boat. Another remarked that we would have made it back... on our own in a half-hour...."

Rachael Krugman's Adventure:

"...being stranded in a boat, miles from shore, in swampy deep mud at night, the solution only showed its face after every other attempt failed. Getting out of the boat was not even an option while I was alone in fear of being completely sunk into my surroundings, so I just waited for Andrea to scoot my way and figure out this situation together. ...we could only laugh at where we were. It was a truly beautiful scene with the city illuminated in the distance and the sky reflecting its glow on the dark waters....The solution came.... We both got out of our boats while stabilizing ourselves with each other's kayak on either side of our bodies. I was holding on waist deep in mud to the front of the boats and Andrea on the back in the same fashion. In unison we trudged about twenty yards and then climbed onto our boats for a quick breather. We continued this course until the welcoming site of the boat ramp...."

Andrea Wolf's Adventure:

"As I sat in my kayak, stuck in the mud, I realized I would be missing a Cajun dance in Berkeley.... I inched my way up to Rachael's kayak using every muscle in my upper body. When she suggested we actually try to walk in the mud, leaning on our Kayaks, I was willing to try. I had no idea when the tide would come in.... If you want to know how to relieve yourself (the bathroom) in that situation, ask one of us. Anyway, we made it back to shore with every square inch of our bodies (free mud facials) and kayaks covered with mud.

"I did make the last two hours of the dance...luckily, I had a change of clothes, and a friend's house in Berkeley to shower."

Ann Dwyer's Adventure:

"Our quartet started later than planned but paddled along at a good pace with all going well until we started noticing mud on the tips of our paddles. We were in sight of the take-out when the going became inching along in the mud with paddles pushing in the goo and bodies joining to make the forward push further. Hard work! Rachael was to our left near the salt grass far from the deeper channel that was somewhere to our right with Arlene inching along behind us. After a quick discussion, Andrea headed over to Rachael with plans for the two of them to figure out how to get to the dock. I sat comfortable in my very stable kayak resting on top of the mud, standing up to change the view and my body, shouting words of encouragement to Arlene as the sky darkened and the lights came on. The water drained out of the mounds of mud, shore birds scooted around feeding, airplanes flew in to land in three different airports, all was peaceful. It was over two hours before the tide started coming back and fast! Arlene was now within talking distance behind me. Mud scooting in a kayak is exhausting, so the tow strap was hooked onto our two kayaks and the double paddling began. We were definitely on our way to the dock when we heard the airboat getting into action for our rescue. How comforting to know there are airboats in the area for 'stuck in the mud' wind surfers and paddlers.

"The clean up took longer than the time we were stuck in the mud. Bay mud does not just wash off; it has to be scrubbed and scrubbed some more. After two days of scrubbing, most of it had gone down the drain to return 'home.'"

NOTE: Andrea's car was at our take-out with her cell phone (although there was a telephone near the dock). Several 911 calls, the report that two women were stuck in the mud and one, 74 years of age, put several agencies into fast action: police, fire, medics, and airboat personnel. To all of them we four wish to express a, THANK YOU! Andrea had moved her car so her bright lights shone on our path to be replaced by the more efficient lights on the top of the fire truck. (I had always wondered what it would be like to be stuck in the mud in the bay. Now I know.)

NOTE: A report of four women stuck in the mud was on the 10 PM news and also a three inch article in a local paper; both without names of the adventurers.

SOUTH BAY AND SAN JOSE RIVERS

Palo Alto to Alviso, 4 bayshore miles

ACCESS: Put-in • Dock at L. Evans Nature & Interpretive Center. East of US-101 Embarcadero exit to end. Rrm. Parking & Telephone.
9 miles to • Alviso Marina Park boat ramp. From SR-237 follow signs to Alviso. Restricted parking & Rrm.

COMMENTS on bay paddling: this is the far south end of San Francisco Bay where a 6' tide at the Golden Gate is about 8.5' in the Alviso area and takes an hour to arrive. Likewise, the time it takes for the tide to go out is about 2 hours after the time at the Golden Gate. Read and heed the tidebook when paddling at the south end of the bay, which has a deep accumulation of black bay gooey mud. Alviso used to be a very important location in the early days before the train delivered goods. Alviso was the port for the comings and goings of the former capitol of California, San Jose. It is now a capitol in another manner—that of world importance—Silicon Valley and the computer industry. This marsh area is fabulous for birding. A paddler can watch birds feeding at close range.

LOS GATOS CREEK & GUADALUPE RIVER

Campbell to Alviso, 13 river miles, Class II

SEASON: Winter & spring BEST FLOWS: 50-300 cfs. BEST TIDE: 4-6'

ACCESS: Put-in • Campbell Park & Los Gatos Creek on E. Campbell Ave. Pkg & Rrm
3.5 miles to • Childrens Discovery Museum parking area at Woz Way under US-280. Parking & Rrm. (NOTE: Woz Way - named for Steve Wozniak of Apple computers, was married to noted kayaker Candy Clark.)
2 miles to • Guadalupe River & Coleman Ave. near SR-87.
3.5 miles to • Trimble Road, .25 mile E. of US-101. Carry around the gate.
4 miles to • Alviso Marina Park. From Gold St., left on Elizabeth, right on Hope St. Parking & Rrm.

BEWARE: Rubble and ribar in waterways, snags, construction debris, and portages may be needed. Not for beginning paddlers!

COMMENTS: San Jose's waterways can be paddled, but be very careful, scout as much as possible. In Campbell, Los Gatos Creek Park with several miles of trail on both sides of Los Gatos Creek can be used for scouting. The Guadalupe River at the confluence with Los Gatos Creek in downtown San Jose has more rubble with rebar, especially between Coleman Ave. and Montague Expressway. The last two miles upriver from Alviso are marshlands with tidal action. (Thank you Larry Johmann for the river information.)

• • • • • • • • • • • • • • • •

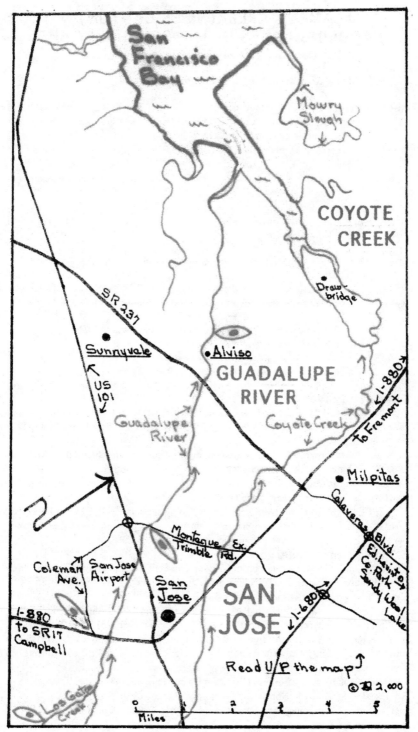

San Francisco Bay

Mowry Slough

COYOTE CREEK

Draw-bridge

SR 237

Sunnyvale

US 101

Alviso

GUADALUPE RIVER

Guadalupe River

Coyote Creek

I-880

to Fremont

Milpitas

Calaveras Blvd.

Ed Levin Co. Park
Sandy Wool Lake

Coleman Ave.

San Jose Airport

Montague Ex.
Trimble Rd.

San Jose

SAN JOSE

I-680

I-880
to SR 17
Campbell

Los Gatos Creek

Read UP the map ↑

© 2,000

0   1   2   3   4   5
Miles

ALAMEDA CREEK(NILES CANYON) & PADDLING LAKES IN THE SOUTH BAY AREA

Niles Canyon, below Sunol, 5 miles, Class II+

SEASON: After a good rain or two BEST FLOW: 300'-600' cfs.

ACCESS: Put-in • below the bridge and after the 5' drop wier. It is 5 miles downstream from Sunol on Niles Canyon Rd. via SR-84. There are train tracks on both sides of the creek (and train rides).

.5 mile to • roadside park with creek access; pkng & Rrm. After a short ways there is another weir. Keep a look out for more weirs.

1 mile to • bridge, possible access, road now on river left. About .5 mile downstream from tunnel for river left train tracks. Limited parking.

1 mile to • bridge, main road crossing to river right.

2.5 miles to • bridge (Old Canyon Rd.) over creek, across from Vallejo Mill Historical Park. Limited parking.

MAPS: AAA — "Fremont, Newark, & Vicinity." DE LORME — p. 105.

BEWARE: 4 weirs! Some can be run, they vary with water flow. They are often after slow water. It's a small rainfed stream; the water level fluctuates quickly.

COMMENTS: It is brushy and there's danger from trees across the waterway. It is not wilderness with the road, that is also a safety factor. Run it twice in a day.

●●●●●●●●●●●●●●●●

Paddling Lakes in the South Bay Area (no map)

Guadalupe River reservoirs:

• Uvas. Near Morgan Hill. S. on US-101, exit on Bernal Ave., west to Monterey Hwy., then S to Bailey Ave., R to McKean Rd., go left (becomes Uvas Rd.) 10 mi. Non-power boats only. Boat ramp.

• Chesbro. (north/downstream from Uvas). From US-101 S. exit on Bailey, left on McKean/Uvas Rd., 4.5 mi. to Oak Glen Ave., left 2+ miles to res. Non-power.

• Lexington, near Los Gatos. From SR-17, exit on Alma Bridge Rd., continue to res. No power boats. Windsurfing very popular. Boat ramp: 408.356.2729.

• Vasona Lake & Los Gatos Creek, Los Gatos. Going south on SR-17, exit at Lark Ave., go east to Los Gatos Blvd., turn right, then right again onto Blossom Hill Rd. Boat ramp. No power boats. Canoe & kayak rentals.

Stevens Creek reservoir:

• Stevens Creek near Cupertino. From I-280 exit on Foothill Exp. go west 3 miles. Non-power boats only. Picnic areas available from the lake shore.

Coyote Creek reservoir parks:

• Cottonwood Lake at Hellyer Co. Park in San Jose. From US-101 south take the Hellyer exit, follow to the park. Small lake with a boat ramp. No power boats: 408.358.3741.

• Lake Cunningham, San Jose (Under City of San Jose Parks Dept.: 408.277.4573). South on US-101 take Tully Rd. exit, go east, follow signs to lake. Used for windsurfing, no power boats. Beach launch. 408.277.4792.

• Sandy Wool Lake near Milpitas in Ed Levin County Park. From I-680, exit on Calaveras Rd. E and follow to park. Non-power boats only. 408.262.6980.

NOTE: Some lakes managed by Santa Clara Co. Parks & Rec. Dept.: 408.358.3741

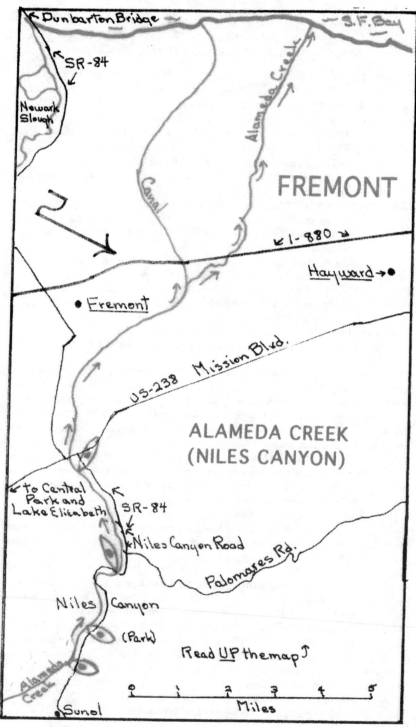

Dunbarton Bridge

S.F. Bay

SR-84

Newark Slough

Canal

Alameda Creek

FREMONT

← I-880 →

Hayward → ●

● Fremont

US-238 Mission Blvd.

ALAMEDA CREEK
(NILES CANYON)

← to Central Park and Lake Elizabeth

SR-84

Niles Canyon Road

Palomares Rd.

Niles Canyon

(Park)

Read UP the map ↑

Alameda Creek

● Sunol

0   1   2   3   4   5
Miles

EAST BAY

San Leandro, Alameda Island/Oakland Estuary

ACCESS: Put-in • San Leandro Marina boat ramp at 40 San Leandro Marina:800.559.7245, near Mulford Landing. (17 miles N of Mowry Slough.) From I-880, exit on Marina Blvd., go W. Parking & restaurant.

8 miles to • San Leandro Bay Park, Airport Bay Park. Hegenberger Rd. exit from I-880 SE to Doolittle (SR-61), N. to ramp at M. L. King Reg. Shoreline Pk. Cafe: 510.881.1833. Gives paddling access to both sides of Alameda Is.

Alameda Island — West Shore (bay side)

Beach launch • Robert Crown Memorial St. Beach. Webster St. tube, across island right on Central, left on McKay Ave.

Boat ramp • Ballena Isle Marina. From the Webster St. tube, go across the island, turn right on Central, left on Ballena Blvd. Parking, Rrm., picnicking.

Boat ramp • Alameda Park. From the Webster Street tube, go across the island, turn right on Central, 1 mile to Main, turn left.

Alameda Island — East Shore (Oakland side)

Boat ramp • End of Grand St, 4 blocks E. of Buena Vista Ave.

Boat ramp • Encinal, 3rd St. & Central Ave. 510.748.4565.

Beach launch • Shoreline Park via Webster St. S. on Atlantic, E. on Triumph Drive.

Oakland Shore opposite Alameda Island

Boat ramp • Embarcadero between Oak Street and 5th Ave.

Boat ramp • Jack London Marina, foot of Broadway at Jack London Square.

COMMENTS: The south end of the Bay to Coyote Hills Slough is part of SF Bay National Wildlife Refuge. North of the San Mateo Bridge is Hayward Regional Shoreline. San Leandro offers a boat ramp. Be wary when paddling north past the Oakland Int. Airport at the south end of the Bay Farm Island. When the planes are taking off the screaming engines are painful to bayside paddler's ears!. (I know. The extreme pain caused me to stop paddling and cover my ears.) Alameda Island is full of activities on both sides, San Francisco Bay or the Oakland Estuary. There are parks and marinas on both sides of the island. It is an important Navy Base and shares the estuary with Coast Guard Island, an extremely valuable base of operations for the Coast Guard services in the bay and ocean. Paddle on the estuary side where there are businesses, marinas, and homes. On weekends this area is alive with sailboats. The bay end is always busy with BIG ships coming and going. Give them lots of room. This is a working harbor plus a recreational boating area. Paddlecraft are the easiest to turn, but the hardest to be seen by the big ships. Attractive Jack London Square (marina) has water access.

Paddling Lakes in the Area

Fremont—Lake Elizabeth. 510.791.4140. Fremont Central Park at Paseo Padre & Stevenson Blvd. Canoe & kayak rentals. Very lovely park. Bring the kids.

San Leandro—Lake Chabot via I-580 & Lake Chabot Road. Canoe & kayak rentals.

Oakland—Lake Merritt. 510.444.3807. Off Grand Ave. at 568 Bellevue Ave. Canoe & kayaks rentals. Fairyland is in the same park area. Ducks to feed.

Castro Valley—Lake Chabot. 510.582.2198. 17930 Lake Chabot Road. Canoe & kayak rentals. Tours of the lake and instruction.

Orinda & El Sobrante—San Pablo Res. via San Pablo Dam Road.

Berkeley—Aquatic Park Lake. 510.548.3730. 80 Bolivar Dr.

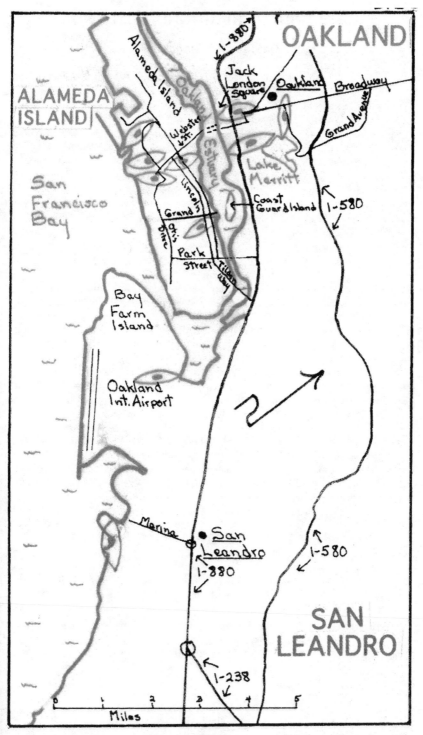

OAKLAND TO RICHMOND & ISLANDS

Oakland to Richmond

ACCESS: Put-in • 6 miles (from Alameda Is.) to Emeryville City Marina boat ramp. From I -80 exit at Powell St. go towards the bay.

3 miles to • Berkeley Marina boat ramp. From I-80 exit at University Ave. going W., turn R. on Marina Blvd., left on Spinnaker Way.

4.5 miles to • Richmond Marina Bay boat ramp. 140 Marina Way, Richmond via I-580, S. on Marina Bay Pkwy, W. on Regatta Blvd, S. on Marina Way S. From I-580 eastbound, S. on Harbor Way S., E. on Hall Ave. to the ramp. (NOTE: there is an old boat ramp on Boat Ramp St. off of W. Cutting Blvd. off of S. Garrard Blvd. close to I-580, at the land end of Santa Fe Channel.)

3 miles to • Keller Beach, Pt Richmond. From I-580 exit on Garrard Blvd. go towards the bay, right after the tunnel turn right to Keller Beach. Short carry to water through the bayside park. Pkg & Rrm.

2.5 miles • Pt Molate beach. Going W. on I-580 just before the San Rafael-Richmond Bridge exit, go N. past the ex-naval depot to beach. Pkng.

BEWARE: The shallow shore areas can have choppy waves in the wind and there can be mudflats at low tides. Sailboats to and from marinas, especially on the weekends.

COMMENTS: The east side of the bay is marshlands, some have been filled for buildings, others are salt producers and the rest natural. From Alameda Island the route goes around the deepwater channel and container docks past the Navy facility, then under the S.F.-Oakland Bridge. From here to Pt. Richmond the shoreline is marsh, marinas, or buildings. Caesar Chavez Park is one of the marsh areas. Paddling under the Richmond - S.R. Bridge is good for photo shots of Mt. Tamalpais. After going around the ex-Richmond ferry pier there's a graveyard of ship hulls in various stages of decay.

Broods Island, 1 mile to island or 4 miles around and back

COMMENTS: Start at the Richmond Marina and paddling around the island. The island has an interesting history: Ohlones lived here; there was oyster harvesting, fruit growing, mining (even a short railroad), and more recently a very exclusive game bird hunting club. The island is restricted, phone for permission, or to join a group. Fee. 510.562.2267 or 510.636.1684. No fee for the sand spit or paddling.

Red Rock Island from Pt. Molate Beach Park, 4 miles r/t

COMMENTS: Red Rock Island (yes, it is red chert) is the meeting point of Marin,Contra Costa, and San Francisco Counties as well as being an old mining site. It has a beach at low to moderate tides. Climbing to the top is difficult. Paddling across the deep channel during a fast tide flow can also present problems.

The Brothers Islands from Pt. Molate, 4 miles round trip

COMMENTS: Situated close to San Pablo are two small islands, The Brothers. The east island was a light station. The islands were sold and turned into a very attractive B&B for weekend guests. (The Sisters Islands are across the bay.)

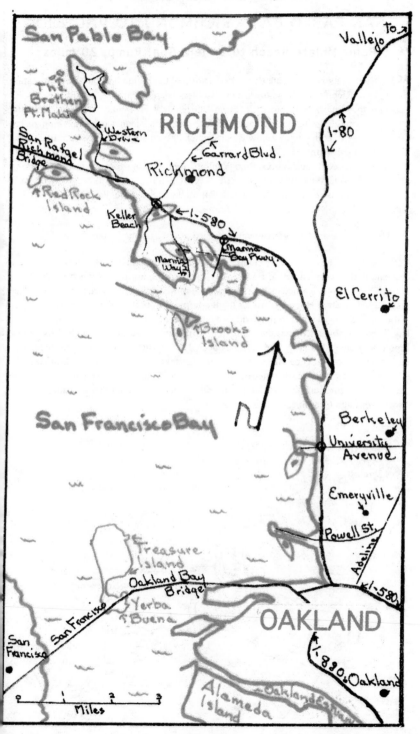

SAN PABLO BAY - RICHMOND TO VALLEJO

Point Molate Beach to Vallejo Boat Ramp, 20 miles

ACCESS: Put-in • Point Molate Beach Park. North of the Richmond end of the San Rafael
- Richmond Bridge toward the Brothers Islands. Parking.

12 miles to • Pinole Bayfront Park. From I-80 go NW on Pinole Valley Rd., .5 mile,
straight on Tennent Avenue, 1 mile to end. Beach launch or a small ramp on the
right, both muddy at low water; launch or take out with almost a 5' tide. Parking & Rrm.

2 miles to • Rodeo, beach at Lone Pine Point or Joseph's Fishing Resort boat ramp. From
I-80 take the Willow Ave. exit (NW) which becomes Parker Ave., in .5 mile
veer left on Pacific Ave. across RR tracks to the shore. Parking.

5 miles to • Vallejo Small Boat Launch Ramp at Curtola Parkway. Parking & Rrm.

BEWARE: There are facing breakwaters at the entrance to Mare Island Strait.

COMMENTS: The ex-Navy installations, fueling station, and The Brothers Islands, the
east one with a very attractive B&B and a "light" on it, are interesting from the shore
going NE. I recently learned that the recreational railroad train that used to run in this area
may be reactivated. Hope so. Watch for the burned timbers of the last active whaling
station in the US. The exceedingly wide way is still there for dragging the whales from the
bay. There are some marinas, and then a very different bay landscape—high cliffs—at Pt.
Pinole Regional Shoreline. The park has posted a long list of activities that does NOT
include paddlecraft. At certain tides paddlers can take a respite on a beach or two. Oil
refineries dot the hillsides on much of this entire route. Take care crossing the bay to get to
Vallejo, the entire drainage of the Central Valley, Sacramento and San Joaquin Rivers, is
flowing through Carquinez Strait.

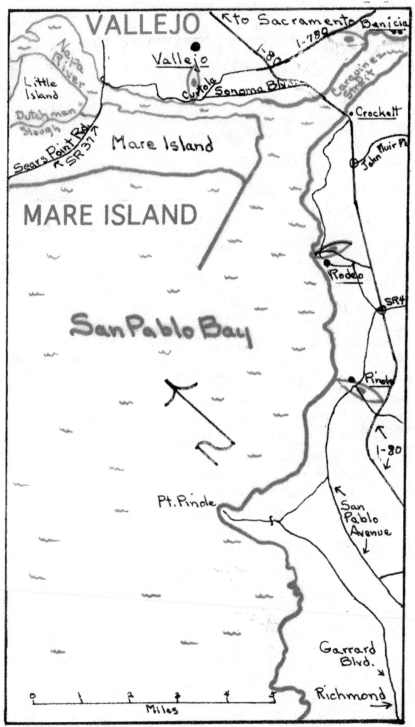

MARE ISLAND

Mare Island Strait, Vallejo, (Napa River - mouth) 3 miles

SEASON: All year. BEST TIDES: 3'-6'. TIDE LOCATION: Vallejo, Mare Island Strait.

ACCESS: Put-in • Vallejo Small Boat Launch Ramp, 42 Harbor Way at Curtola Parkway. E. end of SR-37 bridge over Napa River, go E. on Wilson Ave., right on Mare Island Way, follow shoreline 2 miles to the boat ramp. From I-80, W. on I-780, follow to the ferry, next to boat ramp. Parking & Rrm.

BEWARE: Read the tide tables well to make sure the tide is flowing in the direction favorable to your paddling plans and with enough water. Paddlecraft should be on constant watch and stay clear of larger vessels. With the many marinas on the east side, there is busy boating traffic. The ferry boats stern thrust is so powerful that the PWCs (personal water craft) have a splashing good time playing in the waves.

COMMENTS: This channel, the main terminus of the Napa River, is bordered by the Navy installation on Mare Island, a very important location during WWII. It is now being decommissioned. Many Navy ships were stored in the strait after the war, but most are now gone with a few—the "Moth Ball Fleet"—now in Suisun Bay (E. of Benecia on the N. side of Carquinez Strait). Mare Island creates a protective harbor as the entire southwest side of the strait. It is recommended that paddlecraft explore this strait during the week or on winter weekends to avoid the heavy boating traffic. The mixture of pleasure craft, working boats, and navy ships makes this an interesting area. Paddling up the Napa River, we watched the Mare Island Causeway drawbridge go into action; it lifted up to let a sailboat pass. Nearing the SR-37 bridge, there are quite a few water birds and some barking sea lions. Across the strait is River Park (accessed on Wilson Ave.), a preserved native marsh with trails, old boats "melting" into the mudflats, but no paddlecraft access. Continuing on from Sears Point Bridge into the Napa River is Dutchman Slough to the west that circles around Knight Island then back to the Napa River—about 6 miles around. The marinas in the strait are interesting to paddle into. At the Carquinez Strait end, there are breakwaters on both sides of the entrance. The west end of Mare Island has a 2 mile-long solid breakwater to be paddled around if going from the west side of the island across San Pablo Bay.

NOTE: Vallejo is a city in transition as it, and the Mare Island Navy Base, were closely interrelated. There is great emphasis on this fabulous waterfront with much new marine-like construction. Another water-oriented activity is to take the Vallejo Ferry to San Francisco for a great way to see the bay.

EAST BROTHER ISLAND

BURNED RAMP OF LAST WHALING STATION

VALLEJO FERRY

"MOTHBALL" FLEET, MARE ISLAND

NAPA RIVER

GENERAL INFORMATION: The Napa river is a little known facet of this world-known Napa Valley wine region. It has been paddled in sections from Calistoga to San Pablo Bay into one of the largest and best preserved deltas composed of miles of sloughs. The main flow goes between Vallejo and Mare Island. Second Napa Slough enters the bay near Sears Point (site of the noted raceway) increasing its flow with Sonoma Creek en route.

There have been recent kayaking forays on the upper Napa River organized by a local resident, Andrea Wolf. One of the runs from Calistoga, 8 miles down river, to Pope St. Bridge, west of downtown St. Helena. She reported, "the run at the right water level, could have been very attractive had there not been so many snags requiring frequent portages." I joined her from Yountville Cross Rd. to Oak Knoll Ave. , 5 miles. We enjoyed the obstacle-free portions of the clear river but not the many snags. The 3 miles on down to Trancas St. started with too many snags. We may try it another day.

Trancas Street to Cuttings Wharf, 10.5 miles

SEASON: All year. BEST TIDES: 3'-5'. TIDE LOCATION: Napa River

ACCESS: Put-in • Below the bridge at Trancas St. 1.5 miles north of downtown Napa, 1.5 miles east of SR-29, .5 miles west of SR-121. Limited parking.
2 miles to • Point Park, W. side of the river between 1st & West Streets.
.25 mile to • Boat launch, west side, 1 block south of 3rd St. off of Main Street.
2.5 miles to • Public boat ramp at J.F.K. Memorial Park, E. side of river. End of Streblow Dr. off of SR-29, near Napa Com. College. Parking & Rrm.
3.5 miles to • Cuttings Wharf ramp(west side) public launch ramp off of Cuttings Wharf Road from SR-12 & SR-121, 4 miles to ramp. Parking & Rrm.
NOTE: .5 miles south of Cuttings Wharf is Napa Valley Marina & boat ramp. Also there is river access on east side at the end of Green Is. Rd. off of SR-29.
The Vallejo boat ramp is downsream 12 miles from Napa Valley Marina.

BEWARE: Low tide and mud! Wind, especially in the lower section. High water from river flows after heavy rains. Patrol boat checks for PFDs and water safety.

COMMENTS: Enjoy this paddling experience going past riverside homes and businesses in the upper section of the Napa River. Marshlands with natural vegetation and water birds are an attraction in the lower section. To go without need for a shuttle, put-in at Kennedy Park and paddle to Napa for lunch, then paddle back; but first, make sure the tides are favorable. With the relatively short distances between access points this is an interesting waterway to explore. This is the city of Napa's river, flowing right through town. They are trying to bring more interest to the river with clean-up projects and summer river-oriented programs. For more information contact: Friends of Napa River, 68 Coombs St. Bldg. B, Napa: 707.254.8520. How about an upper Napa River "Clean out the brush" project?

●●●●●●●●●●●●●●●

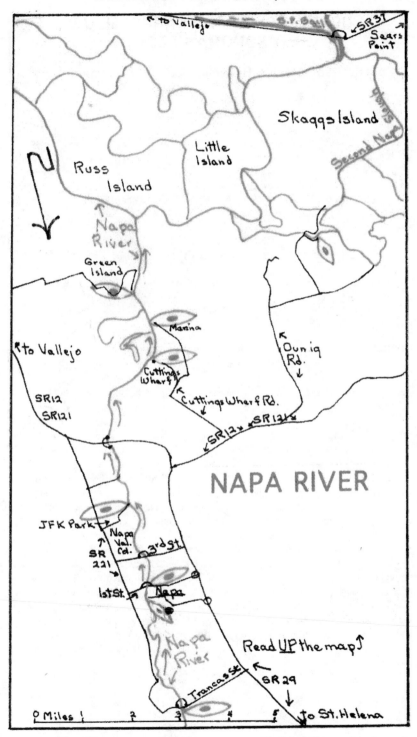

HUDEMAN SLOUGH, SKAGGS ISLAND, & SONOMA CREEK

Second Napa Slough, Hudeman Slough, & Skaggs Island

ACCESS: Put-in • Hudeman Slough boat ramp. E. of Schellville on SR-121, S. on Ramal Rd. to Skaggs Island Rd., R. before bridge to ramp. Parking & Rrm.

COMMENTS: Here is another part of the north bay to explore that has easy access and about four side channels to poke into on the way to SR-37. The iffy take-out at the north of the bridge over Sonoma Creek/Second Napa Slough at SR-37 is best at a 5 foot tide. These small channel paddling areas are seldom used, providing solitude and adventure. Enjoy views of Mt. Tamalpais and Mt. Diablo. We sighted gulls, cormorants, western grebes, coots, and a muskrat.

SONOMA CREEK
Schellville to Hudeman Slough boat ramp, 12 miles

SEASON: All year. BEST TIDE: 5'-6' TIDE LOCATION: Wingo & Sonoma Creek.

ACCESS: Put-in • Under the SR-121 bridge, west side, at Schellville. Parking. Take-out • Hudeman Slough boat ramp (see above).

COMMENTS: This Sept.'98, exploratory trip was an adventure! Sonoma Creek below the bridge near Schellville was 15' wide with plenty of water. We chose the wrong tide which soon resulted in some creek-bottom walking. After we met the incoming tide, the water deepened and marshy mud flats became the sides of the waterway. The entire narrow width of the creek was blocked by interwoven snags which we somehow managed to get by. We found the drawbridge at Wingo, a small community and a drawbridge. After Wingo, we heard the shots and the signs warning us of the hunt club on the right. (The shots came from the left: a non-member?). Several blasts with our whistles kept us "safe." In tidal mud-flat territory we came to a fallen tree trunk about 8" in diameter, across the entire creek, which we each managed to wiggle over only to be in water covered with floating cattails, branches, and wood. Paddling became impossible so we grabbed handfuls of floating cattails to pull the kayaks through the water a foot or so at a time. It was slow going and I'm sure our progress was reported to the "tower" by the small airplanes flying overhead. (Were they taking bets to see if we kayakers would make it?) What they knew and we soon found out was that a larger tree trunk, fifty feet from the first one, blocked our passage at the other end. This one we could not wiggle over AND we could not get out and walk around on the banks of gooey mud. To make it worse there was a stinky 30" long dead fish floating among the cattails. Two of us slowly got out of our kayaks onto the 12" log giving it enough weight for the other two paddlers to get over in their kayaks and pull our kayaks across. MORE! A strong wind came up, the day was ending, and our destination too far. We found a "private" dock, got out and two of us in PFDs "hitched" a ride back to our car. So endeth this saga of Ron, Connie, Andrea, and Ann.

•••••••••••••••

SONOMA CREEK

MORE SONOMA CREEK

HUDEMAN SLOUGH/SKAGGS ISLAND

NAPA RIVER

PETALUMA RIVER, SONOMA COUNTY

Petaluma to Black Point Marina, 14 miles

SEASON: All year. BEST TIDE: 4'-6'. TIDE LOCATION: Petaluma River entrance.

ACCESS: Put-in • Petaluma waterfront, Water Street behind McNears building or off of Washington St. near Petaluma Blvd. Washington St. going west from US-101 goes to Petaluma Blvd. There is a turning basin here with several access locations. Limited Parking.

1.5 miles to • Petaluma Marina dock and boat ramp, 781 Baywood Dr., off Lakeville Hwy. SR-116. Parking. Easy to find and good launching area.

6.5 miles to • Gilardi's Lakeville Marina, 5684 Lakeville Hwy.: 707.763.7555 also known as Gilardi's Landing. Location of Taverna: 707.769.8545. From Petaluma E. on Lakeville Hwy. 6 miles. From SR-37 N. on Lakeville Hwy. 7 miles. Limited parking.

7.5 miles to • Boat ramp, Black Point Boat Launch (fee). Mouth of the Petaluma River, W. side below SR-37 bridge on Harbor Dr. Fee, parking & Rrm.

COMMENTS: This is an easy tidewater paddle going from a small city into the marshlands complete with marsh birds, fishing boats, and winds from the bay. A combination of creek flow and tide water. Or this is a great run with an incoming tide in the fall, paddle from Gilardi's Landing to Petaluma for lunch then back with the tide for dinner at Papas' Taverna. With the tide start at Petaluma, go the entire distance to Black Point boat ramp. At high tides it is possible to wander into and through the many sloughs. One goes through to San Antonio Creek to the west. Half of the run is in the Petaluma Marsh Wildlife Area, so bird watchers bring your binoculars. Paddling up from Black Point, explore the side channels on the left, the third one, about a mile up. The largest is Bahia Lagoon and goes a mile into a bay with homes and two small parks. Elizabeth Terwilliger (Mrs. T) used to have her canoeists get out here, but the reeds have grown, and the channel may or may not be redredged. The next left side creek is Black John Cr. which goes into Rush Creek—the north border of the Rush Creek Open Space Preserve.

HISTORY: Petaluma's nickname was Chickaluma reflecting the many, many chicken houses in the area. It was the egg capitol of California. I remember visiting a hatchery filled with peeping fluffy chicks being carefully packed in boxes, holding about 100 balls of live yellow fluff, to be shipped all over the country. At the southern entrance to the city, there used to be a large statue of a chicken. Times have changed, but the Petaluma River (an act of Congress changed its name from the Petaluma Creek or Slough) is still a commercial waterway. On one of my many paddles on the river, we had to wait while a tugboat, pulling a barge of sand, barely squeezed past the narrow opening of the river below the US-101 overpass. The last remnants of the once very active commercial waterfront can be seen, going from the overpass up to the city center.

•••••••••••••••

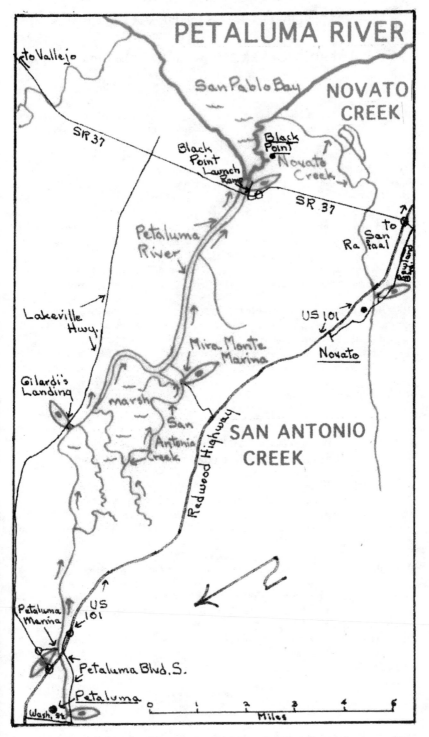

PETALUMA RIVER

SAN ANTONIO CREEK & NOVATO CREEK

San Antonio Creek, (flows into Petaluma River)

Mira Monte Marina up river & back, 7 miles

ACCESS: Put-in • Mira Monte Marina boat ramp (fee). From US-101 N. of Novato and Marin County Airport and S. of Sonoma County line, go E. at Mira Monte Marina sign. Fee, parking, & Rrm.

COMMENTS: The 6.5 foot incoming tide at Mira Monte Marina gave us ample water to paddle up San Antonio Creek. After a serpentine route for 3.5 miles, the creek was contained in a dead-end canal on the west side of the railroad tracks above the cow fields. Neils Island to the northeast was a fresh green carpet dotted with large oaks. The well-groomed Marin County dump was active with earth movers and explosive detonators used to scare away the gulls. It was like throwing up large fire crackers seeing them flare, hearing the explosion followed by smoke puffs. Our exploring route took us past small houses—some intact, others sinking into the mud—named Slue Vue, Marsh Mellow, Aloha. Paddled in Jan. 1998 on a pleasant day, though overcast with a storm brewing.

HISTORY: The former owner has been restoring Mira Monte's important place in boating and water-ski history. This was the site of one of the early water ski schools where renowned skiers of the day trained and a youth water ski summer camp was held. At that time, Kimball fiberglass (revolutionary) water skis were being manufactured in San Rafael by Bill Kimball and engineer Merritt Robinson. The marina was known for its oyster restaurant. Mira Monte was part of Rancho Olompali. The ranch house (burned) site is now just a flagpole on the hilltop

•••••••••••••••

Novato Creek, Marin County
Black Point Marina to Novato, 7.5 miles

ACCESS: Put-in • Black Point Boat Launch (fee). Mouth of the Petaluma River west side of river, beneath SR-37 bridge on Harbor Drive. Pkg. & Rrm.
7.5 miles to • a steep bank behind the buildings one block W., after Redwood Blvd. crosses Novato Creek. From US-101 exit on Rowland Blvd. go towards Novato on Redwood Blvd.

BEWARE: Water releases from Stafford Lake, phone first: 415.897.4133.

COMMENTS: Another creek to explore during high tide. Start at the Black Point boat ramp (see Pet. Riv.) paddling out to San Pablo Bay with a water-eye view of the homes on the hill overlooking the bay. 2 miles W. is the unmarked entrance to Novato Creek. The creek roams around Bel Marin Keys under railroad tracks and SR-37. It then becomes the NW border of the Petaluma Marsh Wildlife Area. Great for water birds. After the second railroad bridge (a low one) its channel is straightened into Novato. Or, paddle from Novato to Black Pt.

•••••••••••••••

LAS GALLINAS CREEK

UNDER THE 101

SANTA VENETIA BOATERS

MARIN COUNTY

Santa Venetia to San Rafael Canal, 11 miles

ACCESS: Canoe dock • J.F. McGinnis Park. From US-101 exit at Lucas Valley Rd. & Smith Ranch Road, follow to the park. So. Fk. Gallinas Creek, 7 bay miles from entrance to Novato Creek past ex-Hamilton AFB. Explore the arms and sloughs of Gallinas creek at high tide, one goes to the lagoon at Frank Lloyd Wright designed civic center, one to an oak tree studded Santa Margarita Island and another under US-101.

Boat ramp • Buck's Landing. Located off of San Pedro Road at the bay, 2 miles from US-101 via San Pedro Road & Santa Venetia. bar & parking. A brickyard was located at Buck's Landing so it has a very firm base as its use dates back well into the 1980's.

Beach launch • China Camp State Park and Historic Area. On San Pedro Road, 5 miles from San Rafael & US-101 and 4 miles via Santa Venetia & US-101. Limited parking at the beach & Rrm. Camping: 415.456.0766. (This is where we used to buy bay shrimp from the Chinese for $.30 a pound.)

3 miles to • McNears Beach County Park. Off of San Pedro Rd., 4 miles from San Rafael via 3rd. Street, and 5 miles from US-101 via Santa Venetia. The Sisters Islands are nearby but may have squirrely water. Paddle east around Pt. San Pedro, past the McNear brickyard to the Marin Islands Nat'l Wildlife Refuge, (Phone Audubon Nat'l society about distance restrictions: 415.388.2524.) about a mile from Loch Lomond boat ramp.

3 miles to • Loch Lomond Marina boat ramp at 110 Loch Lomond Dr. via Third St. W. of San Rafael.

HISTORY: It was on Easter Sunday, 1964, when we viewed the damage to boats in the area of Loch Lomond Marina caused by the tsunami from the Anchorage, Alaska, 8.4 earthquake. Just think of the distance that wave traveled, down the west coast into San Francisco Bay to San Rafael still with power to do damage.

San Rafael Cr./Canal to Corte Madera Creek, 3 bay miles

ACCESS: Dock • at City of San Rafael Beach Park, next to San Rafael Yacht Club. E. of US-101 from 2nd Street, S. on Francisco Blvd. .25 mile to Yacht Club Dr., go to end. Limited parking. This 2 mile long quiet waterway is almost in downtown San Rafael. Marinas, restaurants, businesses, and homes are all a part of its being. At the east end is Pickleweed Park across from homes and a large marina and near Loch Lomond Marina.

Beach Launch • S end of shoreline Park via Francisco Blvd. E, left on Grange Way then right to small parking area & Rrm.

Beach launch • Remillard Park, a popular wind-surfing area and near the uniquely designed Larkspur Ferry Terminal. In going around Point San Quentin, under Richmond-San Rafael Bridg stay clear of San Quentin Prison grounds. And then there was the escaped prisoner who got stuck in the mud wading across Corte Madera Creek, the tide came in, and he drowned.

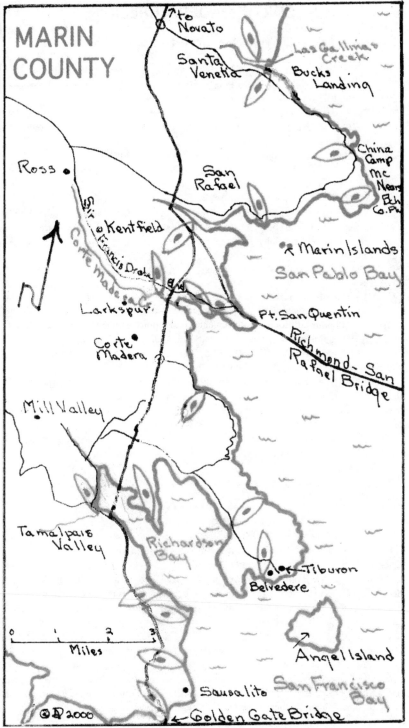

MARIN COUNTY

to Novato

Santa Venetia

Las Gallinas Creek

Bucks Landing

Ross

San Rafael

China Camp inc Marc Neary Bch Co.Pk.

Sir Francis Drake

Kentfield

Corte Madera Cr.

Marin Islands

San Pablo Bay

Larkspur

Corte Madera

Pt. San Quentin

Richmond - San Rafael Bridge

Mill Valley

Tamalpais Valley

Richardson Bay

Tiburon

Belvedere

0   1   2   3
Miles

Angel Island

© AP 2000

Sausalito

San Francisco Bay

Golden Gate Bridge

N

CORTE MADERA CREEK

Corte Madera Creek, Greenbrae to Ross, 4 miles, Class I

ACCESS: Put-in • Marin Rowing Club dock (low level), Greenbrae. From US-101 at Greenbrae, go west on Sir Francis Drake Blvd., S. at 1st light, S. on Barry Way (& Eliseo Dr.), then east on Drakes Landing Road to the end. Pkg.

.5 miles to • Bon Air Landing. Go S. on Bon Air Road 1 mi. west of Barry Way on Sir Francis Drake Blvd., .5 mile to S. Eliseo Dr., .5 mile to Bon Air Landing & water access. Limited parking.

Or • Corte Madera Dock. From US-101 S. of the Corte Madera Creek, take the Lucky Dr. exit, W. (towards Mt. Tam.) to E. side of Redwood High School. Just before Doherty Dr. there is a dock at an inlet. NO parking.

3.5 miles to • Ross (very high tide only). Exit is difficult.

NOTE: Explore the side channels and out towards the bay. Also paddle about .5 mile S. along the marsh to an inlet complete with water and shore birds of all kinds, Corte Madera Marsh. My friend Gerry Reichard was instrumental in its preservations as is the home of burrowing owls. Paddling in the marsh in October with Terry & Gary Haag and Andrea Wolf, we admired the fall colors of the pickle weed; red, rust, and green.

COMMENTS: Mt. Tamalpais is an inspiring backdrop when paddling up the creek. Unfortunately Kentfield is viewed from the concrete ditch the Army Corps of Engineers decided would alleviate flooding. WRONG! Several protesting the concrete ditch, were jailed, including a member of the Kent family. Tamalpais Creek, was the name of a ship built at Marinship during WWII in Sausalito. Since ships have to be named after bodies of water, an unnamed stream flowing down "The Mountain" became Tamalpais Creek and the next ship: "Tamalpais." We paddled past Murray Park—an early thirties airplane landing field. Marin General Hospital, birthplace of three of my four is on the site of the once luxurious Bon Aire Hotel. Only the palm trees that shaded the hotel's swimming pool remain.

MORE HISTORY: It was on Corte Madera Creek near US-101, where I opened my first paddlesport store in 1972, *Canoe Trips West*. After it was sold it was moved and renamed *California Canoe & Kayak*. I taught canoe classes, guided canoe trips pointing out, among other things, the site where Sir Francis Drake's plaque was found. (This created quite a stir among history buffs.)

●●●●●●●●●●●●●●●●

Paddling around Tiburon Peninsula

ACCESS: Beach launch • San Clemente Park via Paradise Dr. & US-101.

Beach launch • Paradise Beach County Park, a short walk from the parking area.

Dock • Sam's Anchor Cafe, 27 Main in Tiburon.

COMMENTS: The prominent enclave at Point Chanucey was the Tiburon Net Depot during WWII. The submarine net spanned the Golden Gate. It is now the Tiburon Oceanographic Center. Along the Tiburon waterfront is the terminal for ferries to Angel Island and San Francisco. Paddlers should be wary of Raccoon Strait, the deep water channel for the Sacramento River going out the Golden Gate. (The first time I canoed to Angel Island we had to change course because of a passing freighter. Merchant ships now pass to the east of Angel Is.)

HISTORY: Tiburon was a very important railroad terminal where the freight trains went on barges to cross the bay to San Francisco. In 1937 when the Golden Gate Bridge was completed, freight could then go by truck across the bridge.

CORTE MADERA CREEK

RICHARDSON BAY, ANGEL IS., & SAUSALITO

Around Tiburon Peninsula, Richardson Bay, & Angel Island

ACCESS: Beach launch • Strawberry Drive from Seminary Dr. from US-101 exit on north side of Richardson Bay. Limited parking.

Beach launch • end of Harbor Drive NE of Broadway.

Boat ramp • Turney St. boat ramp (where Zacks used to be), at Turney and Broadway. Very limited parking.

Beach launch • Schoonmaker Beach via Bridgeway, Marinship Way, and Liberty Ship Way. Limited parking. Rrm.

Beach launch • Gabrielson Park, Sausalito via Broadway, NE on Anchor.

Beach launch • Coyote Creek, Tamalpais Valley, at creek & NE of SR-1 bridge.

COMMENTS: Richardson Bay is dominated in the west by Mt. Tamalpais. Marinas, houseboats of all descriptions and businesses line the west bank. The east shore, Strawberry Point area, is convoluted with 6 miles of natural habitat. Further east and closer to Tiburon Blvd. is The Dickey House (moved from San Francisco), the Audubon Society headquarters. On the eastside are 2 miles of shoreline preserve then Belvedere Lagoon followed by Belvedere Island dotted with multi-million dollar homes with views to match. One 6-foot tide day on this bay, we could paddle up Arroyo Corte Madera del Presidio creek to Locust, half way to Mill Valley from Tamalapis High School. The creek flows from Mt. Tamalpais through Old Mill Park, the site of Captain Richardson's saw mill. Another day we paddled up Coyote Creek flowing into the bay from Tamalpais Valley.

Angel Island via Sausalito, 9 miles around & back, Class II

BEWARE: Watch for favorable tides, (go with the flow), wind (more in the afternoon), and current from the Sacramento River. Strong outgoing tides could give a fast ride out the Golden Gate and on to Hawaii via the Farralones.

COMMENTS: Paddlers should be experienced and trained in rescue skills for paddling to or around the island. Angel Island SP (415.435.1915) has beaches, historical sites, trails, camping, and ferry service! The 360° view from the top on a clear night is spectacular! Paddling to and around Angel Island can be from San Quentin (village), Miller Beach at Pt. Richmond, and Aquatic Park in San Francisco and one of the access locations in Sausalito.

Horseshoe Bay, ex- Ft. Baker, Presidio Yacht Club Marina

ACCESS: Beach launch • via Sausalito Lateral, 1st exit after Vista Point to the right at the north end of the Golden Gate Bridge, down the hill to Bunker Road, then to the water. Going S., exit at Marin City onto Bridgeway, through Sausalito staying to the waterfront, take East Road, or from Waldo Grande, take the Sausalito Lateral.

COMMENTS: Horseshoe Bay is a small protected harbor that can be paddled in an hour—great for a practice session. Or it could be the "jumping off place" to paddle around the bay to Sausalito, out the Golden Gate to Kirby Beach or Muir Beach, or with a very strong out-going tide to Hawaii (?).

MARIN ISLANDS

BEING PHOTOGRAPHED

Burning Desire

ANGEL ISLAND

RICHARDSON BAY

CHAPTER 4 -NORTH COAST

CONTENTS

BOLINAS LAGOON

SEASON: All year. . ST TIDE: 4' - 6'. TIDE LOCATION: Bolinas Lagoon.

ACCESS: In Bolinas go through town continuing on Wharf Road to the end or enroute at the dock across from the College of Marin Marine Lab. There are several (un-marked) waterside access spots from SR-1 between Calle Del Arroyo north of Stinson Beach and Fairfax Bolinas Road. (Watch for heavy weekend traffic.) Limited parking. NOTE: Signs to Bolinas from SR-1 are missing.

MAPS: AAA — "Marin County" and "San Fran. Bay Region." DE LORME — p. 103

GAS, FOOD, and LODGING: Bolinas and Stinson Beach.
CAMPING: Steep Ravine State Park, 1 mile S. of Stinson Beach on SR-1. 415.388.2070. By reservation only: 1.800.444.7275.

WATER: Streams enter the lagoon at the southern and northern ends and a few on the Bolinas Ridge side. The water would be brackish at the recommended tides, it is mostly ocean water, except after recent heavy rains.

BEWARE: The wind blows often. When the tide goes out, it can be fast! Read the tide book well or get stuck in the mud. The lagoon is now mostly shallow.

COMMENTS: The lagoon was absolutely fantastic on a mid-March day, sunny, warm, no wind, incoming tide as we started and outgoing tide as we were ending our 5 mile outing. We paddled along the Bolinas shore up the small creek across trails in the marsh to the main lagoon, then south towards Stinson past the burnt dredge into the shallow marsh behind beach cabins (the causeway has been eroded away). Our return trip was along the lagoon side of the gated residential Sea Drift and along the south end of Kent Island. On other trips, we stared down at leopard sharks resting on the sand bottom—none this time. But we did see a bald eagle, plus gulls, long-billed curlews, willets, American avocets, coots, bufflehead ducks, and many others. We paddled through a school of small fish with terns diving with a splash, just feet away from our kayaks. The lagoon is the feeding ground for the herons and egrets from rookeries in Bolinas and Audubon Canyon Ranch.

MEMORIES: We often spent our summers at Stinson Beach in one of the eight cabins my father built. We dug deep holes in the sand, lit forgotten fire crackers on July 5th, used the ironing board for surfing in the freezing water (pre- surfboard and wet-suit days). We watched each Friday evening to see if The Owl, a motor-sailor, had anchored at Bolinas bringing weekend visitors and a food supply. The lagoon was deeper then. My father was the first one to run the Dipsea Race twice, when it was reactivated after WWII. The first time at night (after his late work day) to see if he could find the route and the second time to enter the race the next day. He came in last, very exhausted, but happy to receive a cup as the oldest competitor.

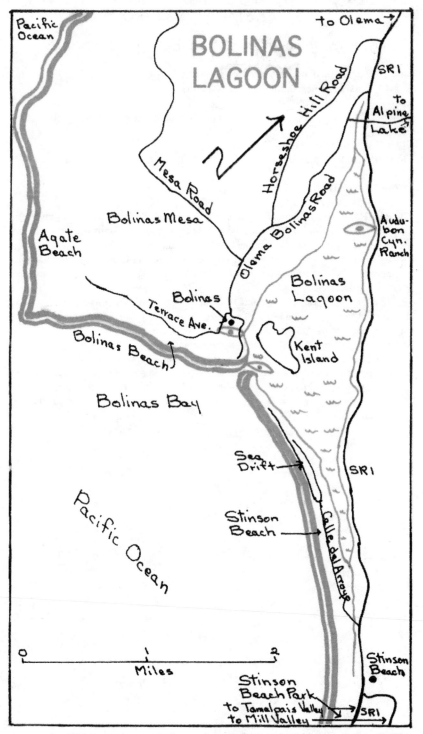

DRAKES BAY/ESTERO

SEASON: All year. SHORE MILEAGE: 15 BEST TIDE: over 2.2' (Pt. Reyes)

ACCESS: Johnson's Oyster Farm. From Inverness stay on Sir Francis Drake Blvd. not quite 5 miles, turn left to the oyster farm. Pkg. & Rrm.

MAPS: AAA — "San Francisco Bay Region" and "Marin County." DE LORME — p. 93.

GAS, FOOD, and LODGING: Inverness.
CAMPING: Olema Ranch Campground, 10155 SR-1, Olema. 415.663.8001.

BEWARE: Wind! Low tides.

COMMENTS: What a fabulous bay to explore nestled behind a high cliff that gives protection from the ocean winds. Notice the way that oysters are now grown protecting them from the hungry sting rays. There are a few beaches for a paddling break or lunch. Explore the arms, Creamery and Barries Bay on the right and Home Bay on the left. An extended trip could be going around the left hill and Drakes Head into Estero De Limantour another 3 miles of paddling.

And then there was that cold day in January when Marty Griffin and I were joining Elizabeth Terwilliger's group paddling on Limantour Bay. Not calling in advance, we failed to learn the trip was canceled due to the freezing weather. Marty and I went canoeing anyway, breaking a good quarter inch of ice with the square metal-tipped ends of our Seda wood paddles. Using our paddles as ice picks was extra work and slow going as well as crunching the canoe through the cracked ice down the creek into the ice-free bay. (Felt a hint of being an ice-breaker. Although they crack ice several feet thick.) Gorgeous clear brisk day with clear water so that we could see 3 inch moon snails on the sandy bottom.

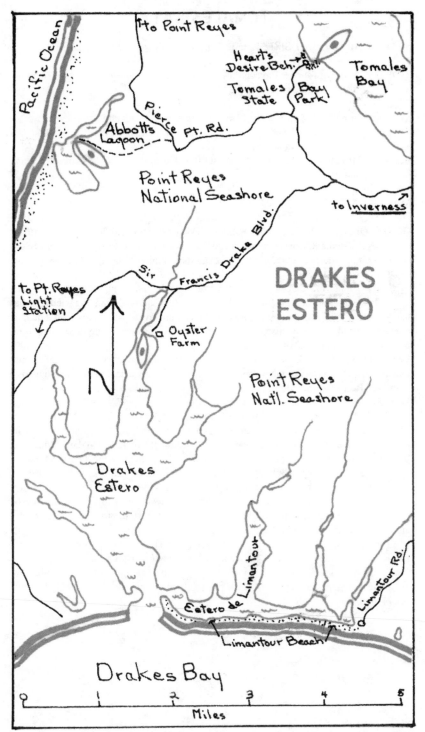

TOMALES BAY

SEASON: All year. BAY SIZE: 12 miles long x 1+ mile wide. BEST TIDE: 3'-6'.

TIDE LOCATION: Tomales Bay; entrance, Blakes Landing (for Walker Creek), Marshall and Inverness (for Lagunitas Creek).

ACCESS: South end • Whitehouse Pool parking area. Parking and Rrm.
West side • Hearts Desire Beach, go past Inverness, right on Pierce Pt. Rd. 2 miles to park
     turnoff. Parking and Rrm.
East side • Millerton Pt. SP, and boat ramp at Miller Co. Park near Walker Creek. Parking
     and Rrm.

MAPS: AAA — "San Francisco Bay Region" and "Marin County." DE LORME — p. 93.

GAS, FOOD, and LODGING: Olema, Inverness (west side), and Pt. Reyers Station.
CAMPING: Olema Ranch Campground, 10155 SR-1, Olema. 415.663.8001. Taylor State
Park, Sir Francis Drake Blvd., 4 miles N. Lagunitas, 4 miles S. Olema, 415.488.9897.

BEWARE: Tidal flow that can erase a few beaches at high tide and the flow of the water
from the tide that can have an effect on the return trip. Winds and changing winds that can
happen very quickly, impeding progress and creating waves. Sting rays with a quickly
released painful barb. Establish a turn-around time as it is a temptation to paddle to the
next cove.and the next cove.
    The mouth of Tomales Bay is a breeding ground of great white sharks. There are also
treacherous currents and rogue waves that have caused many a boat to capsize, some with
lives lost. Rescue is hazardous.

COMMENTS: In spite of the "downside" Tomales Bay is a fabulous paddling location.
Several paddle sport stores offer guided trips as do some outfitters. Some trips may include fresh oysters roasted on the beach or a lunch stop at Hog Island in the middle of the
bay with its plateau with cypress trees. Nearby is Piglet as the teenage, Quentin Canoers,
part of the Marin Canoe Club, named it. (It is more formally known as Duck Island.)
Paddling on the east shore one sees mostly eel grass in the shallow water. The west shore
has starfish, crabs and other sea life. The beach at Heart's Desire SP is a favorite for
swimming and paddling. Stop at a beach up the bay and roast the fresh oysters bought at
an oyster farm from the other side of the bay
    The bay is situated along the Inverness Ridge giving some protection from the wind
and fog. Small communities and private inholdings are the exception with natural vegetation, beaches and rock cliffs being dominant. Bishop pines are plentiful as are wildflowers in the spring. At the ocean end of the bay is a herd of Tule elk. Water birds are plentiful, particulary in the winter.

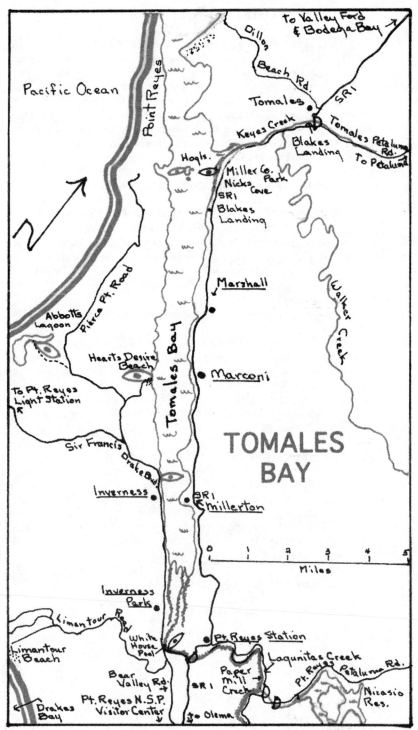

Pacific Ocean

Point Reyes

To Valley Ford & Bodega Bay

Dillon

Beach Rd.

Tomales

SR1

Keyes Creek

Tomales

Tomales Petaluma Rd.

To Petaluma

Blakes Landing

Hogs.

Miller Co. Park

Nicks Cove

SR1

Blakes Landing

Marshall

Walker Creek

Abbotts Lagoon

Pierce Pt. Road

Hearts Desire Beach

Marconi

To Pt. Reyes Light Station

Sir Francis Drake Bud.

TOMALES BAY

Tomales Bay

Inverness

SR1

Millerton

0   1   2   3   4   5

Miles

Inverness Park

Limantour Rd.

Limantour Beach

White House Pool

Pt. Reyes Station

Laquinitas Creek

Bear Valley Rd.

Paper mill Creek

SR1

Pt. Reyes Petaluma Rd.

Drakes Bay

Pt. Reyes N.S.P. Visitor Center

To Olema

Nicasio Res.

TOMALES BAY (con't)

Tomales Bay, what a fascinating spot, an earthquake fault line, caused by the famous San Andreas fault running the length of the bay. Just imagine as you're paddling that the land on the west side is galloping past you, according to geological time, as the land to the east is standing still. The 1906 earthquake drastically moved some property lines. The visitor center at Pt. Reyes Seashore National Park off of Bear Valley Road is worth a visit. The saving of Tomales Bay in as natural state as possible is another interesting story of very recent history. On the west is the quaint town of Inverness, becoming a bit touristy but still charming. Driving around to the east side is Point Reyes Station, a ranch-oriented community, also welcomes tourists.

KAYAK RENTALS: Rentals just north of Inverness and near Marshall.

LAGUNITAS CREEK (PAPERMILL CREEK)

ACCESS: Park and launch at White House Pool Co. Park and paddle southeast toward SR-1 going under a bridge or two as far as the water will support your paddling craft. This means, check the tide tables for the highest flow, watch your head going under the bridges. Or go north into Tomales Bay.

ABBOTT'S LAGOON

ACCESS: Watch for the sign on the left for the way to the lagoons. The long path is surfaced so wheels for your paddlecraft are advised. A long large sand dune borders the ocean with the lagoons nestled behind. There were four of us on the exploratory trip with Dick Brown, a naturalist at this new national seashore park. We were all pleasantly surprised as we watched local naturalist Elizabeth Terwilliger pick up an arrowhead on the sand dune, exclaiming, "This is the first one I've found!" Mrs. 'T's". Abbott's Lagoon canoe trips were launched.

KEYS CREEK to WALKER CREEK

ACCESS: Miller County Park boat ramp. Paddle north along the east shore into the marshy end of keys Creek. SR-1 is parallel to Keys Creek for about two miles, to the confluence with Walker Creek entering from the east. It has a very different feel, more remote, than Tomales Bay and is warmer with less wind. How far up can Walker Creek be paddled? This depends upon the flow in the creek, the tide and the skill level of the paddler.

NOTE: The upper miles of Walker Creek, according to reports, is a Class II stream when there is enough water to run it, but with many snags.

●●●●●●●●●●●●●●●●

STINSON BEACH - BOLINAS BAY SURFING

TOMALES BAY

TOMALES

DRAKES ESTERO - OYSTER GROWING

ESTERO AMERICANO
MURRELET

BODEGA HARBOR

SEASON: All year. BEST TIDES: 3'-6'. TIDE LOCATION: Bodega Harbor Entrance.

ACCESS: Boat ramps at Doran Regional Park, at Doran Beach, at the Westside Park on the way to Bodega Head and at the commercial fishing marina.

MAPS: AAA — "Mendocino and Sonoma Coast Region." DELORME — p. 92.

GAS, FOOD, and LODGING: Nearby town of Bodega Bay. C. of C. 707.875.3422. CAMPING: On the southwest side is Doran County Park at Doran Beach. West the southwest side: 707.875.3540.

BEWARE: Low tide and getting stuck in the mud. Sting rays in and out of the bay and great white sharks at the mouth of the bay.

COMMENTS: Bodega Harbor and vicinity is a kaleidoscopic array of possible activities: paddling small craft, camping at the beach, playing golf, visiting art galleries, studying marine life in the ocean and harbor, hiking on Bodega Head, birding, eating at some of the best seafood restaurants, visiting the town of Bodega where Alfred Hitchcock's thriller, The Birds, was filmed, sailing in the harbor, watching the commercial fishing boats empty their daily catch which could be fish of all kinds, sea urchins destined for Japan, or crabs for local markets. Several times we have paddled in the harbor on a summer evening then enjoyed seafood feast at a local restaurant looking at the harbor.

STORY: There were five of us in Kopapa compact kayaks paddling around the harbor. We paddled to the south seeing many species of water birds, up to the Coast Guard Station near the mouth, along the east shore pausing at the marina to chat with Vancouver B.C. sailors. Then to the jetty where this story really begins. A tall man wearing cowboy boots called to us frantically from the end of the jetty, asking for help. Halfway down the jetty was his fishing rod with a heavy-duty line wound around a large pole in the water. Problem: there was a large fish on the end of his line. One of our paddlers unwrapped the line around the pole and started reeling it in and discovering, yes, there was a large fish on the end. One big enough to drag his kayak as he held on to the pole. So another paddler grabbed a hold of the fish-dragged kayak and another kayaker held on to that kayak so there were now three kayaks slowly being dragged by the "fish"! Or was it a sting ray? Very carefully the fishing pole was placed in the hands of the fisherman on shore who slowly reeled it in. We kayakers watching to see what was going to be landed. It took time and muscle to finally get the big fish to shore AND it was a sting ray! With great care he landed it, killed it with a big hunting knife and kept his boots dry. An adventurous day!

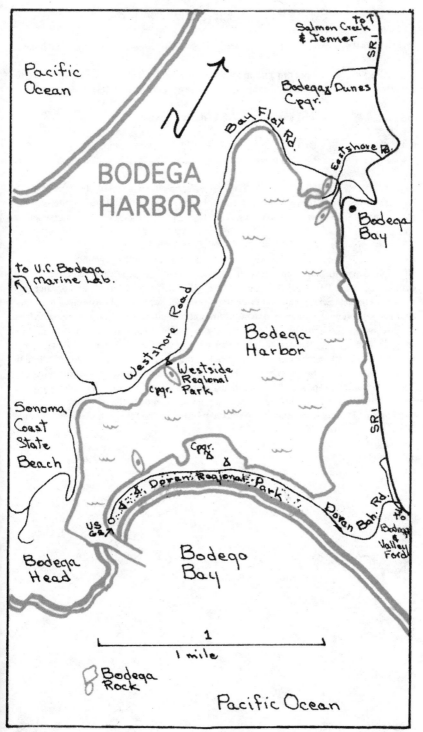

Pacific Ocean

Salmon Creek & Jenner

Bodega Dunes Cpgr.

Eastshore Rd.

BODEGA HARBOR

Bay Flat Rd.

Bodega Bay

to U.C. Bodega Marine Lab.

Westshore Road

Bodega Harbor

Westside Regional Park
Cpgr.

Sonoma Coast State Beach

Cpgr.

Doran Regional Park

Doran Bch. Rd.

to Bodega & Valley Ford

US G&r

Bodega Head

Bodega Bay

1
1 mile

Bodega Rock

Pacific Ocean

ESTERO AMERICANO - Tidal

SEASON: All year. **MILES:** 8-10 round trip. **BEST TIDE** (Bodega Harbor):3' and higher.

ACCESS: SR-1 at Valley Ford SW on Valley Ford Franklin School Road cross the estero turn left on Marsh Rd. then quickly left on a dirt road to the water.

MAPS: AAA — "Sonoma and Napa." DE LORME — p. 93.

GAS, FOOD, and LODGING: Bodega Bay, Santa Rosa, and Petaluma.
CAMPING: Bodega Bay: Dillon Beach, Tomales Bay.

BEWARE: Tide and wind! The tide has more affect on the water flow then the creek so pay close attention to the high and low tides and the times and height differentials of the flows. The wind is more apt to blow up the estero in the afternoon which can give a nice "push" on the return trip.

COMMENTS: Don't be fooled, the route to the ocean is to the left under the bridge; although it may look the other way, it isn't! At lower tide the water pathway is well defined. There are few beaches enroute. About halfway to the ocean half of the water cuts sharply to the left, with a stronger current, go that way. A fence partway across the channel may be in view straight ahead. Not far from here is a false channel, again go left. The countryside is rolling to steep hills mostly bare except for bays, oaks and cattle. There are some art-like rock formationson the south bank and what looks like rock carvings on a low cliff on a north bank. Hiking on the beach at the ocean are the reward for paddling to the end. The water is brackish and yucko! Birds are interesting with both sea birds and land birds: herons, egrets, gulls, cormorants, grebes. We had an interest encounter with a friendly bird, possibly a Guillamot in winter plumage in the middle of summer. It was by itself, seemed lonely so we paddled to it. It pecked at our paddles and hands but ignored our offer bits of crackers.

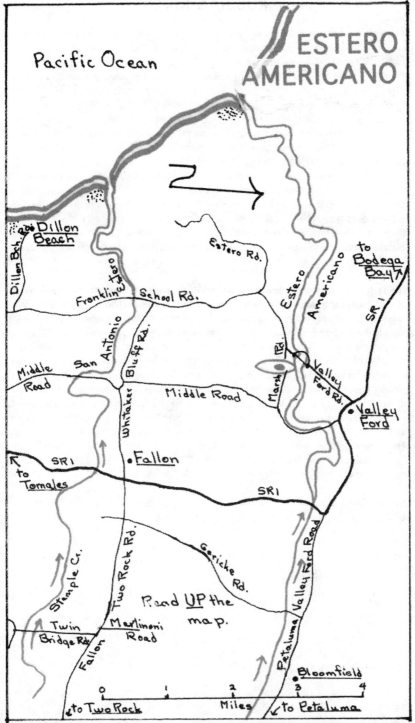

Pacific Ocean

ESTERO AMERICANO

Dillon Beach

Dillon Bch.

Estero Rd.

Franklin

Estero

School Rd.

Estero Americano

to Bodega Bay

SR 1

San Antonio

Whitaker Bluff Rd.

Middle Road

Marsh Rd.

Valley Ford Rd.

Middle Road

Valley Ford

Fallon

SR 1

to Tomales

SR 1

Two Rock Rd.

Geriche Rd.

Stemple Cr.

Read UP the map.

Petaluma

Valley Ford Road

Twin Bridge Rd.

Fallon

Martinoni Road

Bloomfield

0   1   2   3   4

to Two Rock

Miles

to Petaluma

RUSSIAN RIVER

The Russian River is one of my favorite easy rivers with a few miles of excitement for the novice paddler. It is assured a continuous flow, thanks to the man-made diversion tunnel for Eel River water. (BUT the Eel River community wants its water back!) It is close enough to large cities to attract many summer visitors. The scenery varies from water-carved boulders, giant redwood trees, willows and cottonwoods, to miles of vineyards, riverside homes to inviting swimming holes, some with sand or gravel beaches.

In summer the 100 miles of river below Coyote Dam, in Ukiah, to the ocean is mostly class I+ swimming temperature water. The class II & III rapids are between Squaw Rock and Preston. The five, easily portaged, summer dams create lake-like waters. Flow increases from winter rains add a challenge to paddlers.

It's a birder's paradise with varieties of water, sea, and land birds as well a migratory ones. Spindly-legged great blue heron, osprey diving for fish, begging mallards, common mergansers (maybe ducklings on mother's back), double-crested cormorants drying their out-stretched wings, colorful wood ducks, water ouzels walking down rocks under water to feed are just a few of the many species along the way. Seeing harbor seals at Jenner and curious otters add to a river adventure. The river at Jenner, often open to the ocean, is tidal.

HISTORY: So interesting; first the activities of the native Americans, the exploring and sea otter hunting of the Russians for whom the river is named. The coming of the railroad was prompted by the logging of redwoods and Douglas fir. Resorts came soon after inviting fog-bound San Franciscans to enjoy the warm water and sunny weather of the river. They came via the Northwestern Pacific ferry to Marin County, boarded the NWP train bound for Monte Rio, Guerneville or Forestville via the Ross Valley to Fairfax (where mountain biking started) through Whites Hill tunnel and San Geronimo Valley (Papermill Creek country) on to Point Reyes Station along Tomales Bay, inland to Duncan's Mills along the river to Fulton where it connected with the track from Santa Rosa. There was a spur to Cazadero along Austin Creek where the Camp Fire Girls got off at Camp Thayer and the Boy Scouts for the Marin Co. Camp. Also in Russian River country were wine and champaign, oranges from Cloverdale the former citrus capital of California, apples from Sebastopol (Luther Burbank's efforts were in full bloom and yield) and cinnabar from the mines near Cazadero, all carried by train until the line closed in 1935.

NOTE: Today the tourist featured trout in New Zealand arrived by slow boat in the form of Russian River steelhead roe encased in a 3 foot ice cube in the '30's.

RUSSIAN RIVER

CLASS I

REDWOOD STUMP

EGRETS

ROCK "SLIDE"

KIDS LOVE PADDLING

RUSSIAN RIVER, Ukiah to Jenner

Coyote Dam to Talmage, 4.5 miles, Class II
(Below Lake Mendocino, Ukiah)

ACCESS: Put-in • below Coyote Dam spillway, on the east side. From US-101 hwy. east on Lake Mendocino Dr. follow signs to dam. Parking.

3 miles to • Perkins St. Bridge. US-101 Perkins St. exit go east to bridge. Perkins St. is Vichy Springs Road east of the bridge.

1.5 miles to • Talmage Road bridge. From US-101 take the Talmage Road exit, go east to bridge. Parking.

BEWARE: About two miles below the dam is a river-wide rocky outcropping that creates interesting waves and waterflows. Stop and scout on river right at lower water. There can be trees and logs in the river plus overhanging branches.

• • • • • • • • • • • • • • •

Talmage to Old Hopland - 14.5 miles, Class I+, (dam)

ACCESS: Put-in • below the bridge at Talmage.

14.5 miles to • Hopland Road bridge in Old Hopland. From US-101 go east 1 mile from Hopland to Old Hopland. This put-in keeps changing with the change in river banks, property owner's attitudes, and fishing paths. (1997 access was on the northwest end of the bridge. Dirt road parking.)

BEWARE: Be aware of the slow flow of the river a short ways below the Talmage bridge caused by the dam. In kayaks, getting out on the dam is a bit tricky. Over the dam and back in the water is easier. Watch for snags, overhanging trees and old posts. The river changes with each flood, so be wary.

COMMENTS: There is a remote feeling to the river as it flows past vineyards and fruit ranches except for the many pumps and pipes taking water for irrigation. The remains of a few car bodies used for bank stabilization are mostly out of sight and vine covered. Keep alert, enjoy the solitude, some of the area feels like a fern glade. Bay, sycamore, and willow trees dominate the banks with grape vines and Himalayan blackberries in a few areas. A seldom paddled run. The solitude may be interrupted by a train on the closeby track.

Lake Mendocino near Ukaih impounds both arms of the Russian River by Coyote Dam. It is an attractive recreational and camping area.

• • • • • • • • • • • • • • •

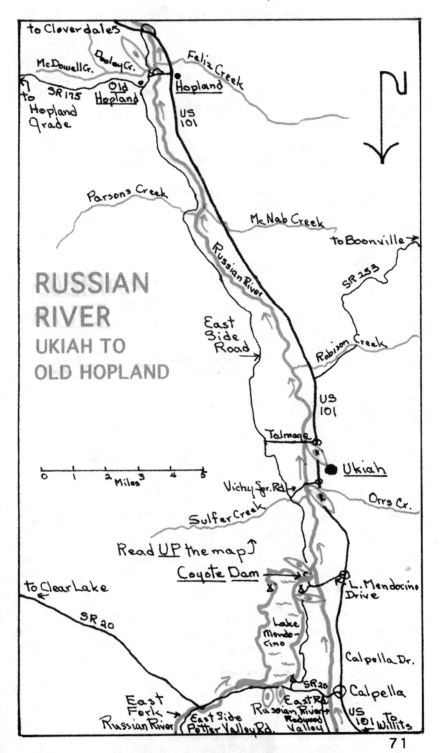

RUSSIAN
RIVER
UKIAH TO
OLD HOPLAND

Read UP the map ↑

Coyote Dam →

RUSSIAN RIVER (con't.)

Old Hopland to Cloverdale, 17 miles, Class II (III)
Old Hopland to beach above Squaw Rock, 6 miles, Class I & II

ACCESS: Put-in • near bridge at Old Hopland, 1 mile east of US-101 at Hopland.
6 miles to • beach above Squaw Rock. There is a path to the beach just before a fence upriver from Squaw Rock. Short steep walk. Limited parking.

GAS, FOOD, and LODGING: Ukiah, Hopland, and Cloverdale.
CAMPING: L. Mendocino, Ukiah. 707.462,7581. Lake Sonoma. 707.433.9483.

BEWARE: Quick turns and river "moods," going from an easy flow to a small drop, turn and faster flow. Snags in and across the river. Three areas for caution: under the US-101 bridge (left), near the end of the valley (right and left), after Pieta Creek pool (right) and after the boulders with Squaw Rock in view (left).

COMMENTS: Easy beginning, scenic and interesting. After US-101 bridge the river flows on the right side of the valley. Not far is the pool where Pieta Creek enters from river left and a mile upriver from Squaw Rock. After paddling between two house-sized boulders (great photo spot) the river twists and Squaw Rock is around the bend but in view at the river left beach. Check the take-out before paddling. Pieta Creek is also an access spot.

• • • • • • • • • • • • • • •

Beach above Squaw Rock to Cloverdale, 11 miles, Class I, II & III

ACCESS: Put-in • at beach above Squaw Rock. Parking.
2 miles to • Comminsky Station Road. From US-101 turn west on Comminski Station Rd. to the river. Several access spots. Gauging station.
2.5 miles to • Geysers Road exit from US-101, east end of underpass. Parking.3.5 miles to • NACO campground (fee), 33655 Redwood Hwy. N. 2 miles south 1.5 miles to • site of Preston bridge. Large turn-out south of NACO cpgr. From First St. bridge in Cloverdale, east to Crocker Rd., north on River Rd., left on Redwood Hwy. N. to large turn-out on the left. Parking.
1.5 miles to • First St. (Crocker) bridge, Cloverdale. From US-101 exit at Citrus Fair Dr., go north on east frontage rd., rt. on First St. to river.

BEWARE: Class III Squaw Rock Slot has changed. Scout before running! The Graveyard is still a tricky rock garden. C-turn is now a low Class III. Watch for rocks, blind turns, snags and strainers. Constant changes.

COMMENTS: The first 5 miles, known as the Squaw Rock Run, are the most challenging on the Russian River, Class II & III. There are rapids, carved rocks, "play holes," and bushes to duck under. From NACO campground the river is Class I+ to Preston then Class I to the bridge, a good short fun run for beginners.

• • • • • • • • • • • • • • •

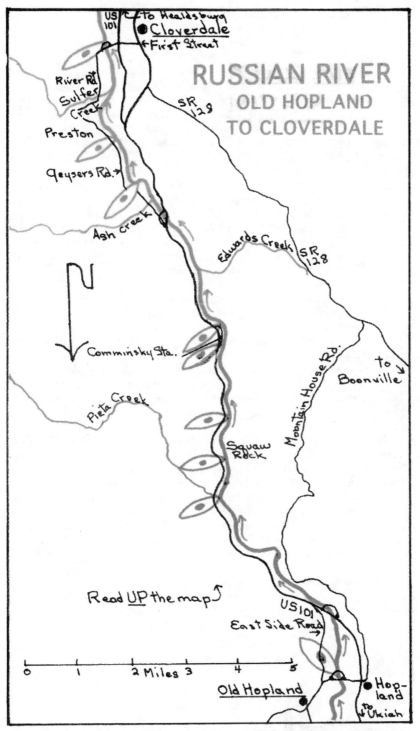

RUSSIAN RIVER
OLD HOPLAND
TO CLOVERDALE

RUSSIAN RIVER (con't)

Cloverdale to Healdsburg, 32 miles, Class I+

ACCESS: Put-in •First St. (Crocker) bridge, Cloverdale. From US-101 exit at Citrus Fair Dr., go north on east frontage road, right on First St. to river. Parking.

5.5 miles to • Asti. From US-101 take Asti exit, turn right on Asti Rd., left on Wash. School Rd. (KOA sign) to bridge (summer only). Limited parking. Winter; long walk from gate near Asti Road.

6.5 miles to • Geyserville bridge. From US-101 follow signs to Geyserville, go east on SR-128 to bridge. Limited parking.

6 miles to • Alexander ValleyBridge, at the campground. From US-101 take the Alexander Valley exit, go south on Healdsburg Ave. to Alexander Valley Rd., turn east 2.5 miles to the bridge. Campground(fee); Parking & Rrm.

11 miles to • Del Rio Woods. From US-101 go east at Dry Creek Rd. exit to Healdsburg Ave., right to Powell Ave., left 2.5 miles. Beach. Parking.3 miles to • Healdsburg Vet. Mem. Beach Co. Park. From US-101 on the south side of the Russian River go east on Healdsburg Ave. to the park (fee). Picnic tables, swimming, parking and Rrm. Carry boats around dam.

GAS, FOOD, and LODGING: Healdsburg, Geyserville, and Cloverdale
CAMPING: Alexander Valley Campground: 707.431.1453.

BEWARE: Upriver winds, mostly in the summer, especially paddling the last three miles to Healdsburg beach with the sun and the wind in the face. Cars parked near the river have been vandalized. This part of the river receives heavy use by those renting aluminum canoes and plastic kayaks from Trowbridge Recreation; some lacking in paddling skills. The last few miles to the Healdsburg beach on a hot summer day can be a "killer" with almost no current, sun in the eyes, wind in the face, and sore muscles!

COMMENTS: The Russian River in this middle section flows past miles of vineyards. The river, now going south, is great for paddling in the spring when the north winds blow. The 14 mile stretch to Healdsburg is picturesque as the river makes large sweeping turns around Black Peak and then Fitch Mountain. There are a few rock outcroppings in the river, one about a mile below Asti and another forming an island near Black Peak.

In late summer the beautiful yellow and silver blazing stars brighten the beaches and the yellow flowering water plant from China enliven the slack water areas. Note: Once when paddling towards the bridge at Geyserville I counted 55 American egrets in a large tree making it look like a leaf-bare Magnolia.

Canoe and kayak rentals: Trowbridge Rec. 707.433.7247.

●●●●●●●●●●●●●●●●

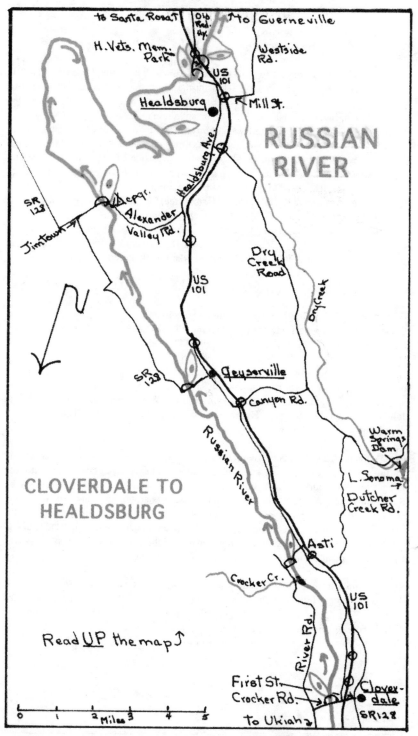

CLOVERDALE TO
HEALDSBURG

Read UP the map ↑

RUSSIAN RIVER (con't)

Sat. 9/16/06
Vet. Mem Park @
9:30AM to Steelhead Beach

Healdsburg to Guerneville, 16 miles, Class I+

10AM - 3p
Faster Part of River

ACCESS: Put-in • Portage to below summer dam at Vet. Mem. Beach Co. park at Healdsburg (fee). From US-101 on the south side of the Russian River exit onto Healdsburg Ave. go north 1 mile to the park on the south side of the river. Parking, picnic tables, Rrm. beach, swimming.

7 miles to • second boat ramp at Maxwell Grove close to Wohler bridge. From south on US-101 take Healdsburg Ave. exit, turn left at first stop light, Mill St. into Westside road. From north turn left at Westside Road, 10 miles to Wohler Road bridge, summer locked gate with pass-through. Go through redwoods to river. NO PARKING nearby in any direction!

* 1 mile to • Burkes Canoe Rentals beach, Mirabel (fee).707.887.7662. Pkg. & Rrm.
.5 miles to • Steelhead Beach County Park (fee). Parking and Rrm.
3.5 miles to • River Bend Resort, 11820 River Road (fee). 707.887.7662.
4 miles to • Johnson's Bch. & Resort, public access. Downriver from bridges at Guerneville. Boat rentals. 707-869.2022. Summer dam. Parking & Rrm.

MAPS: AAA —"Mendocino and Sonoma Coast Region." DE LORME — pp. 93 & 83.

GAS, FOOD, and LODGING: Healdsburg and Guerneville.
CAMPING: Armstrong Redwoods SP, Guerneville: 707.869.2015. Alex. Valley Cpgr., Healdsburg: 707.431.1453. Lake Sonoma: 707.433.2200.

BEWARE: Afternoon upriver winds preceded by morning fogs. Current flowing under overhanging branches. Three summer dams all require portaging: left at Vet. Mem. Bch. at Healdsburg, left at the rubber dam downriver from Wholer Bridge, right at the dam at Johnson's Beach at Guerneville. Highly congested roads between Mirabel and Monte Rio during summer and sunny weekends.

COMMENTS: This is the very friendly heavily used section of the Russian River. except for the first 10 miles which are areas of agriculture and extensive gravel mining leaving large lakes. After Burke's stay to the right. Cook's is the next beach, river left followed by Steelhead Beach Co. Park. The big left-hand sweep is around the vineyards of Korbel Winery with fabulous gardens and tasting room. After Hacienda bridge (gauging sta.) is the summer footbridge of Summerhome Park followed soon by the summer bridge of Old Fellows Rd., then a big left turn and stream on river right that drains the seven canyons of Rio Nido. Popular Johnson's Beach is on the right after two bridges.

NOTE: A mile from the rubber dam, Mark West Ck. enters from river left after flowing down a fairly steep hillside with Class IV rapids then into the flat lands where it is joined by Santa Rosa Creek via the Laguna in Sebastopol. There's a two mile paddle on the Laguna between Occidental Rd. and Guerneville Rd.

• • • • • • • • • • • • • • •

Stayed @ Riverlane Resort Cottage Cabin #6.

Sun. 9/17/06
Steelhead Beach to Johnsons Beach in Guerneville
11 AM - 2:30 pm
slower part of RR

Sept 06

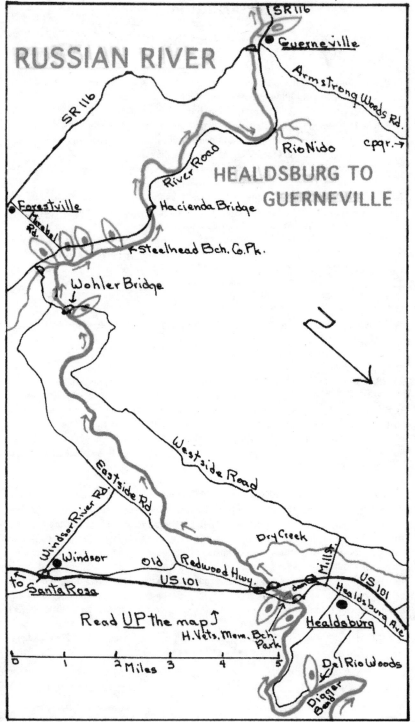

RUSSIAN RIVER

SR 116

Guerneville

Armstrong Woods Rd.

cpgr.→

Rio Nido

River Road

HEALDSBURG TO
GUERNEVILLE

Forestville

Hacienda Bridge

Mirabel Rd.

Steelhead Bch. Co. Pk.

Wohler Bridge

Westside Road

Eastside Rd.

Windsor River Rd.

Windsor

Dry Creek

Old Redwood Hwy.

US 101

Mill St.

US 101

to Santa Rosa

Healdsburg Ave.

Healdsburg

Read UP the map ↑

H. Vets. Mem. Bch. Park

Del Rio Woods

Digger Bend

0   1   2 Miles 3   4   5

RUSSIAN RIVER (con't)

Guerneville to Jenner (ocean), 15 miles, Class I

ACCESS: Put-in • Guerneville, Johnson's Beach and Resort, public access. Downriver from bridges at Guerneville on SR-116. Canoe & kayak rentals: 707.869.2022. Summer dam. Public parking and Rrm.

5 miles to • Monte Rio Beach below north end of Bohemian Hwy. Bridge, boat ramp. Drive to the beach. Parking & Rrm. Canoe & kayak rentals.

2.5 miles to • Rien's Sandy Beach, SR-116 near the confluence with Austin Creek, 3 miles from Monte Rio (fee). 707.865.2102. Parking & cpgr.

.5 mile to • Casini Ranch Family Campground, 22855 Moscow Road (fee). 707.865.2255. Parking, Rrm., campground, store, canoe rentals.

1 mile to • Duncan's Mills Camping Club Beach, 25387 Duncan's Mills Rd., Duncan's Mills (SR-116) (fee). 707.865.2024. Parking, Rrm, campground. Drive to beach at NW end of Mocsow Rd. Bridge. Kayak rentals.

3 miles to• Willow Creek Environmental Camp SP 1 mile south of Jenner off SR-1 on Willow Creek Rd. 707.875.3483 (phone for access). Parking & Rrm. 1.5 miles to • Bridgehaven Campground, 707.865.2473. At SW end of SR-1 bridge, private road to campground and river (fee). Parking & Rrm.

1.5 miles to • Jenner, SR-1, public boat ramp, across from gas station. Pkg & Rrm.

MAPS: AAA — "Mendocino & Sonoma Coast Region." DE LORME — pp. 82, 83, 92, & 93.

GAS, FOOD, and LODGING: Guerneville, Monte Rio, and Jenner.
CAMPING: Armstrong Redwoods SP, Guerneville: 707.869.2015. See above.

BEWARE: Afternoon upriver winds preceded by morning fogs. Highly congested roads during summer and sunny weekends. Portage Guerneville dam on right. The second dam is 2 miles below Guerneville at Vacation Beach. Paddling downstream getting swept out the mouth of the river. Note: One such "swept-out" paddler had to be plucked out of the ocean by helicopter.

COMMENTS: The river receives high use in the Guerneville and Monte Rio areas. A mile downriver from Guerneville is a residential area followed by sharp right hand bend going around the Northwood golf course. After Vacation Beach on the left are the steps from the Grove of the San Francisco-based Bohemian Club. The large riverside rocks often provide deep swimming holes opposite wide beaches. Reins Sandy Beach may not be recognized but it is soon followed by rain-fed Austin Creek just beyond flowing in from the right 6 miles downstream from Cazadero going under SR-116 bridge. On the left is the big sweeping curve around Casini's Family Beach and Campground. Several miles of willow-lined banks and cow pasture on the right give a wilderness feel. Willow Creek enters from the left near Willow Beach Campground up in the trees. The sweeping right turn after Bridge Haven acts as a wind break paddling into Jenner as does Penny Island.

•••••••••••••••

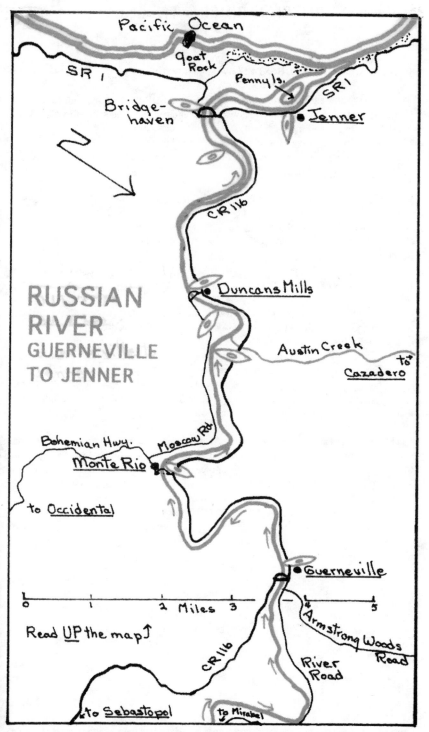

Pacific Ocean

Goat Rock

SR 1

Penny Is.

SR 1

Bridge-haven

Jenner

RUSSIAN RIVER
GUERNEVILLE TO JENNER

CR 116

Duncans Mills

Austin Creek

to Cazadero

Bohemian Hwy.

Moscow Rd.

Monte Rio

to Occidental

Guerneville

0   1   Miles   3   4   5

Read UP the map ↑

Armstrong Woods Road

River Road

CR 116

to Sebastopol

to Mirabel

RUSSIAN RIVER - Tributary

Austin Creek, 7.5 miles, Class 1+

SEASON: Winter & spring. BEST FLOWS: 300-1,000 cfs.

ACCESS: Put-in • Up river from Cazadero on Fort Ross Rd. after King Ridge Rd.
1 mile to • Cazadero, behind the fire house or NE end of the bridge just before Cazadero. Limited parking.
2 miles to • Cazadero Hwy. Bridge, SW end. Limited parking.
4.5 miles to • bridge between Cazadero Hwy. and Austin Creek Rd. Short walk to river on NW end of bridge. Parking.

MAPS: AAA — "Mendocino and Sonoma Coast Region." DE LORME — pp. 82 & 93.

GAS, FOOD, and LODGING: Monte Rio and Guerneville.
CAMPING: Armstrong Redwoods State Reserve, Guerneville, 707.869.5015. Rein's Sandy Beach: 707.865.2102. Casini's Family Ranch Campground: 800.451.8400.

BEWARE: Snags and fallen trees on the side or in the river.

COMMENTS: This is a springtime gem with easy clear water that includes a few fun spots, flowing 'neath the towering redwoods, though there are woodsy homes along the banks. It is rainfed, so the flow is iffy guesswork. We ran it at high-water once, took us an hour, being a skilled group of paddlers we continued on down the Russian to Jenner, another hour or so. This is the run of choice when the Russian is too high or the skill level of the group says "Austin Creek' or if we want just a very pleasant few hours in the relaxing quiet of the redwoods. Sort of a close short version of the Navarro with homes. During the summer residents install summer dams.

NOTE: Summer camps were common on Austin Creek; Marin County Boy Scout Camp at Cazadero, Berkeley Camp (still in operation), Camp Thayer for the Marin and Sonoma Counties Camp Fire Girls (where I went for 6 years as a camper and one on staff) and San Francisco Boy Scout Camp Royaneh on East Austin Creek, still in operation. (My efforts at finding a launch site on East Austin Creek were firmly thwarted.)

• • • • • • • • • • • • • • • •

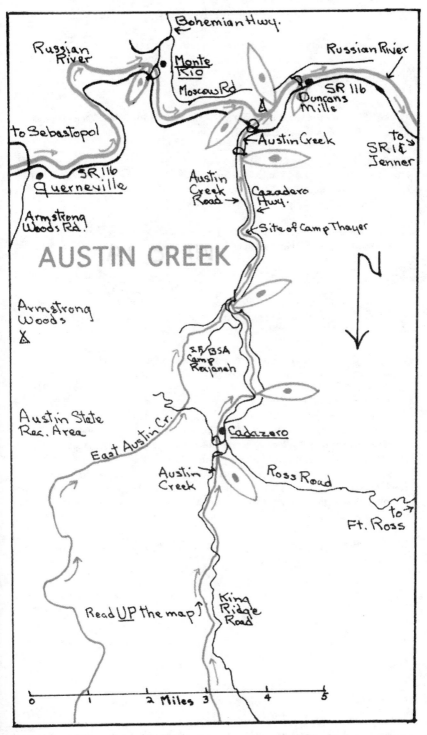

GUALALA RIVER

Wheatfield Branch, House Creek, 27 miles, Class 1 - 1+

SEASON: Spring & early summer. BEST FLOWS: 250 - 600 cfs.
FLOW INFO: http;//cdec.water.ca.gov/misc/stages/html.

ACCESS: Put-in • House Creek: From SR-1 east on Stewarts Point-Skaggs Springs Rd.,
4 miles south of Sea Ranch and 6 miles north of Salt Pt. SP, 16 miles to House Creek
coming in on the left.
5 miles to • "Y" camp on Skaggs Springs Rd.
4 miles to • Annapolis Rd. .5 mile from Stewarts Pt.-Skaggs Spr. Rd., below the bridge.
7.5 miles to • Annapolis Rd., 2 miles from SR-1 on Wheatfield Branch.
6.5 miles to • Double Bridges just upriver from Switchville, also an access.
1.5 miles to • Gualala Redwood Cpgr.
1.5 miles to • SR-1, below the bridge.
1 mile to bar • Summer lagoon when bar closed to ocean.

MAPS: AAA — "Mendocino and Sonoma Coast Region." DE LORME — pp. 72 & 82.

GAS, FOOD, and LODGING: Gualala, about 20 miles north on SR-1.
CAMPING: Gualala Point Regional Park: 707.785.2377 and Gualala Redwood Park:
707.884.3533.

BEWARE: Cold weather because of being so close to the ocean. Trees that could have
fallen across the river and snags.

COMMENTS: California at its best! Over 25 miles of paddling in redwood forests followed by the coast and a sandy beach. Ideal! The river is flowing through mostly private
forest land in active harvesting. What is its future? There is just something special about
paddling beneath trees that are 12 feet in diameter and tower over the land and water by
more than a hundred feet and combining with redwood forest plant life give off a very
characteristic welcoming fragrance. Am I prejudiced? Yes! But, where there are redwoods there is fog! The river flow near House Creek has a bit of interest making it class
I+ with a class II rapid at the YMCA camp. Most ofthe run is class I BUT this could
change very quickly with a storm, wind or logging; be wary.

RENTALS: Kayaks & canoes; Adventure Rents: 707.884.4FUN (386)
● ● ● ● ● ● ● ● ● ● ● ● ● ● ● ● ●

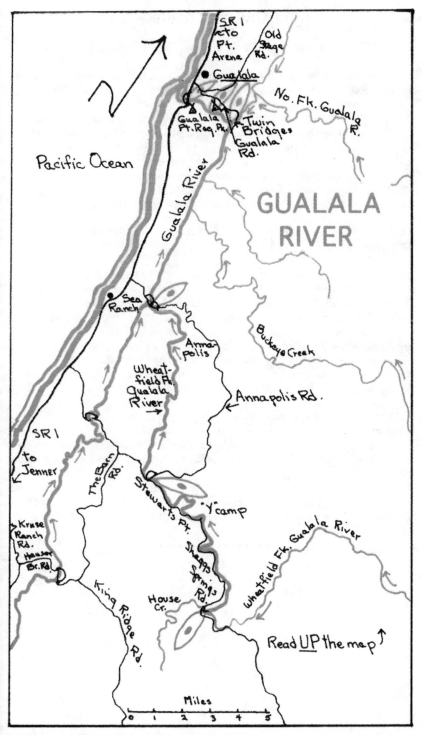

GARCIA RIVER, Point Arena

Voorhees Park to SR-1 bridge, 18 miles, class I, I+

SEASON: Rainy & spring. BEST FLOWS: 1.6'-3'. GAUGE: Eureka Hill Rd. bridge.
FLOW INFO: http://monsoon.water.ca.gov/cig/bin/select. FrOG: 707.882.3086.

ACCESS: Put-in • Voorhees Park. From SR-1 at Point Arena, turn east on Riverside
    Drive that becomes Eureka Hill Rd. 2.5 miles, to Ten Mile Road go 2.5 miles
    to Ten Mile Cutoff, drive 2 miles to end. This is down a steep hill, at the "Y"
    bear, after the gate (which should be open) the dirt road is poor and steep for
    the last 1/4 mile. (Very few signs.) Parking only.
8 miles to • Eureka Hill Road Bridge 4 miles from SR-1.
10 miles to • SR-1 bridge. Take out on river left upriver from bridge. Limited parking.

MAPS: AAA — "Bay and Mt. Section," "Mendocino and Sonoma Coast Region."
DELORME — p. 72.

GAS, FOOD, and LODGING: Pt. Arena. Restaurant: "The Wharf" at the pier.
CAMPING: Manchester Beach SP, 1 mile north of Manchester off SR-1: 707.937.5804.
Manchester Beach KOA, 1 mile north of Manchester on Kinny Rd: 707.882.2375.
Rollerville Junction, 2 mi. north of Pt. Arena: 707.882.2440.

BEWARE: About 3.5 miles downriver from Voorhees Park is a tricky rapid where the
river goes toward a high ridge with willows, followed by a right turn and pool. As a rain-
fed stream watch the weather and check for the recorded feet. Gravel mining contacts
have shot over the heads of paddlers, on one occasion.

COMMENTS: Paddling in the redwoods is very special especially on this intimate river,
much smaller than the Navarro or the Gualala. It definitely is a wilderness run with private property on both sides. The first half of the run the river flows north following the
San Andreas fault like the Gualala River to the south, then it turns left to flow to the
ocean.
    Thanks to the local organization FrOG, Friends Of the Garcia, gravel mining in the
river has been stopped since 1994. For more information: 707.882.3086. Thank you Peter
Dobbins for the information on the Garcia River and for fighting to preserve its watershed.

•••••••••••••••••••

RANCHERIA CREEK (NAVARRO RIVER)

Rancheria Creek, Fish Rock Rd. — Mt. View Rd., 10 mi., Class II+ (-III)

SEASON: Rainy & spring. BEST FLOWS: 200-500 cfs.

ACCESS: Put-in • SR-128 between US-101 & SR-1, 5 mi. NW. of Yorkville & 9 mi. SE of Boonville turn W. on Fish Rock Rd., SE corner of bridge.

10 miles to • Mt. View Rd. N. end of Boonville 4.5 miles to bridge, NW end, between Minnie (upstream of bridge) and Bear Wallow Creeks. This access keeps changing. New property owners installed a fence across the NW put-in, so a very thoughtful person dug steps down the steep slope. Best access is on the upstream end of the bridge. Limited pkg.

MAPS: AAA — "Mendocino and Sonoma Coast Region". DE LORME — p. 82.

GAS, FOOD, and LODGING: Boonville, Cloverdale, and Ukiah.
CAMPING: Hendy Woods SP near Philo: 707.937.5904.

BEWARE: Paddling this run is "Creekin' ". In the beginning the creek is narrow, with trees across, snags to catch the unwary and small drops, plus debris piles. When it leaves the road it widens and flows through farm lands then into a narrow canyon with rocks and drops. The channel changes after each storm.

●●●●●●●●●●●●●●●●

Rancheria Cr., Mt. View Rd. — Hendy Woods, 12 mi., Cl. II+

(See info. above and DE LORME — p. 74.)

ACCESS: Take-out • Hendy Woods SP parking area. Rrm.

BEWARE: Logs across the river, log jams, and sharp rocks from a recent earth slide. As the water gets lower there may be some ducking of overhanging branchs and scraping over rocks. Quick temperature drops! The river wide rock slide of a few years ago is mostly washed out but there was a new rock slide, a bit smaller but still across the river downstream from Ralph's Rapid, and just upstream of the earlier slide. May of 1999 we found a route through on river left. The slide came down from river right, as did the other one.

COMMENTS: A Class II favorite! In the late 70's I read about this run in Dick Schwind's book, called some daring friends, and ran it. (The two of us in inflatable kayaks were able to duck under the large redwood completely across the water.) What a fabulous surprise to have this run close to our homes. It's busy, but not too busy. It has waterfalls, ferns, azaleas, redwoods, clear water, steep banks that twist and turn, a true wilderness. BUT it is rainfed so the flow rises quickly and departs almost as fast. The shuttle is long, the day is long, and it can get cold very fast. The last few miles are slow on the Navarro, new name, after Rancheria, Anderson, and Indian Creeks all join three miles above Hendy Woods SP parking lot.

●●●●●●●●●●●●●●●●

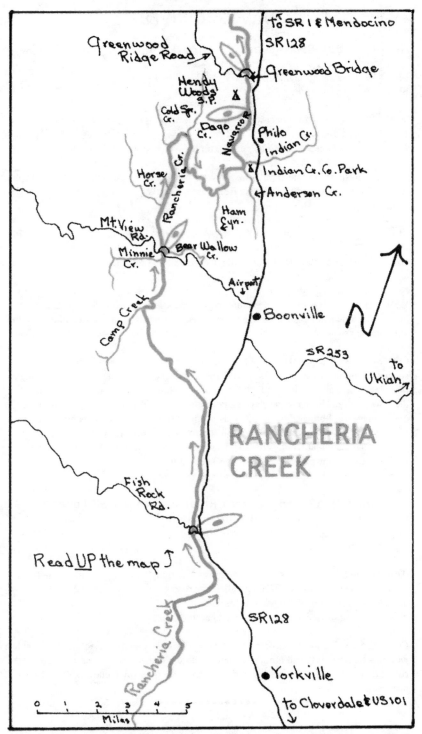

To SR 1 & Mendocino
SR 128
Greenwood Bridge
Greenwood Ridge Road
Hendy Woods S.P.
Cold Spr. Cr.
Dago Cr.
Navarro R.
Philo
Indian Cr.
Indian Cr. Co. Park
Andersen Cr.
Horse Cr.
Rancheria Cr.
Ham Cyn.
Mt. View Rd.
Minnie Cr.
Bear Wallow Cr.
Airport
Camp Creek
Boonville
SR 253
to Ukiah
RANCHERIA CREEK
Fish Rock Rd.
Read UP the map
Rancheria Creek
SR 128
Yorkville
to Cloverdale & US 101
0 1 2 3 4 5
Miles

NAVARRO RIVER

Hendy Woods SP to Dimmick SRA, 12 miles, Class I+

SEASON: Rainy & spring. BEST FLOWS: 200-800 cfs.
FLOW INFO: http://sonic.net/kkct/whitewat.htm.

ACCESS: Put-in • Below Greenwood bridge • From SR 128 3 miles NW of Philo turn W.
    on Greenwood Rd.
12 miles to • Dimmick SRA and Cpgr. (10 mi. NW of Greenwood Ridge Rd.)

Alternate put-in • If the steep hill at Greenwood bridge causes too many problems, try the
river parking lot at Hendy Woods Sp. Be advised, however, that this put-in may be undesirable due to a downstream snag.

MAPS: AAA — "Mendocino and Sonoma Coast Region." DE LORME — pp. 73 & 74.

GAS, FOOD, and LODGING: Boonville, Cloverdale, Ukiah, and Mendocino.
CAMPING: Along the river, Hendy Woods SP and Dimmick SRA.:707.937.5804.

BEWARE: As a Class I+ river it is more likely to be affected by flooding. This can cause
land slides, downed trees across the river, snags, and debris piles. Don't paddle past the
Dimmick take-out.

COMMENTS: This popular canoeing weekend run, camping beneath the redwoods is a
special springtime treat. It is mostly wilderness in a second growth redwood and Douglas
fir forest. The water is clear and cold, flowing in a fairly narrow canyon. Depending on
the flow it can easily be run in a day or 2 hours, as I once did at high water. It can be chilly;
one January trip I brushed the ice crystals off my kayak seat before launching. The take-out at Dimmick is bordered by the north fork of the Navarro River entering from river
right. This is a popular fishing area so fishermen will be indicative of the park being close
by. The beach at the park generally shows signs of use.

•••••••••••••••

Dimmick SRA to Navarro River Redwoods SP (ocean),
8 miles, Class I

(See info. above.)

ACCESS: Put-in • Dimmick SRA, campground, parking and Rrm. (6 miles with several
    access spots as SR-128 parallels the river.)
6 miles to • dirt ramp used by drift boats. Limited parking.
2 miles to • lagoon at river's end. Limited parking.

COMMENTS: The lower run of the Navarro is more open more accessible and sometimes
with more debris. It is still attractive, though more heavily used. Fisherman trails to the
river are usually near off-highway parking areas. The river often ends in a small lagoon
near the ocean.

•••••••••••••••

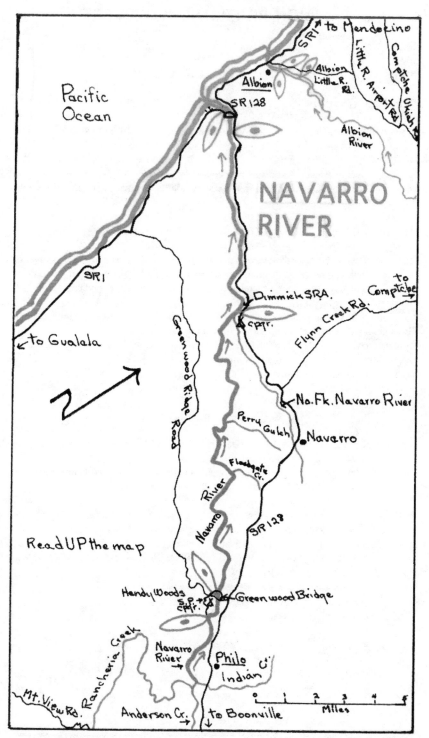

Pacific Ocean

to Mendocino

Albion

SR 128

Albion Little R. Rd.

Little R. Airport Rd.

Comptche Ukiah Rd.

Albion River

NAVARRO RIVER

SR 1

to Gualala

Greenwood Ridge Road

Dimmick SRA.

cmpr.

Flynn Creek Rd.

to Comptche

No. Fk. Navarro River

Perri Gulch

Navarro

Floodgate Cr.

Navarro River

Read UP the map

SR 128

Hendy Woods S.P. cmpr.

Greenwood Bridge

Rancheria Creek

Navarro River

Philo

Indian C'

Mt. View Rd.

Anderson Cr.

to Boonville

0   1   2   3   4   5

Miles

ALBION RIVER AND BIG RIVER

SEASON: All year. WATER: Tidal and river flow. TIDE REF.: Pt. Cabrillo (Casper).

MAPS: AAA — "Mendocino and Sonoma Coast Region." DE LORME — p. 73.

GAS, FOOD, and LODGING: Albion and Mendocino. B&Bs and great food. Mendocino Chamber of Commerce: 707.961.6300.
CAMPING: South of Mendocino at Van Damme State Park: 707.937.5804.

BEWARE: Winds blowing upriver in the afternoon. "Sinker" operations. Trees fallen across the river and snags. Almost no beaches or places to get out! On the Big River, you may find yourself stuck in the mud if you venture too far upstream when the tide is ebbing.

ALBION RIVER HISTORICAL TOUR, 7 mi. round-trip, Class I

ACCESS: Put-in • From SR-1 at the town of Albion go east and down towards the river or public boat ramp in the religious retreat grounds. North side of river, drive down to the harbor, several access locations at the harbor and upriver a bit.

COMMENTS: Paddle past fishing boats on the way up river amid a fascinating array of floating abodes. Channel markers and railroad remnants are here for the historians. The railroad arrived via the north fork of the Navarro River, over the hill and along the Albion, during logging days. Now an interesting hike in the redwoods. Explore the bird refuge lagoon three miles up river. On a calm day paddle a short ways out of the harbor.

●●●●●●●●●●●●●●●●

BIG RIVER, 10 miles, Class I

ACCESS: Up and back • Mendocino Headlands SP from SR-1 at NE end of bridge take road to the river. Plenty of parking.
Or 10 mile run from Mendocino Headlands SP, (Outdoor Center). Go east on Little Lake Rd. off of SR-1 N. of Mendocino, 5.5 mi., turn rt. to river.

COMMENTS: As paddlers go further up river, the usual fog disappears leaving a warm sunny day. The Big River flows into the ocean just south of the historic charming community of Mendocino, now a tourist destination. The recovery of "sinkers", redwood logs that have sunk, is an active operation on the Big River, like moving and lifting a sunken whale.

●●●●●●●●●●●●●●●●

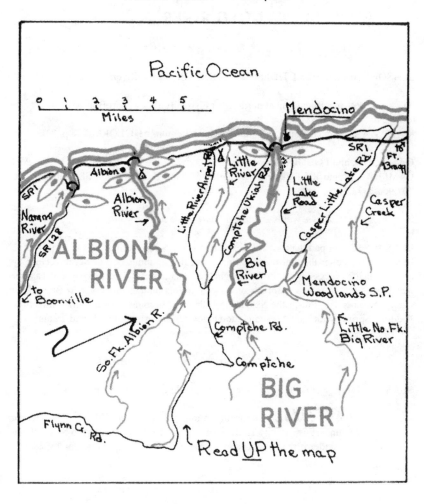

STORY: We were paddling one winter day from the outdoor center to the coast. Not far downstream we saw a large redwood tree, about 8' in diameter across the river. One bank was a vertical crumbling sandstone wall the other very steep saturated mud. Forget "plan A or B" try for "C"! We paddled slowly to the small end of the tree and found just barely enough room for our compact kayaks to sneak through. Wheeeee, made it!

PADDLECRAFT RENTALS: On the south bank, Catch A Canoe rents canoes, some large out-rigger and kayaks. 707-320.2453.

NOYO RIVER

Noyo Harbor, upriver & back, 4 miles rd. trip, Class I

SEASON: All year. BEST TIDES: 3'-6' TIDE REF.: Noyo River.

ACCESS: Put-in • Boat ramp at north side of Noyo Harbor at Fort Bragg.

MAPS: AAA — "Mendocino and Sonoma Coast Region." DE LORME — p. 73

GAS, FOOD, and LODGING: Fort Bragg.
CAMPING: Pomo RV Park and Campground, 1 mi. S. of junction SR-1 and SR-20: 707.964.3373.

BEWARE: Tidal flows, winds and larger boats in the harbor.

COMMENTS: For paddlers who like exploring harbors and marinas, this is a special one because it is smaller than most and has an active fishing industry. The ocean is close by and the sea life processing facilities are right there on the waterfront. It is the end of a river that flows through redwood forests on its way to this lumber town of Fort Bragg. The Pacific Lumber Co. Put-in the Skunk Train that has become a local tourist attraction. Paddling upriver with the tide, and not too much current, is pleasurable and scenic.

* * * * * * * * * * * * * * * *

Northspur (to Noyo Harbor), 14 (22) miles, Class II

SEASON: Rainy. FLOW INFO: Hodges:sonic.net/kkct/whitewat.htm.

ACCESS: Put-in • Skunk Train, Northspur Station. Riding the train from Willits is where the fun begins. Randy Hodges has organized 2 trips using the Skunk Train (now under private ownership) as the means to get upriver—boats, paddlers and all.

BEWARE: Snags and trees, some across the river. Scouting by train was great.

COMMENTS: The two 14 mile day trips I have been on with Randy have been very special. The first year there were about 22 paddlers, the second 43. To be able to shuttle by train, boats and all, was most unusual. On the 1997 run, we scouted twice and ran everything. 1998 being an El Nino year, there were more downed trees so we scouted more and portaged more. A constant obstacle is the dam at one of the camps that is runnable by finding the slot near river right, turning quickly, and going straight through (down!) for the best entry to maneuver the rocks below. There is growth in the river, snags, rocky drops, with some quiet spots. The river is in redwood forests which means cool, damp, waterfalls, and ferns. The take-out for the one day run is questionable but the river could be done as an overnight, paddling to Fort Bragg, 22 miles in all.

* * * * * * * * * * * * * * * *

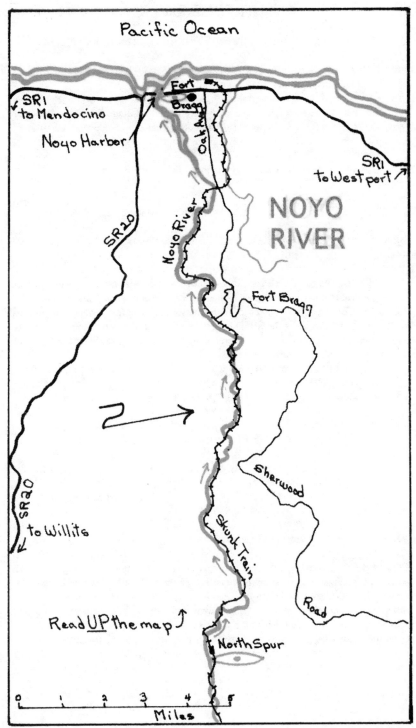

Pacific Ocean

SR1
to Mendocino

Noyo Harbor

SR20

Fort
Bragg

Oak Ave

SR1
to Westport

NOYO
RIVER

Noyo River

Fort Bragg

SR20

to Willits

Sherwood

Read UP the map

Skunk Train

Road

North Spur

0   1   2   3   4   5
Miles

MATTOLE RIVER

Ettersburg to Honeydew, 17 miles, Class I+ & II (III+)

SEASON: Rainy (about 300" a year). BEST FLOWS: 250-900 cfs.
FLOW INFO: http://cdec.water.ca.gov/misc/stages.html.

ACCESS: Put-in • Ettersburg is at the crossroads of Wilder Ridge Ettersburg Honeydew
Rd. and Briceland Thorne Rd. west of Briceland via Redway & US-101.
17 miles to • bridge at Honeydew, river right take-out.

MAPS: AAA — "Northern California Section." DE LORME — p. 52.

GAS, FOOD, and LODGING:: Garberville and Redway.
CAMPING: AW Way Park 12 mi. W. of Honeydew on Mattole Rd. 707.445.7651.

BEWARE: Entirely rainfed. The water rises and falls fast. Be wary. A new slide with 4
drops .3 mile long, Class III+.

COMMENTS: The run is an easy Class II until about 3 miles from the end, where the
rapids increase in difficulty. The most difficult are when the river is parallel to the road. At
the start of the run the river passes through a narrow tree and fern covered canyon, with
waterfalls. Next a broad cattle-raising valley. Old roads lead to a few homes. Ettersburg
was named for the Etter family who were famed botanists in the early part of the 1900's
developing apple-sized strawberries.

But trying to find water in the Mattole at the right time is a real problem. During
heavy rains George Hagen and I drove to the Mattole thinking "Of course there would be
water in the river." There was! Too much! Maybe next time.

●●●●●●●●●●●●●●●●

Honeydew to Petrolia, 22 miles, Class I+

ACCESS: Put-in • Near the bridge at Honeydew. US-101 go west on Mattole Rd. at Bull
Creek Flats about 20 miles of winding road to Honeydew.
13 miles to • AW Way County Park. Cpgr., swimming beach, and boatramp.
9 miles to • Mattole Rd. Bridge 1 mile S. of Petrolia.

BEWARE: Low water and upriver winds.

COMMENTS: This is a great two-day run, easy water and mid-way campground.   The
river winds through sheep pastures and past a few homes. The hillsides have been heavily
logged. A resident told me how a logging company asked to buy her timber during the
'40's and '50's housing boom. They said they would be logging above her timber and the
remaining slash would ruin her grove when washed down by the heavy rains. She and
other timber owners sold. Now the heavy rains have destroyed the streambeds leaving a
big mess. Another timber situation is the Kings Range which has received publicity in
recent years.

●●●●●●●●●●●●●●●●

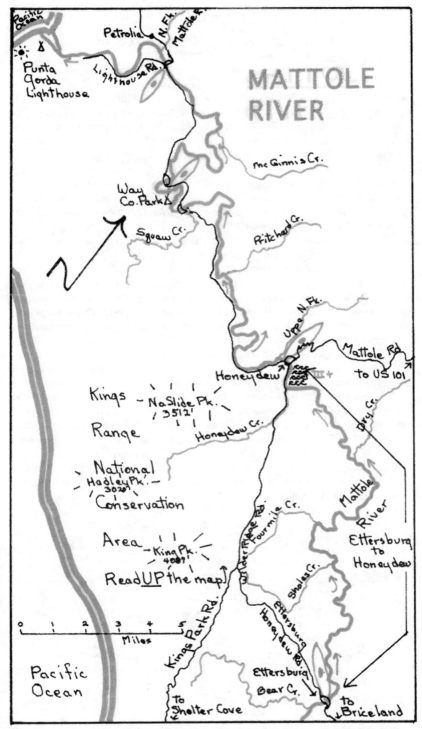

EEL RIVER SYSTEM

Main, South Fork, and Van Duzen River

FLOW INFO: 707.445.7855 or 916.368.8682 or Hodges: http//sonic.net/kkct.

The Eel River system is one of the most fabulous and free-flowing (mostly) in the state of California. The US-101, Redwood Highway parallels the South Fork for 75 miles in the redwood country, adding to the scenic beauty of the ride. It makes those vehicle-bound wish they could be in or on the river as they follow along seeing "swimming holes" and clear turquoise flowing waters. Much of the main stem flows through wilderness in redwood forests or oak-dotted hillsides. The total Eel River system offers paddlers over 200 miles of Class I and II waterways. There's river running for all abilities and paddlecraft except during the summer when more water is diverted into the Russian River. The demands on the Russian River far exceed the available flow AND the Eel River area residents want their water back; another water fight?

For more skilled paddlers there are the runs like the Branscomb on the South Fork, Pillsbury on the main, as well as the north and middle forks. These are mainly rainfed waterways except for the snowmelt from the 7,000 foot Yolla Bollys. The greatest flows on the Eel are in January and February at 39,000 acre feet dropping to 27,000 in December and March, reduced more in November and April, dwindling in May and June with little flow the rest of the year. Due to the heavy winter flows, beaches are water-scoured leaving large expanses of rocks and/or sand and rocks that are artistically sculpted. Large logs are sometimes left atop huge rocks.

May and June are two of the favored months as the flow is comfortable and the days and water have warmed up a bit. July is often a low water month with algae blooms in the "pools". The season is usually a month behind the bay area.

Logging of the trees is on-going. It started with the sugar pines then moved on to the redwoods. Azaleas, rhododendrons and dog wood add color to the forests in the spring. On some of my trips we were privileged to have botanists: Clare Wheeler, Wilma Follette and/or Elizabeth Terwilliger sharing their knowledge. Three different orchids were found and the colorful firecracker flower, Brodaeia Ida Mae. The petroglyphs on Squaw Rock near Eel Rock, the female ceremonial rock and a new find reported by Steve Hart were left by earlier native peoples. The whole area abounds in history, geology, and botany. A very special treat for paddlers.

EEL RIVER

BASIN CREEK

PETROGLYPHS

CAMPING - DOS RIOS RUN

SLIDE RAPID - S. FORK

DOS RIOS RUN - CLASS II

CLIFFS ACROSS FROM CAMP GRANT

EEL RIVER (main stem)

Hearst to Outlet Creek, 17 miles, Class II - II+

SEASON: Spring run-off. BEST FLOWS: 400-800 cfs.

ACCESS: Put-in • Below the bridge at Hearst. From Willitts go east on Commercial then left on Hearst Willitts Rd. 15 miles to the Eel River.
17 miles to • east end of bridge over Eel R. at Outlet Creek confluence. From US-101 at Longvale go E. on SR-162 (Covelo Rd.) 6.5 miles. Parking.

MAPS: AAA — "Northern California Section." DE LORME — pp. 64 & 74.

GAS, FOOD, and LODGING: Willits.

BEWARE: The Class I river drops into a large boulder, the river turns left then out of sight, Class II+ - III rapid. Scout on river right, private property. Log jam.
The shuttle is long about 2 hours, 45 road miles one-way, some slow.

COMMENTS: This is a great Class II run with a rapid just where the paddler wants the next bit of excitement, like Rancheria Creek, and with the same remote feeling. Bears are often seen. The big rapid is in the beginning where the flow goes out of sight to river left and may contain a pile of debris. Shoot? Yes, the first kayakers to scout this 17 mile run were threatened with a gun to get off the private property, or else. On our first run in open canoes the irate property owner Mr. Ramsing, came out to watch and chatted with us. A "local" newspaper reporter and kayaker, Steve Hart interviewed Mr. Ramsing and changed his feelings about kayakers. This overnight run is seldom paddled because of the long shuttle and short paddling season as the flow is diverted into the Russian River in early June.

●●●●●●●●●●●●●●●

Outlet Creek to Dos Rios, 6.5 miles, Class II+ (-III)

ACCESS: Put-in • Confluence of Eel R.iver & Outlet Creek, SR-162 to Covelo (see above). 6.5 miles to • Confluence of Eel River and Middle Fork Eel River.
NOTE: There are several locations of accessing this run from SR-162.

BEWARE: Snags.

COMMENTS: What a fun spot to practice Class II+ paddling skills. The run is interesting with a variety of situations and parallel to the road.

●●●●●●●●●●●●●●●

NOTE: After the Class III Pillsbury Run on the Eel there is a 4 mi. Class I+ run from Bucknell Cr. to Van Arsdale Dam reached via Potter Valley from SR-20.

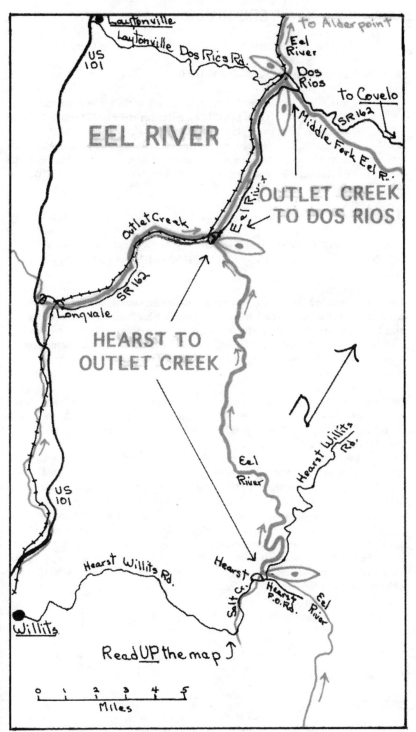

to Alderpoint

Eel River

Dos Rios

to Covelo

SR 162

Middle Fork Eel R.

EEL RIVER

Lauftonville

Lauftonville Dos Rios Rd.

US 101

Eel River

OUTLET CREEK TO DOS RIOS

Outlet Creek

SR 162

Longvale

HEARST TO OUTLET CREEK

US 101

Eel River

Hearst Willits Rd.

Eel River

Hearst Willits Rd.

Hearst

Salt Cr.

Hearst P.O. Rd.

Eel River

Willits

Read UP the map ↑

0 1 2 3 4 5
Miles

EEL RIVER (con't)

Dos Rios to Alderpoint, 49 mi. (46 RR mi.), Class II - III

SEASON: Late spring. BEST FLOWS: 400-1,200 cfs.

ACCESS: Put-in • Take the dirt road to the Middle Fork of the Eel near the confluence with the Main Eel. Or from SR-162 a mile after crossing the Middle Fork the road to Dos Rios, turn right after bridge across the Eel (main).

49 miles to • Alderpoint, 22 miles E. of Garberville off of road to Redway E. on Alderpoint Rd. At Alderpoint stay on main road past the bridge, stay W. of the river 1 mile past bridge go left down a dirt road past a water tank to the railroad. Walk or drive to the river.

MAPS: AAA — "Northern California Section." DE LORME — pp. 53, 54, & 64.

GAS, FOOD, and LODGING: Willits and Garberville.
CAMPGROUNDS: Standish-Hickey SRA: 707.925.6482 and Richardson Grove SP: 707.247.3318.

BEWARE: Check the flow as higher water makes this a Class III run. The more difficult rapids are at Spyrock (a high rock spire on river right), Blue Rock Cr. enters from the left, Island Mtn. (RR mi. #194. Island Mtn. Falls upriver from bridge and tunnel, scout on river left), a tricky spot at the end of the "tunnel loop", Kekawaka Falls, 5 miles upstream of the creek and "mile 201" rapid half of a mile below RR mi. #201, that now is considered one of the most difficult.

COMMENTS: The access spots change. One year they were mining gravel on the beach on the Middle Fork just upriver from the confluence so the road to the beach was in good condition. Check locally. The shuttle is long, over 150 miles on some slow roads, about 4 hours via Garberville.

Great for solitude, almost no other people, no roads, just you and your group. The roads that came to the river at Spyrock and Island Mtn. are now private and gated. This is in the "green triangle" a marijuana growing area from the Eel River north to the Trinity and Klamath Rivers. Take care exploring the hills from the river. The growers might do to you what they have done to the once plentiful deer who munch on their frilly green leaves.

The railroad once had a repair crew living at Island Mtn. Twice we aborted trips at Island Mtn. in the early 70's when there was a community there. The last time was when the tunnel had been closed from a fire isolating five engines north of the tunnel. TheRR was in process of moving the engines by flat car from Alderpoint to Island Mtn. after first widening and smoothing the country roads. The engines could generate revenue to the south but not where they were.

The Budd passenger car no longer runs. We used it once as a shuttle.

• • • • • • • • • • • • • •

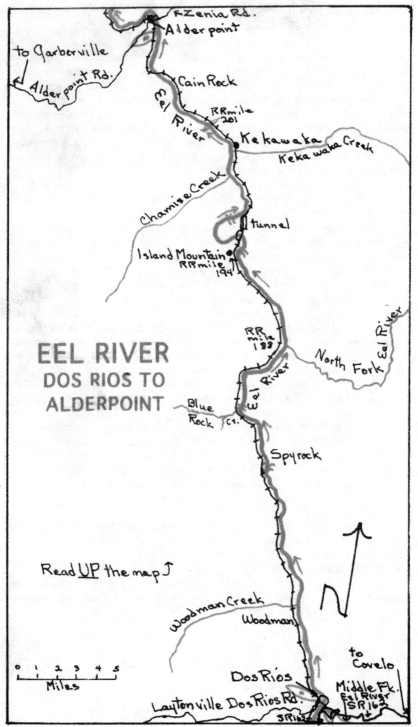

EEL RIVER
DOS RIOS TO
ALDERPOINT

Read UP the map ↑

MEMORIES OF "DOS RIOS" EEL RIVER TRIPS

FLORA & FAUNA: Being asked to identify the black (very dark brown) and white (light cream) rattle snake living in a shaded area. It was definitely a rattlesnake but with almost king snake coloring but with the irregular strips not the smooth ones of the king snake.

Then there was the late-day search for a campsite. We found a good one but there was a 2 foot long rattler under the 8 foot log that must be passed on the way to the sleeping area; plus we had children in the group. A council was held, everyone told about the snake under the log and were warned to give it "wide berth" as the snake was at "home" under the log. The snake stayed put (probably too scared to move) until the next day when the canoes were loaded and boarded. I took a long stick and gently urged the snake to move so I could see its rattles; there were only about 5.

Watching the decapitated rattlesnake wiggle for three hours so we could cook it. It was about 18", so our bits of snake fried in butter & garlic were small. Saw a small rattlesnake swim across the river.

Being lead canoe I saw the bird first, bouncing up and down and chirping on the rock just like a road runner, but the bird books say road runners live in the southwest and this was the northwest. We saw an "illiterate" road runner.

Hiking up to see the small plot of cannabis growing near the RR tracks.

Wondering what was making a shambles of the gravel areas on the beaches? Pigs root for bugs and worms on rotting wood. We saw their tracks then the piglets of feral pigs.

ROYALEX CANOES: The run in 1969 by the Marin Canoe Club Dos Rios trip had some Royalex canoes which were new to the west coast. Quite by accident I learned of Royalex canoes made by Rivers and Gilman in Maine, when I was traveling through Maine the summer before and visited their factory. During the year I convinced six others to buy them, sight unseen, which arrived just before the Dos Rios trip in late June. Gwen Kleeman had researched the material learning that it was soften by heat. This was valuable knowledge when one of the canoes was buried in the river when being lined down a rapid and had both ends touching when it was pryed out of the river. I went up the river with the rest of the crew to organize a portage as a few were left to the reconstruction task. When I arrived back the canoes were lined up on shore ready to leave. All eyes were watching as I looked behind rocks for the discarded canoe, then counted the loaded canoes. The crew had successfully reshaped the craft, loaded it with gear ready to go on down the river. We all became Royalex canoe converts.

SUPER SPECIAL ROCKS: It was a large artistically sculptured rock with room for two people to sleep in it which Molly and Bill Bricca did. Lowell, my geology major son, was curious about the dark red spots in the rock. The small chip he took to be analyzed showed they were garnets in a granite base.

Another rock of memory on the 1969 run is pictured here. It was out of the flow, surrounded by deep water ideal for diving, easy to climb up to its relatively flat surface. Dreamtime rock! The group reluctantly paddled on.

EEL RIVER, ALDERPOINT RUN

ROCK FORMATIONS

NELSON EDDY ROCK, DOBBYN CR.

CREEK ORCHIDS

RIVER SCULPTURED ROCK

EEL RIVER (con't.)

Alderpoint to South Fork, 30 miles, Class I+

SEASON: Spring & early summer. BEST FLOWS: 300-1,000 cfs.

ACCESS: Put-in • Alderpoint. From Garberville go towards Redway turn right on Alderpoint Rd. to Alderpoint. Go past the bridge staying on the right 1 mile to dirt rd. left down to the RR tracks past a water tank. River left.

7.5 miles to • Fort Seward beach .5 mile upriver from the bridge. Turn left from the Alderpoint Rd. on the Dyerville Loop follow signs to Ft. Seward. Beach is SE of "town".

10 miles to • Eel Rock. North of Miranda turn right on Eel Cr. Rd., right on Dyerville Loop left on Eel Rock Rd. to RR or down to the beach.

5 miles to • Whitlow (Sequoia): See above directions to Whitlow which is N. of Eel Rock. Go N. on RR down path to river. Do not cross Sonoma Creek.

2 miles to • McCann location of a low-level summer bridge. Drive through Founders Grove staying on Dyerville Loop Rd. 4.5 miles. to bridge.

5.5 miles to • South Fork beach. North on US-101, take the Dyerville, Bull Creek, So. Fork exit to South Fork via Founders Grove, cross RR tracks down dirt road to beach, go south to take out.

MAPS: AAA — "Northern California Section." DE LORME — pp. 52 & 53.

GAS, FOOD, and LODGING: Garberville, Miranda, and Rio Dell.
CAMPGROUNDS: Humboldt Red. SP: Burlington and Hidden Springs. 707.946.2409.

BEWARE: Snags, strong upriver winds especially going into Sequoia and So. Fk.

COMMENTS: This is a paddler's dream, sort of. The water is fairly clear and warm with a moderate flow. There may be low water going under the bridge at Alderpoint. There are easy rapids below Steelhead Creek (former hatchery site) & Dobbyns Creek (site of Nelson Eddy Rock and an interesting creek hike to Blocksburg). After Ft. Seward bridge there is sometimes a drop going towards Boehne Butte where the river turns sharply to the left. Expect more fog closer to South Fork and more wind. Paddlers often take out at Eel Rock (blown up) beach. Squaw Rock up from Coleman Creek with a few petroglyphs can be seen from here.

Many campsites, but they're on private property. Please be careful and leave the campsite as you found it or better. Burn or take out all trash, bury campfires deeply. Return unburned wood to where it was found. Use a trench latrine 6 inches deep away from the river, leave it well covered. When I started paddling this run in the late sixties, I personally contacted the property owners saying how we would leave the campsites. Thank you fellow paddlers for caring and doing.

The majestic grove of redwoods at the former Boy Scout Camp was logged soon after the Pacific Lumber Company was sold to Maxxim. The litter from logging was left making it unsuitable for camping or even walking through.

•••••••••••••••••

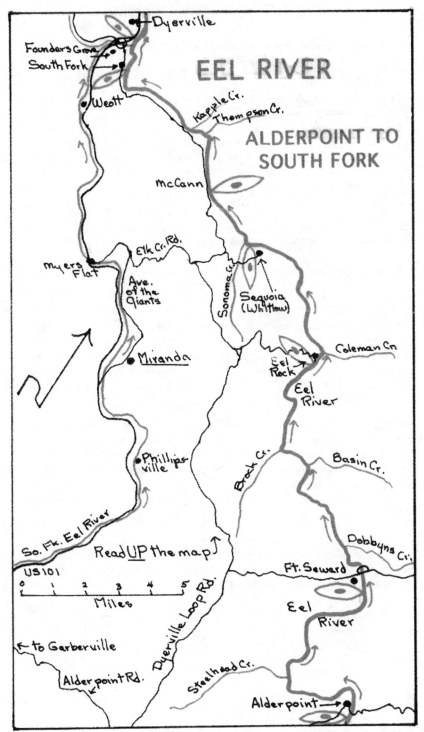

EEL RIVER

ALDERPOINT TO
SOUTH FORK

Dyerville

Founders Grove
South Fork

Weott

Kapple Cr.
Thompson Cr.

McCann

Elk Cr. Rd.

Myers Flat

Ave. of the Giants

Sonoma Cr.

Sequoia (Whitlow)

Coleman Cn.

Miranda

Eel Rock

Eel River

Phillipsville

Brock Cr.

Basin Cr.

So. Fk. Eel River

Read UP the map

Dobbyns Cr.

US 101

0   1   2   3   4   5
Miles

Ft. Seward

Eel River

Dyerville Loop Rd.

← to Garberville

Alderpoint Rd.

Steelhead Cr.

Alderpoint

EEL RIVER, SOUTH FORK

Big Bend to Benbow Lake SRA, 25 miles, Class I & II (II+)

SEASON: Rainy & early summer. BEST FLOWS: 250-950 cfs.

ACCESS: Put-in • Big Bend Lodge (707.984.6321) 1 mile to river and lodge from Drive
        Thru Tree Rd. 3 mi. S. of Leggett or 3 mi. N. of Cummings (fee). Parking and
        Rrm.
3 miles to • Millbank bridge on SR-1 near Leggett.
.5 miles to • beach via dirt rd. N. through ball field .5 mi. W. on SR-1 via US-101.
4 miles to • Standish-Hickey SRA. Easy summer access. Winter, walk to river from locked
        gate. Campground, parking, and Rrm (fee).
2.5 miles to • Smithe Redwoods SP, Wayside on US-101. Parking and Rrm(?).
3 miles to • SR-271, dirt road to river S. of McCoy Creek. Limited parking.
6.5 miles to • Richardson Grove SP. Campground, parking, and Rrm. (fee).
5.5 miles to • Lake. Benbow Lake SRA. Campground, parking, and Rrm.

MAPS: AAA — "Northern California Section." DE LORME — pp. 53 & 63.

GAS, FOOD, and LODGING: Garberville. Paddlers welcome at Benbow Lodge.

BEWARE: Rocks, drops, and snags. Before Smythe Redwoods watch for Slide Rapid,
with a large rocky beach on river left and a steep bank up to the highway and rock slide.
The river flows through a rock garden, turns abruptly and goes over a 4 foot drop into a
chute—Class II+. Scout? The entrance is a bit trickier than the drop. After Red Mountain
Cr., there's a bit of a tricky drop and squirrely water where there's a high rock wall on
river left. The highway is over the hill.

COMMENTS: The river from Big Bend to Standish-Hickey flows through picturesque
redwood forests with a few rocks and drops, some swimming holes and Class II rapids.
On one trip there was a fast chute below the bridge at Standish-Hickey with an easy
portage for rerunning. Here my grandchildren got a taste for fast moving water as their
fears changed to thrills on each rerun.
    From Standish-Hickey to Smythe Redwoods there are a few easy Class II rapids.
After going under the US-101 bridge the river is mostly Class I+ to Benbow.

FLORA & FAUNA: Evergreen trees: redwoods, Douglas firs, and sugar pine are the most
common, tanoak, madrone, live oak and dogwood are on the hillsides alder and several
species of willows grow along the river banks. Wildflowers abound. Birds of all kinds in
abundance including herons, eagles and osprey.

• • • • • • • • • • • • • • • •

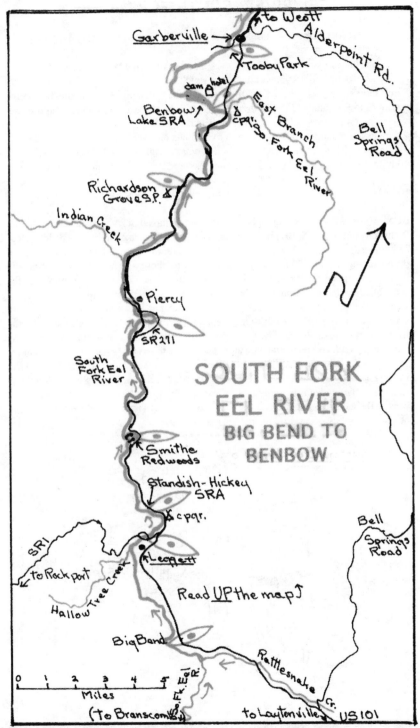

EEL RIVER, SOUTH FORK (con't.)

Garberville to Dyerville, 37 miles, class I+

ACCESS: Put-in • Garberville, Tooby Park. From Garberville W. on Sprowel Cr. Rd. to Tooby Park, Rrm, parking, and picnic tables.

8 miles to • Dean Creek Resort. On the river at Dean Creek off ramp. Parking and Rrm.

9.5 miles to • North of Phillipsville just upriver from US-101 off ramp to bridge across river. Dirt road to river on river right.

2.5 miles to • County park 2 miles north of Miranda on river right.

7 miles to • Myers Flat below US-101 bridge on river right.

10 miles to • Dyerville boat ramp near underpass on Ave. of the Giants.

BEWARE: Sand and/or gravel bars in summer. Upriver winds. Snags.

COMMENTS: Ever look longingly at the turquoise thread of river when driving on the Redwood Highway (US-101) in the area of Garberville. It is a great river to paddle, clear and interesting. But, the flow drops in a hurry as it is entirely rainfed; the drainage is from the coast range only 4,000 feet in height. However for those who want good flows, paddle it in the spring, and for those who don't mind walking the shallow parts, enjoy it in the summer when the swimming holes have warmed up. The highway is there but not obtrusive. Camping along the river does present a problem as land owners object. There are several state park campgrounds along the way, but campsites are often away from the river. The river is sandwiched between the Redwood Highway and Avenue of the Giants from Phillipsville to Myers Flat with more people and towns along the way. The Founders Tree, once the tallest tree, can be found growing between the South Fork and the main Eel River. The tall redwood trees at Redwood NP are also growing by the water, Redwood Creek. Did the silt deposits from flooding add to their growth? Stop at Founder's Grove to walk in the redwoods and look up at one of the tallest trees in the world. Not for too long or neck pains may occur!

• • • • • • • • • • • • • • • •

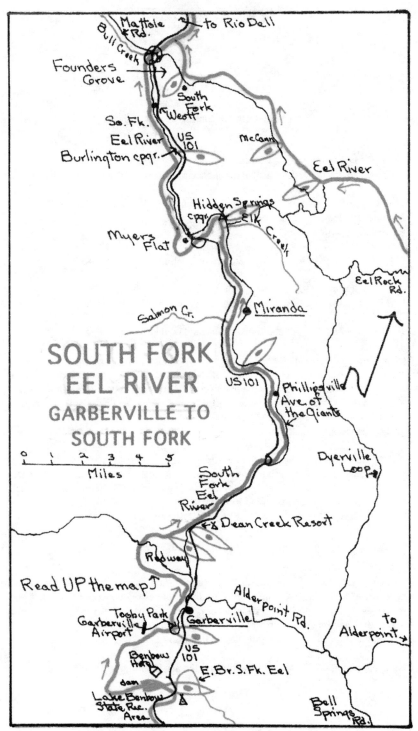

to Rio Dell

Mattole Rd.

Bull Creek

Founders Grove

South Fork Weott

So. Fk. Eel River

McCann

Burlington cpgr.

US 101

Eel River

Hidden Springs cpgr.

Elk Creek

Myers Flat

Eel Rock Rd.

Salmon Cr.

Miranda

SOUTH FORK
EEL RIVER
GARBERVILLE TO
SOUTH FORK

US 101

Phillipsville
Ave. of the Giants

0 1 2 3 4 5
Miles

Dyerville Loop

South Fork Eel River

Dean Creek Resort

Redway

Read UP the map

Alder Point Rd.

Toohy Park
Garberville Airport

Garberville

to Alderpoint

US 101

Benbow Hotel

E. Br. S. Fk. Eel

dam

Lake Benbow State Rec. Area

Bell Springs Rd.

EEL RIVER (con't)

South Fork (confl.) to Ocean, 44 miles, Class I (1 dam)

SEASON: All year. BEST FLOW: 500-3,000 cfs. BEST TIDE: 3'-5'
FLOW INFO: River Report: 707.445.7855. Tide Location: Humboldt Bay.

ACCESS: Put-in • Just upriver from the confluence across the gravel bar on the South
Fork.
9 miles to • Shively.
10 miles to • Scotia.
2.5 miles to • Rio Dell, end of Painter St. and Nally's RV Park, end of Davis St.
707.764.5420.
11 miles to • Fortuna park. Drive towards river on River Walk Dr. Parking & Rrm.
2.5 miles to • Fairgrounds at Fernbridge.
8 miles to • Pacific Ocean.

MAPS: AAA —"Northern California Section." DE LORME — pp. 42 & 52.

GAS, FOOD, and LODGING: Rio Dell, Fortuna, and Fernbridge.
CAMPING: Grizzly Cr. Red. SP: 707.777.3683, Fortuna KOA: 707.725.3359.

BEWARE: Small dam at Scotia. Winds, tide and sand bars.

COMMENTS: Here's another 44, and more, miles of Eel River to paddle on and delta to
explore. This last section of the Eel is from the redwood forests past farm lands and into a
marshy area with water birds and a few mammals in from the ocean. En route the river
goes in a wide sweeping bend in the Rio Dell area. The steep right bank is sandstone
imbedded with large clam shells. Here the railroad is cut out of the cliff and train passengers can receive a close look at the shells.

NOTE: Not far after Fernbridge the Eel River waters are spread out in a tidal delta area,
with various passageways and islands, not unlike but smaller than the delta of the Sacramento and San Joaquin Rivers. Some of the area is preserved. The north side of the delta
is accessible via Cannibal from Eel River Dr. in Loleta.

●●●●●●●●●●●●●●●●

HUMBOLDT BAY

An active harbor area oozing with history from the early logging days to the rejuvenated
"Old Town" area of Eureka. Ships of all kinds, an interesting variety of birds, and some
mammals create an entertaining paddling day. There are boat ramps west of Fields Landing, three boat ramps just south of the bridge to the Samoa Peninsula, and 2 boat ramps at
the south end on the bay side of the Samoa Peninsula.

Humboat Rentals: 707.444.3048. Paddlecraft rentals, sales and trips.

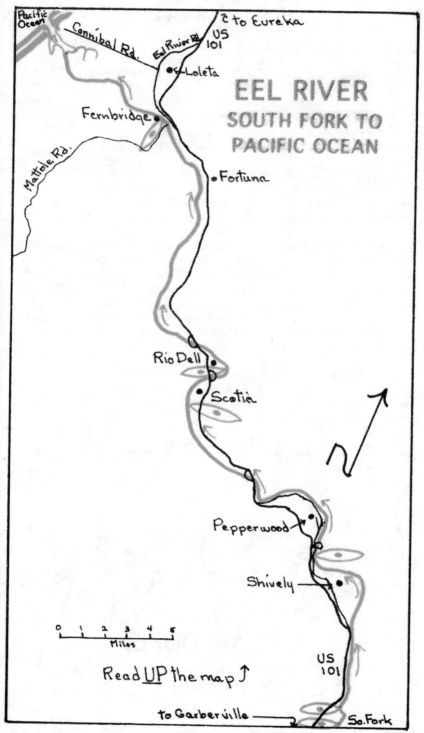

EEL RIVER
SOUTH FORK TO
PACIFIC OCEAN

Pacific Ocean

Cannibal Rd.

Eel River Rd.

US 101

to Eureka

Loleta

Fernbridge

Mattole Rd.

Fortuna

Rio Dell

Scotia

Pepperwood

Shively

US 101

0 1 2 3 4 5
Miles

Read UP the map ↑

to Garberville

So. Fork

VAN DUZEN RIVER

Little Golden Gate to Yager Creek, 23 miles, Class I+ & II+

SEASON: Rainy - short. BEST FLOWS: 400-800 cfs. FLOW INFO: 707.445.7855.

ACCESS: Put-in • Little Golden Gate subdivision south of the river, go to upriver end of
road. Path to the river.
10 miles to • Rainbow Bridge, upriver form Grizzly Redwoods SP.
13 miles to • Yager Cr. near Carlotta., across gravel bar where the red. begin.

MAPS: AAA — "Northern California Section." DE LORME — pp. 42, 52, & 53.

GAS, FOOD, and LODGING: Fortuna and Eureka.
CAMPING: Grizzly Redwoods SP, 707.777.3683, 17 mi. E. of US-101 on SR-36.

BEWARE: There is a surprise when putting in at the NE end of Little Golden Gate as
launching is at a Class II+ rapid. The trail to the river may be through poison oak. The
flow level fluctuates quickly. The feet measured at the gaging station at rainbow bridge
varies from year to year as to the corresponding cfs. After Grizzly Red. SP the river goes
into a gorge, Devils Elbow, a .3 mile long
     Class II+ to -III rapid with tricky maneuvering. At the beginning of the gorge be very
watchful of a concrete riprap section that has been undermined with enough space to
allow a canoe to get caught and held by river pressure.

COMMENTS: This river is nearby for those living in the Eureka area like the Six Rivers
Canoe Club. Members have been very helpful in providing information. Look at a map of
the flow of the Van Duzen and notice how close at the town of Mad River and again at
Dinsmore where they are about a mile apart. The Mad then flows north as the Van Duzen
flows west into the Eel.

• • • • • • • • • • • • • • • •

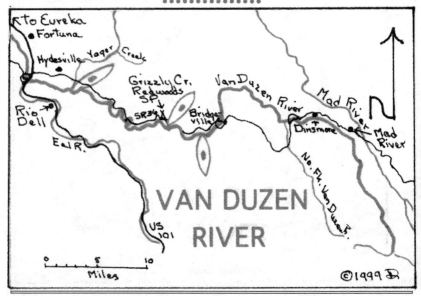

SLIDE RAPID - RANCHERIA CREEK

RALPH'S RAPID - RANCHERIA CREEK

NAVARRO RIVER

ALBION RIVER

NOYO RIVER TRAIN SHUTTLE

NOYO RIVER

CHAPTER 5 - EUREKA TO OREGON

CONTENTS

EUREKA to OREGON

The waterways from Eureka to Oregon are some of the best in the state, especially the Klamath/Trinity River combination, topped by the pristine Smith River in the far north. They offer many miles of challenging paddling for novices—day runs or longer river camping excursions. They are protected by the Wild & Scenic Rivers Act. The area is quite fascinating with Big Foot sightings, an active gold mining region, lumber, and salmon fishing. And how can the "State of Jefferson" be viable without any taxes? Many of the river miles are through Indian Reservations. It is a place for paddlers to enjoy!

Humboldt and Arcata Bays: With the popularity of sea kayaking this bay needs to be in the book. Bay paddling is interesting, especially for bird watchers and just a day for relaxed paddling.

Mad River: The lower run on the Mad River is closeby for those living in Arcata and Eureka. The Butler Valley run has rock slides requiring several portages. Local paddlers suggested I remove it. Terry and Gary told me about a run below Ruth Lake they liked, it has been added.

Redwood Creek: There are two runs to paddle on Redwood Creek, an easy one with a long downhill carry to the river and the whitewater run with Class III and IV rapids. (The Best Whitewater in California by Holbek and Stanley includes this section.) This coastal stream flows through Redwood National Park and past an impressive redwood grove containing the former tallest tree.

Klamath and Trinity Rivers: The Klamath River system is one of California's most impressive. It has about 200 miles of Class I and II waters. When added to the Trinity's 95 miles, they provide many happy paddling hours. The rivers wind their way to the ocean from the Cascades, Marble Mountains, Trinity Alps, and the Yolla Bollys in the south. Then there are the runs for more advanced paddlers including Class VI Ishi Pishi Falls on the Klamath and Class IV and V Burnt Ranch Gorge on the Trinity. The US Forest Service has supplied the area well with campgrounds, though camping can be done on the river as well.
Wildlife is abundant: otter, eagles, deer, bear (frequently seen), mountan lions (heard and sometimes seen on the lower Klamath) and BIG FOOT? It's a Mecca for birders, botanists, fishers, and gold miners. There are many rafting companies that do runs on both the Trinity and Klamath Rivers. Canoeing outfitting and instruction are available on both rivers. A noted kayak school at Otter Bar Lodge is held on nearby Salmon River.

Smith River: The Smith River is one of the most beautiful rivers in this section, but so far away. Like the Klamath River it comes from Oregon with its crystal clear water but it has a short paddling season being mostly rain-fed.. Its average rain fall is 92 inches a year, so the supply is good and frequent. Smith River paddling often gets rained out.

EEL RIVER, DOS RIOS TO ALDERPOINT, CLASS II+

HUMBOLDT AND ARCATA BAYS

SEASON: All year, tidal

ACCESS: Put-in • Boat ramp, Arcata Boat Launching Facility at the foot of I St., Arcata 707.822.8184.
Boat ramp • below SR 255 bridge to Samoa Peninsula near Waterfront Drive, Eureka.
Boat ramp • Samoa. New Navy Base Rd. near Samoa Dunes Recreation Area. 707.445.7651.
Boat ramp • Eureka Mooring Basin, at the foot of Commercial St at 531 K St., Eureka. 707.441.4230.
Boat ramp • E-Z Landing Marina, 5 miles S of Eureka at 1875 Buhne Dr., Eureka. 707.442.1118
Boat ramp • Fields Landing Park, 7 miles S of Eureka at end of Railroad Avenue. 707.445.7651.

MAPS: AAA — "Eureka, Arcata..." & "North CA Section." DE LORME — p. 42.

GAS, FOOD, AND LODGING: Arcata and Eureka.
CAMPING: Eureka KOA, 4 miles NE of Eureka at 4050 N US 101. 707.822.4243.

BEWARE: Heed similar precautions to paddling San Francisco Bay. Humboldt Bay is smaller but it still has commercial ship activity. Tides and winds are also to be considered when paddling.

COMMENTS: Choose a calm morning and go bay exploring. There are many locations for paddling. At high tide Mad River slough between Arcata and the coast can be explored or Swain Slough south of Eureka. Or paddle to one of the several islands near the Samoa bridge, Indian Island a wildlife refuge and Woodley Island which is also accessible by road from US 255. South Bay has sloughs to paddle up and sand dunes on the ocean side for hiking. Beside just going paddling this area is fascinating. Paper mills along the bay have "scented" the air in Eureka for years. Lumber is still exported from the docks. South Bay and Fields Landing south of King Salmon are the primary commercial areas. Arcata Bay has little large ship activity and more marshy areas for birding.

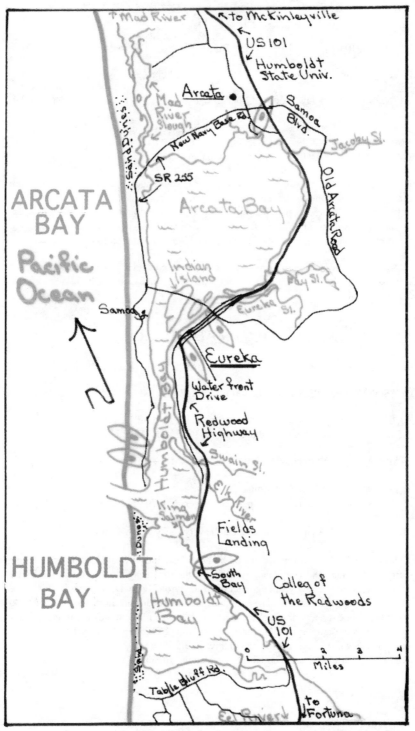

MAD RIVER

Blue River to Mad River Boat Ramp, 11 miles, Class I+

SEASON: Rainy & spring. BEST FLOWS: 400-1,000 cfs.

ACCESS: Put in • below West End Road bridge .5 N. of Blue Lake and 6 miles E. of US 101.
11 miles to • Mad River Boat Ramp on Mad River Rd. near ocean.
MAPS: AAA — "Northern CA Section." DE LORME — p. 42
GAS, FOOD, & LODGING: Guinella, Arcata, or Eureka.

COMMENTS: This run is quite easy except for the drop under the US-101 bridge where the riverbed below the concrete has eroded. As the river slows, it tends to form new channels during heavy flows, called braiding. Some are dead-ends and some the main flow. Go with the most water and strongest flow. Know the tide flow as it affects the water closer to the ocean. This run is not recommended during high wind conditions.

NOTE: The Butler Valley run was just deleted because of several rock slides making the run more difficult. The 10 miles up-river of the Butler Valley run is Class IV, reported in *The Best Whitewater in CA.*.

●●●●●●●●●●●●●●●●

(UPPER) MAD RIVER

Ruth Lake (Res.) to SR 36, 7.5 miles, Class II

SEASON: Spring. BEST FLOWS: 300-600 cfs. FLOW INFO: Mad River FS RS

ACCESS: Put in • .5 miles below the dam on a side road off Lower Mad River Rd. 7.5 miles to • take out below bridge off of SR 36 61 miles E. of US-101.

MAPS: AAA — "Northern CA Section" DE LORME — p. 42

GAS, FOOD & LODGING: Fortuna.
CAMPING: Ruth Lake (Res) FS cpgrs. Six Rivers NF: 707.574.6233.

BEWARE: The flows are critical as it can be very rocky at low flows.

COMMENTS: This run was written up by Dick Schwind in West Coast River Touring. Terry Sauter Haag and Gary Haag recently did the run, using the information in Dick's book. "We tried it a few years ago and liked it." wrote Terry. Dick writes: "This run is much more pleasant than would be expected, particularly driving along the road and looking down at the river. A dozen or so short rapids. Some of the rapids are in gravel bars. Other rapids are among medium-sized rocks. None of the rapids are particularly difficult." The down side, it is a good two to three hours of winding roads to get to Ruth Lake either from Fortuna area or Garberville each on the 101 highway.

●●●●●●●●●●●●●●●●

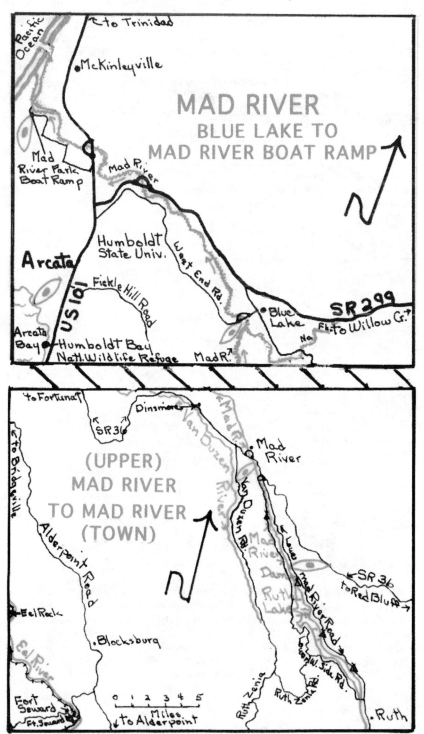

MAD RIVER
BLUE LAKE TO
MAD RIVER BOAT RAMP

(UPPER)
MAD RIVER
TO MAD RIVER
(TOWN)

LAGOONS

There are three large lagoons adjacent to US-101 between Patricks Pt. SP and Orick (Redwood NP) with easy paddlecraft access. Besides being very scenic in view of the ocean, they offer excellent wildlife viewing—river otter, Roosevelt elk, deer, waterfowl that are permanent and migratory. There are cpgrs. at each.

Freshwater Lagoon is part of Redwood National Park on the east side of US-101 across the highway from a long sandspit. INFO: 707.464.6101.

Stone Lagoon, on the west side of the highway, is larger than Freshwater. One of its two campgrounds is a boat-in. There is a sandspit between the brackish lagoon and the ocean which is breached about twice a year allowing water to pour directly into the ocean. At this time, the lagoon is affected by tidal action. INFO: 707.488.2041.

Big Lagoon is the largest of the three lagoons with a campground at the south end. It also has many wildlife species in and around it. Its long sandspit is breached about 4 times a year. Like Stone Lagoon, duck hunting and power boats are allowed. INFO: Humboldt Co. Parks.

• • • • • • • • • • • • • • • •

REDWOOD CREEK

Tall Trees to Orick, 8 miles, Class I

SEASON: Rainy & spring. BEST FLOW: 400-1,000 cfs. GAGING STATION: Orick
FLOW INFO: Hodges: http//sonic.net/kkct/whitewat.htm.

ACCESS: Put-in • Tall Trees Grove, US-101 to Balk Hills Rd. to Redwood NP. Drive to the end of the road where the trail goes a mile to the grove.
8 miles to • US-101 bridge.

MAPS: AAA — "Northern California Section." DE LORME — p. 32 "Redwood." Redwood NP: 707.464.6101.

GAS, FOOD & LODGING: Orick and Trinidad to the south.
CAMPING: Freshwater Lagoon Campground, Stone Lagoon Campground, and Stone Lagoon Boat-in Campground.

BEWARE: Water too high or too low and wind.

COMMENTS: Redwood Creek has two sections, one a Class III with a IV+ that simmers down to a Class I as it flows past the Tall Trees. Getting to the water at the Tall Trees Grove is a long carry or push on a narrow trail. The creek is easy; it flows through the flat area of Redwood NP and into the plains of Orick. The tallest tall tree lost about 15 feet of its "crown" and thus was dethrowned in 1999. Now the tallest tree is in Montgomery Woods, northwest of Ukiah.

• • • • • • • • • • • • • • •

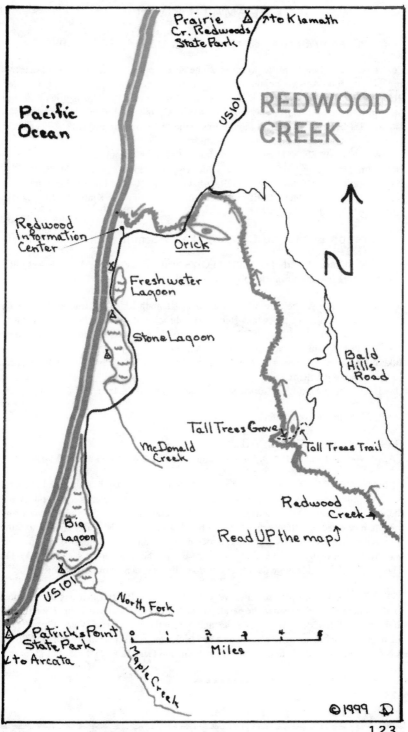

Prairie Cr. Redwoods State Park

↗ to Klamath

US 101

REDWOOD CREEK

Pacific Ocean

Redwood Information Center

Orick

Freshwater Lagoon

Stone Lagoon

Bald Hills Road

Tall Trees Grove

Tall Trees Trail

McDonald Creek

Redwood Creek

Read UP the map ↑

Big Lagoon

US 101

North Fork

0 1 2 3 4 5
Miles

Patrick's Point State Park

↙ to Arcata

Maple Creek

© 1999

KLAMATH RIVER

Oregon Border to the Pacific Ocean, 200+ miles

Before paddling, first learn the location of the access points, which are not all marked, and the river flow. As a very experienced Klamath River canoe instructor and guide, Neil Rucker said: "The higher the flow, the more difficult the rapids." This is true of most of the rapids, unless the higher water provides "sneak" routes. This "pool-drop" river has mostly Class II and II+ rapids or wave-trains in the center or near the banks. Check at the nearest Forest Service Ranger Station for information.

FLOW INFORMATION: Hodges: http//sonic.net/kkct/whitewat.htm.
Gov.: http://water.usgs.gov/nwc/ or www.cdec.ca.gov. K-Phone: 916.368.8682.
Gaging Stations: John Boyle Res. in OR, Iron Gate Dam, Copco Lake and Orleans.
MAPS: AAA —"Northern California Section." and USFS — Klamath N.F., Yreka: 530.842.6131, and DE LORME.

Oregon Border to Copco Lake, 5.5 miles, Class II - III

SEASON: Summer & early fall. BEST FLOWS: 950-2,500 cfs. G.S.: J. Boyle Res OR. Allow 3 hours for water from JC Boyle to reach the put-in.

ACCESS: Put-in • At the take-out for the upper Klamath River raft trips at the Oregon border. From US I-5, take Henley/Hornbrook exit, go east, then R on Ager Rd., and L on Ager Beswick Rd. south of Copco Lake. Pass Copco Lake and follow dirt rd 6 mi. to state line. Parking & Rrm.
Take-out • Fishing Access #1, 1/2 mile on road to put-in above bridge to Lake Copco. Parking & Rrm.
Or • Boat-ramp behind Lake Copco Store at the NE end of the lake. Pkg & Rrm.

MAP: DE LORME — pp. 26 & 27.

GAS, FOOD, and LODGING: Yreka.
CAMPING: FS Tree of Heaven Campground, 12 miles NW of Yreka on US-96.

BEWARE: The flow is often augmented about noon of each day by scheduled releases, almost tripling the flow from 950 cfs to 2,500 cfs. The lower water is not as pushy but there are many rocks in the rapids to be avoided or scraped over. At the higher flow, many rocks are covered, but there are almost no beaches or eddies, the water is cold, and the flow is powerful. A mile downstream is a rock dam with ditches on both sides and no easy way to scout at high water. On the road to the put-in, the weir can be seen. STUDY IT! The paddling route down the dam is one-third of the way across from river left.

COMMENTS: What a pleasant discovery, a Class II+ to III- run that has been almost totally ignored. The dirt road to the parking area is easy compared to driving down the hill to the river—full of deep ruts. This is the take-out for the upper Class IV and V run. There are many rock gardens, wave trains, and a few tricky spots. With the afternoon high flows, it is fast flowing. But it's fun. (Terry Salter-Haag and Gary Haag told me about this run. Thanks!)

●●●●●●●●●●●●●●●●

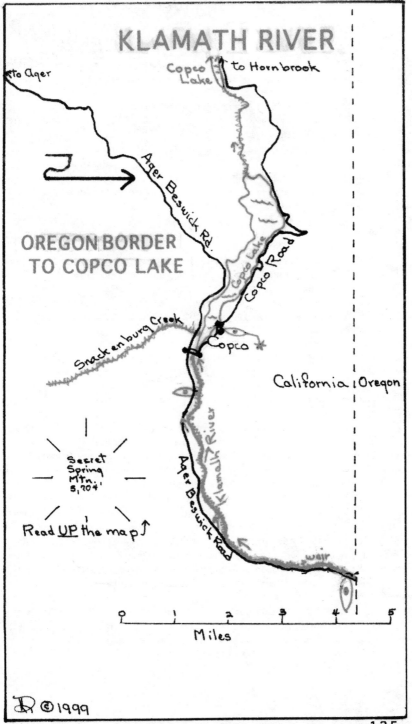

KLAMATH RIVER

to Ager

Copco Lake

to Hornbrook

Ager Beswick Rd.

OREGON BORDER TO COPCO LAKE

Copco Lake

Copco Road

Snackenburg Creek

Copco

California | Oregon

Secret Spring Mtn. 5,704'

Read UP the map ↑

Ager Beswick Road

Klamath River

weir

| 0 | 1 | 2 | 3 | 4 | 5 |

Miles

℗ ©1999

KLAMATH RIVER (con't)

Iron Gate Dam to Tree of Heaven Campground, 17.5 miles,
Class I+ - II+

BEST FLOW: 1,000 cfs is the usual summer release from Iron Gate Dam.

ACCESS: Put in • From US I-5 Henley-Hornbrook exit, east on Copco Road to launch
ramp.
5.5 miles to • Klamathon and Ager Rd. bridge.
6 miles to • behind store just upstream from the Shasta River confluence.
.5 miles to • 100 yards upstream of Collier Rest Area, on dirt road on river left.
2.5 miles to • Ash Creek, across the bridge and down the river a bit.
3.5 miles to • FS Tree of Heaven Cpgr., on SR-96, 5.5 miles west of US I-5 exit.

MAPS: DE LORME — pp. 25 & 26.

GAS, FOOD, and LODGING: Yreka.
CAMPING: Ash Creek and Tree of Heaven FS Campgound. Very attractive campground
on the river with mowed grass, trees, pit toilets, gentle-sloping boat ramp. Parking &
Rrm. Fee for camping, but day use is free.

BEWARE: After the Shasta River enters on River left, the difficulty increases with a few
Class III rapids. Check first.

COMMENTS: The easiest river access is downriver on river right; you may be able to
drive part way. Park upriver. Bogus Creek enters from river left near the gaging station,
1.5 miles later is Dry Creek on river right, in another mile after passing R Ranch is a
footbridge, followed by Kutskey Lodge in another mile. Between here and Ager Rd. bridge,
Willow Creek enters from river left. Cottonwood Creek enters from river right a half-mile
before US I-5, then after going under the freeway, the river flows parallel to the freeway
for three miles. The Collier Rest Area is very evident on river left; there is easy water
access 100 yards upstream on river left. This is an easy run with good flow until the
Shasta River enters on river left. A mile downstream is a Class II+ and three Class III-
rapids. Ash Creek rapid, the first is just upstream from Ash Creek on river right, stay right
of center, (cpgr. on river left across the bridge) followed by Badger Creek rapid in a half
mile, again stay right. The third rapid is less than a half mile away. Tree of Heaven Cpgr.
(when driving from the east, turning off SR-96 is fairly tricky due to the bend in the road.
Be careful.) is 2 miles further on river right. As the river flows into the restricted canyons
with sculptured rocks to go through, over and around, the character changes, offering
more of a remote feeling. This run is fun, has a good flow as it passes through a wide
valley past bridge remnants and under bridges increasing in difficulty when it goes into
the canyon.
The campground, Tree of Heaven, is at a wide bend in the river on level ground with a
boat ramp for easy access. Trees and mowed grass make for a comfortable stay. At the
downstream end of the campground are the Trees of Heaven, native to China.

●●●●●●●●●●●●●●●●

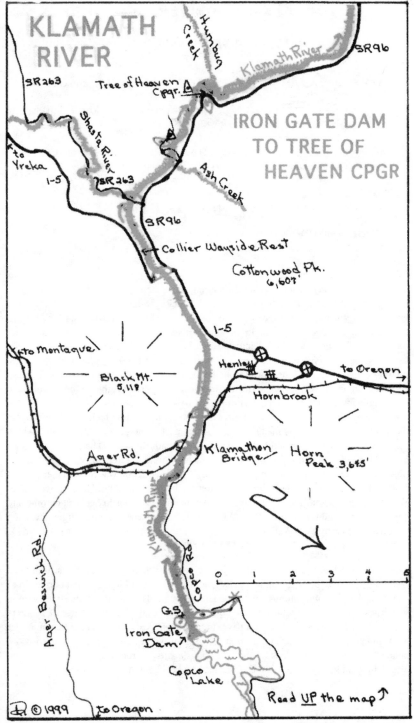

KLAMATH
RIVER

Humbug
Creek

Klamath River

SR96

SR263

Tree of Heaven
Cpgr.

IRON GATE DAM
TO TREE OF
HEAVEN CPGR

to
Yreka

I-5

Shasta River

SR263

Ash Creek

SR96

Collier Wayside Rest

Cottonwood Pk.
6,607'

I-5

to Montague

Henley

to Oregon

Black Mt.
6,118'

Hornbrook

Ager Rd.

Klamathon
Bridge

Horn
Peak 3,645'

Klamath River

Copco Rd.

0   1   2   3   4   5

Ager Beswick Rd.

G.S.

Iron Gate
Dam

Copco
Lake

© 1999

to Oregon

Read UP the map ↑

KLAMATH RIVER (con't)

Tree of Heaven Cprg. to Brown Bear Access, 22.5 miles, Class II+ - III-

SEASON: Summer & early fall. BEST FLOWS: 700-3,000 cfs. G.S.: Iron Gate Dam.

ACCESS: Put in • Tree of Heaven Campground, SR-96. Parking & Rrm. (Cl. II)
3.5 miles to • Skeahan Bar. SR-96. Parking. (Cl. II+)
3.5 miles to • Gottville. SR-96. Parking. (Cl. II)
5.5 miles to • Klamath River (town). Ask at Quigleys. SR-96. Pkng & Rrm. (Cl.II+)
10 miles to • Brown Bear access, well marked. SR-96. Parking under trees. (Cl. I+)

MAPS: DE LORME — pp. 25 & 26.
MANAGING AGENCY: Happy Camp Ranger Sta..: 530.493.2894.

GAS, FOOD, and LODGING: Yreka.
CAMPING: FS Tree of Heaven Cpgr. upriver, or Sarah Totten FS Cpgr. downriver.

COMMENTS: Here the Klamath begins to have greener scenery with more mountains and interesting water. After Skeahan Bar on the right, 3.5 miles downriver, the next two miles have some Class II+ (III-)drops—Dutch Creek (creek enters from river right) and Honolulu. A great surfing wave at 700 to 1300 cfs has School House Rapid, a Class II, between Dutch Creek and Honolulu. In 7 miles Beaver Creek enters from the right (cpgr. 4 mi. up creek) and the town of Klamath River is 1 mile further. Through the area of the town of Klamath River, the river is easy flowing and continues with a few Class II rapids, nothing with a name. It is also away from the highway though there is a road on river left and a few homes along the banks. Brown Bear access is on river right; be sure to note how to recognize it from the river. (Latest run: 8-98.)
Stop in two or three of the local businesses and notice the different feeling, you are now in the state of "Jefferson," as many of the "locals" wish. The state of "Jefferson" (which included southern Oregon and California in the Klamath River area) had its wishful start in 1852 but failed to win approval of either state legislature. "Jefferson" was to be "free of obnoxious taxes, no sales, income or liquor tax.." Positive action was revived in the fall of 1941 only to be stopped short three days after the bombing of Pearl Harbor. Because of WWII, a road was built along the river, SR-96, making it easier to haul out chrome and copper ores needed for the war effort. While in "Jefferson" eat a buffalo burger; the bison are raised in nearby Scott Valley.

• • • • • • • • • • • • • • • •

The Klamath River is for all paddlers. Beginners have three good locations: Iron Gate Dam to Klamathon bridge, a bit more challenging is the Class I to II run just upriver from Curley Jack Cpgr., and Happy Camp area. Then for a good camping trip, the 40 to 50 mile wilderness run from Weitchpec to the coast is mostly Class I and I+. Class II paddlers have over 120 miles of the Klamath River to hone their skills on from the Oregon border to Weitchpec. There are several sections of exciting whitewater for the Class III & IV boaters. There are some Class III and IV rapids downriver from Happy Camp and again after Ishi Pishi Falls (Somes Bar) to Orleans, The Ikes being the best known.

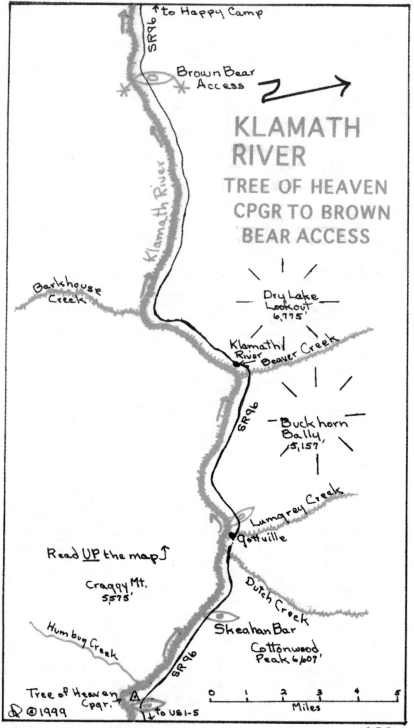

to Happy Camp

SR96

Brown Bear Access

KLAMATH RIVER
TREE OF HEAVEN
CPGR TO BROWN
BEAR ACCESS

Klamath River

Barkhouse Creek

Dry Lake Lookout 6,775'

Klamath River

Beaver Creek

SR96

Buckhorn Bally 5,157'

Lumgrey Creek

Gottville

Read UP the map

Craggy Mt. 5,575'

Dutch Creek

Humbug Creek

Skeahan Bar

Cottonwood Peak 6,607'

SR96

Tree of Heaven Cpgr.

to US I-5

0 1 2 3 4 5
Miles

©1999

KLAMATH RIVER (con't)

Brown Bear Access to Portuguese Creek, 24 miles, Class II, II+, & III

ACCESS: Put in • Brown Bear Access. SR-96. Parking under the trees.
7.5 miles to • Blue Heron Access. SR-96. Parking.
2 miles to • Sarah Totten Cpgr. SR-96. Parking & Rrm.
5 miles to • O'Neil Creek Cpgr. SR-96. Parking & Rrm.
7.5 miles to • Sluice Box Access. SR-96. Parking.
2 miles to • Portuguese Creek with access on either side of the river, Ft. Goff Cpgr. and Savage Rapids Access, in close proximity, about .5 mile between each. SR-96. Parking.

MAP: DE LORME — pp. 24 & 25.

GAS, FOOD, and LODGING: (Seiad Valley) and Happy Camp.
CAMPING: FS Sarah Totten Cpgr. and FS O'Neil Creek Cpgr.

COMMENTS: A mile downstream the highway passes over the river to be on river left for the next 15.5 miles, then it goes back to the right side near Seiad Valley. This is mostly Class I water for the next 6 miles until after the entrance of the Scott River on river left followed shortly with Tom Martin Creek and riffle on river left. Knowing that Hamburg Falls is coming soon I have credited Tom Martin riffle, a bit tricky, for being Hamburg Falls. No way! But first, take a break at Sarah Totten Cpgr. on river left. Not far downstream is Hamburg Falls and it is a Class III! It is at a sharp right bend with big boulders in the channel. Scout on river right or left or portage on river left.
It is followed by several miles of Class I & II water then into Seiad Valley where the river is away from SR-96. Grider Road is on river left until Grider Creek comes in on the left. The Pacific Crest Trail crosses the river here and does some "peak-bagging" or close to it as it goes north then east in the Rogue River National Forest. The flow in this open valley is gentle until the canyon narrows and the big waves of Sluice Box (II+) challenge the paddler. (Last run: 8-98.)

NOTE: The SCOTT RIVER flows into the Scott Valley from the Trinity/Marble Mountains. For 30 miles it leisurely winds its way through this scenic valley of cattle ranches before cascading 21 miles in Class III to V rapids, in some sections dropping at 90 feet per mile before gently sliding into the Klamath River. Scott Valley property owners along the river do not welcome paddlers on these many miles of Class I water as access points are barred and posted. Maybe some year local residents will establish riverside parks. (The whitewater section is written up in both; The Best Whitewater in California by Holbek & Stanley and California Whitewater by Cassady & Calhoun.)

• • • • • • • • • • • • • • • •

Portuguese Creek (Fort Goff) to Seattle Creek, 6 miles, Class III-

Here's Upper Savage, a Class III- rapid with holes and boulders and Otter's Play Pen, a Class III- with big rock labs dividing the river, according to CA WW.

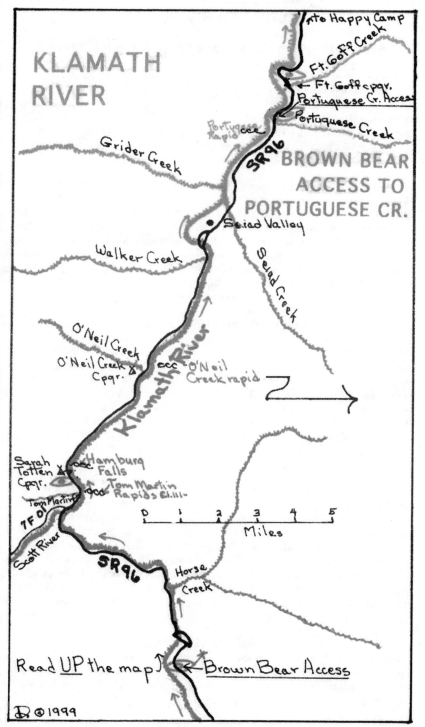

KLAMATH RIVER

nto Happy Camp

Ft. Goff Creek

← Ft. Goff cpgr.
Portuguese Cr. Access

Portuguese Creek

Portuguese Rapid ccc

SR96

BROWN BEAR ACCESS TO PORTUGUESE CR.

Grider Creek

● Seiad Valley

Seiad Creek

Walker Creek

O'Neil Creek

O'Neil Creek Cpgr.

ccc O'Neil Creek rapid

Klamath River

Sarah Totten Cpgr.

Hamburg Falls

ccc

Tom Martin Rapids Cl.III—

Tom Martin

0   1   2   3   4   5
        Miles

7F Ol

Scott River

SR96

Horse Creek

Read UP the map ↑ ← Brown Bear Access

R ©1999

KLAMATH RIVER (con't)

Seattle Creek to Curley Jack Cpgr., 17 miles, Class II

ACCESS: Put-in • Seattle Creek FS Access. Nearby is Shinar Creek. SR-96.
4 miles to • China Point FS Access. SR-96.
5 miles to • Gordon's Ferry.
5 miles to • Happy Camp Bulk Plant.
2 miles to • Indian Creek FS Access. Used by outfitters. Parking & Rrm.
1 mile to • FS Curley Jack Cpgr. Across the Elk Creek Rd. Bridge (access below the
   bridge) turn right, follow signs to USFS campground. Easy.

MANAGING AGENCY: FS Happy Camp Ranger Station: 530.493.2243.

COMMENTS: This next stretch is a good respite from the more demanding flows as it
goes away from the highway in a big bend leisurely flowing through the valley. Don't
relax too much. There are still some Class II's for fun. It is also a good mid-river introduction to the Klamath River, like the 6 mile run from Iron Gate Dam to Klamathon Bridge.
Curley Jack Campground, with Happy Camp nearby for supplies, makes a good base
camp for three classes of Klamath River flows. Last date run: 8/13/98.

•••••••••••••••

Curly Jack Cpgr. to Dillon Riffle, 23 mi., Cl. II+, III, & IV

COMMENTS: The river enters a narrow section around a mile after the put-in for some
challenging rapids, especially the Class III Kanaka Falls (A.K.A. Rattlesnake), followed
by several Class II+ drops like: Mixmaster, Funnel and The Trench. Where Clear Creek
enters from the right are the sacred ceremonial grounds of the Karok Indians. These are
on both sides of the river for the next three miles. During the 5-week World Renewal
Ceremony held here, boaters should not stop but go quietly through. Rumor has it that
Dragon's Tooth (IV) suffered some involuntary reconstruction in 1998. It is the BIG rapid
in this run, that can be portaged on river right.

•••••••••••••••

HISTORY: Gold was discovered on the Klamath in the 1851 following the discovery of
the precious metal by John Scott in the valley bearing his name. Miners found what they
sought and left their feelings with the name Happy Camp. Some of the Klamath River
banks are covered with large rock piles from gold mining. There are miners today clad in
wet suits, weight belts, and masks seeking the best spot at river bottom for their hoses to
vacuum the gravel to the sluice boxes on the floating dredges. They have claims and do
hardrock mining. There's still gold in "them thar hills" as evidenced by the annual gather-
ing of gold seekers to Happy Camp. Up river, at Sarah Totten Campground, mounds of
shale, left from the mining, separate campsites. Many miles of these mounds are visible
from the river.

MORE KLAMATH RIVER RUNNING INFO:

Stateline to Weitchpec: *Handbook to the Klamath River Canyon* by Quinn & Quinn. 1983.
Happy Camp to Dillon Creek Cpgr.: *The Best Whitewater in California* by Holbek &
Stanley. Sarah Totten Cpgr.(Hamburg) to Weitchpec: *California Whitewater* by Cassady
& Calhoun.

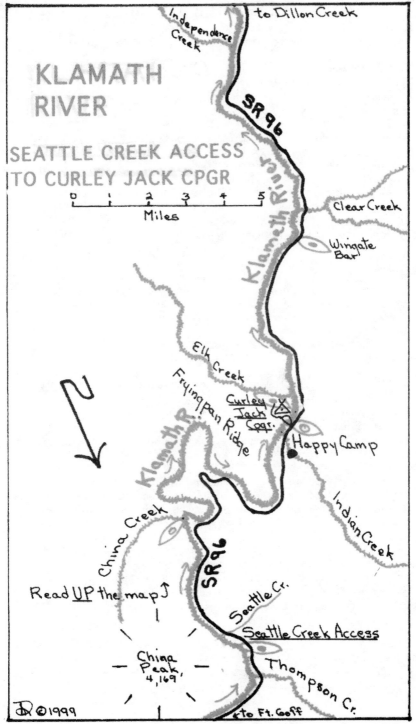

KLAMATH
RIVER

SEATTLE CREEK ACCESS
TO CURLEY JACK CPGR

0 1 2 3 4 5
Miles

to Dillon Creek

Independence
Creek

SR 96

Klamath River

Clear Creek

Wingate
Bar!

Elk Creek

Curley
Jack
Cgr.

Frying Pan Ridge

Happy Camp

Klamath R.

China Creek

Indian Creek

SR 96

Read UP the map ↑

Seattle Cr.

Seattle Creek Access

China
Peak,
4,169

Thompson Cr.

to Ft. Goff

© 1999

KLAMATH RIVER (con't)

Dillon Creek to Green Riffle, 12.5 miles, Class II+

ACCESS: Put-in • Dillon Creek Cpgr. SR-96. Steep downhill over shale to river.
3 miles to • Persido Bar FS Access. SR-96.
1.5 miles to • Ti Bar FS Access. SR-96. Easy drive to river. Parking & Rrm.
8 miles to • Green Riffle FS Access. SR-96. Steep road down to river.

MANAGING AGENCY: FS Happy Camp RS: 530.493.2243.

CAMPING: FS Dillon Creek Campground.

COMMENTS: Here's a fun stretch with Class II+ rapids. Just downriver from Dillon Creek the highway crosses to be on river left. In the next 9 miles it crosses twice where the river makes a tight bend to the east, then it stays on the east of the river until Orleans. Some of the river can be scouted from the highway including a distant view of Ishi Pishi Falls (Class VI), near the road to the Yurok ceremonial site, 3 miles upriver from Somes Bar. The Ti Bar take-out is easy; a great spot to swim and pan for gold. Green Riffle, 8 miles further is the last take out before the unrunnable Ishi Pishi Falls (not an easy portage). We ran from near Dillon Creek to Ti Bar on 8/14/98; The Green Riffle take out was still unfinished at that time.

●●●●●●●●●●●●●●●●

Somes Bar to Dolans Bar, 6 miles (incl. The Ikes), Class III & IV

COMMENTS: Somes Bar is at the confluence of the Cal. Salmon River with the sizable flow early in the season. Next are The Ikes! These are the BIG rapids! They are just a short ways down the river but they can be scouted from the highway, high above, or on the dirt road (marked The Ikes) down to the river for a closer look. The first one, Little Ike (III-), has a big rock outcropping in the middle, the warning that Big Ike (IV) is just ahead, then Super Ike (III+) which has a difficult ledge drop at lower flows.

NOTE: Reg Lake, a Class V kayaker, rafting guide, river explorer (Sierra & Chile), and kayak instructor (teaching for Otter Bar on the Cal Salmon), told me about a 4 mile, Class II+ run from Oak Bottom Cpgr. to Somes Bar on the Salmon River early in the season.

●●●●●●●●●●●●●●●●

HISTORY: The last Indian Reservation authorized by the US government was the Hoopa Reservation that included the Hoopas, Yuroks, and Karuks—the last two being primarily on the Klamath River. There have been some recent changes making the three tribes more autonomous. The Karuks are near Somes Bar; Ishi Pishi Falls area is the site for one of the tribal gatherings; the Yuroks are headquartered near Weitchpec.

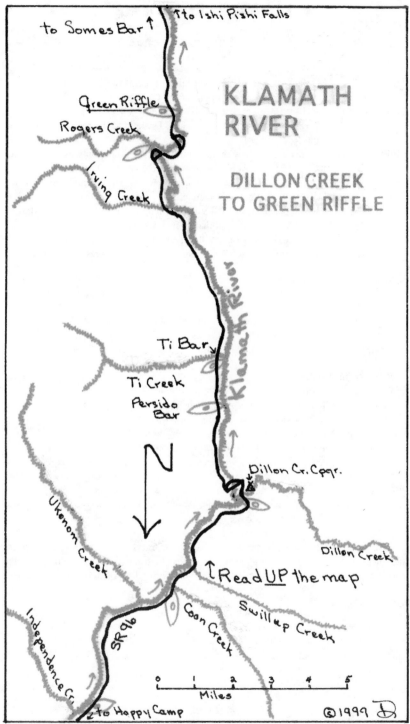

to Somes Bar ↑   ↑to Ishi Pishi Falls

KLAMATH RIVER

DILLON CREEK TO GREEN RIFFLE

Green Riffle
Rogers Creek
Irving Creek

Klamath River

Ti Bar
Ti Creek
Persido Bar

Dillon Cr. Cpgr.

N

Ukonom Creek

Dillon Creek

↑ Read UP the map

Swillup Creek

Independence Cr.

SR 96

Coon Creek

0 1 2 3 4 5
Miles

© 1999

↙ to Happy Camp

KLAMATH RIVER (con't)

Orleans Bridge or Dolans Bar to Weitchpec, 15 miles, Class II+ to III-

ACCESS: Put-in • Dolans Bar on SR-96, river left a mile upstream from Orleans. Parking. (Or access the river below the bridge at Orleans.)

3 miles to • FS Long (Big) Bar Access. Easy road to the river. Parking & Rrm.

6 miles to • FS Aitkens Creek Cpgr.(not in service). Drive in to the rock bluff over the river. Parking.

6 miles to • Weitchpec & confluence with the Trinity River. The take-outs are shortly after the bridge, one just upstream of the confluence with the Trinity where a steep trail goes up to the back of the Weitchpec store OR paddle into the confluence around the bend to the boat beach launch site on river right. No. Weitchpec Bar Rd. goes to the beach shortly after the Weitchpec bridge on SR-169, Martins Ferry Rd. It's a narrow dirt road that goes down past a few homes and a brush dance site to a sand plateau above the river. (This is the only rd that goes L for mi.!) Don't get stuck in the sand! Respect the homes and residents. Parking.

MAPS: DE LORME — p. 33.
MANAGING AGENCY: FS Ukonom/Orleans RS: 530.627.3291. Gag. Sta.: Orleans.

GAS, FOOD, and LODGING: Orleans, Hoopa, and Willow Creek.
CAMPING: FS Pearch Creek Cpgr. on the east side of the bridge to Orleans. FS E-Ne-Nuck Cpgr. near Bluff Creek: 530.627.3291. (Bluff Creek Cpgr. not in service)

COMMENTS: The run is mostly Class II and II+ until Slate Creek rapid (III) that comes in from the right forming a river-wide big-rocks rapid. Scout on river left (good photo spot). In a half-mile is Bluff Cr., entering from the right and a rapid just upstream from the bluff. It's a big long rock garden in a dropping waterway. If there is a good flow, scout on the right, there may be a run on the far right. Portage on river left. Below the bluff is a great swimming hole! (Fishermen: there was big excitement here on one trip. We watched a large sturgeon being caught. They are a fascinating ugly-looking boneless fish.) The third challenge is right after the sturgeon pool where Aitken Creek enters from river right. It starts with a left turn, the water then looks like a river-wide water slide with the river forming a giant "pillow" against the far bank. About half of the flow goes river right and the rest creates a giant swirling eddy on river left. Paddle hard to stay in the right-turning flow. Scout and/or portage on river right.

"Fun & games" simmer down to the usual Class II wave-trains, at most. Closer to Weitchpec the river flows rather straight with the highway fairly high above on river right. Below the SR-96 bridge at Weitchpec is the confluence of the Trinity River entering from river left.

• • • • • • • • • • • • • • • •

AVERAGE KLAMATH RIVER ANNUAL FLOWS:

The California Water Atlas Info:
Jan. to April: 64,000 cfs - Dec & May: 45,000 cfs - Nov. & June: 25,000 cfs
July: 10,500 cfs - Aug. & Sept.: 6,500 cfs.

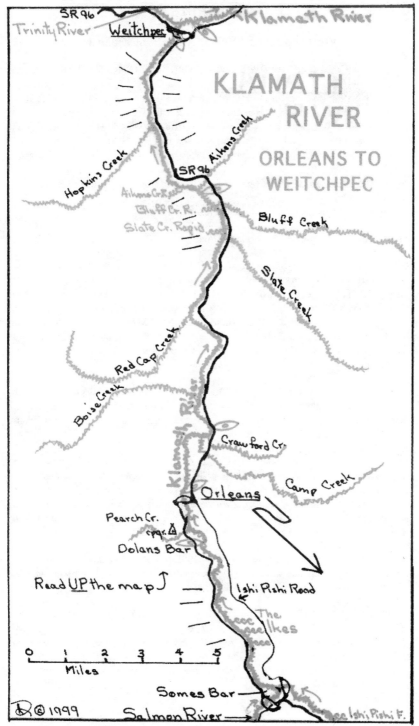

KLAMATH RIVER (con't.)

Weitchpec to Requa, 46 miles, class I+

SEASON: All year.   BEST FLOWS: 5,000-10,000 cfs. GAGING STATION: Orleans.

ACCESS: Put-in • Weitchpec store on SR-96; down the steep trail behind the store towards the Klamath R. near the confluence with Trinity R. Pkg.
.5 miles to • No. Weitchpec Bar Rd., narrow dirt road that goes down to the beach to the
left off of SR-169 Martins Ferry Rd., shortly after the Weitchpec bridge. Road
ends on the beach. Respect private property.
20 miles to • Johnsons, end of SR-169 (This is Yurok country, be respectful.)
20 miles to • Klamath Glen boat ramp, 7 miles upriver from Klamath, north side.
2.5 miles to • Klamath (US-101).
3.5 miles to • Requa near the mouth of the Klamath River.

MAPS: AAA — "Northern California Section." DE LORME — pp. 22, 32, & 33.

GAS, FOOD, and LODGING: Hoopa, Willow Creek, Eureka, Klamath, & Crescent
City.CAMPING: FS cpgrs. in Willow Creek area: 530.629.2118, Orick, and Klamath
areas.SHUTTLE: Forever! Martins Ferry Rd. ENDS at Johnsons. To get from Weitchpec
to the Klamath River at Klamath on US-101,the quickest routes are: SR-96 to Willow
Creek, right on US-299 to US-101, north to Klamath OR Martins Ferry Rd., across Martins Ferry bridge on Bald Hills Rd. to US-101, north of Orick then 17 miles north to
Klamath. OR, maybe the jet boat will take up your group for an easy 2-3 day return:
800.887.JETS.

BEWARE: Just downriver from the confluence of the Trinity and the Klamath can be a
series of large standing waves, one with a large rock just under the water. Sometimes gill
nets are anchored by the Native Americans part way across the river. Watch for them!
Upriver winds, mainly in the afternoon.

COMMENTS: This lower section of 40 to 50 miles of easy water is mostly wilderness
and very scenic, ideal for a camping trip. "The run goes through one of the most picturesque parts of the Klamath River; broad moving river, sand beaches, in-stream boulders,
waterfalls and side streams" *Canoeing Waters of California.*. This is in the Yurok Indian
Reservation. The jet boat will sometimes ferry a group, boats and all, up river. Info. on Jet
Boat Tours: 1.800.887.JETS.

FLORA & FAUNA: The madrone, oak, and pine forest of up river has changed more to
Douglas fir, pine, and canoe and Port Orford cedars. There are many birds of land and
water. Animals: deer, otter, bear, squirrels, and mountain lions.

MOUNTAIN LIONS: Campers at Roach Creek have reported seeing mountain lions at
night. One Sierra Club Nat'l Outings leader reported a lion in a tree above them that
growled for two hours. Another sighting was on a trip I was leading; my college-age
daughter reported seeing a mountain lion on the ledge across from where "the group" was
sleeping. They eyed each other for 20 minutes before the lion retreated. Lion's night calls
sound like a baby crying.

●●●●●●●●●●●●●●●●

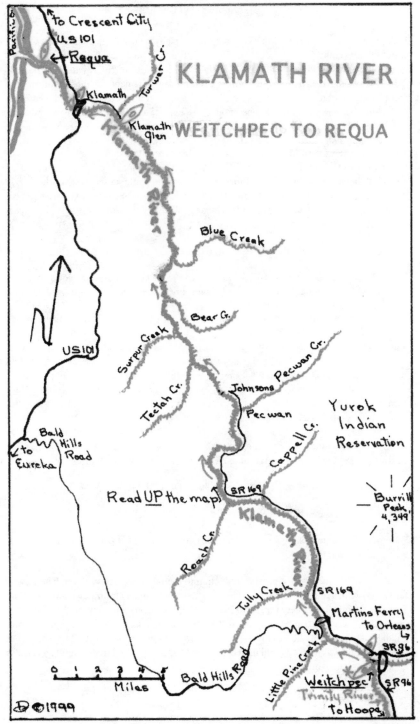

KLAMATH RIVER

WEITCHPEC TO REQUA

to Crescent City
US 101
Requa
Klamath
Klamath Glen
Turwer Cr.
Pacific
Klamath River

Blue Creek

Bear Cr.

Surpur Creek

US 101

Tectah Cr.

Johnsons

Pecwan Cr.

Pecwan

Yurok Indian Reservation

Cappell Cr.

Bald Hills Road
to Eureka

Read UP the map!

SR 169

Burrill Peak 4,349'

Klamath River

Roach Cr.

Tully Creek

SR 169

Martins Ferry to Orleans

SR 96

0 1 2 3 4 5
Miles

Bald Hills Road

Little Pine Creek

Weitchpec

SR 96

Trinity River
To Hoopa

© 1999

TRINITY RIVER

Paddlers have favorite rivers; this is a favorite for many who want a friendly river, warm water, good weather and scenery. The Trinity more than qualifies. This river also holds big excitement, the Pigeon Point Run to Big Flat, five miles of river with four Class III rapids, including Hell Hole. But there is even more excitement for those who run the Burnt Ranch Gorge with six miles of Class IV and V rapids. Cassady and Calhoun in, *California Whitewater*, call it "...one of the finest expert runs in the West." But sandwiching this expert run are miles of Class I and II waters. Enjoy!

HISTORY: The story of Major Reading and his discovery of gold in the area is an interesting chapter of California history and one that is still in the making. On the shuttle, stop and look closely at the highway exhibit of the hydraulic pump and the size of the nozzle that bored into the hills, turning them into giant mud slides. Take some extra time to visit the historical museum and Chinese Joss House in Weaverville. This west side of the state is gold rush town.

Steel Bridge Rd. to Pigeon Point, 27 mi., Class I, I+, & II

SEASON: Spring & summer. BEST FLOWS: 300-1,500 cfs. GS: Lewiston Dam.
FLOW INFO: K-Phone: 916.368.8682. Hodges: http//sonic.net/kkct/whitewat.htm.

ACCESS: Put-in • BLM Steel Bridge Cpgr. 7 mi. NE of Douglas City on Steel   Bridge Rd.NW of SR-299.
 OR • Additional put-ins: Browns Mt. Rd., a paved road to and across the river,   access downstream of bridge. 2 mi. to Lewiston and 3 miles to-SR 299.   Rrm. Old Lewiston Bridge, large parking area, and Rrm. Store & coffee   shop. (NOTE: Just downstream is a weir, runnable on river left.)
8 miles to • BLM Douglas City Cpgr., 6 miles south of Weaverville, .5 mi. W. of   Douglas City off SR-299. Parking & Rrm.
14 miles to • Junction City where the river is close to SR-299, near town, or at   Canyon Creek. Junction City Campground.
5 miles to • Pigeon Point Campground, river right just beyond the North Fork.

MAPS: AAA — "Northern California Section."   DE LORME — pp. 44 & 45.

GAS, FOOD, and LODGING: Weaverville.

BEWARE: Trees across the river and snags. Below Douglas City are remnants of extensive gold mining. Be wary.

COMMENTS: This run is a great introduction to the fabulous Trinity River. The flow is fairly easy with a minimum 300 cfs. release (often much higher) from Lewiston Dam. The 14 miles from Douglas City (cpgr.) to Junction City (cpgr.) is a fun outing for a long day or an easy overnight trip because the difficulty only increases a bit throughout the run. Paddle past the private homes on river left before looking for a campsite. This somewhat remote section was actively gold mined. The next 5 miles, parallel to the highway is Class I, easy and picturesque.

●●●●●●●●●●●●●●●●

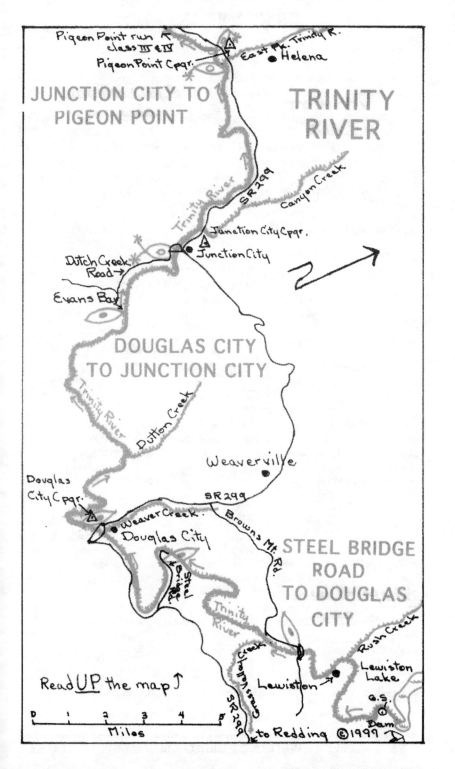

Pigeon Point run
class III & IV

Pigeon Point Cpgr.

East Fk. Trinity R.
Helena

JUNCTION CITY TO PIGEON POINT

TRINITY RIVER

Trinity River

SR 299

Canyon Creek

Junction City Cpgr.
Junction City

Dutch Creek
Road →

Evans Bar

DOUGLAS CITY TO JUNCTION CITY

Trinity River

Dutton Creek

Weaverville

Douglas
City Cpgr.

SR 299

Weaver Creek
Douglas City

Browns Mt. Rd.

STEEL BRIDGE ROAD TO DOUGLAS CITY

Steel Bridge Rd.

Trinity River

Rush Creek

Grass Valley Creek

Lewiston

Lewiston
Lake

G.S.

Read UP the map ↑

Dam

0   1   2   3   4   5
Miles

SR 299

to Redding   ©1999

TRINITY RIVER (con't.)

Big Flat to Cedar Flat, 18 miles, Class II & II+

SEASON: Spring, summer, & fall. BEST FLOWS: 400-1,200 cfs. GS: Lewiston Dam.
FLOW INFO: Hodges: http//sonic.net/kkct/whitewat.htm. K-Phone: 916.368.8682.

ACCESS: Put-in • Trinity River Cpgr. in Big Flat on SR-299 (private) right on the river
    with a store and small restaurant. Very convenient! Parking & Rrm.
2.5 miles to • Big Bar near the Bottom Rd. bridge off SR-299, across the river   from the
    FS Big Bar Ranger Station.
9 miles to • FS Hayden Flat Cpgr. Around the bend past the trees to a small   sand beach
    and pool. Parking area at the west end of the lower cpgr.
6.5 miles to • Cedar Flat, FS picnic area. Short walk to the road and parking area.

MAPS: AAA — "Northern California Section." DE LORME — pp. 44 & 45.

GAS, FOOD, and LODGING: Weaverville to the east, Willow Creek to the west.
CAMPING: FS Shasta-Trinity Cpgrs.: 530.246.5222: Big Flat, (on the river), Big Bar
(2.5 miles, SE Big Bar Ranger Station) and Pigeon Pt. (2 miles W. of Helena & No. Fk.
Trinity & Trinity River). Hayden Flat Cpgr. is often used as a staging area with camping
on both sides of the highway.

BEWARE: High water from heavy rains or during the snowmelt.

COMMENTS: This river "has it all!" The scenery is spectacular—forested mountains on
both sides, gold mining, flowers unique to the area, birds abound as well as deer, mountain lions, otter, mink (watched a mother mink move her brood while sitting in my canoe),
fabulous summer weather, and few paddlers.
This is a fun run. It has well-spaced rapids—some with boulders, some with simple standing waves, and some with a few rock gardens. Most can be boat-scouted. "When in doubt
get out and scout!" This is especially true of a border-line Class III- at Don Juan Point, a
sharp right turn in the river after a natural weir. The preceeding rock garden has few good
routes. Scout and/or portage on river right. The large pool below the weir helps in rescu-
ing.

STORY: Can plastic (linear polyethylene) kayaks be punctured? Yes! Here's what happened on the rapid at San juan Point. One paddler was a little too far right when dropping
over the natural weir so her kayak came down hard on a pointed rock. Someone commented after watching the impact, "Wasn't she lucky to be in a plastic boat." Then she
started yelling as she floated in the pool below the weir. "There's water filling up my
kayak, I'm sinking! My legs are numb". A close look at the kayak, showed an 8 inch slit
below the seat which was mended with duct tape. Chest pains the following day sent her
to a doctor; she had two fractured ribs. The observers knew she had hit rock hard, but hard
enough to split her kayak, fracture two ribs, and cause her legs to be numb? AND this is
only a Class II+ to III- rapid. (The seat of her kayak lacked flex space.)

DANGER! The next run is THE BIG ONE, Burnt Ranch Gorge, Class IV & V. It is well
documented in, *The Best Whitewater in California* and *California Whitewater*.

●●●●●●●●●●●●●●●

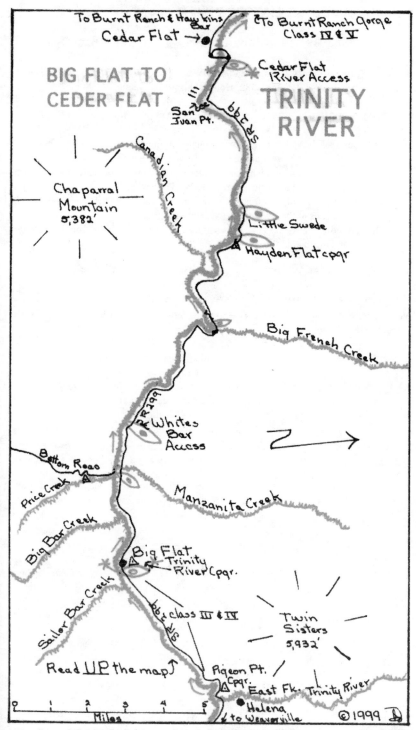

To Burnt Ranch & Hawkins Bar
Cedar Flat

To Burnt Ranch Gorge
Class IV & V

Cedar Flat
River Access

**BIG FLAT TO
CEDER FLAT**

San Juan Pt.

**TRINITY
RIVER**

Canadian Creek

Chaparral
Mountain
5,382'

Little Swede

Hayden Flat cpgr

Big French Creek

FR 199

Whites
Bar
Access

Bottom Road

Price Creek

Manzanita Creek

Big Bar Creek

Big Flat
Trinity
River Cpgr.

Sailor Bar Creek

class III & IV

Twin
Sisters
5,932'

Read UP the map ↑

Pigeon Pt.
Cpgr.

East Fk. Trinity River

Helena
to Weaverville

0 1 2 3 4 5
Miles

© 1999

143

TRINITY RIVER (con't)

Hawkins Bar to Willow Creek, 15.5 miles, Class I+

SEASON: Spring, summer, & fall. BEST FLOWS: 400-2,500 cfs. G. Sta.: Cedar Flat.
FLOW INFO: K-Phone: 916.368.8682, Hodges: http://sonic.net/kkct/whitewat.htm.

ACCESS: Put-in • Hawkins Bar on SR 299. Access also used by commercial outfitters.
   Pkg.
4 miles to • Devil's Elbow. The river flows around a prominent narrow ridge   where the
   "locals" access the river at the end of Tunnel Flat Rd. (dirt).
3 miles to • Salyer, a very small town with a bridge to a small residential area on the north
   side of the river. Fairly steep trail at NE end of bridge.
1.5 mile to • Confluence with South Fork of the Trinity River and a fairly easy take-out. A
   dirt road goes to the river on the NE end of the bridge.
7 miles to • Willow Creek access near the airport off of SR-96 across from the Ranger
   Station. Dirt road to the river. Parking & Rrm.

MAPS: AAA — "Northern California Section." DE LORME — p. 43.

GAS, FOOD, and LODGING: Willow Creek.
CAMPING: Salyer: Lazy Double B RV Park: 530.629.2156. FS Tish Tang Cpgr.:
530.629.2118. Or camp along the river.

BEWARE: Possibly a summer rain shower and afternoon upriver winds.

COMMENTS: This part of the river offers a mixture of "away from it all" feelings interspersed with a few homes visible from the river, an occasional view of the highway, and
local residents also enjoying the river. The Class II features of the river are evidenced
soon after launching at Hawkins Bar and continue with many sections of easy water,
giving a respite. Approaching Willow Creek, the river becomes mostly class I+ until after
the air strip then the "fun" resumes. The river makes a large bend around the community
of Willow Creek that includes Camp Kimtu with river access. The flow goes under a
bridge that leads to a residential area. Not far beyond is Big Rock access. From Willow
Creek on SR-299 is an hour of forested mountain highway to Eureka on the coast.

●●●●●●●●●●●●●●●●

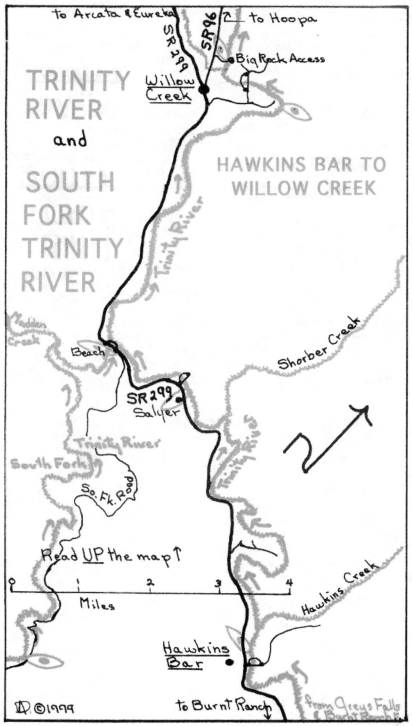

TRINITY RIVER
and
SOUTH FORK TRINITY RIVER

HAWKINS BAR TO WILLOW CREEK

to Arcata & Eureka
SR 299
SR 96
to Hoopa
Big Rock Access
Willow Creek

Trinity River

Madden Creek

Shorber Creek

Beach

SR 299
Salyer

Trinity River

South Fork

Trinity River

So. Fk. Road

Read UP the map ↑

0   1   2   3   4
Miles

Hawkins Creek

Hawkins Bar

to Burnt Ranch

from Greys Falls & Burnt Ranch

TD.©1999

TRINITY RIVER (con't)

So. Fork of the Trinity River to Trinity R., 9 mi., Class II

SEASON: Spring. BEST FLOWS: 300-1,200 cfs. FLOW INFO: Laughing Heart Adv.: 530.629.3516, www.pcweb.net/laughingheart, e-mail: laughingheart@pcweb.net.

ACCESS: Put-in • On Forest Service land via South Fork Rd. off of SR-299 west of Salyer about 9 miles up river on the east side at low bridge (washed out). There may be a barbed-wire fence to get over plus a steep drop to the river. Check at the ranger station first: 530.629.2118 or Laughing Heart Adv.: 530.629.3516.
8 miles to • Sandy Bar located upriver from the bridge on river left. Ask locally. Parking.
1 mile to • Confluence with the Trinity R. Take out at old road, right side after SR-299 bridge; long easy walk to highway.

MAPS: AAA — "No. CA Section." DE LORME — p. 43. FS Six Rivers NF map.

GAS, FOOD, and LODGING: Willow Creek, 6 miles north.
CAMPING: FS Boise Creek Cpgr. 2 miles west of Willow Creek: 530.629.2118.

BEWARE: Put-in is still iffy. Low water in summer. Class III at rock slide.

COMMENTS: I've only done this run once. I really liked it and want to do it again in spite of the put-in and limited running season. The river winds past high cliffs, complete with waterfalls and sand beaches with Class I and II rapids for paddling fun. It is a very scenic wilderness run until the sweeping right turn, a mile upriver from the bridge, and confluence where there is a large public beach with easy access on the west side of the river.

NOTE: The land at the put-in is public but "locals" are objecting to boaters.
● ● ● ● ● ● ● ● ● ● ● ● ● ● ● ● ●

BIG FOOT: This is Big Foot country. There is a chain-sawed wooden Big Foot on display for those driving into Willow Creek from the west. Many rumors abound about this mystical creature. There is the story about a Humboldt State College student who did a research project on Big Foot. The student gathered all the information on the sightings of the creature and plotted them out as to elevation, vegetation, climate, terrain and other criteria. The student found several positive correlations. Maybe Big Foot did (does) exist.

GOLD MINING: California and the discovery of gold has been such a fascinating part of our state and it is a current element in running some of our rivers. The Trinity being a great example. One of my kayak dealers told me about being part owner of a mine on the Trinity River and having to spend a given amount of time "working" the mine each year or lose the claim. The way to buy nuggets is directly from a gold dredger. Ask when paddling past.

TRINITY RIVER

EEL RIVER

TRINITY RIVER (con't.)

Willow Creek to Weitchpec, 26 miles, Class II, II+ (III)

SEASON: All year. BEST FLOWS: 600-3,000 cfs. Gaging S: Cedar Flat & Hoopa.
FLOW INFO: K-Phone: 916.368.8682. Hodges: http://sonic.net/kkct/whitewat.htm.

ACCESS: Put-in • Big Rock access near the airstrip & SR-96. Parking & Rrm.
10 miles to • FS Tish Tang Cpgr. Camping, SR-96. Parking & Rrm.
5 miles to • SR-96 bridge at Hoopa. Parking.
10.5 miles to • Weitchpec store. Parking.

MAPS: AAA — "Northern California Section." DE LORME — p. 43. USFS: Six Rivers
Ranger S.: 530.629.2118.

CAMPING: Knight's Park: 530.629.3219. FS Tish Tang Cpgr.: 530.629.2118

BEWARE: Highwater and gill nets across the river in the gorge.

COMMENTS: After the easy put-in below Willow Creek the flow is gentle with a few
rapids until after the tight left turn at Horse Linto Creek (stop for a swim in the deep pool).
The river is now in a gorge away from the road, with Sugar Bowl Ranch and a Class II+
rapid at the sweeping right turn a short ways from Horse Linto. A special surprise on one
trip was a hillside orange with blooming tiger lilies. Tish Tang FS Campground is located
on the left in a sweeping left turn across from Tish Tang A Tang Creek.
The Hoopa tribe has an adjacent camp ground at Tish Tang. From here the river is flowing
through the Hoopa Indian Reservation to Weitchpec. The flow is gentle around the town
of Hoopa (stop at the market or visit the museum). When the houses on river right end and
the highway climbs, the rapids begin. Very scenic with ferns and waterfalls. Bear, otter,
and the water ouzel (dipper bird) may be seen. If camping in the gorge, the night cries of
the mountain lions can be heard; they sound like a baby crying. The flow can be a bit
tricky as the water flows around large rocks in the narrow canyon with drops and swirling
eddies. Weitchpec Falls, the big one, is in sight of the store at Weitchpec. It changes often
and is easily scouted and portaged. The take-out is either on the Trinity below the store
with a long steep climb, or from the Klamath River. Take care in the sweeping wave train
before the take-out at the far end of the big beach on river right. The first time I saw the
Klamath River from the Trinity I thought it was a big side creek. What a surprise when we
paddled in its size and power.
On another trip we were taking out on the beach on river right of the Klamath River with
a long way to walk across the hot burning sands to the vehicles, during a heat wave with
the temperature over 100. The directive was to "submerge in the river before each load to
the cars." Everyone survived!

• • • • • • • • • • • • • • • •

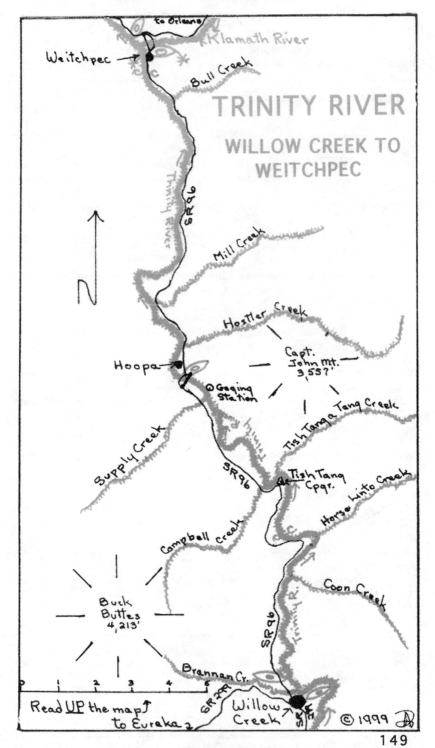

TRINITY RIVER
WILLOW CREEK TO
WEITCHPEC

© 1999

SMITH RIVER

When we were paddling the Smith river in late May of 1998, the El Nino year, the water was fantastic and so were the wildflowers—including blooming fragrant azaleas and crimson rhododendrons. The drive north through redwood forests with dogwood in bloom was also beautiful. We rented a fascinating retreat high above the So. Fk. of the Smith that welcomed paddlers. (Owners: Jim & Pam Matthews:707.458.3231 or Escape Hatch:707.464.2614.)

The Forest Service, State Park, and National Park all have jurisdictions and rangers in the area and are quite knowledgeable about the river access points, dangers, and campgrounds. A recent floral gift with huckleberry foliage reminded me of seeing notices posted outside a Smith River ranger station listing designated plots and harvest times allocated to Northern California florists.

There will be only two runs with write-ups in this section as the others are classified as Class III or better—one ends near the ocean and the other above a Class V gorge. Pay close attention to take-outs! The Class II - III runs on the South Fork end in a narrow Class V gorge. (See*CA WW* and *Best WW in CA..*)

Middle Fork, Panther Flat to above Oregon Hole, 8 miles, Class II+ - III

SEASON: Spring & early summer. BEST FLOWS: 400-2,000 cfs. GAGE: Smith SP FLOWS: K-phone:916.368.8682, Hodges:http//sonic.net/kkct/whitewat.htm., & h2o.usgs.gov. Smith River Info. Line: 707.457.3313.

ACCESS: Put-in • Panther Flat Cpgr., US-199, 4 miles NE of Gasquet, on the M. Fk.
2 miles to • Gasquet. Access behind the self-serve laundry.
2.5 miles to • take-out before the Oregon Hole Gorge. The location of the path to the river
    is at Caltrans highway mile marker 9.09. (Thanks Jim,   *CA Whitewater*, it
    worked!)

MAPS: AAA — "Northern California Section." DE LORME — p. 22. USFS: "Whitewater/ Smith R. Watershed."

GAS, FOOD, and LODGING: Hiouchi and Crescent City.
CAMPING: Panther Flat USFS Cpgr., Gasquet: 707.457.3131, J. Smith SP, Hiouchi: 707. 464.9533.

BEWARE: Mark the takeout before Class V Oregon Hole Gorge. Have three paddlers locate three positive signs visible from the river to make sure of the take out. When paddling watch for Hardscrabble Creek entering from river right 3 miles below Gasquet and 2.5 miles upriver from the take-out. Do not paddle the Smith when the river is rising. It quickly rises to dangerous levels.

COMMENTS: This is a fabulous run, on a fabulous river, with fabulous scenery! It is Class II+, bordering on III but friendly. The North Fork of the Smith enters the Middle Fork at Gasquet. Have three paddlers walk down to the river and identify three things to view when paddling downriver to recognize this important take-out.

●●●●●●●●●●●●●●●

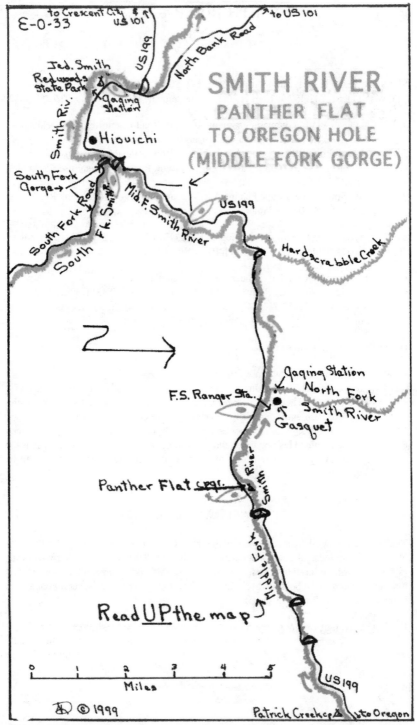

E-O-33

to Crescent City
US 101
US 199
to US 101
North Bank Road

SMITH RIVER
PANTHER FLAT
TO OREGON HOLE
(MIDDLE FORK GORGE)

Jed. Smith
Redwoods
State Park
Gaging Station
Smith Riv.

Hiouchi

South Fork
Gorge →
South Fork Road
South Fk. Smith R.
South
Mid. F. Smith River
US 199

Hardscrabble Creek

Gaging Station
North Fork
Smith River
F.S. Ranger Sta.
Gasquet

Panther Flat cegr.
Smith River

Read UP the map →

Middle Fork

0   1   2   3   4   5
Miles

Ⓐ ©1999

Patrick Creek cⓖ   to Oregon

151

SMITH RIVER (con't.)

Hiouchi (So. Fk.) to Crescent City Boat Ramp, 9 miles, Class I - II

SEASON: Rainy & early summer. BEST FLOW: 500-2,000 cfs. GS: J. Smith SP
FLOW INFO: SP:707.457.3313 or Hodges: http://sonic.ne/kkct/ K-phone: 916.368.8682.

ACCESS: Put-in • Public launching area on So. Fork Road just north of Hiouchi across
the river. Road to the beach, paved parking area, Rrm.
2 miles to • Jed Smith SRA off US-199. Parking & Rrm. Inflatable kayak trips.
4.5 miles to • Ruby VanDeventer Park off of No. Bank Rd, cpgr. & day use. Parking &
Rrm.
2.5 miles to • Smith River Public Fishing Access boat ramp off of North Bank Rd. 2 miles
west of US-101. Parking.

MAPS: AAA — "Northern CA Section." DE LORME — p. 22. Smith River NRA:.
707.457.3131. "Whitewater of the Smith River Watershed."

GAS, FOOD, and LODGING: Hiouchi and Crescent City.
CAMPING: Jedediah Smith Redwoods SP, Hiouchi: 707.464.9533, Panther Flat FS, 4
mi. NE of Gasquet:707.457.3131, Crescent City Redwoods KOA, 6 miles north of Crescent City on US-101: 707.464.5744., and VanDeventer County Park.

BEWARE: Low flows in summer. Some whirlpools at higher water. Upriver wind.

COMMENTS: This a great warm-up for the "rest and best yet to come." At higher water
it is definitely a Class II. The put-in is just upriver from the So. Fk. confluence—watch for
squirrely water here. There are some very attractive homes along the banks. Ruby
VanDeventer Co. Park and J. Smith Redwoods SP have camping and easy river access.
Redwoods are on both sides of the river until US-101 bridge. The last few miles have been
extensively gravel mined leaving holes and gravel mounds. Two miles from US-101 is the
boat ramp, not easily recognized from the river as it slants downstream. A car can be
parked in view of the river.

●●●●●●●●●●●●●●●●

LAKE EARL, WILDLIFE AREA

This is a unique two-lake area located at the tip of California's north coast, 5 miles north
of Crescent City. The lakes are in a marsh area adjacent to the ocean, teaming with birds,
especially during migration. The headquarters is staffed and organized hikes, as well as
birding, bicycling, and boating, are some of the activities. There are several boat access
points. Hunting is allowed in season.

INFO: CA Dept. of Fish & Game, Lake Earl Wildlife Area: 707.464.2523.

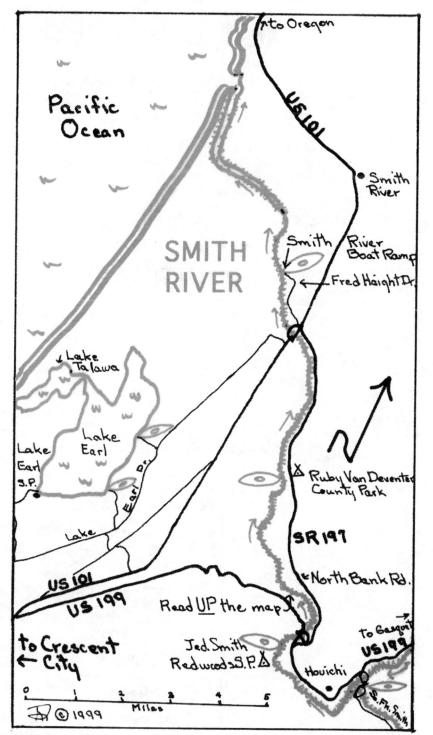

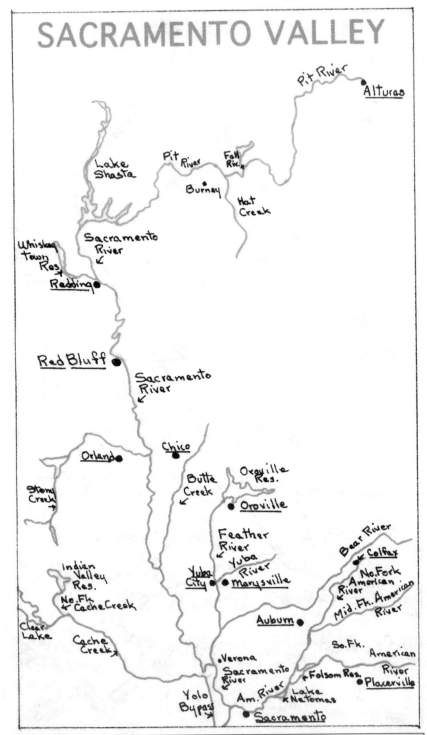

SACRAMENTO VALLEY

CHAPTER 6 - SACRAMENTO VALLEY

CONTENTS

PIT RIVER

Canby Run, SR 139 to Stone Coal Rd., 21.5 mi., Cl. II & I

SEASON: Spring & early summer. BEST FLOWS: 500-1,000 cfs.
FLOW INFO: h2o.usgs.gov

ACCESS: Put-in • SR-299 & SR-139 and Pit River Road, 4 miles SW of Canby.
10 miles to • (Class II) Stone Coal Rd. bridge, 4 miles W. of SR-299 & SR-139.
9 miles to • (Class II) Stone Coal Rd. 3+ miles east of Lookout Hackamore Rd.
2.5 miles to • (Class I) Gaging Station near Lookout Hackamore Rd.

MAPS: AAA — "Northeastern California" & "No. CA Section". DE LORME — p. 39.

GAS, FOOD, and LODGING: Alturas, 19 miles east.
CAMPING: Modoc NF: 530.233.5811; Howards Gulch, 1.5 mi. NW of Canby off SR-139 and Lower Rush Creek, 7.5 mi. NE of Adin off SR-299.

BEWARE: Snags.

COMMENTS: The Pit River flows through high desert country (el. 4,000'+) across the state to the McCloud then into L. Shasta, from very dry climate to wet. The annual rainfall at nearby Alturas is 12 inches, whereas the PG&E Power House #5 on the east side of Mt. Shasta receives 74 inches. The region abounds in springs and caverns. (Info, thanks to Charles Albright.)

• • • • • • • • • • • • • • • •

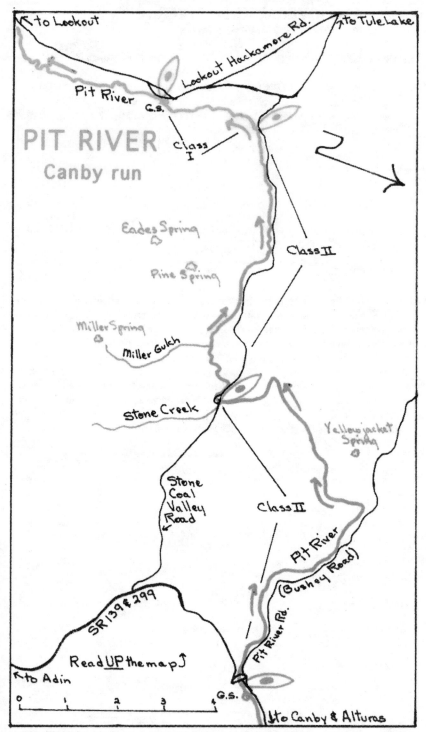

to Lookout

Lookout Hackamore Rd.

to Tule Lake

Pit River

G.S.

PIT RIVER
Canby run

Class I

Class II

Eades Spring

Pine Spring

Miller Spring

Miller Gulch

Stone Creek

Yellowjacket Spring

Stone Coal Valley Road

Class II

Pit River

(Bushey Road)

Pit River Rd.

SR 139 & 299

Read UP the map ↑

to Adin

G.S.

to Canby & Alturas

0   1   2   3   4

FALL RIVER & TULE RIVER, Class I & I+
AHJUMAWI LAVA SPRINGS STATE PARK

SEASON: All year. BEST FLOWS: 300-1,000 cfs. FLOW INFO: 800.444.7275.

ACCESS: Put-in • So. end of Big Lake. 3 miles N. of McArthur, SR-299, on Rat Farm Rd.
　　　　beyond the fairgrounds. Boat ramp across the canal.
4 miles to • Tule River flowing out of Horr Pond then into Fall River to McArthur Rd.
7 miles to • Fall River on Glenburn Rd.
9 miles to • Fall River Lake boat ramp. Parking, Rrm., and picnic area.

MAPS: AAA — "Northern California Section." DE LORME — p. 38.

GAS, FOOD, and LODGING: Fall River Mills.
CAMPING: Nine Environmental Campsites (all boat-in only), 3 near Ja She Creek, 3 at
Crystal springs, and 3 on the north shore of Horr Pond at Ahjumawi SP. (INFO: McArthur-
Burney Falls Mem. SP: 530.335.2777.)

BEWARE: Winds and water level are the two main concerns.

COMMENTS: Ahjumawi Lava Springs SP is an ideal area for paddlers. There are lakes to
paddle through, springs bubbling up from the lava tubes, picturesque Mt. Shasta in the
right location for morning photographers, and Tule River flowing to the south into Fall
River. Tules and birds, and birds in tules, are the foreground to Mt. Shasta in the SW on
the way to the boat-in campgrounds. This is a fascinating part of our state and well worth
a visit or two. The Tule River originates in the lake flowing south soon joining Fall River
which twists and turns to Glenburn. Paddlers are at eye-level with the cow pastures and
smiling at friendly cows staring down from waters edge. Fall River is dammed at Fall
River Lake, a popular local water ski and picnic spot frequently used by Fall River Mills
residents. Besides usual agricultural products from Fall River Valley, they also grow wild
rice and have a diatomaceous earth industry.

●●●●●●●●●●●●●●●●

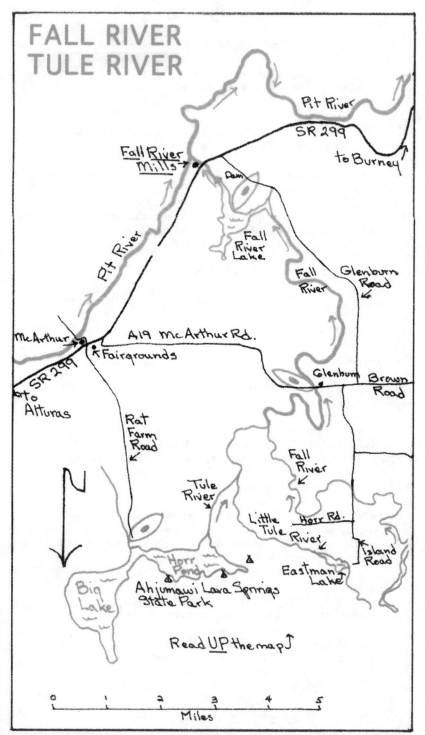

FALL RIVER
TULE RIVER

PIT RIVER (lower run)

Pit River Power H.#1, to SR-299 bridge, 3 mi., Cl. II & III

ACCESS: Put-in • The road to Pit River Power House #1, 2+ miles W. of Fall River Mills on SR-299 is marked. Cpgr. (PG&E: 800.743.5000, ask for supervisor.)
3 miles to • SR-299 bridge.

BEWARE: "Tubers" have fun on this run, don't upset them. I road scouted some of the run and there are some definite low Class III's.

COMMENTS: This run was submitted by Bob Foote, a Class V open canoe paddler. The summer weather is warm to hot and the water is comfortable for swimming. The Pit River and Hat Creek flow into the 9 mile long Lake Britton, part of McArthur-Burney Falls Mem. SP and Cpgr. Lava flows from Mt. Shasta cover much of this large NE area of the state—preserved in Lava Beds NM and Ahjumawi SP.

• • • • • • • • • • • • • • • •

HAT CREEK

Hat Creek, Hat Cr. Powerhouse Rd. to SR-299, 5 mi., Cl. I

ACCESS: Put-in • Hat Creek Powerhouse Rd. 1+ miles E. of Cassel Rd., 2 mi. S. of SR-299.
5 miles to • SR-299 bridge.

INFO: McArthur-Burney FM SP: 530.335.2777., Fall River Valley C.of C.: 530.336.5840., & Burney Basin C.of C.: 530.335.2111.

MAPS: AAA — "Northern California Section." DE LORME — p. 48.
GAS, FOOD, and LODGING: Burney and Fall River Mills.
CAMPING: Cassel PG&E Cpgr., Cassel Cpgr., and McArthur-Burney Falls Mem. SP.

BEWARE: Dam to portage at the end of Lake Baum.

COMMENTS: Ancient lava flows leaving springs and caves, and sea bed mounds (diatomaceous earth) make this area unique. It is mainly agricultural. Many cpgrs. great fishing, warm summer weather plus rivers and lakes for all paddling abilities. Hat Creek starts here in a lake, is then a creek before it flows into the Pit River.

• • • • • • • • • • • • • • • •

McArthur-Burney Falls Mem. SP
Paddle on Burney Creek then 9 miles on Lake Britton then on to the Pit River.

Lakes of Lava Beds & Warner Mountains
Juanita Lake in Klamath NF., cpgr. boat launch. 530.398.4391.
Tule Lake, Tule Lake Nat'l Wildlife Refuge. Cpgr. 530.667.2231.
Blue Lake, E of Likely. Warner Mtn. Ranger Dist. 530.279.6116.

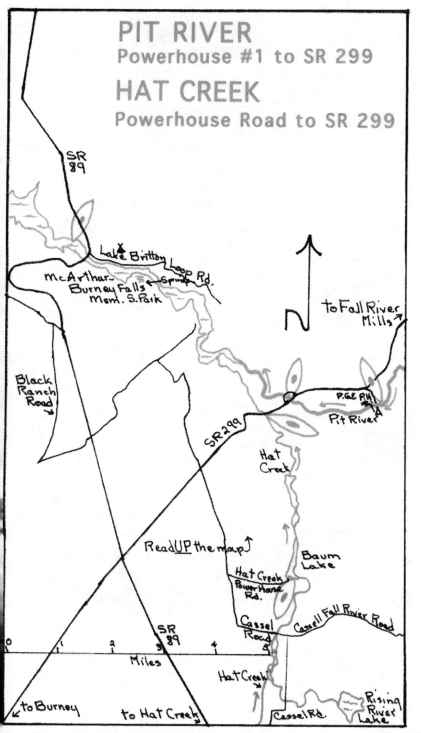

PIT RIVER
Powerhouse #1 to SR 299
HAT CREEK
Powerhouse Road to SR 299

SR 89

Lake Britton Loop Rd.

McArthur-
Burney Falls
Mem. S. Park

Spring

to Fall River
Mills

N

Black
Ranch
Road

P.G.E. P.H.

Pit River

SR 299

Hat
Creek

Read UP the map

Baum
Lake

Hat Creek
Power House
Rd.

Cassell Fall River Road

Cassel
Road

0   1   2   3   4   5

SR
89

Miles

Hat Creek

to Burney

to Hat Creek

Cassel Rd.

Rising
River
Lake

SACRAMENTO RIVER

Redding to Sacramento, 239 miles, Class I+ (1 dam)

SEASON: All year. BEST FLOW: 8,000-20,000 cfs. FLOW INFO: 916.368.8682.

GENERAL INFORMATION

The Sacramento River is California's largest and longest river, draining over 26,000 square miles of the north and central areas of our state. High flows of January through April average 24,000 to 48,000 cfs.; the low flows average about 14,000 cfs. The two principal tributaries are the Feather and American River systems. The Sacramento Valley is an agricultural region of worldwide importance. It's a big part of our California "bread-basket!" Rice is a prime product. After harvesting it is shipped to many countries of the world.

It was in 1917 that the Sacramento River Flood Control Project was authorized by Congress. This was the beginning of the miles of levees, dams by the hundreds, and riprapped banks along the waterway, all in efforts to control the flooding. One of the first dams in the Sierra was built in 1855 at Kidd Lake.

On the Sacramento River a paddler can go with only one portage, the dam at Red Bluff, for 300 miles to the San Francisco Bay, in fact, all the way to Hawaii! Camping on the river banks is possible in some areas, but not all. We did this 300 mile run one October during twelve beautiful Indian Summer days. What we noticed were very few fellow paddlers, power boats were common, and a few swimmers, and many, many people fishing. The river was channelized in many areas with is banks kept in place with sharp quarried rock (riprap), not the natural habitat for the indigenous river life. I felt sad thinking of the plants and animals that used to depend on the natural river banks. We paddled past many miles of wilderness, a wilderness that has looked the same for centuries. The flow is Class I+ all the way except for Chinese Rapids after Bend (boat ramp) upriver from Ide Adobe State Park. Take out at Bend to avoid Chinese Rapids.

We no longer have the sky blackened with migrating waterfowl as was reported by the early settlers. The salmon run isn't what it used to be. The grasses "as high as the horses heads" have been replaced with economically viable species. (We found a rare sample of the tall grass on top of Billy Goat Peak, when hiking up from the Eel River, it was 6'2" high, as tall as Dick Brown my "measuring stick." It was growing high on a rocky hill top out of reach of the browsing cattle.) But the river is still there, a bit modified, but very runnable by paddlecraft. Enjoy the flow.

STORY: California native plant rediscovered! A special find on our 300 mile journey was a plant that had an attractive fall display, roundish-shaped leafless delicate stems, each a different hue of tan, brown or gold, unknown to our fellow paddler, botanist Clare Wheeler. She showed our "find" to "botanist supreme" John Thomas Howell. He exclaimed (Clare said, he NEVER exclaims) the plant had not been seen since 1924 when it had been identified in Redding by Alice Eastwood.

SACRAMENTO R. SCENES

VERY FEW BRIDGES

NOAH'S ARK?

HARD DAY AT THE OFFICE!!!

WAYWARD NATIVE PLANT

GRAPEVINES TO THE SKY

SACRAMENTO RIVER (con't)

Redding to Woodson Bridge SRA (Corning), 78.5 miles,
Class I+

SEASON: All year. BEST FLOW: 9,000-24,000 cfs.

ACCESS: Put-in • Redding boat ramp behind the Civic Auditorium. Exit from US I-5 on Lake Blvd., go west to Auditorium Dr., follow signs to boat ramp. Parking & Rrm.

21.5 miles to • Balls Ferry Public Boat Ramp. Balls Ferry exit from US I-5, go east, turn left on CR-A17, 3 miles, right on Ash Creek Rd., 1 mile to ramp across from Balls Ferry Fishing Resort.

18.5 miles to • Bend Bridge Public Boat Ramp. From US I-5 north of Red Bluff take the Jellys Ferry Road exit, go east. Follow the signs to Bend RV Park: 916.525.6289. The ramp is just behind the park.

10.5 miles to • Ide Adobe Historical SP dock.

2 miles to • Red Bluff River Park boat ramp. From US I-5 take the Red Bluff exit, go west, at the second stoplight, turn left on Main St., go four blocks to park entrance. Boat ramp at the end of the parking area on the left. Parking & Rrm.: 530.934.3316.

2 miles to • Red Bluff Lake Recreation Area near the dam. From US I-5 in Red Bluff on the east side of the river take the Susanville-Hwy. exit, go east, turn right on Sale Lane which ends at the Sycamore USFS Cpgr. Parking and Rrm.

100 yds. to • Boat ramp below dam of Red Bluff Lake Rec. Area. Parking & Rrm.

24 miles to • Woodson Bridge State Rec. Area east of Corning. From US I-5 at Corning go east on South Avenue, 9 miles to the park. Beach & boat ramp launch site: 530.839.2112.

WATER: The water is moving at a moderate rate, good volume and quite cold as it has recently come from the bottom of a dam or two—Shasta and Keswick.

MAPS: AAA — "Northern California Section." "Redding." "Anderson." & "Red Bluff." DE LORME — pp. 46, 56, 57, & 67.

GAS, FOOD, and LODGING: Redding, Red Bluff, and Corning.
CAMPING: Woodson Bridge State Rec. Area: 530.839.2112. Red Bluff; Sycamore USFS Cpgr. at Diversion Dam: 530.934.3316. (See RV Park at Bend.) We camped between Redding and Red Bluff. It was difficult to find a campsite where we could get off the river, that was not in sight of buildings, where we could build a small fire for cooking, a latrine site away from the water, and have level ground for sleeping. Between Red Bluff and Woodson Bridge there is an island that is commonly used for camping.

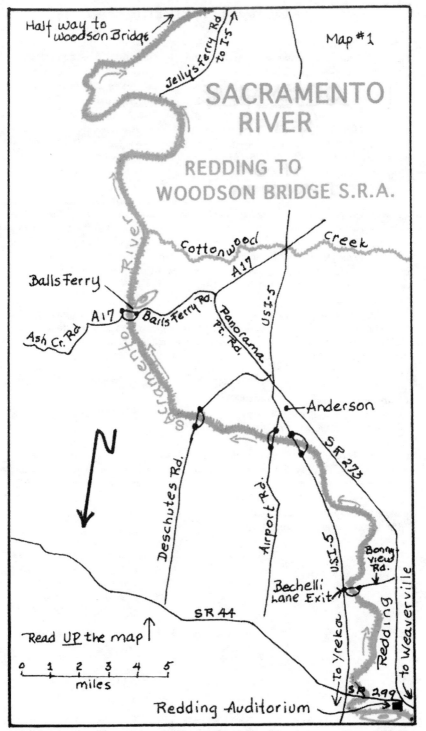

Half way to woodson Bridge

Jellys Ferry Rd

to I-5

Map #1

SACRAMENTO RIVER

REDDING TO WOODSON BRIDGE S.R.A.

Cottonwood Creek

A17

Balls Ferry

A17

Balls Ferry Rd.

Ash Cr. Rd

Panorama Pt. Rd.

US I-5

Anderson

N

Deschutes Rd.

Airport Rd.

SR 272

US I-5

Bonny View Rd.

Bechelli Lane Exit

To Yreka

Redding

to Weaverville

SR 44

Read UP the map ↑

0 1 2 3 4 5
miles

SR 299

Redding Auditorium

BEWARE: Personal Water Craft (a.k.a. Jet Skis), especially in the more lake-like areas of the river. Cold water, fairly fast moving in a wide river that makes a rescue much more difficult. (One of our canoeists capsized in the swirling currents next to an undercut bridge piling, not far from Redding. He was momentarily trapped in the undercut bank and had to push out before he could surface. The same currents made rescue assistance difficult.)

COMMENTS: The first riffle in the right bend of the river as it flows around Turtle Bay Park can be "upsetting" to those not quite used to the flow and their craft. Around this bend the river flows under the US-299 bridge with the Cypress Ave. Bridge 1.5 miles down river. The weather can be very hot, as Redding is known for its hot summer days. Be prepared with appropriate clothing, sunscreen, and drinking water. Sycamores are a common riverbank tree. 4.5 miles further is the So. Bonnyview Rd. Bridge with an island just below it. The river and the river banks are quite attractive—green with a few custom designed riverside homes. The US I -5 bridge crosses at Anderson with the Airport Bridge a mile further and a boat ramp in another mile. Gravel mining on river right followed in 2.5 miles by the Deschutes Rd. bridge. Three miles further down is Balls Ferry bridge and boat ramp. Even though there have been a few areas of natural habitat, there are more after Balls Ferry with fewer evidences of habitation. As the river rounds Wildcat Point, the buildings and marina can be seen at this resort area.
Even though I looked, I never did find Jellys Ferry, washed out by the floods, maybe, though the road is on both sides of the river. The river meanders a bit here with wide turns and large gravel beaches. Blackberries may be ripe in late summer. The bridge at Bend may come sooner than planned. This is important to watch for, if it is your planned take-out. Chinese Rapids are just around the bend. They are formed by sculpted out river-worn sandstone at a left bend in the river and a narrowing of the channel. The water gets squirrely creating whirlpools as it flows down the uneven bottom past the hollowed-out river banks—like separate booths in cafes or side-opening large wine barrels. Otter slides were seen on the side of the island down river from Red Bluff.

STORY: On our 300 mile October saga, it was in this area that we experienced an annual river happening. Our first sign of change was air pollution, next was the humming sound, both of which increased as we progressed down the river. I imagined the start of an invasion or maybe a huge fire. Then I saw the cause: a large eddy in the river filled with motorized fishing boats with motors going, hence smoke and hum. Being curious, I asked what was the event—a Fishing Derby.

● ● ● ● ● ● ● ● ● ● ● ● ● ● ● ●

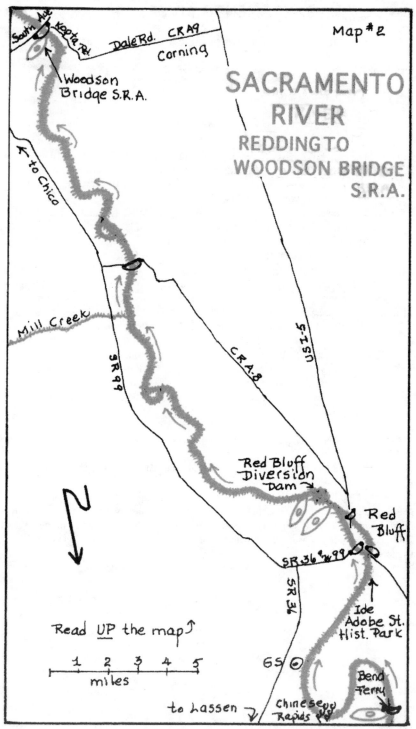

Map #2

SACRAMENTO
RIVER
REDDING TO
WOODSON BRIDGE
S.R.A.

South Ave
Kopta Rd
Dale Rd. CRA9
Corning

Woodson
Bridge S.R.A.

← to Chico

Mill Creek

SR 99

CRA-8

US I-5

Red Bluff
Diversion
Dam →

Red
Bluff

SR 36 & 99

SR 36

Ide
Adobe St.
Hist. Park

Read UP the map ↑

1   2   3   4   5
miles

GS ●

to Lassen ↓

Chinese
Rapids

Bend
Ferry

167

SACRAMENTO RIVER (con't)

Woodson Bridge SRA (Corning) to Colusa, 74.5 mi., Cl. I+

SEASON: All year.BEST FLOWS: 9,000-24,000 cfs.

ACCESS: Put-in • Beach at Woodson Bridge State Rec. Area, east side of river. From US I-5 just south of Corning go east on South Ave. 8 miles, OR from SR-99 SE of Vina go west on South Ave., CR-A9 4 miles. Camping, parking, & Rrm.: 530.839.2112.

22 miles to • Irving Finch River Access and boat ramp. 1 mile south of SR-32, 10 mi. east of Orland and US I-5 to Hamilton City, 1 mile east of and across the river from Hamilton City OR from the east side and SR-99 take SR-32 (8th St., to Walnut Ave. to Nord Ave.) west 11 miles. Pkg. & Rrm.

2.5 miles to • Bidwell-Sacto. River SP and boat ramp. From US I-5 follow directions to Irving Finch River Access go south on River Road 1.5 miles. From the east, in downtown Chico take W. Sacramento Ave. off of SR-32, go west to River road, then south to access.

29 miles to • Butte City. Boat ramp. From US I-5 go east 16 miles to Willows on CR-162 which turns south then across the river and east to Butte City. From SR-99 go west on SR-162, Butte City Hwy. 17 miles to the river.

21 miles to • Colusa Sacramento River State Rec. Area. Boat ramp. Go east on SR-20 from US I-5 to Colusa, then north on Colusa Princeton Rd. (CR-45) to the park. Go west from Yuba City & Marysville, take SR-20 to Colusa, then to the park. Parking & Rrm. Note: This park was a riverside dump during the days of waterways being places to dump "whatever." A forward looking local politician changed the dump into a very attractive riverside park. His name: Edmund G. Brown. He went on to become governor of the state of California, as did his son Jerry.

MAPS: AAA — "No. CA Section." "Bay & Mt. Section." DE LORME — pp. 67 & 77.

GAS, FOOD, and LODGING: Colusa, Corning, Chico, Yuba City, and Marysville.

BEWARE: Flood-control banks that often are large sharp shale rocks, not easy to use for getting out of the river. Few beaches. Mosquitoes, during warm weather that can last all night during the heat of summer and Indian Summer. Big bare dead trees in the river. During duck hunting season (check with fish & game) you could be a moving target for a trigger-happy hunter.

• • • • • • • • • • • • • • • •

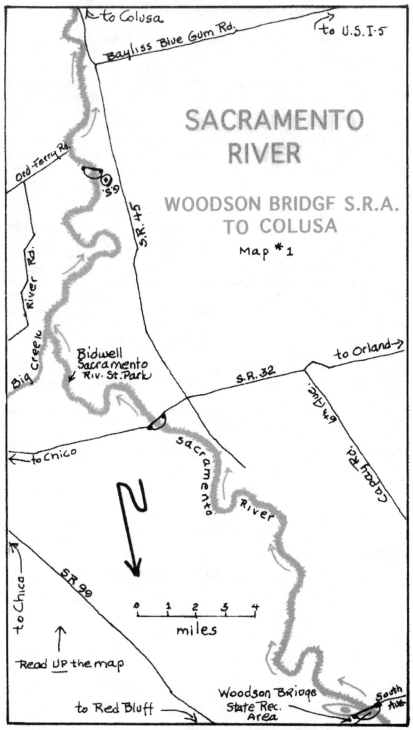

to Colusa

Bayliss Blue Gum Rd.

to U.S.I-5

SACRAMENTO
RIVER

WOODSON BRIDGE S.R.A.
TO COLUSA

Map #1

Ord Ferry Rd.

S.9

S.R. 45

Big Creek River Rd.

Bidwell
Sacramento
Riv. St. Park

to Orland →

S.R. 32

Capay Rd.

6th Ave.

← to Chico

Sacramento

River

← to Chica

S.R. 99

0 1 2 3 4
miles

↑
Read UP the map

to Red Bluff ←

Woodson Bridge
State Rec.
Area

South Ave.

COMMENTS: Many small streams enter the Sacramento River in this stretch, two that will receive special attention: Stony Creek from the west and Butte Creek. The latter is a fabulous stream with a Class II+ run between Paradise and Chico that flows into Butte Basin Slough and then into the Sacramento River about 10 miles downriver from Colusa. The river is still quite attractive and interesting with ox-bows resulting from the slowing down of the flow causing large twists and turns in the river. An ox-bow is caused when a large bend is cut by the river no longer taking the long way around but cutting across the bend leaving the curved remnants of a former flow area. It then becomes a back water dead end or a separate lake. This area is rich farm land that grows a variety of crops. At Colusa look to the east at the mountains in the middle of the valley, the Sierra Buttes. They are very unique, privately owned, and well preserved. There are guided hikes in the spring to see the rare wild flowers.

STORY: Our "ox-bow incident": (Many years ago there was a popular murder mystery called, *The Ox-bow Incident*, which was subsequently made into a movie.) It was dusk, the paddling day long, we kept hoping "around the next bend" to see the bridge we were seeking, our meeting spot. We came to a fork in the river; we all followed the lead boat going left, no one questioned. Fatigue had numbed our brains. It was a long left hand turn, almost dark, no bridge, we had paddled in the remnants of an ox-bow. Darkness dictated that we find a spot to camp. The bank was steep but we saw where we could get up the 15 foot climb, with enough room at the top for sleeping bags. The houses were not too close, but the dogs barked our presence. No fires. We shared what ready-to-eat food we had, then to sleep. I was up when I heard the pickup truck on its way. Would he be angry? Would we be shot? When his truck stopped I walked over and introduced myself then explained why we were there. After we chatted a bit, me trying to create a relaxed feeling, he trying to decide what to do, I asked,"Do you happen to know any of the Wurlitzer boys?" The words were magic, of course he knew some of the Wurlitzers, so I added that we had had dinner with their father, a friend of mine, the previous night. Immediately he "unrolled the welcome mat." Then he gave me his phone number so I could call in advance, next time.

●●●●●●●●●●●●●●●●

WOODSON
BRIDGE S.R.A
TO COLUSA-
SACRAMENTO
RIVER S.R.A.

Map #2

Read UP the map

0 1 2 3 4
miles

Butte Creek

Colusa

Colusa-
Sacramento R.
S.R.A.

Lurline Ave.

Maxwell Rd.

to Maxwell

Sacramento River

SACRAMENTO
RIVER

Princeton

Princeton
Ferry

Norman Rd.

Butte
City

Riz Rd.

SR 162

S.R. 45

S.R. 162

S.R 162

to Willows
and
I-5

SACRAMENTO RIVER (con't)

Colusa to Discovery Park, Sacramento, 86 miles, Class I+
(confluence with the Amercian River)

SEASON: All year.BEST FLOWS: 9,000-24,000 cfs.

ACCESS: Put-in • Colusa Sacramento River State Rec. Area. Boat ramp. From US I -5 go east on SR-20 to Colusa, follow the signs to the park just upriver on river right. From Yuba City go west from SR-99 on SR-20 across the river to Colusa, follow the signs. Parking & Rrm.

6 miles to • Boat ramp on river left on Butte Slough Road 5.5 miles southeast of Colusa and confluence with Butte Creek. From SR-20 on east side of the river go north 6 miles on Meridian Rd.

60 miles to • Verona marina and boat ramp. Confluence with the Feather River off of Garden Highway. From US I-5 on the east side the river go north on Garden highway about 6 miles. Parking & Rrm.

9.5 miles to • Boat ramp at US 1-5 and Garden Highway.

10.5 miles to • Boat ramp at catch basin at Discovery Park just up river from the confluence with the American River. Or paddle up the American River to beach take-out.

MAPS: AAA — "Bay and Mt. Section." "Sacramento Valley Region." DE LORME — pp. 77, 85, & 86.

GAS, FOOD, and LODGING: Colusa, Yuba City/Marysville, and Sacramento. There are motels very close to Discovery Park in Sacramento.
CAMPING: Verona Marina.

BEWARE: Power boats, jet skis, water skiers, winds.

COMMENTS: The agricultural fields and native habitat change to riverside commercial enterprises the closer to Sacramento the river flows. A great variety of boats are in use on the river that are much larger in size than those upriver.

HISTORY: During the gold rush days, sand and gravel from hydraulic mining were washed down the Feather and American Rivers and into the Sacramento. Entire hillsides were washed away by powerful hoses whose nozzles were mounted like cannons. As the river flow slowed in the valley, the gravel and sand were deposited causing the Sacramento River to lose much of its depth, which increased the flooding in Sacramento during high water. Levees have been built along the river banks to help prevent flooding and make use of the rich soil for agriculture.

Half way to Sacramento

China Bend

Bullock Bend

Kirkville

Sacramento River

Hershey Line Rd.

U.S. I-5

White Rd.

Grimes Tule Rd.

Tisdale Rd.

SR 45

SACRAMENTO RIVER
COLUSA TO SACRAMENTO
DISCOVERY PARK
Map #1

Garmire Rd.

Meridian Rd.

SR 45

Read UP the Map

SR 20

Colusa
Sacto. Riv.
S.R.A

SR 20 SR 45

Pass Rd

River Rd.

Colusa

0 1 2 3 4
miles

LAVA SPRING - AHJUMAWI S.P.

LAKE SISKIYOU & MT. SHASTA

GEESE ON THE AMERICAN R.

BEAVER WORK - AMERICAN R.

PELICANS ON CLEAR LAKE

INDIAN VLY. RES. SPILLWAY-DRY YEAR

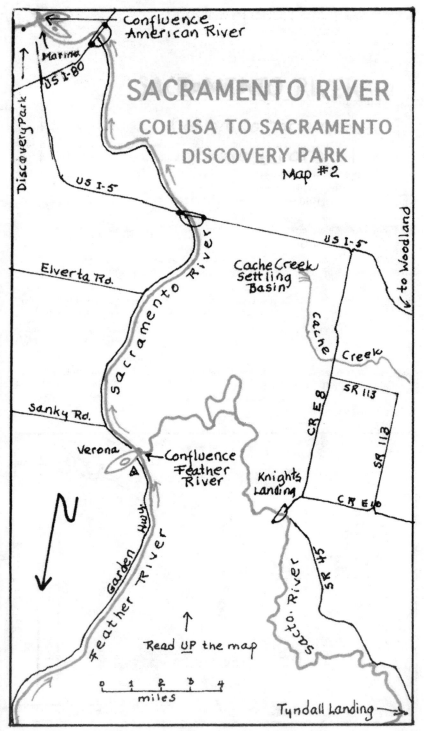

Confluence
American River

Marina

US I-80

Discovery Park

SACRAMENTO RIVER
COLUSA TO SACRAMENTO
DISCOVERY PARK
Map #2

US I-5

US I-5

to Woodland

Elverta Rd.

Sacramento River

Cache Creek
Settling
Basin

Cache Creek

CREEK

SR 113

SR 113

Sanky Rd.

Verona

Confluence
Feather River

Knights
Landing

CREEK

N

Garden Hwy

Feather River

Sacto. River

SR 5

Read UP the map

0 1 2 3 4
miles

Tyndall Landing

175

BUTTE CREEK
(East side of the Sacramento Valley near Chico & Paradise)

Steel Bridge to Covered Bridge, 6 miles, Class II+

SEASON: After several rains or snow-melt. BEST FLOWS: 400-1,000 cfs.
FLOW INFO: Hodges: http//sonic.net/kkct/whitewat.htm.

ACCESS: Put-in • From US-99, just south of Chico, take Skyway exit, go towards Paradise, at the bridge go to Centerville. Leave a car at Honey Run Covered Bridge Park. Continue on 6 miles to Centerville & the NE end of the steel bridge. OR upriver at end of road across from Centerville public building. Put in downriver from the low-water dam.
6 miles to • Covered Bridge, day use park area.

MAPS: AAA — "Northern California Section." DE LORME — p. 68.
GAS, FOOD, and LODGING: Chico.

BEWARE: Snags or fallen trees in the river, some tricky maneuvering.

COMMENTS: This was a fun run. I was invited to join a Paradise group of Kopapa Paddlers to run Butte Creek. It is a fairly fast flowing, technical run that is "busy" with some pools. It's very scenic, with a few homes. Quoted from Terry Sauter-Haag: "The run is characterized by many rocky, technical rapids with some short pools. " Randy Hodges (April '98, 950 cfs run) reported: "The action is pretty continuous, Class II and II+ sections, one or two rapids border on low Class III." Sharon Schumacher wrote a detailed account for the PNB, May 2000 issue.

●●●●●●●●●●●●●●●

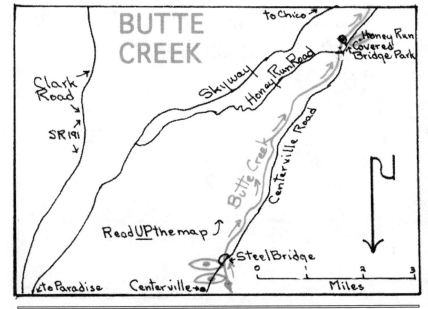

BUTTE CREEK

BUTTE CREEK

COVERED BRIDGE ACCESS
BUTTE CREEK

"THE" FUN RAPID - STONY CREEK

STONY CREEK VALLEY

STONY CREEK

SACRAMENTO VALLEY — Chapter 6
STONY CREEK (west slope)

Stonyford to Road 303, 7 miles, Class II+

SEASON: Rainy & spring run off. BEST FLOWS: 400-1,200 cfs.
FLOW INFO: Orland Irrigation District: 916-865-4126.

ACCESS: Put-in • North across the river from Stonyford (in the hills west of Williams, Maxwell & Willows), turn on road that is down river.
7 miles to • Rd. 303 E. of bridge from Rd. 306 N. from Stonyford.

MAPS: AAA — "Bay and Mt. Section." "No. CA Sec." DE LORME — pp. 66 & 76.

GAS, FOOD, and LODGING: Stonyford and Maxwell.
CAMPING: East Park Res. & Black Butte Lake: 530.865.4781 or NFS: 530.934.3316.

BEWARE: Low water, very rocky, OR high water, very swift.

COMMENTS: After exploring this area by car and seeing what Stony Creek looked like from the road, it seemed to be an ideal class II run. I kept searching for information and located two reports. The week after Terry and Gary did the run and gave me a verbal report, I was on my way with Andrea Wolf and Dan Phy. It was FUN! Busy, with drops and rocks. Definitely Class II, bordering on low Class III. Terry told us to stay right on the first important drop or scout on river left and watch for the snag in the river on the right. The flow was about 730 cfs. The water is clear, snow-melt from the S. Yolla Bollys, 7,400 foot Black butte and 6,000 foot Mt. Sanhedrin. The flow is fairly fast with rocks of all sizes and many willows. One of the most spectacular wild flower areas in CA, especially Bear Valley or the Leesville Rd. west of Williams off of SR20. Date: 5/2/98.

●●●●●●●●●●●●●●●●

Stony Gorge Res. to Grindstone Creek, 7.5 miles, Class II

ACCESS: Put-in • At the base of Stony Gorge Dam from Road 306 go north to just before Grindstone Creek enters Stony Creek.
7.5 miles to • Grindstone Creek, upstream of confluence. Park along the road.

BEWARE: The first two miles are rocky and technical. The rapid just south of SR-162 can be scouted from the road, scout before putting on the water.

COMMENTS: Scout the first rapid before doing the run. It is a ledge just upstream from the bridge—the most technical rapid and gage for water flow. If there is not enough water flow it will be too low. After this the river becomes wider and less rocky. Wildlife abounds; we saw woodpeckers, mergansers, wood ducks, blue herons, quail, and swallows. Terry Sauter-Haag report on 4/26/98 run.

●●●●●●●●●●●●●●●●

RESERVOIRS (south to north)
East Park: Near Stonyford, pleasant lake, camping & boating.: 530.963.3128.
Stony Groge: Near Elk Creek, SR-162, interesting dam built in 1928.
Black Butte Lake: Between Newville & US I-5 on Newville Rd.: 530.865.4781.

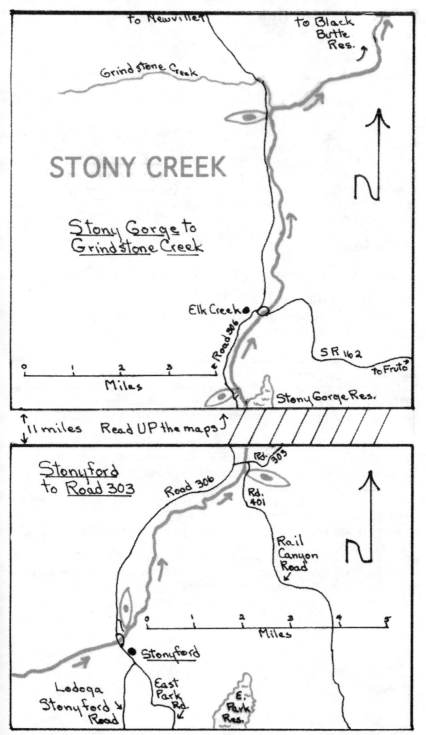

STONY CREEK

Stony Gorge to Grindstone Creek

to Newville

to Black Butte Res.

Grindstone Creek

Elk Creek

Road 306

SR 162

to Fruto

Stony Gorge Res.

11 miles   Read UP the maps ↗

Stonyford to Road 303

Road 306

Rd. 303

Rd. 401

Rail Canyon Road

Stonyford

Lodoga Stonyford Road

East Park Rd.

E. Park Res.

FEATHER RIVER (below Oroville Dam)

Oroville to Verona, 64 miles, Class I+ (II+)

SEASON: All year. BEST FLOWS: 1,000-5,000 cfs. FLOW INFO: 916.368.8682.

ACCESS: Put-in • Bedrock Park, Oroville, Feather River Blvd. and 5th via Business SR-70. Parking and Rrm.
10 miles to • bridge at E. Gridley. West side of the river.
9 miles to • Live Oak. West side of the river.
16 miles to • Marysville/Yuba City. Both sides of the river.
11 miles to • Star Bend near, junction of Algodon Rd. & Feather R. Blvd., E.side.
1 mile to • Boyd's Pump boat ramp. West side off of Garden Hwy.
9 miles to • Beer Can Beach. End of Lee Rd. Parking. East side of river.
8 miles to • Verona. Private marina with facilities & cpgr. parking (fee). E. side.

NOTE: There are very few bridges across the Feather River.

MAPS: AAA — "Sacramento Valley Region." DE LORME — pp. 68, 78, & 86.

GAS, FOOD, and LODGING: Oroville, Marysville, and Yuba City.
CAMPING: Live Oak Park, 1 mi. E. of Live Oak at 1100 Pennington Rd., on the west side of the river: 530.822.7410.

BEWARE: Snags and duck hunting season. Rip-rap dam 1 mile below Live Oak. Portage over dam. Shanghai Rapids, Class II, a mile or so below Marysville, is a riverwide curving clay ledge that can be run by experienced paddlers and portaged on river right. The water level is a big factor for this run. At high water, there is no problem. There are sand bars at low water. Upriver winds can create fairly high waves.

COMMENTS: Another multi-day river run with the excitement of Shanghai Rapids in warm agricultural country with warm water and a few beaches. Much of the route is bordered on both sides by levees. The levees are not as high nearer Oroville. Good public access and some private. The Yuba River enters just above Marysville and the Bear River downstream (however it was not found by my searching eye). Lake of the Woods Wildlife Area is across the river from the confluence with the Bear River. (Chet Dunbar just told me about an island in the Feather River at the mouth of the Bear River.)

NOTE: I ran t he Feather River again from Star Bend to US-99 bridge. The take out was just downstream of the bridge on river left. It was a Mother Lode Chapter of the Sierra Club outing in May that Chet Dunbar was leading.

● ● ● ● ● ● ● ● ● ● ● ● ● ● ● ●

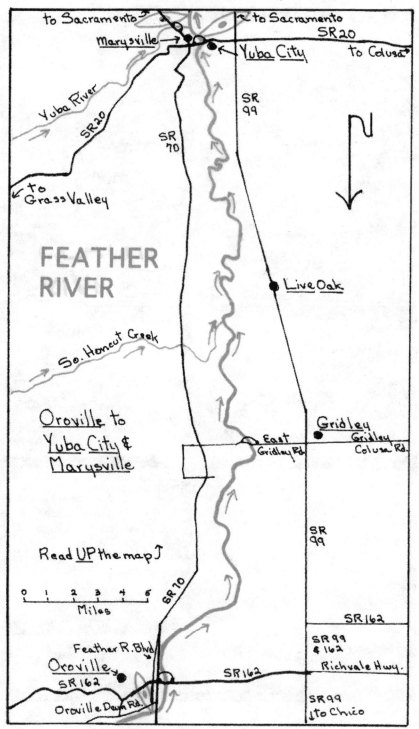

to Sacramento

to Sacramento
SR 20

Marysville

Yuba City

to Colusa

Yuba River

SR 20

SR 99

SR 70

to Grass Valley

FEATHER RIVER

Live Oak

So. Honcut Creek

Oroville to Yuba City & Marysville

Gridley

East Gridley Rd.

Gridley Colusa Rd.

SR 99

Read UP the map

0 1 2 3 4 5
Miles

SR 70

SR 162

SR 99 & 162

Richvale Hwy.

Feather R. Blvd.

Oroville

SR 162

SR 162

Oroville Dam Rd.

SR 99 to Chico

FEATHER RIVER

FEATHER RIV

SHANGHAI RAPIDS - FEATHER RIVER

BEAR RIVER - COLFAX

YUBA RIVER & SNOWY SIERRA

YUBA RIVER - GOLD MINING ROCE

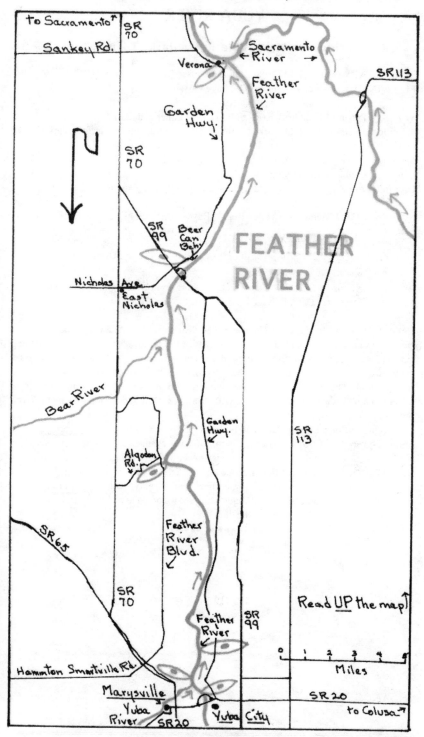

183

YUBA RIVER

SR-20 bridge to Marysville River Park, 14 mi., Class I+

SEASON: All year. BEST FLOWS: 300-1,000 cfs.
FLOW INFO: K-Phone: 916.368.8682. "Lake Oroville."

ACCESS: Put-in • SR-20 bridge (a.k.a. Parks Bar) either end. Parking.
4.5 miles to • Dry Creek (not marked from the river) Sycamore Ranch (fee). Parking and
    Rrm.
5.5 miles to • End of Hallwood Blvd.
4 miles to • Yuba City boat ramp.
Or 5 miles to • Marysville River Park and boat ramp. Parking and Rrm.

MAPS: AAA — "Sacramento Valley Reg." "Bay & Mt. Section." DE LORME — p. 78.

GAS, FOOD, and LODGING: Marysville and Yuba City.
CAMPING: Sycamore Ranch (Coast to Coast Cpgr.): 530.743.7959.

BEWARE: About 1 mile below Dry Creek, entering from river right, is DeGuerre Point
and a dam, DeGuerre Dam. Portage on river left.

COMMENTS: Put-in was easy. The water was clear and cold with a very good flow. The
river flows through a wide relatively flat area with a few willows struggling to regain their
size that were greatly reduced by the floods. The hills from the gold mining tailings start
about two miles down the river, but the steep hills from the river's edge would make it
hard to climb. The river has a few riffles and turns, but it is mostly easy water. The Yuba
River has long been a canoeing favorite with an all year flow and camping along the river
before the rock piles.

DeGuerre Point Debris Dam was built in 1935 to catch the tailings from the gold
mining, but is now filled in. After the dam, the river changes character; there is a rock
garden just below the dam, then the flow is slower as it continues on for the Hallwood
Blvd. take out. (Warning: the flow may be on river left with the road on river right and a
large beach in between.) 0r paddle a few miles past the gravel mining to Marysville or
Yuba City into the Feather River. In August of 1998, we opted to paddle up Dry Creek and
take out at Sycamore Ranch before the dam.

• • • • • • • • • • • • • • • •

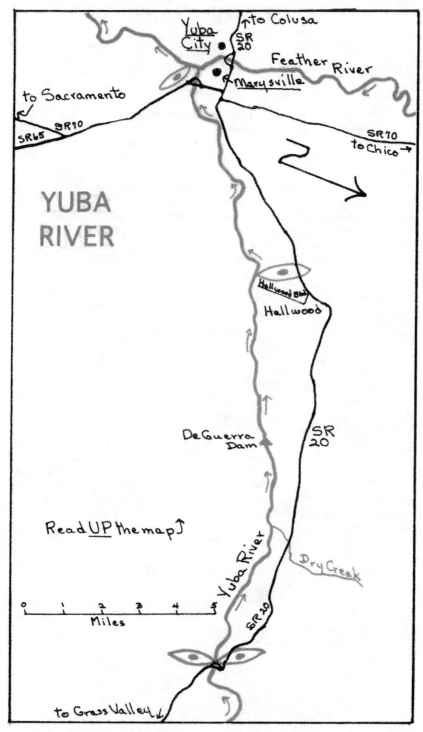

YUBA
RIVER

Read UP the map ↑

BEAR RIVER (Colfax)

Ben Taylor Rd. to Dog Bar Rd., 3.5 mi., Class II & II+

SEASON: Spring & early summer. BEST FLOWS: 300-1,000 cfs.
FLOW INFO: Nevada Irrigation Dist.: 530.273.8571., E-mail: yubabear@foothill. net

ACCESS: Put-in • East end of Ben Taylor Rd. In Colfax go N. on Church St. over hill, R.
on Ben Taylor Rd., go down the hill to the end of the dirt road.
1.5 miles to • Bear River Cpgr. Several put-in spots. Parking & Rrm.
2 miles to • Dog Bar Bridge. Bit of a steep climb up to the road. Limited pkg.

SHUTTLE: Ben Taylor Road is parallel to the river in the hills. Follow the signs to the
Bear River Campground, take this road west along the river and as it goes back up to the
hillside, turn right, watch for the Dog Bar Rd. sign, follow it down to and across Dog Bar
Bridge. The shuttle is longer than the river.

MAPS: AAA — "Bay and Mt. Section." DE LORME — p. 79.

GAS, FOOD, and LODGING: Colfax or Auburn. Try one of the Colfax eateries—yum.
CAMPING: Bear River Campground (on the run).

BEWARE: Cold water. High water makes the run more difficult.

COMMENTS: This run is short but delightful. It has beautiful scenery, clear water, and is
a popular tubing river. When I first ran the Bear River, there were some railroad cars in the
river, which are no longer there. As Charlie Martin wrote in, *Sierra Whitewater*: "In 1971
we came upon several railroad cars in the river above Dog Bar. I missed the chance of a
lifetime to boat in one door of a box car and out the other side." Gold mining is still going
on and nuggets are taken from the Bear River.
Date of last run: August 13, 1998. We put-in at the campground—an easy flow of 340
cfs. The Class I+ to II rapids are formed by shale rock which can be sharp. Everything was
fairly easy until we came to a rocky area with drops and bigger waves. There was an
obvious scouting rock and portage route on river left. We were able to river scout the
Class II+ rapid on river right. The route was between two rocks on river right down a 2
foot drop then a quick left turn to be in position to run the waves on river left. Dog Bar
Bridge was soon in sight.

●●●●●●●●●●●●●●●●

Below Camp Far West Res. dam, 14 miles, Class I+

SEASON: Rainy or snow melt. BEST FLOW: 200-600 cfs.

ACCESS: Put-in • near bridge at SR-65 (near Wheatland).
5 miles to • bridge at Rio Oso and Forty Mile Rd.
3 miles to • SR-70 bridge flows into the Feather River.
6 miles to • Nicholas on the Feather River.

BEWARE: Short season, strainers going through a riparian jungle, 2 foot clay bank drop
upstream of SR-70 bridge. (Thank you Chet Dunbar!)

●●●●●●●●●●●●●●●●

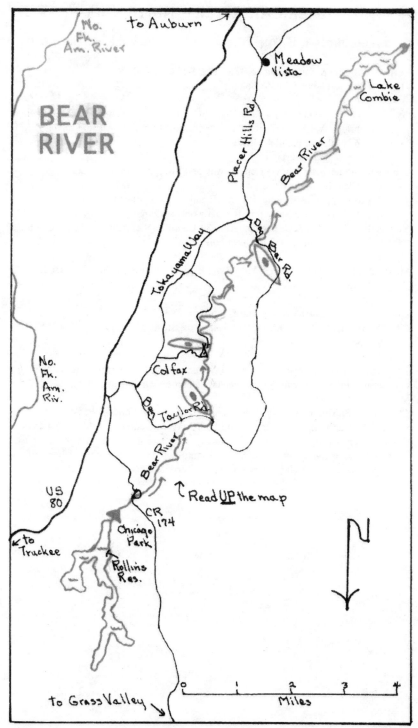

AMERICAN RIVER - North Fork

Yankee Jim's Rd. to L. Clementine, 13.5 mi., Class I & II+

SEASON: Spring & early summer. BEST FLOW: 700-1,400 cfs.
FLOW INFO: K-Phone: 916.368.8682.

ACCESS: Put-in • Yankee Jim's Road, (narrow, steep dirt road) on river left, upstream of bridge. Yankee Jim's Rd. (sign: "Foresthill 13 mi.") is east of Canyon Way, E. of I-80, and parallel between Colfax and Wiemar exits. Limited parking and Rrm. Class II+ run to:

4 miles to • Ponderosa Way via Canyon Way and I-80, river left upstream of the bridge. Class II run to:

4.5 miles to • Upper Clementine Rd. at NE end (beginning) of the lake. Rd. closed between October and April. It usually opens Mem. Day weekend.

5 miles to • SW end of Lake Clementine. I-80 1.5 miles N of Auburn take Foresthill Rd. exit, in 3 mi. go left to North Fork Dam.

MAPS: AAA — "Feather River & Yuba River Region." "Bay & Mt. Section." DE LORME — pp. 79 & 87.

GAS, FOOD, and LODGING: Auburn.
CAMPING: Auburn KOA, 3.5 mi. N of Auburn off SR-49 and Rock Cr. Rd. at 3550 KOA Way: 916.885.0990.

BEWARE: Strong upstream winds are very common on Lake Clementine. Long shuttle compared to the run, driving up and then down narrow winding dirt roads.

COMMENTS: This is the Big Bend section of the North Fork of the American River below the Chamberlin Falls run and Shirttail Canyon. Definitely gold mining country. The flow is primarily snow melt, so be aware of hot late spring days that could cause a good, but not too good, flow. The canyon is beautiful, the water is clear, and the wildflowers display in full color. (Information thanks to Terry & Gary Haag.)

• • • • • • • • • • • • • • •

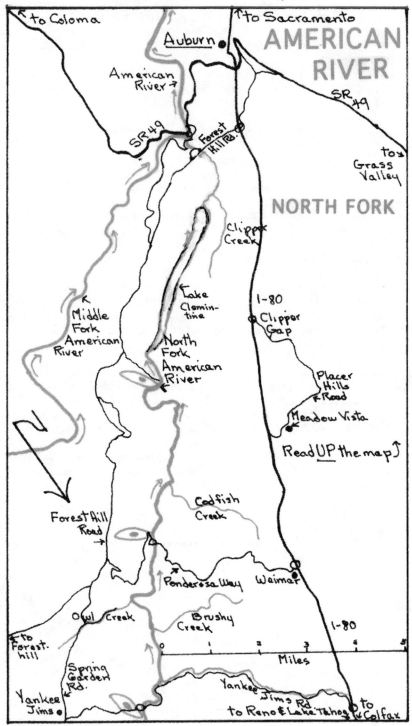

to Coloma

to Sacramento

Auburn

AMERICAN
RIVER

American
River

SR 49

SR 49

Forest
Hill Rd.

to
Grass
Valley

NORTH FORK

Clipper
Creek

Lake
Clemin-
tine

I-80

Clipper
Gap

Middle
Fork
American
River

North
Fork
American
River

Placer
Hills
Road

Meadow Vista

Read UP the map

N

Codfish
Creek

Forest Hill
Road

Weimar

Ponderosa Way

Owl Creek

Brushy
Creek

I-80

to
Forest.
hill

0   1   2   3   4   5
Miles

Spring
Garden
Rd.

Yankee
Jims

Yankee Jims Rd
to Reno & Lake Tahoe

to
Colfax

AMERICAN RIVER — Middle Fork

SEASON: Summer BEST FLOW: 800-1,500 cfs. FLOW INFO: K-Ph.: 916.368.8682.
INFO: Map & Info: Dept. of Boating & Water and Dept. of Parks & Recreation:
530.885.5648.

ACCESS: Put-in • Greenwood Bridge site; North of Auburn take the Foresthill Rd., 9
              miles, rt. on Driver's Flat Rd., go left at fork to the end of the road (a bit rough)
              to Ruck-A-Chucky Campground. Rrm. & parking.
7 miles to • Mammoth Bar. Take Foresthill Rd. from confluence with No. Fk. 2+ mi. R. on
              Mammoth Bar Rd. goes to Mammoth Bar. Parking.

MAPS: AAA — "Feather River & Yuba River Region." "Bay & Mt. Section". DE LORME
— pp. 87 & 88.

GAS, FOOD, and LODGING: Auburn.

BEWARE: Rough going to the put-in by car and carry. The two most difficult rapids are
shortly after the put-in. Just downstream from Mammoth Bar is Murderers Bar, a Class V-
VI rapid with serious strainers. The gate .5 mile up the road at Mammoth Bar is locked at
sundown. It takes the flow 5 hours from the dam to arrive at the put-in. It arrives about 2
p.m.

COMMENTS: This clear water, Class II run has many "play" spots. Years ago I did this
run and I remember the poor road to the river, the carry the rest of the way, the dirt road to
Mammoth Bar, and the take-out before the bad portage around the Class V-VI rapid at
Murderers Bar. Fortunately I was with three eager muscular male teens who fed our two
canoes through the rocks so we could paddle the last two miles to SR-49 and the confluence
with the North Fork. The high-up bridge has been built, but no dam...yet! Rep. Doolittle is
still pushing for the dam. There is a rumor that the water may be diverted out of the tunnel
below the confluence so it can be paddled and fished. Also a rock slide has created a Class
III+ rapid in the area that can be scouted. (Update info. thanks to Terry and Gary Haag.)

NOTE: The take-out is sometimes reserved by OHV groups who charge admission. Paddlers are generally not charged.

●●●●●●●●●●●●●●●

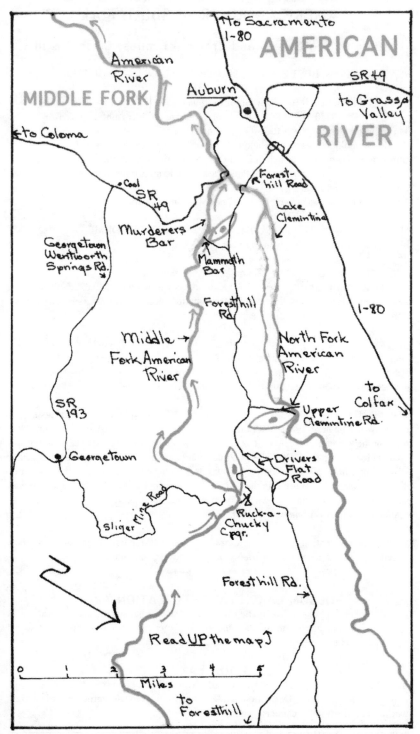

to Sacramento
I-80

AMERICAN

American
River

MIDDLE FORK

Auburn

SR 49

to Grass
Valley

RIVER

to Coloma

Forest-
hill Road

Cool
SR
49

Lake
Clemintine

Murderers
Bar

Mammoth
Bar

Georgetown
Wentworth
Springs Rd.

Foresthill
Rd.

Middle
Fork American
River

North Fork
American
River

I-80

SR
193

to
Colfax

Georgetown

Upper
Clemintine Rd.

Drivers
Flat
Road

Sliger Mine Road

Ruck-a-
Chucky
Cpgr.

Sliger

Foresthill Rd.

Read UP the map ↑

0   1   2   3   4   5
Miles

to
Foresthill

AMERICAN RIVER — South Fork

Chile Bar to Greenwood Creek, 11 miles, Class II & III

SEASON: All year. BEST FLOWS: 500-2,000 cfs. FLOW INFO: 530.621.6616.

ACCESS: Put-in • Chile Bar, 6 mi. SE of Coloma on SR-49 (near Placerville) turn left on SR-193, 3 mi. to R. Downstream of bridge on river right. Pkg. & Rrm.
5 miles to • American River Resort (see below).
.5 mile to • Coloma Resort (see below).
.5 mile to • (put-in only) Marshall Gold Disc. State Historical Park.
2 miles to • Henningsen-Lotus Co. Park. Parking & Rrm. A river running facility.
1 mile to • Camp Lotus.
2 miles to • Greenwood Creek BLM access. Very limited parking.

MAPS: AAA — "Lake Tahoe." "Bay and Mt. Section." DE LORME — pp. 87 & 88. BLM map is available locally at the river.

GAS, FOOD, and LODGING: Coloma, Lotus, and Placerville.
CAMPING: American River Resort, 6019 New River Rd., Coloma: 530.622.6700. Coloma Resort, opp. SP, E of SR-49 at 6921 Mt. Murphy Rd.: 530.621.2267.
Camp Lotus: 530.622.8672.

BEWARE: The very popular and heavily used Chili Bar run is fun but not until the afternoon after most of the rafts have floated down river, during the week, or during the off season. The Class III rapids are a challenge. There is a quiet zone on this river starting upriver from Trouble Maker and extending to Greenwood Creek.

COMMENTS: The Chili Bar run is a bit of a stretch for the perimeters of this book but I feel it should be here. Practice on the Coloma or Lotus to Greenwood Creek run a few times or the Klamath and Trinity Rivers. They have some good Class II+ sections to warm up on before trying Chili Bar. The water is swimming temperature, the weather is generally warm to hot, and there is a good flow release during the summer. Bob Foote introduced me to the Chili Bar run in the late 70s in open canoes—Larry Busby and I tandem and Bob solo. A few years ago when I kayaked it, one of my fellow Kopapa paddlers was running his third river and he did great.

NOTE: For information about 9 mile Class III (4 Class III rapids) Gorge run that starts at Greenwood Creek consult *CA Whitewater* by Casady & Calhoun.

•••••••••••••••••

FOLSOM LAKE STATE RECREATION AREA

ACCESS: Auburn Folsom Rd. on the west side of the lake has several access locations as well as access on the east shore. The American river is stopped and stored giving recreation to power boats and paddlecraft.

LOON LAKE

In the Sierra north of US 50 past Union Valley Res. is Loon Lake (reservoir) nestled in a granite setting bordering Desolation Wilderness with boat-in campgrounds. It is a great weekend destination for canoeists and kayakers.

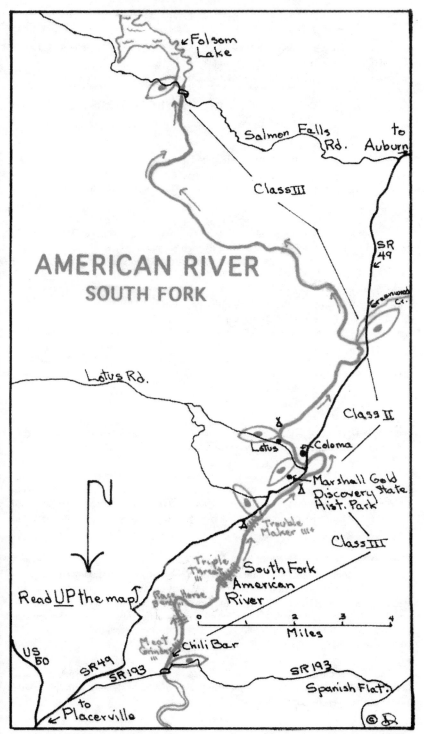

Folsom
Lake

Salmon Falls
Rd.   to
Auburn

Class III

SR
49

Greenwood Cr.

AMERICAN RIVER
SOUTH FORK

Lotus Rd.

Class II

Lotus   Coloma

Marshall Gold
Discovery State
Hist. Park

N   Trouble
Maker III+   Class III

Triple
Threat
III   South Fork
American
River

Read UP the map   Race Horse
Bend   0   2   3   4
Miles

US
50   Meat
Grinder
III   Chili Bar

SR 49
SR 193   SR 193
Spanish Flat.

to
Placerville   © D

193

LAKE NATOMA

ACCESS: Negro Bar. Greenback Lane to Natoma Lane to Negro Bar. Park & Campground. Or the boatramp at the SW end of lake off of Hazel Ave.
A scenic 5 mile paddle, with some current, gold mining channels, and rock walls.

AMERICAN RIVER in Sacramento

Sailor Bar to Discovery Pk. (Sacto. R.), 22 mi., Cl. I+ (II)

SEASON: All year. BEST FLOWS: 2,000-9,000 cfs. FLOW INFO. K-Ph. 916.368.8682.
BEST INFO: Info & map: "The American River Parkway", $3.00. Proceeds benefit parkway. Purchase at R.E.I.: 916.965.4343 or Am. R. Pkway. Found: 916.456.7423.

ACCESS: Put-in • Sailor Bar. N. side of river: US-50 towards Folsom, L. on Hazel Ave.
    cross river, L. on Winding Way, L. on Illinois Ave. Parking & Rrm.
1+ miles to • Sunrise Blvd. S. side of river, Bridge St., parking & Rrm.
4 miles to • Ancil Hoffman Park, N. side. Fair Oaks Blvd. to Van Alstine to CA Ave. to
    Tarshes Dr. Parking & Rrm.
1.5 miles to • Goethe Park, S. side, Rod Beaudry Dr. off Folsom Blvd. Pk. & Rrm.
4 miles to • Watt Ave., south side of river, parking & Rrm.
1 mile to • Howe Ave. south side of river. Parking & Rrm.
8.5 miles to • Discovery Park at confluence with Sacto. R. NW of Capitol off Jibboom St.
    via Richards Blvd. & I-5. Beach & boat ramp. Pk & Rrm.
NOTE: There are many other river access points by paddlecraft. Most of those listed above offer facilities and charge $7.00.

MAPS: AAA — "Greater Sacto. N. Area." "Bay & Mt. Sec." DE LORME — pp. 86 & 87.

GAS, FOOD, and LODGING: Sacramento.
CAMPING: Sacramento-Metro KOA in W. Sacto. at 3951 Lake Rd: 916.371.6771.

BEWARE: San Juan Rapids, these are the BIG ones located just before a sharp left bend in sight of a tudor-style large house built near the river. The rapids are formed by a lateral tilted sandstone strata that is almost river wide, nearer to the right bank. Try the sneak route on river left. Arden Rapids are after Hoffman Park, a constriction in the river with faster flow and a few waves.

COMMENTS: These last miles of the American River flowing through Sacramento are a pleasure to paddle. Almost the entire river corridor is a parkway for hiking and bicycling as well as paddling and swimming. What a pleasant change from 30 years ago when I wrote my first river guide book and had to warn the readers of the dangers in running this stretch because of the many dead trees in the waterway that caused drownings every year. Local news requested that people stay out and off of the river. Now the river is cleared of dead trees and body-trappers. At the confluence is a floating Good Humor "man," music included.
    The river is clear with a moderate flow. It is slower nearer the confluence, has an abundance of wildlife, side channels for exploration, and is in full color with spring wildflowers. It is a gem!

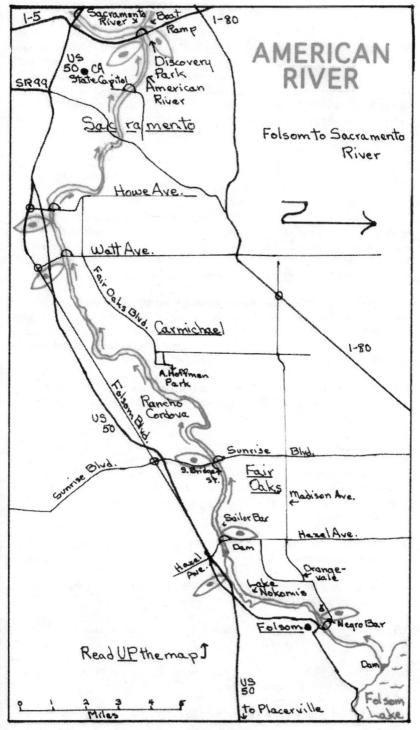

I-5

Sacramento
River SP · Boat
Ramp

I-80

US
50 · CA
State Capitol

SR99

Discovery
Park

American
River

**AMERICAN
RIVER**

Sacramento

Folsom to Sacramento
River

Howe Ave.

Watt Ave.

Fair Oaks Blvd.

Carmichael

I-80

A. Hoffman
Park

Rancho
Cordova

US
50

Folsom Blvd.

Sunrise Blvd.

Sunrise Blvd.

S. Bridge St.

Sunrise Blvd.

Fair
Oaks

Madison Ave.

Sailor Bar

Hazel Ave.

Hazel
Ave.

Dam

Orange-
vale

Lake
Nokomis

Folsom

Negro Bar

Read UP the map ↑

Dam

Folsom
Lake

0 1 2 3 4 5
Miles

US
50
to Placerville

CLEAR LAKE

If you haven't paddled on Clear Lake yet, you have some interesting days in store for you. Clear Lake is the largest natural freshwater lake in California. It warms to a comfortable swimming temperature in the summer making it ideal for water skiing and water sports of all kinds. Canoeing and kayaking are especially suited at most times of year, but NOT during the hot summer days when power boats and PWC's dominate the lake.

A few years ago, a research team drilled two miles deep learning that Clear Lake is the oldest lake in the continental United States. Most lakes of this antiquity have turned into meadows. Perhaps the geothermal activity of Mt Konocti, at the lake's west rim, has aided in keeping it a lake. Anyway, enjoy!

Suggested Clear Lake Day-trips

1. NW end; put-in at Lucerne. Cut off paddling up Rodman Slough past Rodman Ranch, about 2.5 miles in length being fed by Scotts Creek which comes from Blue Lakes on the south and Middle Creek from the north. There is a public park up Scott Creek—a good lunch location. Birds abound. It is a Great Blue Heron nesting site, Western and Clarks Grebes are here, and it is on the flyway for migratory birds.

2. Lakeport is "water friendly" with several launching sites. Paddle north 2 miles to Berger Bay or 5 miles to Rodman Slough, go east to Lakeside County Park about 4 miles or 2 miles further to Clear Lake State Park: 707.279.4293. This state park has a Sycamore tree canopy over the campsites(very hot in the summer) with the largest Sycamore leaves I've ever seen. Cole Creek, which flows through the park, is another bird habitat.

3. From the state park, paddle SE 2 miles to the far shore of Soda Bay and sit in the open large thermal sulfurous pool located on an island near Mt. Konocti. There's a tale about a secret tunnel in the mountain.

4. At the far southeast end, not far from the dam and beginning of Cache Creek is Anderson Marsh State Historic Park: 707.944.0688. They found artifacts that date back 10,000 years—among the oldest in California. Here the natives paddled in reed canoes, wove baskets, and made arrowheads from locally found obsidian points. Paddling in the marshy area today is like going through a tree-covered park complete with chirping birds. Phone ahead for the entrance location and best water level.

5. Put-in at Clearlake Park, paddle west to Monitor Island or into Konocti Bay where there are several marinas.

6. From the public beach and boat ramp in Clearlake Oaks paddle around Rattlesnake Island (private) and see if the exotic animals are still there.

7. Launching at Glenhaven is a short distance from The Narrows and across the lake from Buckingham Park and Anderson Island.

8. The Community Beach at Nice is open to the public. Paddle to Lucerne or beyond to enjoy the rocky, high cliff side of the lake.

WARNING: Watch for afternoon winds, the lake can get rough very quickly.

CACHE CREEK

Long Valley to Guinda, 45 miles, Class I-III

SEASON: Spring & summer. BEST FLOWS: 400-1,000 cfs.
FLOW INFO: K-phone: 916.368.8682 (Rumsey); Hodges: http://sonic.net/kkct/
whitewat.htm. http://cdec.water.ca.gov/cgiii-progs/queryF?RUM. Beware: the flow is
greatly reduced as crops ripen.

MAPS: AAA — "Bay & Mt. Sec." "Mendocino & Lake Co." DE LORME — p. 76

GAS, FOOD, and LODGING: Clear Lake area via SR-20 & SR-53, Woodland.
CAMPING: Cache Creek Canyon. Reg. Park, SR-16. (No reservations.)

COMMENTS: Cache Creek has become very popular for private boaters as well as commercial "paddle yourself" small rafts. It flows through an agricultural area into the Sacramento Valley where it is channeled into the Yolo By-Pass. Two dams supply the primary
flows, one from Clear Lake spewing out warm, somewhat polluted water, with an occasional dead fish. On the North Fork is Indian Valley Reservoir releasing water near the
bottom of the lake that is cool and clear.
    The fantastic floral display on the hillsides in April of vibrant-colored wildflowers,
including cerise-hued red bud is worth the drive. At the BLM parking area there is a trail
leading up the hill and over to the Class IV section of Cache Creek. Elk are often seen as
well as an occasional bear, beaver, bald eagle, or wood duck; mountain lions and coyotes
also share this wilderness area. The tilted strata and geothermal features are fascinating
and make for occasional river-wide ledges and vertical rock walls. And there are hot springs.
It is definitely wilderness, so be prepared
    "Mad Mike," the rapid near the end of the Eagle Run in sight of SR-16, is easy to
scout, river right, and portage. Rowboat Rapid downriver from SR-16 bridge is best scouted.
In the late 60's as kayakers and canoeists started doing the run there was a rowboat
"wrapped" around the big rock in the rapid.

LAKES IN THE AREA

Blue Lakes: 12 miles east of US-101 on SR-20 are two charming lakes protected from
much of the wind and connected with a stream. Each of the mile-long lakes have homes,
resorts, and campgrounds, but still much of it is in wilderness. It is very attractive for a
pleasant short paddling day. Easy access.

Indian Valley Reservoir: Reached via Walker Ridge Rd. It is formed by the North Fork of
Cache Creek. Boating is welcome; it can be accessed by boat ramps at each end.

CLEAR LAKE PELICANS

ANDERSON MARSH - CLEAR LAKE

CLASS II+
RAPID AFTER BEAR CREEK

CACHE CREEK - TILTED STRATA

CACHE CREEK - RUMSEY BRIDGE

CACHE CREEK, EASY RAPID

CACHE CREEK (con't)

Beaver Run: Long Valley to SR-20, 9 miles, Class II

ACCESS: Put-in • From SR-20 go west to New Long Valley Rd., go right on Spring Valley Rd., right on Wolf Cr. Rd., right on Chalk Mt. Rd., right before bridge to river bank. Or at the campground (phone first).
1 mile to • bridge over Long Valley Creek.
10 miles to • Cache Creek Rec. Area. From SR-20, west side of Cache Creek & No. Fk. bridge take the dirt road to (BLM) Cache Cr. Rec. Area. Parking & Rrm.

BEWARE: Beaver-felled trees into/across the river, snags, and shallow water.

COMMENTS: "There is a class IV+ rapid, difficult to portage." These words came from Jim Kirwan. I thought I remembered hearing the same words from Randy Hodges. Terry Sauter-Haag said she had done the run and it was a Class I - II but brushy. With four other "explorers" in search of the IV+ rapid, which we failed to find, we had a delightful, though low-water run. The side streams about doubled as they joined the flow.

Beaver evidence was on both banks where they had cut and feasted on the small, hot dog roasting size willow sticks. At this low water level, the route along the banks was sometimes complicated by overhung beaver-cut trees. Double the flow would have made for a much easier run but higher waves, with some Class II+ rapids. There were a few swimming holes and some water-carved sandstone boulders creating the artistic look. It was a fun 11 mile run on a beautiful April day with a drive of a little over an hour. (Date paddled: 4-24-98.) (Returned the next day for a wild flower/elk viewing walk to the main Cache Creek.)

A year later we did the run again and feel it is one of the best fast-paced Class II runs that is fairly closeby. We could boat-scout everything at the 410 cfs. flow, but this was very often at the last minute, just before being "committed." It's technical but not difficult and requires quick maneuvering skills.

●●●●●●●●●●●●●●●●

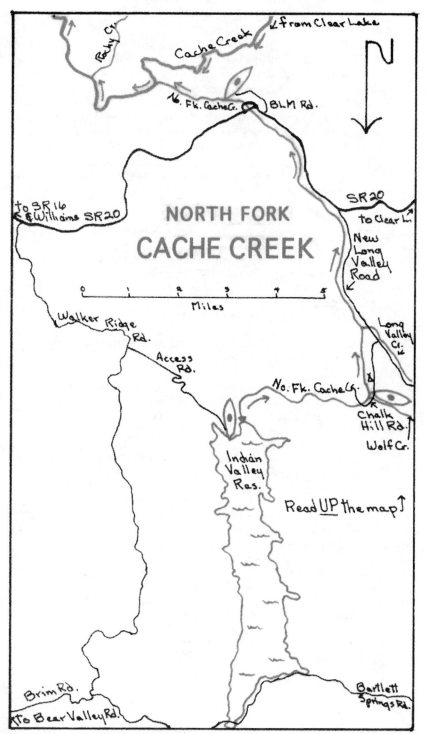

NORTH FORK
CACHE CREEK

Rocky Cr.

Cache Creek

← from Clear Lake

N. Fk. Cache Cr.

BLM Rd.

to SR 16 & Williams SR 20

SR 20

to Clear L.

New Long Valley Road

0 1 2 3 4 5
Miles

Walker Ridge Rd.

Access Rd.

Long Valley Cr.

No. Fk. Cache Cr.

Chalk Hill Rd.

Wolf Cr.

Indian Valley Res.

Read UP the map ↑

Brim Rd.

To Bear Valley Rd.

Bartlett Springs Rd.

CACHE CREEK (con't)

Eagle or Wilderness Run
SR-20 to Yolo County Reg. Pk., 22 mi., Class II+ (III)

ACCESS: Put-in • BLM Cache Creek Recreation Area 1 mi. downstream from SR-20 W. end Cache Creek Bridge. Parking & Rrm.

18 miles to • Upper Cache Creek Canyon Reg. Park Beach. From SR-16, 2 miles below the confluence with Bear Creek is the upper Cache Cr. Cyn. Reg. Park. Short walk to parking & Rrm. Note: Taking out at Bear Creek is discouraged.

BEWARE: Snags or overhanging branches. Rattlesnakes. Watch for the low-water bridge where the valley is wider and the flow slower, left side portage.

COMMENTS: This run definitely feels like wilderness. This is a fabulous summer run during hot weather. And it gets HOT in this valley! This run has become progressively more difficult as erosion digs the gravel bars away and digs a deeper channel. It used to be a great overnight trip for canoeists going on their first camping trip. Now it is reclassified as a bonified Class II, with one or two low Class IIIs, ideal for more experienced canoeists and kayakers. It's a long, long one-day run, but an easy two-day camping trip. Some of the canyon is under the BLM.

●●●●●●●●●●●●●●●●

Cache Creek Canyon Reg. Park to Camp Haswell, 7 miles, Class II+ (III)

ACCESS: Put-in • Cache Creek Canyon Regional Park (upper): 530.666.8115. The lower parking area is easy walking distance to the river off SR-16.

1 mile to • Lower Cache Creek Canyon Regional Park (lower).

2.5 miles to • SR-16 bridge just upriver from Rowboat Rapid.

1.5 miles to • Camp Haswell (Former Boy Scout Camp with remnants of a stone building and a very rocky parking area.) Road goes down to the parking area from SR-16 about 2 miles east of SR-16 bridge over Cache Creek.

BEWARE: Class II+ rapids, some ledges to paddle over and then Class III Rowboat Rapid just after the bridge. Scout on either side, though left is best. The run is generally to the right of the big rock(where the row boat was) or there may be a sneak route closer to the trees on river right followed. Sharp left turn follows.

COMMENTS: Great run for novice to experienced paddlers. The ledges formed by the tilted strata that crosses the river make for interesting drops and surfing waves. Scout Rowboat Rapid (sometimes called The Mother) on river left; it may be too brushy on the right. It can sometimes be run on river right or it may be better to start center and go right around the big rock. Camp Haswell is about a mile downstream.

●●●●●●●●●●●●●●●●

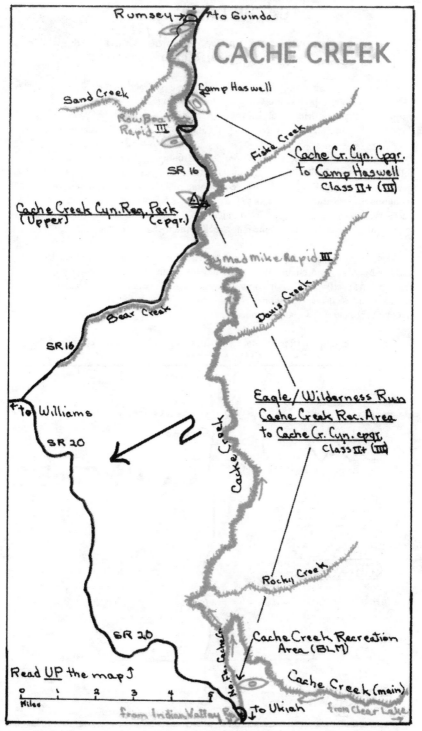

CACHE CREEK

Rumsey→ ↑to Guinda

Sand Creek

Camp Haswell

Row Boat Rapid III

Fiske Creek

SR 16

Cache Cr. Cyn. Cpgr.
to Camp Haswell
Class II+ (III)

Cache Creek Cyn. Reg. Park
(Upper)   (cpgr.)

Mad Mike Rapid III

Bear Creek

Davis Creek

SR 16

←to Williams

SR 20

Eagle/Wilderness Run
Cache Creek Rec. Area
to Cache Cr. Cyn. cpgr.
Class II+ (III)

Cache Creek

Rocky Creek

SR 20

Read UP the map ↑

0 1 2 3 4 5
Miles

from Indian Valley Res.

No. Fk. Cache

Cache Creek Recreation
Area (BLM)

Cache Creek (main)

↓to Ukiah

from Clear Lake

203

CACHE CREEK (con't)

Camp Haswell to Rumsey, 2 miles, Class I+ & -II
Rumsey to Guinda, 7 miles, Class I+

ACCESS: Put-in • SR-16 , 2 miles south of bridge over Cache Creek at the remains of
BSA Camp Haswell. Well used area. Parking.
2 miles to • Rumsey Bridge. Just off of SR-16 at Rumsey, population 8.
7 miles to • Guinda, Vernon A. Nichols Co. Park near the bridge. Parking & Rrm.

BEWARE: The first drop can present problems. Going straight means a long rocky drop
followed by a sharp left turn and going right means a drop under the branches of an
overhanging tree and over rocks. There are some rocky drops that can be boat-scouted,
including the irrigation ditch going to the right with a 3 foot drop on river left. The tricky
one is the rapid where the river drops quickly to the left but looks as if the best route is
straight ahead..and then there's the long "rock garden" that is challenging.

COMMENTS: This is an ideal novice run with a variety of natural river obstacles for the
paddler to "read" and choose the best route. It was an excellent training run for river
reading that I used when I taught compact kayak classes. The take-out is at Rumsey Bridge,
soon after the well-marked commercial take-outs, so scout before doing the run. Rumsey
to Guinda is easy; it's a good beginner run.

NOTE: From Guinda to Capay Dam, river access is greatly discouraged.

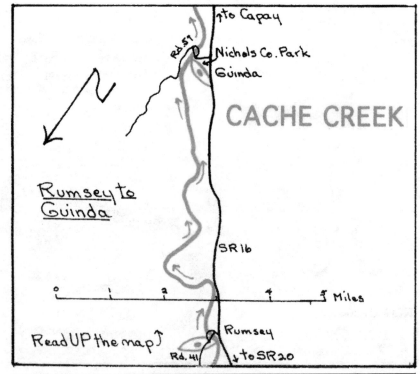

S. FK. AMERICAN RIVER

PHOTO BY BOB FOOTE

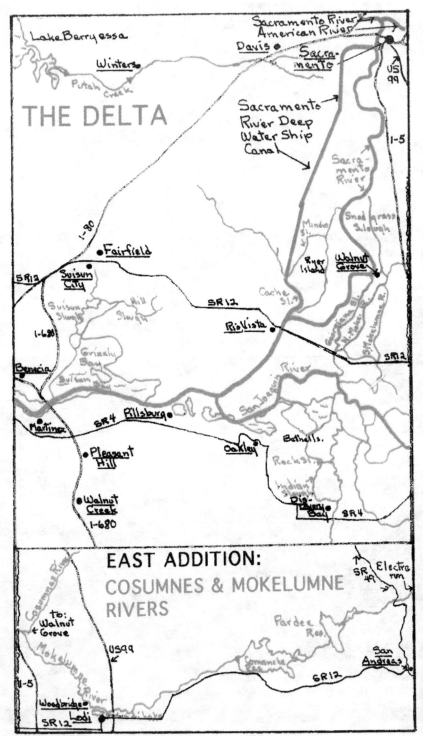

CHAPTER 7 - THE DELTA
of
THE SACRAMENTO & SAN JOAQUIN RIVERS

CONTENTS

GENERAL INFORMATION

Yes, I've heard of The Delta for years, but I had just experienced small bits of it until I was writing this book. It's a fascinating, fabulous area, and ideal for paddling, covering some 1,000 miles of flat water. A quote from "Discover the California Delta" describes it best: "The official Delta, which includes portions of Stockton and Sacramento, is comprised of 738,000 acres in six counties. The five major rivers of the Delta system, plus their tributaries, carry 47 percent of California's runoff water. Most land in the inner Delta—reclaimed islands—is below sea level, from minus 21 feet on Brannan Island to minus 3 feet in New Hope Tract. The Delta annually sees 12 million user days of recreation. It's a busy area for fishing, water skiing, houseboating, and bird hunting. The annual gross value of its crops is over $500 million. It's home to 230 species of birds, 45 mammal species, 25 reptile and amphibian species, and 150 species of flowering plants. If birding is your pleasure, arrive at The Delta in late fall, take in the Sandhill Crane Festival (October in Lodi-Galt), and wander around the Delta. You'll see islands thick with snow geese and great white swans.

The Delta is great but paddlers should be cautious:
- Know how to (and do) read the tide book.
- Heed the weather patterns and forecasts.
- Learn where and when the wind generally blows.
- Know where and when the water skiers, jet skiers, fast moving power boats, houseboats, and ocean-going cargoships are happening, as well as when and where the hunting season happens.

Water skiers and jet skiers generally follow the four W's:
- Water—warm and deep enough for power boats.
- Weather—warm (slow morning risers).
- Wind protection.
- Weekends.

Canoe and kayak paddlers should learn the access spots for the meandering, little-used side channels with the birds, otter, beaver, and exotic flowers. Drive along the levees, seeing water on one side of the road higher than the farm houses way below on the other side. Cross the sloughs on one of the 11 ferries (mostly free). Marinas and resorts are plentiful, often with RV parks, boat ramps, and restaurants. Paddle around an island. Don't get lost. It's easily done!

HISTORY: Gold-seekers in the mid-1800s went from an oceangoing sailing ship to a river boat through The Delta on their way to the gold fields. The gold miners with their bags of nuggets used these same river boats getting back to the Big City via The Delta. Read the fascinating stories about races between river boats—some putting on so much speed that they blew up! After the transcontinental railroad was built, some of the Chinese laborers settled in The Delta. Their town is Locke, which is one mile upriver from Walnut Grove. On our most recent Delta outing, we paddled past an old owner-remodeled Navy vessel that boasts an inside swimming pool. The stories are fascinating and numerous.

BEWARE

The **weather** can turn from calm to very windy as quickly as a wood duck flies out of sight. It can be very hot in the summer to exceedingly cold in the winter when the tule fog hugs the ground. The Delta is a **highly used area** for many kinds of power and sail boats that includes water skiing, houseboats, and PWCs. They generally use the deeper and straighter waterways, ignoring the smaller ones better for paddlecraft and wildlife viewing. This was the advice of Hal Schell (owner of Delta Books and Maps) when I called him: "Go where the others don't." Because there are two primary water currents, the **river flow** and the **tidal flow**, first determine which is the best flow for your excursion at the time you will be on the water. (There is a separate tide book for The Delta.) Using Mt. Diablo as a **navigational aid** be aware that it is south of Suisun, southwest of Rio Vista, and west of Stockton. Take along a compass and map!

LAUNCHING and FEES: An $8-10 fee per boat (even an 8-foot kayak) is a common charge. (Pleasant note: Discovery Bay Marina allows paddle craft that are carried down the ramp to launch free.) Roads next to the water often have "down the bank" access, thanks to fishermen. Much of the land is privately owned, please be respectful. Some of the sloughs have no spots for getting on shore, so be prepared to be boat-bound for several hours.

MORE INFORMATION

- California Delta Chambers, P.O. Box 6, Isleton, CA 95641: 916.777.5007 or 707.374.6134; www.californiadelta.org; e-mail: caldelta@californiadelta.org
- Hal Schell's Delta Books & Maps, Hal Schell Publications, P.O. Box 9140, Stockton, CA 95208: 209.951.7921; e-mail: hal@gotnet.net
- California Dept. of Parks and Recreation, Brannan Island State Recreation Area, 17645 SR-160, Rio Vista, CA 94571: 916.777.6671
- Calif. Dept. of Fish & Game, Region II Office, 1701 Nimbus Rd., Rancho Cordova, CA 95670: 916.355.0978
- Sacramento County Dept. of Parks & Recreation, 4040 Bradshaw Rd., Sacramento, CA 95827: 916.366.2072
- San Joaquin County Dept of Parks & Recreation, 4520 W. Eight Mile Rd., Stockton, CA 95209: 209.953.8800
- Solano County Dept. of Parks & Recreation, Sandy Beach Park, Rio Vista, CA 94571: 707.374.2097
- Stockton Chamber of Commerce, 445 W. Weber Ave., Suite #220, Stockton, CA 95203: 209.446.7066
- Fish-N-Map Company: 303.421.5994. Waterproof map: "The Delta"
- U.S. Coast Guard, Rio Vista Station: 707.374.6477
- Dept. of Boating & Waterways, 1629 S Street, Sacramento, CA 95814: 916.445.2616

MAPS: AAA — "Bay and Mt. Section"
Delta Tide Book — available at Delta marinas

PUTAH CREEK

Monticello Dam (L. Berryessa) to Solano County Park,
5 miles, Class I+ - II+

SEASON: March - Sept. BEST FLOWS: 500-650 cfs. FLOW INFO: 800.675.3833

ACCESS: Put-in • S. side of Putah Creek near the dam off of SR-128 on either side of the
    highway. Parking.
.5 miles to • Sierra Pacific Resort. (Private.)
1+ miles to • Putah Creek fishing access #1. Parking & RRm.
.5 miles to • fishing access #2.
1 mile to • fishing access #3.
2 miles to • Lake Solano County Park. On Pleasant Valley Rd. across the creek from SR-
    128. Parking & campground.
(1.5 miles to • Putah Diversion Dam at east end of Lake Solano.)

MAPS: AAA — "Sacramento Valley Region". DE LORME — pp. 85, 86, & 95.

GAS, FOOD, and LODGING: Winters.
CAMPING: Lake Solano County Park: 530.795.2990.

BEWARE: Snags, trees across the river, log jams, low-hanging branches!

COMMENTS: This is a fun run, but it is fairly fast flowing and has quick turns; a paddler
can get trapped very quickly. A short quick-turning craft that can be exited in a hurry
would be best, along with the appropriate paddling skills. The water is cold! But the air
can be very hot, over 100 in the summer. For safety there are people fishing in several
areas and the highway is closeby. Special...we paddled past a pair of gorgeously colored
wood ducks sitting on a branch at eye-level, that did not fly away.

NOTE: There is access just below the diversion dam for a possible 12 - 15 mile run to
U.C. Davis. However, most of the water is diverted into the Putah South Canal at the
diversion dam for agricultural purposes, so the flow could be quite low. Possibly a spring
run?

●●●●●●●●●●●●●●●

ABOVE LAKE BERRYESSA: Putah Creek can be accessed north of Middletown between Mt. St. Helena and Clear Lake. Dick Schwind's book, *West Coast River Touring*,
has information about an 18 mile run to Lake Berryessa. with some Class IVs in it. I have
heard that there is an easier shorter section closer to the lake.

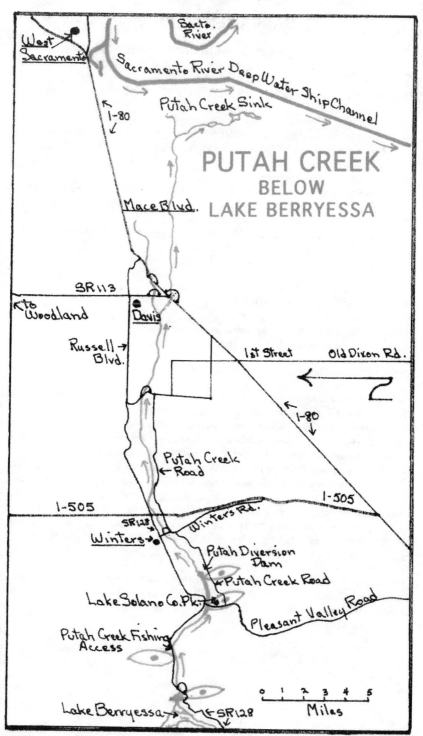

PUTAH CREEK
BELOW
LAKE BERRYESSA

West Sacramento

Sacto. River

Sacramento River Deep Water Ship Channel

Putah Creek Sink

I-80

Mace Blvd.

SR 113

to Woodland

Davis

Russell Blvd.

1st Street

Old Dixon Rd.

I-80

Putah Creek Road

I-505

I-505

SR 128

Winters Rd.

Winters

Putah Diversion Dam

Putah Creek Road

Lake Solano Co. Pk.

Pleasant Valley Road

Putah Creek Fishing Access

Lake Berryessa

SR 128

0 1 2 3 4 5

Miles

SACRAMENTO RIVER

Discovery Park, Sacramento to Rio Vista
48 miles, Class I

SEASON: All yr. BEST FLOWS: 9,000-25,000 cfs. FLOW INFO: K-ph: 916.368.8682.

ACCESS: Put-in • Boat ramp, Discovery Park Marina or beach at SW end of the park on the American River. From US I-5 & US-99 just north of the Am. River take the Garden Hwy. exit, go east to Discovery Park road, go SW and follow signs. Take Jibbom St. bridge to cross the Am. River to Cape Tiscornia Park and Beach. Parking & RRm.: 916.366.2061.

3 miles to • Sacramento Marina in Miller Park east side of river across from Barge Canal, SW of the intersection of US-99 and US I-5 via Front St. and Broadway at 2701 Ramp Way. Parking & RRm.: 916.264.5712.

21 miles to • Clarksburg Boat Ramp, 2 mi. S of Clarksburg on South River Rd. Yolo Co. Parks & Facilities: 916.666.8115.

13 miles to • Walnut Grove Merchants Dock at Walnut Grove.

14 miles to • Rio Vista boat ramp.

MAPS: AAA — "Sacramento Valley Region." DE LORME — pp. 86 & 96.

GAS, FOOD, and LODGING: Sacramento and Rio Vista.
CAMPING: Brannon Island SRA, 3.5 mi. S of SR-12 off S-160: 916.677.6671.

BEWARE: Power boats, water and jet skiing, winds, no beaches, few access areas.

COMMENTS: The launching at Discovery Park is quite easy, either at the boat ramp or from the beach. Paddling along the Sacramento waterfront is like reliving history, especially when passing Old Sacramento. A waterfront area that has recooped its "days of yore" feeling with train rides, steamboat paddlewheeler rides, railroad museum, old-time saloons, and tourist shops (of course). Plus floating restaurants with river views as you eat. The boating activity in the river is curious. The old boats are being refurbished and there are pleasure craft and a few smaller commercial vessels that include the River Otter Taxi Company's cute little boats to use when getting around on the waterfront. After leaving Sacramento, the river has a canal like feeling with riprap rock-faced banks. The next bridge is 11 miles down the river at Freeport; it is another 12.5 miles to the next bridge at Paintersville. As long as everything is going well, this is a fun run, even though the access points are scarce, the bridges are few, and the afternoon wind blows upriver!

Locke, a town founded by Chinese is a mile north of Walnut Grove, chock-full of stories and history. Chinese were gold miners as well as laborers working on installing the railroad tracks. Some have settled here incorporating their culture. Do some shopping and visit the museum.

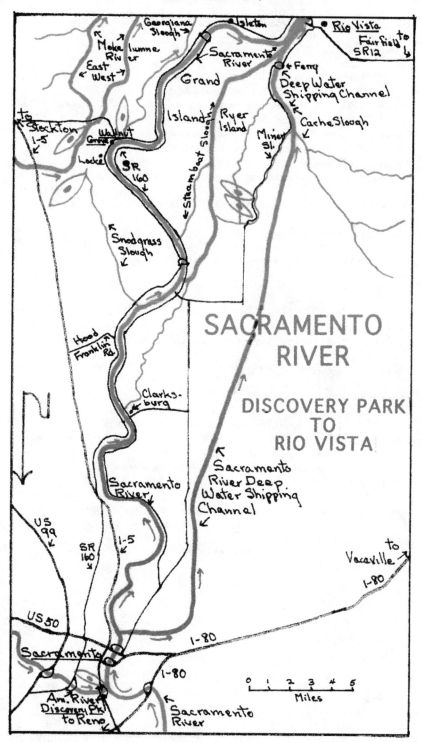

SACRAMENTO RIVER

Rio Vista to Benecia, 31.5 miles, Class I

ACCESS: Put-in • Boat ramp at Rio vista, river right, 1 Main St.:707.374.6451. (SR-12, goes through Rio Vista.) Parking and Rrm.

1.5 miles to • Sandy Beach Park Boat ramp, river right, end of Beach Dr., down river from Rio Vista. Camping: 707.374.2097. Parking and Rrm.

1.5 miles to • Inlet, river left. 1 mile to Brannan Island SRA boat ramp (largest in the Delta, 6 trailered boats wide). Camping, parking, and Rrm.: 916.777.7701.

9 miles to • Boat ramp at Pittsburg Marina, 51-E Marina Blvd.:510.439.4958.

15.5 miles to • Ninth Street launching ramp at W 9th and 1st Streets, Benecia: 707.746.4285.

MAPS: AAA — "Sacramento Valley Region." DE LORME — pp. 95 & 96.

GAS, FOOD, and LODGING: Rio Vista.
CAMPING: Brannon Island SRA, 3.5 miles S of SR-12 off of SR-160, E. side of the Sacramento River. Camping & launching fees. Delta tours. Parking & RRm.

BEWARE: Wind, waves, tides and other watercraft of all sizes!

COMMENTS: From Walnut Grove to the west end of Grand Island, the river is similar to the upper stretch, but from here on to San Pablo Bay it is a more serious waterway. Steamboat Slough (the alternate route from Courtland to Rio Vista) and the deep water channel join the main Sacramento River, now much wider and less "friendly," The winds become a large paddling and comfort factor.

My aircraft generated river maps (thank you Howard!) showed a 300 mile mark at Redding and a "0" on the river opposite Pittsburg. This terminated our 300 mile, 12 day "Indian Summer" oddessy of paddling from Redding to Ross (we substituted Pittsburg). Paddling friends came and went as their schedules allowed. The final three craft, two kayaks and one canoe. Joe Tilt, Herb and Mary Fitz, and I paddled the last three miles in the sunset to the boat ramp at Pittsburg. The next morning, Joe and I were the only ones left to complete the venture "Paddling from Redding to Ross" with San Pablo Bay and Corte Madera Creek yet to paddle. As we looked at the two to three foot waves generated by the cold upriver wind and knowing there was an incoming tide for several hours, Joe and I both decided; enough is enough! We had paddled the Sacramento River; going on to Ross could be another adventure.

•••••••••••••••

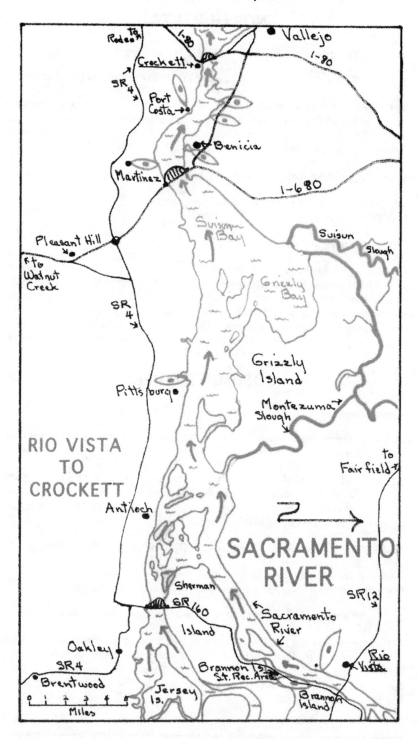

NORTH DELTA

Snodgrass Slough — Delta Meadows River Park

SEASON: Most of the year, except high water. FLOW INFO: Brannan Island SRA.

ACCESS: Put-in • Drive beside the north side of the Delta Cross Canal just north of Walnut Grove off River Road, take the first left dirt road on the old railroad track. Short ways to water access on the right. Storage facility for Brannon Island SRA canoes used for tours.

MAPS: AAA — "Bay and Mt. Section." DE LORME — p. 96.

GAS, FOOD, and LODGING: Rio Vista and Sacramento.
CAMPING: Brannon Island SRA: 916.777.6671.

BEWARE: Winds, low water, and getting lost.

COMMENTS: Take the right route; the left route parallel to the old railroad goes to borrowing pits (so named as dirt was borrowed though never returned). The state is in the process of removing some dwellings in Delta Meadows River Park near the beginning of the paddle to Snodgrass Slough. First go east, then north in the slough that goes about 8 miles. Native Americans knew about the higher ground leaving remnants of their culture from having lived there. Guided tours are conducted by Brannan Island SP. 916.777.6671.

• • • • • • • • • • • • • • •

COSUMNES RIVER

Cosumnes River Preserve adm. by The Nature Conservancy

SEASON: Spring and Summer. FLOW INFO: 916.684.2816 or email:crp@ns.pnet. www.cosumnes.org

ACCESS: Put-in • Behind the Cosumnes River Preserve Vistor Center at 13501 Franklin Blvd., J8, south of Twin Cities Rd., E13, north of New Hope Rd. between Galt and Walnut Grove.
.5 miles to • SE end of Franklin Blvd. Bridge.

MAPS: AAA — "Sacramento Valley Region." DE LORME — p. 96. Delta maps.

GAS, FOOD, and LODGING: Lodi
CAMPING: Brannan Island SRA., SE of Rio Vista, SR-160: 916.777.6671.

BEWARE: Water level for paddling up or downstream, snags, and getting lost.

COMMENTS: This is a fabulous birding area which can be reached by paddlecraft or walking. There are over 220 species of birds and many other animals. The Nature Conservancy Vis. Ctr. offers guided canoe trips. In talking to long-time Cosumnes River Paddler, Bill Griffith, he said access spots upriver are closed to paddlers; likewise for Dry Creek.

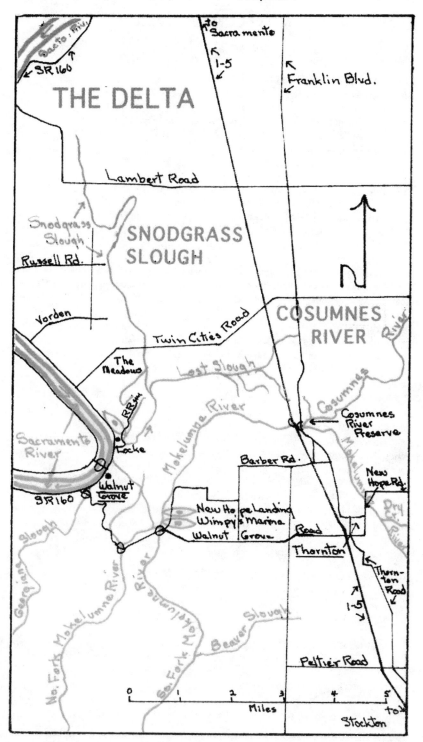

THE DELTA

SR 160

to Sacramento

I-5

Franklin Blvd.

Lambert Road

Snodgrass Slough

SNODGRASS SLOUGH

Russell Rd.

Yorden

COSUMNES RIVER

Cosumnes River

Twin Cities Road

The Meadows

Lost Slough

RR Jct.

Mokelumne River

Cosumnes River

Sacramento River

Locke

Cosumnes River Preserve

Barber Rd.

New Hope Rd.

Walnut Grove

New Hope Landing
Wimpy's Marina
Walnut Grove Road

Dry Cr. River

SR 160

Georgiana Slough

No. Fork Mokelumne River

Mokelumne River

Thornton

Thornton Road

I-5

So. Fork Mokelumne River

Beaver Slough

Peltier Road

0   1   2   3   4   5

Miles

to Stockton

reccomended by sunshine rafting of staneslause river

MOKELUMNE RIVER

Electra Run: 4.5 miles, Class II+

SEASON: All year. BEST FLOWS: 600-2000 cfs.
(In the summer the Electra Powerhouse releases about 800 cfs. to the river.)

ACCESS: Put-in • At the public beach downriver from Electra Powerhouse. SR-49 north on Electra Road. Parking & RRm.
3.5 miles to • Roadside takeout.
4.5 miles to • Below SR-49 bridge.

MAPS: AAA — "Bay & Mountain Section." DE LORME — p. 98.

GAS, FOOD, and LODGING: On SR-49: 7 miles N. to Jackson, 8 miles S. to San Andreas.
CAMPING: New Hogan Lake via SR-26, S. of SR-49: 209.772.1343.

BEWARE: The water flow is controlled by the East Bay Municipal Utilities Distract (East Bay MUD) which could mean a low flow until air conditioners go on in Oakland. The cold water release from the bottom of the dam increases the flow fairly fast. Tubers? Yes! This is a popular tubing run.

COMMENTS: This has been a kayakers favorite for years with a good supply of fun rapids and a road alongside for safety or scouting. It's short—allowing for several reruns. Depending on the flow it can have 3 foot standing waves or it can have several rock gardens. Fun for canoeists in training who want to move into whitewater. Great for kayaks!

The first time I did this run I was soloing an open canoe with Bob Foote and others. We sat impatiently on the beach waiting for the release and for the water to be deep enough to run. Our "mental message" was for East Bayers to hurry and turn on their air conditioners. The rapid above the run was Maytag; it had a washing machine type of action. Another rapid near the end was the Elevator Wave; if your canoe was in the right spot on river left the wave would send it across to the eddy on river right. Great fun!

In the beginning of my kayaking days, this was the location of the river run for the seven of us who had made our own fiberglass kayaks (1972?). We had learned flat water kayak strokes and were ready for a river experience. Three of the group loved kayaking, three found it much too frustrating, and I decided to design my own kayaks. My brain was in full-speed, "designing mode," all the way home; years later the end result: (Hydra Minnow), Kopapa and Kiwi Kayak Co.

●●●●●●●●●●●●●●●

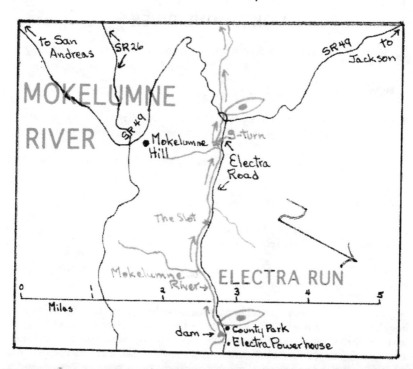

"S"- TURN, MOKELUMNE RIVER

MOKELUMNE RIVER

Comanche Dam to Stillman Magee Co. Pk. (Clements),
4.5 miles, Class I

SEASON: All year. BEST FLOWS: 600-2,000 cfs. FLOW INFO: K-Ph: 916.368.8682

ACCESS: Put-in • Comanche Dam Fish Hatchery (near). From SR-12 turn north on McIntire Rd., follow to parking before fish hatchery. Walk to the river. Parking & RRm.
4.5 miles to • San Joaquin County Park. On SR-12 and SR-88 in Clements turn north on Mackville Rd. to county park (fee) river access. Parking & RRm.

MAPS: AAA — "Bay & Mountain Section."DELORME — p. 97

GAS, FOOD, and LODGING: Lockford.
CAMPING: New Hogan Lake. (See above.)

BEWARE: Trees in the river blocking the route. No easy take-outs between the parks. Private property on both sides of the river.

COMMENTS: Much of this run is like paddling through a lovely park with over- hanging branches shading the river on a hot day, which is not unusual. There are some homes with lawns to the river and a few ranches along the waterway. To remind the paddler that this is a wild river (at times) there are downed trees, piles of tree trunks, and branches left from the last flooding and an occasional tree that blocks the the passageway. This moderately fast flowing cold river has always been a favorite. There are a few bends with a small wave or two, nothing beyond a Class I+ at this water level. Last paddled: 8/29/98.

CONTINUING ON: There are about 20 more miles of river to Lodi Lake. The flow is slower and there could be more snags as the river winds through the valley. Unless a property owner has given permission for you and your party to camp on the property or have access across the property to a public road, the river area is closed.

• • • • • • • • • • • • • • • •

Lodi Lake in Lodi

The Mokelumne River snakes around Lodi Lake and some of it is captured enroute to fill this very attractive recreational park with the lake as a centerpiece. Swimming, paddling, children's play pool, rental kayaks and pedal boats are some of the of activities available. A pleasant spot to picnic under the oaks, learn at the Discovery Center, or walk or bicycle around the lake. Open in the summer months. Rangers patrol on horseback. It is on Turner Road, 2 miles west of US-99, .5 mile north of SR-12. Boat ramp. Parking & RRm.: 209.333.6742.

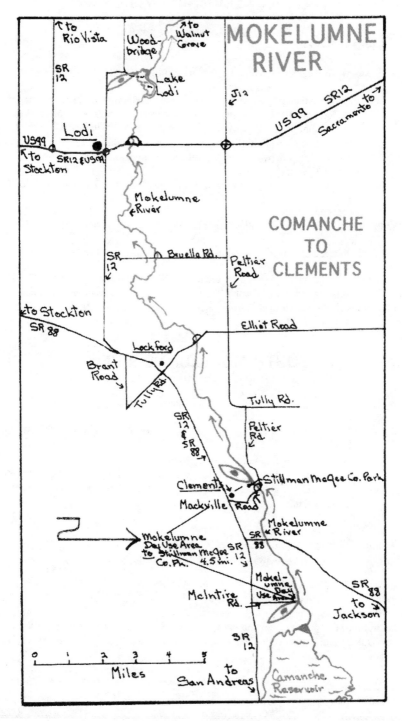

MOKELUMNE RIVER

Woodbridge Reg. Park to New Hope Rd. Br., 12 mi.,
Class I+

SEASON: All year. BEST FLOWS: 300-1,000 cfs. FLOW: K-Ph: 916.368.8682.

ACCESS: Put-in • Woodbridge Reg. Park. Go west on Woodbridge Rd. (from Woodbridge
on Sacramento Rd. NE of Lodi via Turner Rd. west of Lodi Lake) to
Mokelumne, N. on Meadowlark to the end. The small entrance is in a residential area with a walk to the river and semi-steep banks.
12 miles to • New Hope Rd. below bridge, north end. A bit of a steep carry up to the road.
Limited parking.
(4.5 miles to • New Hope Landing. By road W. on New Hope Rd., S. on Co.R-J8 then W.
on Co.R-J11 to Walnut Grove.)

MAPS: AAA — "Sacramento Valley Region." DE LORME — p. 96 & 97.

BEWARE: Snags in the river, downed trees, private property and WINDS.

COMMENTS: The public access after the dam in Woodbridge is a bit hard to find and
requires a fairly long carry to the water. The river twists and turns as it flows past ranches.
In 4 miles is Peltier Rd. Bridge. The next major bridge is New Hope Rd. Bridge. Take out
on river right; it's a bit of a climb.

●●●●●●●●●●●●●●●●

SOUTH MOKELUMNE RIVER
New Hope Landing to Terminous, 10 miles, Class I

BEST TIDE: 3' & above. TIDE LOC.: Mokelumne R. at New Hope Br. & Terminous.

ACCESS: Put-in • Wimpy's Marina ramp, 3 miles west of Thornton, 14001 W Walnut
Grove Rd.: 209.794.2544.
1 mile to • New Hope Landing ramp. 13945 Walnut Grove Rd.: 209.794.2627.
10 miles to • Westgate Landing Co. Park. 1 mile north of Terminous, (11 miles east of Rio
Vista on SR-12 or 5 miles west of US I-5) at West Gate Landing Co. Park. Pkg,
RRm, & camping. High docks, walk to parking.

FOOD and GAS: New Hope Landing, Wimpy's, and Terminous.
LODGING: Rio Vista and Lodi. About 15 miles each way, east or west.
CAMPING: West Gate Landing County Park (see above).

COMMENTS: This run is an easy ten miles with access at both ends, but none in the
middle. To lengthen the paddling day, there are three sloughs to be explored. Three of us
in March of 1998, averaged 3 miles an hour starting with a good flow from recent rains
that was slowed down by the incoming tide waters. Mt. Diablo became more dominate as
we paddled south on this very pleasant day. The long wooden downhill steps to our cars
became a great kayak slide.
NOTE: The No. Mokelumne River, west of our run is another route to paddle.

●●●●●●●●●●●●●●●●

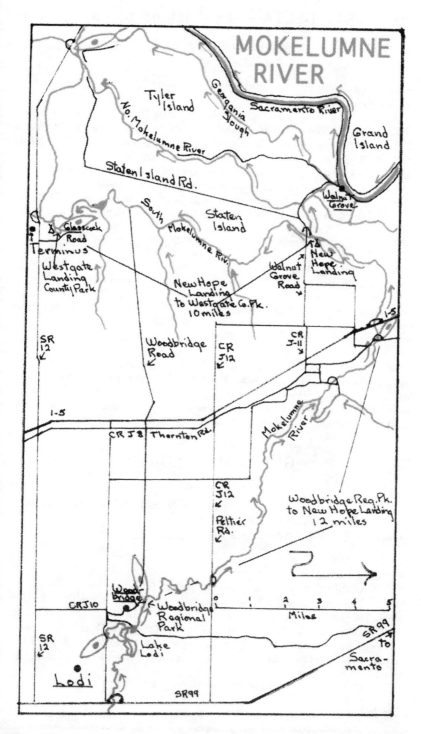

CENTRAL DELTA — Ryer Island to Rio Vista

Miners Slough, Cache Slough & Deep Water Channel, 10-12 miles

SEASON: All year. BEST TIDE: 3'-5'. TIDE LOCATIONS: (Sacramento River) Rio Vista and Steamboat Slough.

ACCESS: Put-in • West side of Ryer Island. SR-12 to Rio Vista N on Ryer Island Rd. to ferry (free) to Ryer Island, west side of Ryer Island to Golden Gate Island Resort Marina, launch fee $8 per boat of any size.
10 miles to • Ryer Island Ferry (not a good take-out).
2.5 miles to • Boat ramp, Rio Vista Launching Ramp at river end of Main St.
1.5 miles to • Boat ramp at Sandy Beach Co. Park. Go east on Main St, south on S. 2nd to Beach St to end. Parking, RRm., & camping: 707.374.2097.

MAPS: AAA — "Sacramento Valley Region." DE LORME — p. 96.

GAS, FOOD, and LODGING: Rio Vista.
CAMPING: Brannon Island St. Rec. Area, 3 mi. S. of Rio Vista off SR-160: 916.777.6671.

BEWARE: A few snags in Miners Slough and Cache Slough. The Sacramento Deep Water Shipping Channel is wide with low banks making it subject to winds and more power boats. It was very boring and uninteresting!

COMMENTS: Driving on Ryer Island levee after the ferry crossing is very scenic. Farms are 25 feet below the road on this side, while on the slough side the water is about 10 feet below the road—higher than the roofs of the farm houses. It's a weird sight. There were many birds; our trip included a barn owl that kept a few yards ahead of us as we paddled along. A resident beaver surprised us by slapping its tail on the water.

●●●●●●●●●●●●●●●●

GEORGIANA SLOUGH
Walnut Grove to SR-12, 13 miles, Class I

ACCESS: Put-in • SW side of the slough (down the bank) near Walnut Grove before Walnut Grove Rd. crosses Georgiana Slough.
13 miles to • B & W Resort Marina near SR-12.

BEWARE: Winds and tide.

COMMENTS: There are three waterways that go south from the Walnut Grove and New Hope Landing area, the north and south forks of the Mokelumne River and the Georgiana Slough. The Georgiana Slough is more affected by tidal flow and less by the extended river flow. It seems to be the least used and smallest of the three. There were numerous birds on the run, especially herons. There's a parallel road on river left for a mile, access at 6 miles, a bridge at the end of Tyler Island Rd., and a resort, trailer park, and Ox Bow Marina at 10 miles.

●●●●●●●●●●●●●●●●

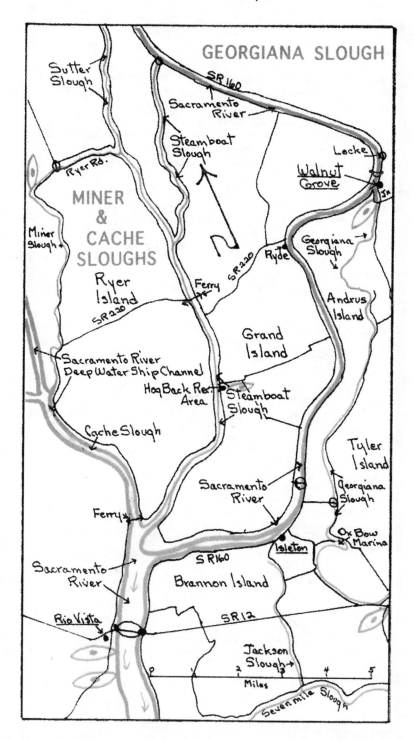

EAST DELTA

Bethel Island - Circumnavigation, 12 miles

SEASON: Calm weather, very little wind. BEST TIDE: 2' minimum. TIDE LOCATION: (San Joaquin River) Three-mile Slough.

ACCESS: Put-in • Boat ramp at Sunset. Harbor Hwy., SR-4, follow signs to Bethel Island, south of Oakley go east on Cypress Road, north on Bethel Island Road. Sunset Harbor (on the right before crossing the bridge).
3 miles to • Sugar Barge Marina, the end of Sugar Barge Road if paddling counterclockwise.
12 miles • paddling circumference.

GAS, FOOD, and LODGING: Bethel Island & Oakley. DINING: Sugar Barge Restnt.

BEWARE: In paddling around the island, make sure to paddle in the best direction according to the tidal flow, wind, and late-day fatigue. There are usually prevailing winds from the west in the afternoon. Paddling into the wind can be tiring but a tail wind can create a "following sea" which makes for tricky maneuvering. Tidal height is 40% lower than at the Golden Gate.

COMMENTS: After carefully assessing our paddling venture in April of 1998, we chose to go counterclockwise around the island, taking all the left channels without "dead ends." We were paddling between islands in sloughs about 50 to 100 feet wide. On the northeast side was a remnant of a levee giving some shelter from the large bay that is a part of Franks Tract State Recreation Area. "Locals" suggested we explore an adjoining bay that had an abundance of birdlife, but we were reluctant because of the wind and we still had a long way yet to paddle. This was typical delta country with man-made sloughs and maintained islands with reeds, willows, and blackberries. Mixed in with the tall grasses were tall bright yellow iris, very unusual and attractive. We saw an 8 inch turtle, but very few birds.

HISTORY: Sugar Barge Marina, boat ramp, and restaurant. The Sugar Barge Restaurant was built where the sugar barge "M.V. Mokulii" was docked (retired) and turned into a restaurant after it was used for hauling freight, including sugar, in the bay and delta area. She sank, was raised, sank again, then was sold and moved to the Holland tract and sank again in shallow water! (On our recent paddle to Holland Riverside Marina, I photographed a misshapen partially sunk vessel. Was it the sugar barge?) All aspects of the restaurant; food, drinks, service, prices, inside and outside dining areas, and adjacent boat ramp are worth mentioning and worth a return visit. 800.799.4100.

•••••••••••••••

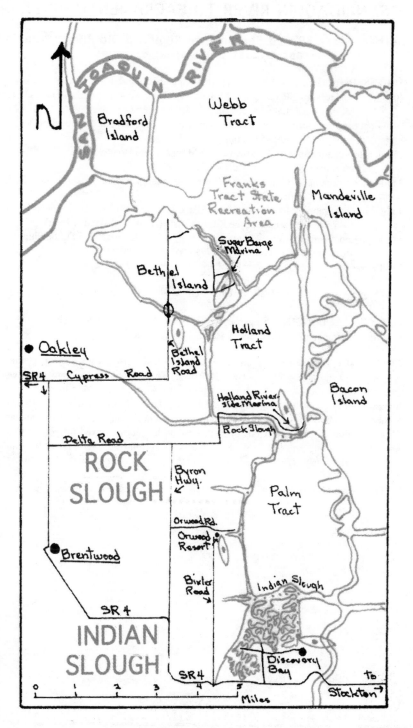

SAN JOAQUIN RIVER TO SACRAMENTO RIVER

Durham Ferry SRA to Sacramento River via Old River, Frank's Tract in East Delta area, 65 miles

ACCESS: Beach launch • Durham Ferry SRA .Cpgr. parking & RRm.
10 miles to • boat ramp. SR 120 below Mossdale Bridge at Mossdale Park, 10 miles W on Mossdale Rd, Lathrop. 209.982.0348.
OR • boat ramp just north and across the river at 19010 Manthey Rd. San Joaquin Dept of Parks & Rec. 209.953.8800.
25 miles to • boat ramp at Holland Riverside Marina. From Brentwood go N on SR-4, E on Delta Rd to Holland tract on Old River.
5 miles to • boat ramp at Bethel Island at Piper Slough. SR 4 in Oakley E on Cypress Road then N on Bethel Island Road.
4 miles to • boat ramp, Eddo's Harbor & RV Park. (510.757.53124) Off SR 160 at 19530 Sherman Island East Levee Rd, Rio Vista (across the island & river).
5 miles to • boat ramp at Antioch (Antioch Municipal Boat Ramp) at 225 Fulton Shipyard Road via Wilbur Avenue. (510.779.6957)
5 miles to • Sacramento River near Pittsburg.

MAPS: AAA - "Sacramento Valley Region" DE LORME: PP 95, 96, & 106.

GAS, FOOD, & LODGING: Stockton, Bethel Island, Rio Vista and Antioch.
CAMPING: Brannan Island SP, Sandy Beach Co. Park, Rio Vista.

COMMENTS: Yes, the San Joaquin River is Stockton's river BUT it shares the channel with the big ships (Deep Water Channel) between Stockton and the Sacramento River. This route is not recommended for paddlecraft. The old and middle San Joaquin Rivers bypassed Stockton so this is the route that has been chosen. It is more intimate, probably less busy, with houseboats, water skiing and jet skiing providing a more interesting paddling day. Frank's Tract SRA NE of Bethel Island has been allowed to recover to its natural state inviting water birds of many species. Read well *Hal Schell's Delta Map* and/ or the waterproof map *The Delta*.. Buy them in marine supply stores in the Delta area.

NOTE: It is easy to get lost in The Delta, especially if it is foggy or overcast.
••••••••••••••••

RIVERS TO THE DELTA

PUTAH CREEK SWALLOW NESTS

PUTAH CREEK

MOKELUMNE RIVER

MOKELUMNE RIVER

SOUTH DELTA – Indian and Rock Slough

Discovery Bay Marina to Holland Riverside Marina, 7 miles

SEASON: All year. BEST TIDE: 3'-5'. TIDE LOCATION: Orwood.

ACCESS: Put-in • Discovery Bay Marina. From SR-4, 7 miles SE of Brentwood and 75 miles west of Stockton on SR-4. Enter on Discovery Bay Blvd., follow signs to marina. Parking & RRm.

3.5 miles to • Orwood Resort. From Discovery Bay turn west on SR-4, in one mile turn north on Bixler Rd. 2.5 miles to Orwood Resort. An attractive riverside resort in view of the main channel with a sand beach, picnic area and boat ramp.

3.5 miles to • Holland Riverside Marina. Stay on SR-4 going west of Discovery Bay 2 miles to Byron Hwy., go N. 5 miles, then E on Delta Rd. 4.5 mi.

MAPS: AAA — "Bay & Mountain Section." DE LORME — p. 106.

GAS, FOOD, and LODGING: Brentwood, Antioch, and Stockton.
CAMPING: Orwood Resort, 4451 Orwood Road, Brentwood: 925.634.7181.

BEWARE: Tides, winds, getting lost, and other access points.

COMMENTS: It was a 1998 mid-December Wednesday that four of us tried to decide if we should paddle downriver or upriver. Which current, the river flow or the incoming tide had more effect on our route between Discovery Bay to Holland Riverside Marina. We chose to go against the tide. After the forty-minute shuttle we were soon happily water-borne paddling west on Indian Slough past some very impressive Discovery Bay water-side homes. We paddled against a bit of current which was non-existent three hours later near our destination where the water was mirror smooth. Several times we consulted the Delta Map; we were very glad we brought it. Mt. Diablo served as our western beacon. Much of the route was channelized, going straight with a few right-angle bends. Where the banks were more natural birdlife was more abundant. We saw herons, egrets, king-fishers, gulls, and a few "LBB's" (little brown birds). We almost stopped at Orwood Resort, a good halfway spot. A very large beaver lodge was at one of the river bends. The row of marina-bound boats were interesting to paddle past. This was just before the boat ramp and our take-out. Snack foods, maps, and Delta Tide Book ($1), as well as free literature on the Delta and Delta knowledge from "locals," were all at the small store.

Because of our limited time, we did not go the route we would have preferred, paddling on the Old River (San Joaquin) with its curvy shoreline and a few small islands. We were told there would be more power boats on the east side. So, we took a low bridge route that presented a problem for power boats.

* * * * * * * * * * * * * *

BENECIA REGATTA

CARQUINEZ BRIDGE

PHOTO BY PAT DUCLOS

CACHE SLOUGH

RYER ISLAND (FREE) FERRY

PHOTO BY PAT DUCLOS

WEST DELTA

Hill Slough and Grizzly Island near Suisun

SEASON: All year. **BEST TIDE:** High 5'-5.5' at Suisun City Marina or Joyce Island, Suisun Slough. (Be sure and check tide levels as well as tide times.)

ACCESS: Put-in • East 1 mile of Suisun on SR-12, S. on the Grizzly Is. Road, 1+ miles to the 1 lane bridge. Parking. Easy access at high tide, slippery bank at low tide.

ROUTE: Paddling 'upstream," north, there are several channels to explore, one that leads to Suisun. Going "downstream," south, leads to the Grizzly Island area with several choices. One has a lunch spot under a tree.

MAPS: AAA — "Fairfield/Suisun City." "Bay & River Area." DE LORME — p. 95. "The Delta."

GAS, FOOD, and LODGING: Suisun or Fairfield.
CAMPING: Sandy Beach County Park, .5 miles So. of Rio Vista, off SR-12 via 2nd St.: 707.374.2097. Delta Marina RV Park, .25 miles So. of Rio Vista, on 2nd St. on 100 Marina Dr.: 707.374.2315.

BEWARE: Winds, low tides, and getting lost in the tulles. HUNTING SEASON!

COMMENTS: The intimate sloughs in the massive Delta area are the most interesting for small boat paddlers. Hill Slough is a prime example. The access is easy being so close to towns and highways. The route twists and turns, with side channels to explore and lush large blackberries to munch on in September. We may have seen a Northern Harrier, but it wouldn't let us see its identifying marks to know for sure. We kept looking for otter or otter slides, as we were told they are there, but we did not see any. Late spring would be an ideal time to explore further when the wildflowers are in bloom. The purple/blue seed pods looked as if they may have been the remains of blooming scabiosa, though smaller than the garden variety. There was some protection from the wind that blows often as indicated by the bent and sculptured trees. Suisun means *"the place of the west wind."* It blew us up-slough as we started and was fairly easy to paddle against on the return trip as the many turns gave us lee shores to hug. At high tide there were dirt and mud shores for launching, however there was a drop-off at lower water making it more difficult to get out of our kayaks. Civilization was nearby judging from the constant hum from US I-80 and the frequent cargo planes taking off at Travis Air Force Base.

This is very close to the Grizzly Island Wildlife Complex managed by Calif. Dept of Fish and Game. It is maintained for wildlife preservation, primarily waterfowl and elk, for managing the hunting that takes place for both at specific times of the year. There are many trails in the complex and an interpretive center as well as bicycle trails and other sloughs for paddling, though some are closed to boating. For INFO: 707.425.3828. Nearby working ranch, Rush Ranch, is open to the public with hiking trails, field trips and an interpretive center: 707.421.1351.

●●●●●●●●●●●●●●●●

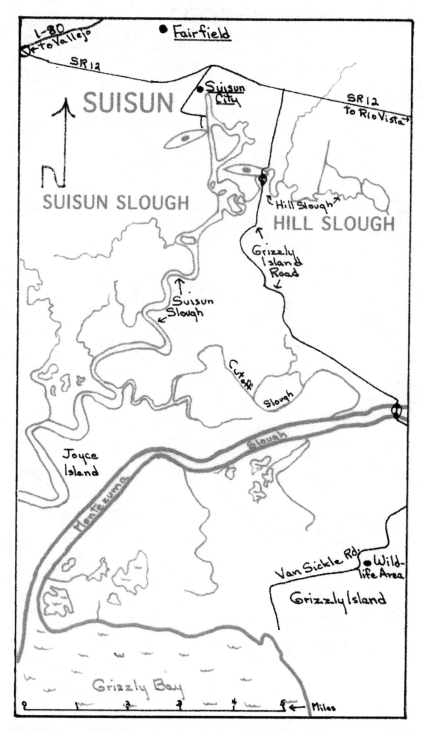

WEST DELTA
CARQUINEZ STRAIGHT

Benicia Bay & North

SEASON: All year. BEST TIDE: 3'-5'. TIDE LOCATION: Carquinez Strait & Benecia.

ACCESS: Public boat ramp at Commodore Jones Point at the end of W. 9th St. Parking & RRm. From US I-780 take the W. 7th exit, go south to W. K St. turn west to W. 9th St. Also near the end of W. K St. at Southampton Bay & Benecia State Recreation Area there is water access. Parking & RRm.

MAPS: AAA — "S. F. Bay Region" & "Vallejo, Benecia & Vicin." DELORME — p. 95.

GAS, FOOD, and LODGING: Benecia & Vallejo.
CAMPING: Skyline Wilderness Park RV & tent, 2201 Imola Ave., 3 mi. SE of Napa. T.: 707.252.0481.

BEWARE: Paddling in the Carquinez Strait can be very interesting BUT very busy. This is the only way ocean ships go to Sacramento and Stockton and where pleasure craft pass between San Francisco Bay and the Delta. The channel is especially narrow at Point Benecia, further west at Dillon Point and on east at Port of Benecia Wharf and Army Point near the Benecia-Martinez Bridge. At these narrow spots the water is squeezed, fast-moving and eddies can be strong. Know the flow of the water and the primary direction. Also be aware of the currents during the tide movements. WINDS? yes, they are a very real factor for paddlecraft as they blow through the strait. Take heed and be careful!

COMMENTS: It was a beautiful April Sunday (1997) when seven of us launched at the 9th St. boat ramp headed towards Suisun Bay. We paddled to the rhythm of the Dixieland Jazz Band playing at a waterside restaurant. Across the strait was a yacht race with color-ful spinnakers in full array. The strong currents at Benecia Wharf kept us from making our destination, but the outing was great!

BENECIA TOUR: Benecia was the first capitol of California, a visit to the historical buildings can be included in an outing. The scenic views are varied: historic government buildings, old large munitions manufacturing facilities, attractive homes on the waterway, new residential complexes, shipping facilities and some natural habitat all with rolling hills and two bridges for backdrops. Also visit some of the other historic buildings or the waterfront parks.

●●●●●●●●●●●●●●●●

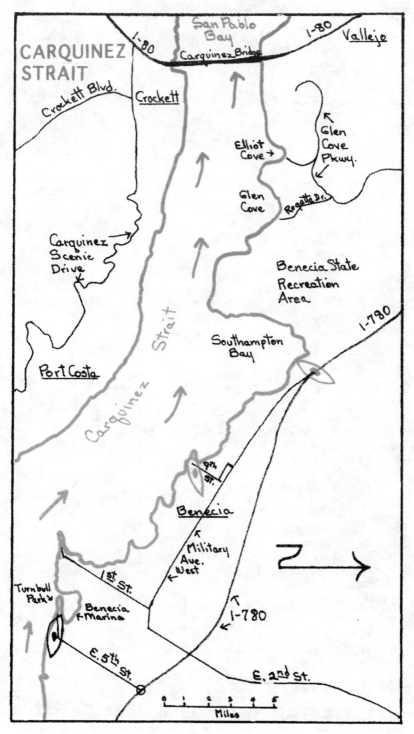

MERCED RIVER, YOSEMITE VALLEY

CHAPTER 8 - SAN JOAQUIN RIVER AREA

CONTENTS

SAN JOAQUIN RIVER AREA

Have you explored the Sierra rivers south of the American? Besides having fabulous Class III and IV, there are over 200 miles of easy paddling waters on the San Joaquin, the Merced, Tuolumne, and Stanislaus Rivers.The most popular are the Stanislaus, Merced in Yosemite, and the new parkway on the San Joaquin near Fresno. The San Joaquin River ends in The Delta (see The Delta chapter) diverting into many sloughs before flowing into the Sacramento River.

There are several river parkways, the Stanislaus and the San Joaquin, and other designated river access locations on all of the rivers. Most of the runs are Class I and I+. The Merced River west of Yosemite has some good Class II water.

STANISLAUS RIVER
Knights Ferry to Caswell Memorial State Park and into the San Joaquin River to Durham Ferry SRA

TUOLUMNE RIVER
La Grange to Shiloh Fishing Access and into the San Joaquin River to Durham Ferry SRA.

MERCED RIVER
Yosemite Valley
Millers Gulch to Briceburg
Snelling to SR-59 Bridge
McConnell SRA to Hatfield SRA

SAN JOAQUIN RIVER
Millerton Lake to US-99, Fresno

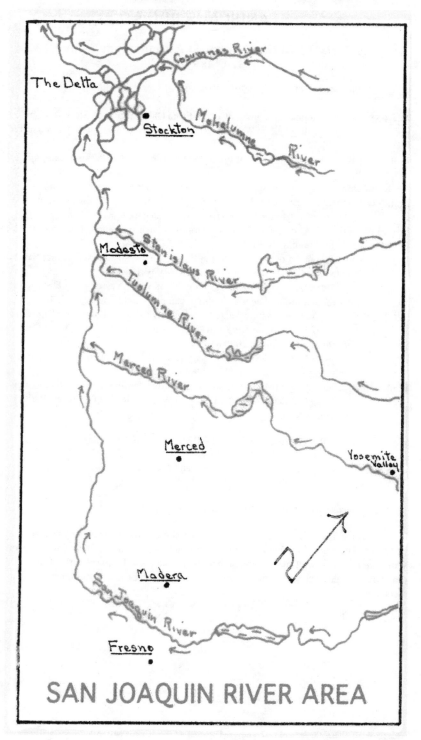

SAN JOAQUIN RIVER AREA

STANISLAUS RIVER

Knights Ferry to Durham Ferry SRA (San Joaquin River), 37 miles, Class I+ (II)

SEASON: All year. BEST FLOWS: 200 -2,500 cfs. FLOW INFO: 209.881.3517.

ACCESS: Put-in • Knights Ferry Visitor Center. From Oakdale go E on SR-120. 12 miles E. of Oakdale go N. on Williams Rd., cross the river, go right to parking area. Rrm.

4 miles to • Horseshoe Rd., river right off of Orange Blossom Rd. Parking, camping, & Rrm.

1 mile to • Honolulu Bar, river right, off of Orange Blossom Rd. Parking & Rrm.

2 miles to • Orange Blossom access area, river right. From SR-120 & SR-108 turn north on Orange Blossom Rd., cross river, go left to parking area. Rrm.

2 miles to • Valley Oak, river right. downstream of Orange Blossom off of Rodden Rd. Parking, camping, & Rrm.

2 miles to • Oakdale. Take out on river left at the bridge. Small shopping center SW of bridge on Oakdale/Waterford Hwy. (CR-J9). Parking.

14 miles to • McHenry Ave. access on river right. N. of McHenry bridge go E. on River road about 2 miles to access. Parking, camping, and Rrm.

(NOTE: the above river information relates to the Army Corps of Engineers, *Stanislaus River Parks Recreation Guide,* available at the Knights Ferry Visitor Center. For info & reservations: 209.881.3517.)

12 miles to • Caswell Memorial State Park, river right. Go E on Ripon Rd, S on Austin. Camping, parking, & Rrm.: 209.599.3810.

12 miles to • Durham Ferry SRA, river right, (4 miles from confluence on the San Joaquin River) 209.953.8800. On CR-J3, Airport Way 6 miles S. of Manteca. Parking, camping, & Rrm.

MAPS: AAA — "Bay & Mountain." DE LORME — pp. 107 & 108.

GAS, FOOD, and LODGING: Tracy, Manteca, and Modesto.
CAMPING: (see above).

BEWARE: Snags, winds, and fellow river users.

COMMENTS: This is a very attractive river with some cliffs, wooded banks and a clear waterway. There are some homes along the way and a few cattle further down stream. With camping areas well spaced along the route, this can be a 4-day river trip. The 4 mile run above Knights Ferry, Goodwin Canyon, is a whitewater Class V run for expert paddlers only.

● ● ● ● ● ● ● ● ● ● ● ● ● ● ●

[handwritten notes: Pretty + moves fast + pretty. Did this Trip in 2004 went from Knights Ferry to Oakdale 1st Day all Day Trip It and I I a lot went from Knights Ferry to Orange Blossom 2nd Day 1/2 Day Trip]

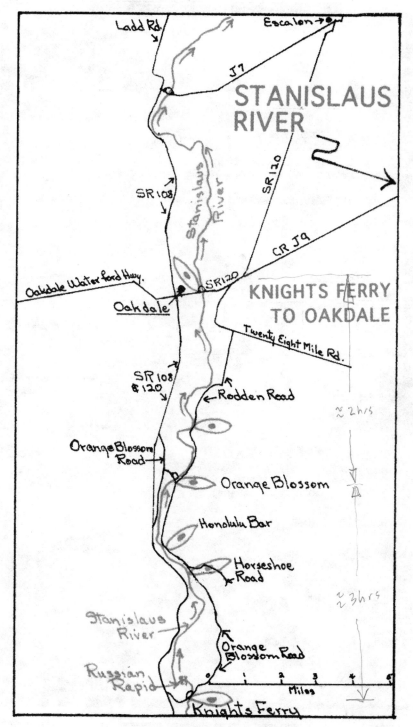

TUOLUMNE & SAN JOAQUIN RIVERS

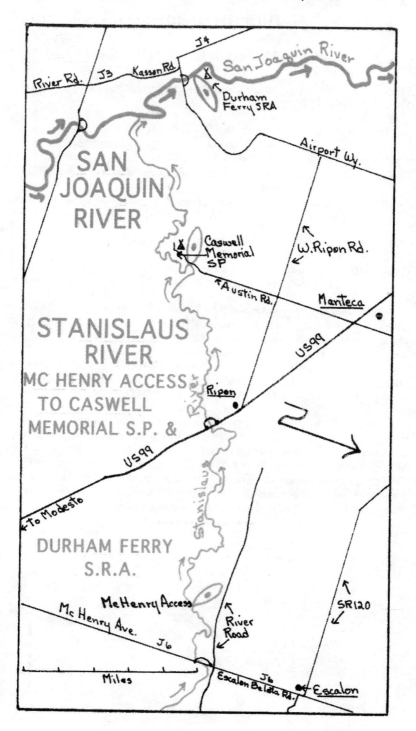

TUOLUMNE RIVER

La Grange to Waterford, 23 miles, Class I

SEASON: Nov.-April. Best Flows: 200-800 cfs. Flow info: Turlock Irrigation Dist.: 209.632.3861 or La Grange: 209.853.2212.

ACCESS: Put-in • S. side of river at old bridge in La Grange via SR-132. Or 100 yards down river from dam-keepers quarters. Or N. side of new bridge.
3 miles to • bridge at Basso Park, 3 miles W. of La Grange. Parking & Rrm.
7 miles to • Turlock Lake SRA Cpgr. (#13 campsite nearest to boat ramp) via SR-132 & Lake Road. Parking & Rrm.
13 miles to • Big Bear Park, Waterpark, & Campground .5 mile E. of Waterford via SR-132. Parking & Rrm.

MAPS: AAA — "Bay & Mountain." DE LORME — p. 108.

GAS, FOOD, and LODGING: Waterford and Modesto (larger).
CAMPING: Big Bear Park, Waterpark, and Campground. Camping Res.:209.874.4000.

BEWARE: From La Grange to Turlock Lake SRA the river goes through brush—mostly willows and blackberries. There are several "S" turns to be aware of, one a double "S" turn at 5.7 miles. The left channel is the one of choice, but it cannot be scouted. This is the same for another similar route further down river.
From Turlock Lake to Waterford, there are three good drops, the third at Roberts Ferry bridge. At mile 9.5 the Hickman Flume enters the river and could double the flow; be wary. The Turlock Irrigation District operates the flume: 209.632.3861.

COMMENTS: These are interesting runs to see the migrating salmon in action in the late fall or to marvel at the many hues of the blooming wild flowers in early spring. The water flows from the nearby New Don Pedro Res. that releases it clear and cold. Turlock Lake SRA is between the Tuolumne River and the lake with the campground on the river side. The river and grasslands attract a variety of water and shore wildlife. Piles of rock are left from the gold-mining operation of the La Grange Dredging Company. They operated there from 1905 to 1952, digging holes 30 feet deep in search of gold.

•••••••••••••••

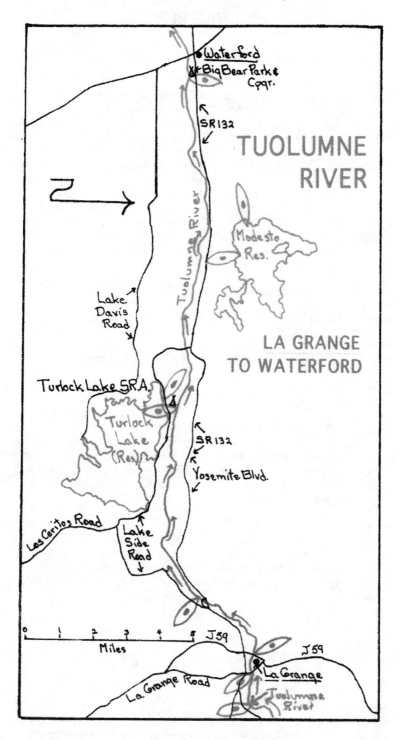

TUOLUMNE RIVER

LA GRANGE TO WATERFORD

TUOLUMNE RIVER (con't)

Waterford to Shiloh Fishing Access, 30 miles, Class I

SEASON: Rainy & spring. BEST FLOWS: 200-1500 cfs. FLOW INFO: CA Dept. of Water Res. Cal Data Exchange: http://sdes.water.ca.gov Dream Flows: www.dreamflows.com/flows.html USGS: http://water.wr.usgs.gov.

ACCESS: Put-in • Waterford via SR-132, N. of Waterford on SR-132 at Big Bear Park. Parking & Rrm.
7 miles to • Fox Grove Fishing Access (ramp), via SR-132 S. on Geer Rd. 1.5 miles. Parking.
6 miles to • Santa Fe Railroad Bridge via SR-132 to Empire, S. on Santa Fe 1 mile.
2 miles to • Big Bear Park, Waterford, .5 miles E. of CR-J9 on SR-132.
4 miles to • Legion Park, Modesto, SR-132 S. Santa Cruz 1 mile. Parking & Rrm.
11 miles to • Shiloh Fishing Access, SR-132 S. on Hart or Gates to Paradise. Shiloh is S. of Paradise between Hart & Gates and crosses the river near the access. Parking.

MAPS: AAA — "Bay & Mountain." DE LORME — pp. 107 & 108.

GAS, FOOD, and LODGING: Modesto.
CAMPING: Turlock Lake SRA, 11 miles E. of Waterford via SR-132: 209.874.2008. Durham Ferry SRA, E. of Modesto via SR-132 W., then N. on W. side of San Joaquin R., N. via CR-J3: 209.953.8800. Big Bear Park & Cpgr.: 209.874.1984.

BEWARE: Mitchell Flume about 2 miles below Santa Fe RR Bridge could increase the flow. Power boats below Fox Grove.

COMMENTS: Looking for Class I water? Here's 30 miles on the Tuolumne River as it flows across the Central Valley from the Sierra to the San Joaquin River. There are riparian woodlands, a few homes, a bridge or two, but mostly just pleasant paddling. Part of this could be a moonlight paddle, or in the hot days of summer, perfect for a swimming break. The Tuolumne River Preservation Trust has been formed to help in restoring the salmon runs and preserve the river environment.

HISTORY: One of John Fremont's camps was near the Santa Fe RR bridge which was also the site of Empire City, which was served by paddle wheelers until about 1870. Imagine traveling by a paddlewheel boat from San Francisco through the San Pablo Bay and Carquinez Straits to the San Joaquin River, then flowing through the southeast delta, south to the Tuolumne River, then up the Tuolumne to Empire City! The search for gold is a fabulous lure.

●●●●●●●●●●●●●●●

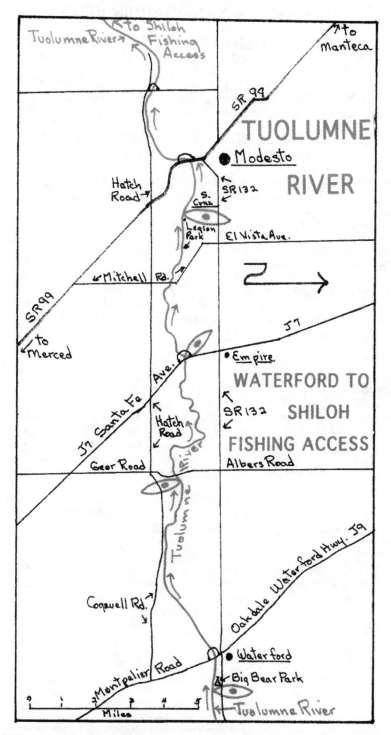

TUOLUMNE & SAN JOAQUIN RIVERS

Shiloh Fishing Access(T) to Durham Ferry SRA (SJ), 20 miles, Class I

SEASON: Rainy or snow melt. BEST FLOWS: 500-2000 cfs. FLOW INFO: CA Dept. of Water Res. Cal Data Exchange: http://sdes.water.ca.gov DreamFlows: www.dreamflows.com/flows.html USGS: http://water.wr.usgs.gov

ACCESS: Put-in • Shiloh Fishing Access. From SR-132, 7 miles west of Modesto, go south on Paradise, south on Shiloh, cross the Tuolumne River and immediately turn left.

20 miles to • Durham Ferry S.R.A., reached via SR-132 by going north 3 miles on Kasson Rd., right on Airport Way, cross river, turn left in about 1 mi.

MAPS: AAA — "Bay & Mountain Section." DELORME — p. 107.

GAS, FOOD, and LODGING: Modesto, 8 miles.
CAMPING: Durham Ferry SRA: 209.953.8800.

BEWARE: Snags in or on the side of the rivers. Be careful going in the left channel after the horseshoe bend and just before SR-132 bridge; it can be shallow and windy and "the long way around" but it does go back to the river. Stay right. At high water there were a few swirling eddies and very few beaches.

COMMENTS: What a delightful day paddling the end of the Tuolumne and fifteen miles of the fast moving San Joaquin. This was all possible because of the very high rainfall year thanks to El Nino which filled the reservoirs and created the releases. Everything was green, the mosquitos were absent, and the sky was in puffy clouds against the blue background and the sun. Perfect! The three of us did 20 miles in four and a half hours including paddling against some strong upriver winds. We labored against both wind and 18 inch waves in the large shallow "lake" before going under the SR-132 bridge. Much of the time we had a good current, which kept us flowing at a fast pace—faster than a person could walk. We all agreed it was a very pleasant way to spend a day in May (5-8-98).

FLORA & FAUNA: The 50 foot tall riverbank trees of willow, cottonwood, and oak provided a wonderful wilderness feeling. There were a few water-oriented birds—mallards, cormorant, great egrets, great blue herons mixed with swallows, magpies, California jays, blackbirds, and several species of LBBs (little brown birds).

SCENERY: With high water and low, or no, levees, the scenery was tall riverbank trees, some fields and pastures, coast range, and a few beaches giving a remote wilderness feeling except for an occasional building.

•••••••••••••••

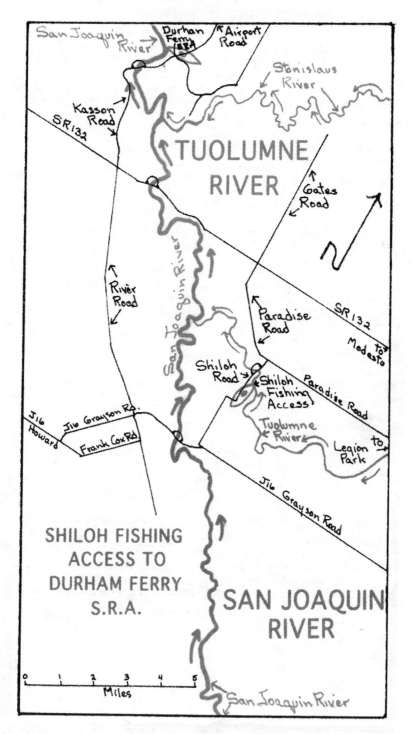

SHILOH FISHING
ACCESS TO
DURHAM FERRY
S.R.A.

SAN JOAQUIN
RIVER

MERCED RIVER

Yosemite National Park, Yosemite Valley
Bridge at Curry Village to Cathedral Br., 4.5 miles, Cl. I

SEASON: Spring & early summer. BEST FLOWS: 200-500 cfs. FLOW INFO: 209.372.0200. CA Dept. of Water Res. Cal Data Exchange: http://sdes.water.ca.gov Dream Flows: www.dreamflows.com/flows.html

ACCESS: Put-in • Below the stables bridge, limited parking.
1 mile to • Curry Village bridge.
4.5 miles to • Bridge at Cathedral beach. Parking & Rrm.

MAPS: AAA — "Yosemite." "Bay & Mountain." DE LORME — p. 110.

GAS, FOOD, and LODGING: Yosemite NP, Oakhurst, and Mariposa.
CAMPING: Yosemite NP

BEWARE: Snags and water level. A week of hot weather with a heavy snow-pack can fill the river so there isn't room under the bridges for paddler's heads! Also heavy rains in the High Sierra in summer can cause a deluge in the valley.

COMMENTS: This is a river run to "die for" when it comes to scenery, beauty, clarity of water, white sand beaches, and wild life. The flow is a Class I, but there are still riffles and log jams. Bring a camera! Photos, with backgrounds like Half Dome, Yosemite Falls, or El Capitan just don't happen very often. The run itself is a winding flow over a white sand bottom, through the pine, oak, and cedar forests—possibly with some dog wood in bloom. The water is clear and cold. We know the glacier-sculptured granite creating Yosemite Valley is one of the most beautiful valleys in the world. Seeing it from a canoe or kayak adds to its charm, especially on a warm summer day "away from it all."

HISTORY: In the '60's, the Merced River in Yosemite Valley was closed to paddlecraft. I wrote to the Superintendent of Yosemite NP requesting the river be opened. A phone call from John Goode, Ass't. Superintendent, a canoe paddler, resulted in six of us running the river from the Stables Bridge to El Capitan Bridge. I brought along Gerry Reichard, a photographer, and we each added a teenaged daughter; the Head Park Ranger, Jack Morehead, a Grand Canyon rafter, paddled with John. This beautiful day of seeing the famous rocks from a different angle resulted in opening the river and to the introduction of river clean-ups by the Quentin Canoers, the teenage section of the Marin Canoe Club. The clean-ups were a great way to spend a few days in Yosemite, compliments of the park, and do a public service at the same time. The natural pool below Cathedral Bridge yielded a big pile of water-logged, sand-filled, terry-cloth towels and a few shoes.

●●●●●●●●●●●●●●●

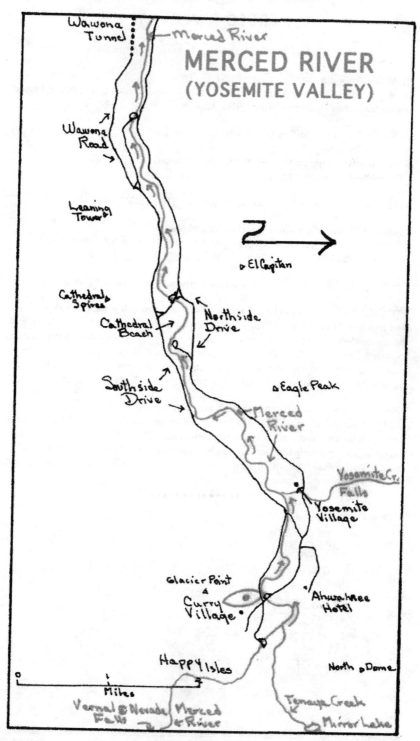

MERCED RIVER
(YOSEMITE VALLEY)

MERCED RIVER (con't)

Millers Gulch to Briceburg, 6 miles, Class II+ - III-

SEASON: Spring & early summer. BEST FLOWS: 500-1,500 cfs. FLOW INFO: CA
Dept. of Water Res. Cal Data Exchange: http://sdes.water.ca.gov Dream Flows:
www.dreamflows.com/flows.html USGS: http://water.wr.usgs.gov

ACCESS: Put-in • At Millers Gulch downriver from Ned's Gulch, 6 miles upriver from
        Briceburg.
6 miles to • Briceburg on SR-140, 8 miles from Mariposa. via SR-140.
NOTE: There are several access locations along the highway.

MAPS: AAA — "Yosemite." "Bay & Mountain." DE LORME — p. 110.

GAS, FOOD, and LODGING: Yosemite NP and Mariposa.
CAMPING: Downriver from Briceburg, on dirt road. Yosemite NP: 209.372.0200.
Indian Flat, SR-140 between El Portal & Briceburg. FS: 209.297.0706

BEWARE: The water level is critical on this very rocky run. Watch for snags and brush.

COMMENTS: This is a fun busy 6 mile Class II+ run just below the Class IV run from
Red Bud near El Portal. SR-140 to Yosemite is parallel to the river, just a few feet above
the water. Most of the run is in view of the highway which also provides alternate access
locations. The water is fairly fast and the rapids frequent. With the popularity of Yosemite,
it might be wise to do this run mid-week, or better yet, in the spring when the wildflowers
are coloring the hillsides and the side streams are gushing down the gulches.

The Merced River travels from the High Sierra through Yosemite into Lakes McClure
and McSwain. It then crosses the San Joaquin Valley into the San Joaquin River. There is
a commercial whitewater run between Briceburg and Bagby before the river is calmed at
Lake McClure. A hiking trail parallels the whitewater run for those who wish to check it
out or have the vicarious thrill of what it would be like to run it in a raft or kayak with the
necessary skills and equipment.

• • • • • • • • • • • • • • • •

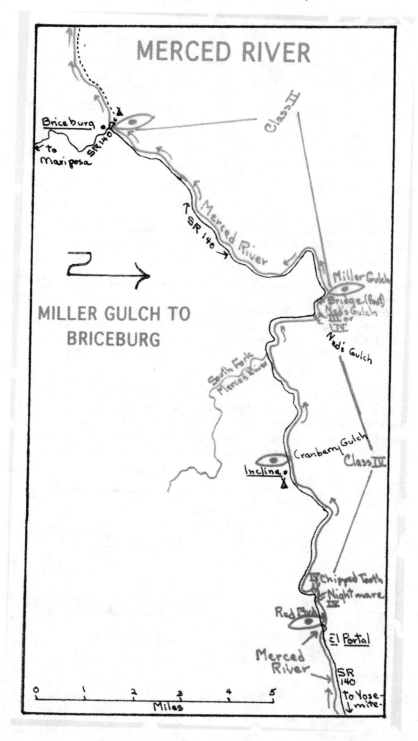

MERCED RIVER

MILLER GULCH TO
BRICEBURG

Briceburg

to
Mariposa

SR 140

SR 140

Merced River

Class II

Miller Gulch

Bridge (foot)
Ned's Gulch
III or
IV

Ned's Gulch

South Fork
Merced River

Cranberry Gulch

Incline

Class IV

IV Chipped Tooth
IV
Nightmare
IV

Red Bud

El Portal

Merced
River

SR
140

to Yose-
mite

0   1   2   3   4   5
Miles

MERCED RIVER (con't)
Snelling to SR-59, 12 miles, Class II

SEASON: Spring & Fall. BEST FLOW: 600-800 cfs. FLOW INFO: Modesto Bee. CA
Dept. of Water Res. Cal Data Exchange: http://sdes.water.ca.gov Dream Flows:
www.dreamflows.com/flows.html USGS: http://water.wr.usgs.gov

ACCESS: Put-in • 3 miles E. of Snelling, (CR-J17 & SR-59 E. of Turlock) on CR-J16,
        road to Merced Falls Co. Park a short ways after river and road are together.
        Difficult put-in to find. Park on side road.
12 miles to • SR-59 bridge, 7 miles SE of Snelling.

MAPS: AAA — "Bay & Mountain Section." DE LORME — pp. 108, 109, & 118.

GAS, FOOD, and LODGING: Merced and Turlock.
CAMPING: McConnell SRA, Livingston. 5 mi. SE of Delhi of SR-99 via El Capitan
Way: 209.394.7755. Lake McSwain Rec. Area, 2 mi. E. of Merced Falls off CR-J16:
800.468.8889.

BEWARE: "Should be Class II due to brushy conditions making rescue difficult."

COMMENTS: "Not heavily used. Not many beaches but you can find a place for lunch,
etc. Type of flow 10/10/82 was moderate at 1200 cfs, with a few fast chutes. Run becomes
more challenging (fun) at lower water. Drops on what appear to be summer dams. A few
rapids where lack of control could put the unsuspecting into the bush (a challenge). They
could be tricky or hazardous."

(NOTE: The information and quotes are from Bill Hitchings report Oct. 10, 1982.
Bill chatted with me each year at the S.F. Sport and Boat Show as I was exhibiting my
paddlesport products. He always asked when my guide book to California easy waters
would be finished. Bill passed away this past year leaving a void in our local paddling
community. We lost a great paddler and paddlesport promoter. My efforts to complete this
book were not quite soon enough.)

• • • • • • • • • • • • • • • •

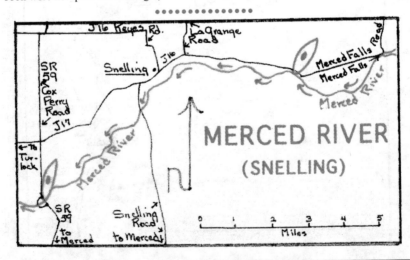

LOON LAKE

LOON LAKE TUNNEL EXPLORING

MERCED RIVER LOG JAM

MERCED RIVER (con't)

McConnell SRA to Hageman Co. Pk. to Hatfield SRA, 19 miles, Class I+

SEASON: All year. BEST FLOWS: 250-1,000 cfs. FLOW INFO: Modesto Bee.

ACCESS: Put-in • McConnell SRA. From Delhi on US-99 take Schendel exit, go E. to Vincent, S. to El Capitan Way, E. 3.5 miles, S. on Pepper St. to park. From Livingston, go NW on Cressy Rd. 4 miles, N. 3 miles on Santa Fe Dr., W. on Bradbury Rd., S. on Ballico Ave., W. on El Capitan Way, S. on Pepper St. to park. Campground, parking, & Rrm.

11 miles to • Hageman County Park, river left. From Livingston, go W. on Westside Road (River Rd.) to the Lander Rd. bridge. The park is large and may not be well marked. Parking & Rrm.

8 miles to • Hatfield SRA., river right near CR-J18 (from US I-5), Kelly Rd., via Turner Rd. from Central Ave. 8.5 miles S. of Ceres & US 99 and River Road/Westside Road, N. on Lincoln Blvd. to Livingston. Cpgr. & Rrm.

(NOTE: Upriver from McConnell is a put-in near Cressey at the Santa Fe RR Bridge extending the run about 3 miles.)

MAPS: AAA — "Yosemite." "Bay & Mountain." DE LORME — pp. 117 & 118.

GAS, FOOD, and LODGING: Turlock & Livingston; Mexican restaurants, a specialty.
CAMPING: Hatfield SRA: 209.632.1852. McConnell SRA: 209.394.7755.
Fisherman's River Bend Campground, (San Joaquin River) Newman: 209.862.3731.

BEWARE: High water, snags, and log jams in the river.

COMMENTS: The put-in at McConnell SRA requires a short walk but has shade trees to keep parked cars cool. During the agricultural growing season there is a good supply of water in the river that makes for a comfortable flow. It even suggests just "going with the flow," though some paddling would be a good idea on the lower stretches when the river slows a bit. The first few miles are through agricultural land followed by cattle country. The water, which is cold and brown, and the air, reflect the change. The flock of ducks that kept darting off their roosts then on down river were acting like wood ducks. They could have been those gorgeous creatures. Heron, kingfishers, and magpies were also sighted. Beavers had been chewing at some of the trees. A park-like setting was created by the large sycamore and oak trees growing along the river banks. It was especially pleasant to be under the canopy as the day was very hot. There were few beaches. Grey high water marks were on many of the large trees. The flowing water was very smooth with the highest wave about 6 inches. The takeout at Hagemen Co. Park was very easy, although the park is heavily used on weekends. (Date run: 8/30/98.)

NOTE: McConnell to Hatfield is a very long day-run, so take-out or put-in at Hageman County Park, but camp at McConnell or Hatfield.
NOTE: Going downstream an additional 3 miles from Hatfield SRA into the San Joaquin River brings you to a take-out at Fisherman's River Bend Campground.

●●●●●●●●●●●●●●●

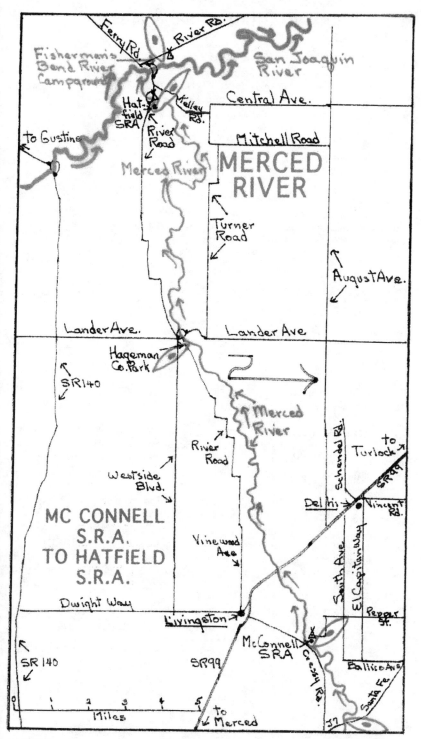

SAN JOAQUIN RIVER — Fresno

Lost Lake to Camp Pashayan, 20 miles, Class I+

SEASON: All year. BEST FLOWS: 200-1,500 cfs. FLOW INFO: Fresno Bee. CA Dept. of WaterRes. Cal Data Exchange: http://sdes.water.ca.gov Dream Flows: www.dreamflows.com/flows.html USGS: http://water.wr.usgs.gov

ACCESS: Put-in • Lost Lake Recreation Area. Campground, parking & Rrm. North of Fresno via SR-41 and Friant Road.
8 miles to • Fresno County Sportsman's Club: 559.434.7618. N. of Fresno N. side of the SJ River via SR-41. Day use fee. Parking & Rrm.
1 mile to • Fort Washington Beach, N. side of river via SR-41.
2 miles to • Sycamore Island, day use and camping: 559.439.9238. Pk. & Rrm.
9 miles to • Camp Pashayan just upriver from SR-99 bridge at end of N. Weber Ave. via W. Herndon. Parking, Rrm, and kayak rentals: 559.248.8480.
NOTE: There are about 40 miles of San Joaquin River to the Mendota Pool at the confluence of the Fresno River, 2 miles N. of Mendota on Bass Road.

MAPS: AAA — "Bay & Mtn. Section." DE LORME — "So. & Central CA," pp. 22 & 23.

GAS, FOOD, and LODGING: Fresno.
CAMPING: Sycamore Island (see above). Lost Lake Rec. Area. Millerton Lake SRA: 559.822.2332.

BEWARE: Snags in the river and brushy banks. Dead-end channels left from gravel mining operations. Stay on the river away from private property.

COMMENTS: With a constant summer and year-round flow, the San Joaquin is an ideal river of easy waters for canoes and kayaks. The San Joaquin River Parkway and Conservation Trust (559.249.8480) is doing a commendable job at preserving and encouraging the use of the river parkway for the 20 miles below Friant Dam to SR-99 just north of Fresno. It is not unlike the American River Parkway in Sacramento. They are incorporating the existing park areas, both public and private, and adding more. A three-event race, similar to the Eppies Race that draws hundreds of entrants on the American River every year, is now an annual event on the San Joaquin River. The San Joaquin Parkway is also exploring the 40 miles of river on down to Mendota, location of the Mendota Pool at the confluence with the Fresno River. This is where the river turns north, draining the Southern Central Valley. It ends in the Delta where it joins the Sacramento River as it flows into San Francisco Bay.

CANOE TRIPS: The River Parkway Trust has a full schedule of canoe trips, the Upper Reach, the Lower Reach, and After-work 3-hour trips: 559.248.8480.

●●●●●●●●●●●●●●●

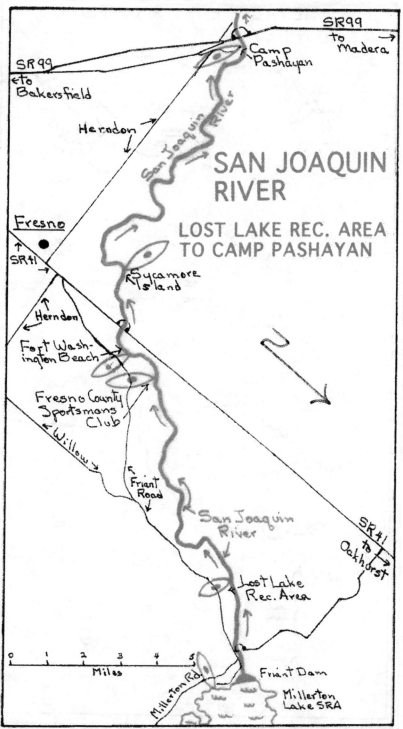

SR99
to Madera →

SR99
←to
Bakersfield

Camp
Pashayan

Herndon →

San Joaquin River

SAN JOAQUIN RIVER

LOST LAKE REC. AREA TO CAMP PASHAYAN

Fresno

↑
SR41

↑
Herndon

Sycamore
Island

Fort Wash-
ington Beach

Fresno County
Sportsmans
Club

Willow

Friant
Road

San Joaquin
River

SR41
to
Oakhurst →

Lost Lake
Rec. Area

0 1 2 3 4 5
Miles

Millerton Rd.

Friant Dam

Millerton
Lake SRA

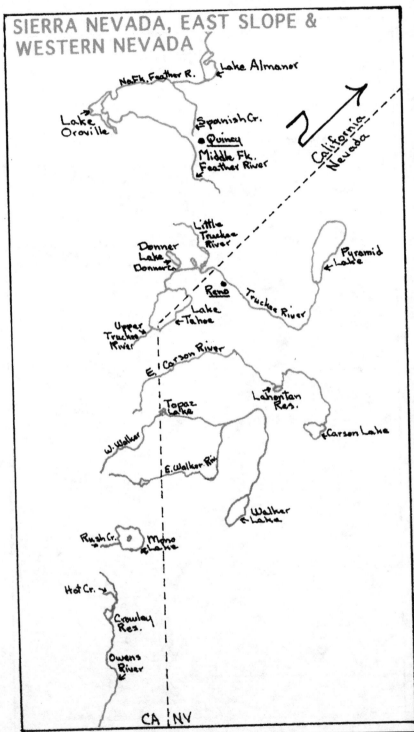

SIERRA NEVADA, EAST SLOPE &
WESTERN NEVADA

Lake Almanor

No.Fk. Feather R.

Lake Oroville

Spanish Cr.

● Quincy

Middle Fk. Feather River

California
Nevada

Little Truckee River

Donner Lake

Donner

Pyramid Lake

Reno ●

Truckee River

Upper Truckee River

Lake Tahoe

E. Carson River

Topaz Lake

Lahontan Res.

Carson Lake

W. Walker

E. Walker Riv.

Walker Lake

Rush Cr.

Mono Lake

Hot Cr.

Crowley Res.

Owens River

CA | NV

CHAPTER 9 - SIERRA NEVADA, EAST SLOPE, AND WESTERN NEVADA

CONTENTS

Note: Some of the runs in this chapter may be more difficult than indicated.

SIERRA/EAST SLOPE & WESTERN NEVADA

California's spine, the Sierra Nevada mountain range is the source of much of California's water. The rains, snow, and a few glaciers water the rich Central Valley from the west flowing rivers. The East Slope, in the rain shadow, receives less precipitation, hence a semi-arid region. Lakes abound in the mountain crevices of the eastern Sierra; Lake Tahoe is the largest and most famous. The rivers, winding their way down the steep slopes, end in lakes. The Truckee River ends in Pyramid Lake, the Carson River drains into Carson Lake, the Walker River enters Walker Lake, the Owens River fills Owens Lake, and Rush Creek is one of the tributaries of Mono Lake. The river systems also fill a few reservoirs enroute. Since half of these lakes are in western Nevada, the coverage of the rivers will be by water course not by stateline. The exception is the Feather River—the middle fork originates near the Nevada border and adds the north fork as it flows through the gap between the Sierra and the Cascades to be impounded in Lake Oroville. These forks will be considered East Slope waterways. Coverage on the East Slope will be from north to south.

It is difficult to find a reliable source of water-flow information on the North Fork of the Feather River and tributaries. PG&E impounds the water (Lake Almanor and other nearby reservoirs) to release the amount needed to generate electricity, which is too high of a flow for safe boating. Since the primary use of the water is to generate electricity, it is not economical to release lower flows just for paddlecraft. Efforts for known releases for the North Fork are in process.

Thanks to the paddling and perceptive skills of Charles Albright, a paddling competitor and promoter now living in Reno, much of the information on the East Slope runs is available due to his continued efforts. He has created a large paddling community with pool sessions weekly in two Reno pools and convinced the authorities that paddling should be allowed on the Truckee River as it flows through Reno. He is a paddling promoter in the best way.

Dr. Leon Dura, a.k.a. Dr. Death, a Class V paddler in Portola, was also very generous with his time and knowledge. The local National Forest Service Districts were very cooperative in my search for waterways, some having river-oriented specialists, as were many others.

More Information

Lassen National Forest: 530.258.2141
Plumas National Forest: 530.836.2575
NFS, Quincy: 530.283.0555
Plumas Co. Chamber of Commerce at Quincy: 530.283.6345

LINING CANOE DOWN ISLAND MT. WATERFALL, EEL RIVER

NORTH FORK of the FEATHER RIVER

Northwest of Chester to Chester, 5 miles, Class II
SEASON: Spring - early summer or high water. BEST FLOWS: 200-400 cfs.

ACCESS: Put-in • Take Warner Valley Rd. to FS-312 west of Chester that follows the
river, in about 3 miles take a dirt logging road that goes to the river, there are
several, or ask at Bowfish in Chester.
5 miles to • Chester, on 1st Ave. after the bridge turn right into the museum and library
area, continue to the river.
OR - Along the causeway. OR on to Lake Almanor.

MAPS: AAA — "No. CA Section." DE LORME — p. 59. USFS: "Lassen NF."

GAS, FOOD, and LODGING: Chester.
CAMPING: High Bridge FS Cpgr. located above dam: 530.258.2141 (Lassen NF).

BEWARE: Be sure to put-in below the diversion dam down-river from the High Bridge
Campground. The run from High Bridge Cpgr. to the dam is very rocky.
COMMENTS: While running rivers in the Feather River area, I learned of this popular
summer tubing section from the owners of Lake Almanor Resort (530.596.3337) and
Bowfish owner of Quiet Mountain Sports (530.258.2338) in Chester. I found a put-in and
a take-out, but had no time to do the run. It looked great—the clear water flowing through
pine forests past backyards into Chester. It passes through the west end of town with
several possible take outs.

Lake Almanor, el. 4,482'
This PG&E reservoir with the looks of a sierra lake has many access spots, campgrounds
and resorts as well. At the NW corner is the quaint small city of Chester. Wilson's Camp,
in Prattville on the west side of the lake, serves delicious meals, especially desserts, where
paddlers can eat on the lakeside deck.

Bucks Lake, el. 5,153'
The scenic, paved, twisting road to Bucks Lake is worth the drive. The lake is a blue gem
in its mountain with campgrounds, resorts, and a road on one side only! Afternoon winds!
Compact kayak rentals available.
MANAGING AGENCY: Plumas NF.: 530.283.0555.

Indian Creek (upper section from map), 6 miles, Class 1

SEASON: Spring. BEST FLOWS: 300-600 cfs FLOW INFO: Beckworth: 530.832.5161

ACCESS: Put-in • Flournoy bridge. N on SR 89 at Greenville "Y" 5.5 mi. , R on A22
across valley R on Genesee Rd, 5 mi. to Flournoy bridge. R turn.

MAPS: DE LORME P 60 & FS - Plumas.

COMMENTS: The run is wilderness though the road is near, through a wooded valley in
cattle country. Very rocky at low water with tricky rapids. Genesee Store is famous; "Last
chance for tofu."

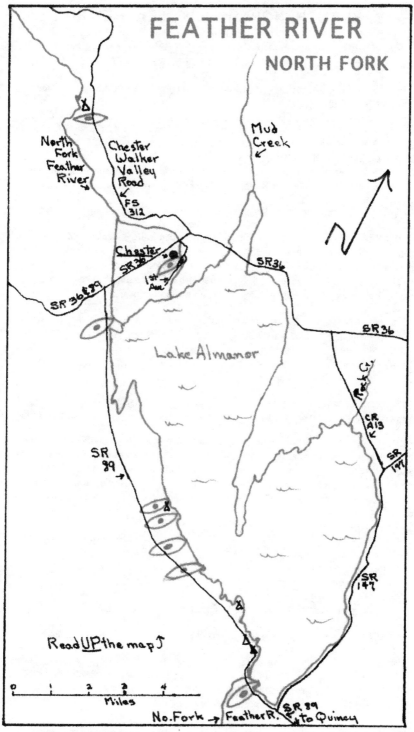

FEATHER RIVER

NORTH FORK

Mud Creek

North Fork Feather River

Chester Walker Valley Road

FS 312

Chester

SR 36

1st Av.

SR 36

SR 36 & 89

SR 36

Lake Almanor

Rock Cr.

CR A13

SR 147

SR 89

SR 147

Read UP the map ↑

0 1 2 3 4
Miles

No. Fork → Feather R.

SR 89 to Quincy

E. BRANCH/NORTH FORK, FEATHER RIVER
Spanish Creek
Quincy to Oakland Camp, 4.5 (8.5) miles, Class I

SEASON: Spring and summer, after rains. BEST FLOWS: 250-1,000 cfs.

ACCESS: Put-in • Bridge near Gansner airport north of Quincy on SR-70 & SR-89.
3 miles to • Chandler Road.
.5 miles to • .5 mile before Oakland Camp is a low water bridge..

MAPS: AAA — "No. CA Section." DE LORME — pp. 59 & 69. USFS — "Plumas NF."
GAS, FOOD, and LODGING: Quincy: 530.283.6345.
CAMPING: Deanes Valley FS Cpgr. 11 miles SW of Quincy. Spanish Creek FS Cpgr. on
SR-70 & SR-89 1 mile north of Keddie. Hallsted FS Cpgr. at Twain on SR-70.

BEWARE: Cattle country, fences (6), low water bridge at Oakland Camp crossing.

COMMENTS: Spanish Creek flows through American Valley, ideal for cattle grazing,
then into a small picturesque gorge that is part of Oakland Camp. There are fern-lined
pools in the lower part that invite swimmers on hot days.
NOTE: By putting in at the bridge to Spanish Ranch off of the Bucks Lake Rd. in Quincy,
the run can be extended about 4 miles. However this section is Class II.

●●●●●●●●●●●●●●●

Oakland Camp to Greenville "Y", 10.5 miles, Class II+-III

ACCESS: Put-in • .5 miles before Oakland Camp. Follow signs from US-70 & US-89.
7 miles to • Keddie, below the bridge.
1 mile to • Spanish Creek FS Campground. 2 miles to • Greenville Y where SR-89 goes
    north to Lake Almanor.

BEWARE: Paddlers should have low class III paddling skills. There are two waterfalls to
be portaged, downed trees and ledges. Above 1500 cfs this run is a high Class III to IV!

COMMENTS: A very scenic, semi-remote paddle trip with lots of easy Class II - III
drops. There are some very tight spots, some downed trees, and lots of rocks! There are
some tricky ledge-type drops near Oakland Camp. 3 miles downstream is a Class V drop,
portaged on river left. More Class II - III to Keddie. From Keddie is a semi-remote area
'till a 15 foot waterfall .5 mile from the Y, portage—river left is the rocky route. There is
an old dam after Keddie. Hwy. along the lower half.

●●●●●●●●●●●●●●

Greenville "Y" - Virgilia, 10.5 miles, Class II+ (III)

ACCESS: Put-in • Greenville "Y" where US-70 and US-89 split.
1.5 miles to • Paxton bridge.
4 miles to • Twain.
3.5 miles to • Hallsted Campground. Parking & RRm.
2.5 miles to • Virgilia, on US-70 above waterfall upstream from Rush Creek.

BEWARE: Take-out before the 6 foot waterfall above Rush Creek. Rocks & snags.

COMMENTS: From the put-in down about 4 miles to the hot springs on river right by
Woody's resort, is a Class III run. There is a Class III rapid about 2.5 miles down. A bit
below Paxton bridge the river turns left and flows over a rock shelf area. This is very
tough at higher flows, scout, and portage on river right.

●●●●●●●●●●●●●●●

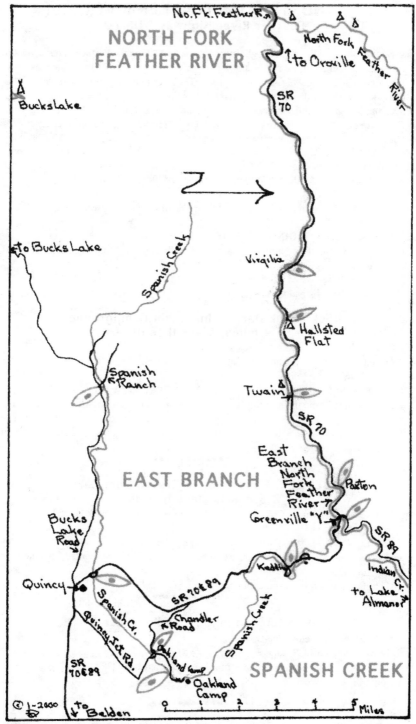

NORTH FORK FEATHER RIVER
Feather River Highway - US 70

Any car-bound paddler on this highway can't resist searching the Feather River below for easy put-ins and paddling routes along the many miles of this beautiful waterway that runs alongside the highway and railroad track. The river-running driver has divided attention—look at the road or look at the river. When the situation becomes dangerous, pull-over and just look at the rapids in the river and how best to run them. I love this highway. There are dams and lakes behind dams and rapids. Here are reports on three short runs going from east to west, downriver.

SEASON: Spring or during dam releases. BEST FLOWS: 400-1,500 cfs.
MANAGING AGENCIES: PG&E and Plumas NF.:530-283.2050.

MAPS: AAA — "Northern CA Section." DE LORME — p. 69. USFS: "Plumas NF."

GAS, FOOD, and LODGING: Quincy and Oroville.
CAMPING: Gasner Bar, North Fork, and Queen Lily NF Campgounds on Caribou Road 1.5 miles east of Belden Town and Injun Jim Campground.

BEWARE: Class III- paddlers only!

Rock Creek Dam to Injun Jim Campground, 4 miles, Class II to III

ACCESS: Put-in • .5 mile below Rock Creek Dam.
Take-out • .5 mile below Injun Jim Campground and 1 mile above Class IV and V rapids by US-70 bridge.
COMMENTS: This fun run is in clear water, beautiful scenery with lots of rocks! Most of it can be scouted from the highway. Be prepared to get out and scout when in doubt! Low water can present a few rather steep drops and high water makes it more difficult. The flow is dam-controlled and often non-existent. There are several Class III drops that should be scouted or portaged.

•••••••••••••••

Bucks Ck. Powerhse. to Cresta Dam Lake, 2.5 miles, Class II to III-

ACCESS: Put-in • Bucks Creek Powerhouse, near Bucks Lake Creek Powerhouse.
Take-out • Cresta Dam Lake.
COMMENTS: A short run with no major rapids, but many minor ones. The highway makes scouting easy, although there are some drops that should be scouted from the river before running.
NOTE: For a longer run paddle, there is more on Cresta lake.

•••••••••••••••

Poe Dam to Pulga, 1 mile, Class II

ACCESS: Put-in • below Poe Dam.
Take-out • Pulga off US-70.
COMMENTS: This is a good starter run. No major rapids. STOP at Pulga as the rapids become Class IV & V+.

•••••••••••••••

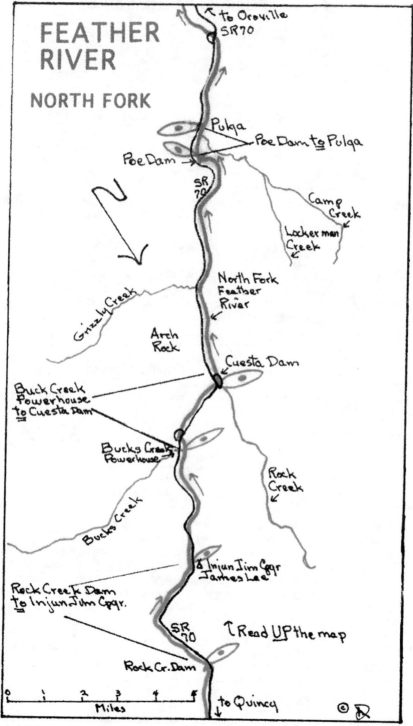

FEATHER RIVER

NORTH FORK

to Oroville
SR70

Pulga

Poe Dam to Pulga

Poe Dam

SR 70

Camp Creek

Locker man Creek

Grizzly Creek

Arch Rock

North Fork Feather River

Cuesta Dam

Buck Creek Powerhouse to Cuesta Dam

Bucks Creek Powerhouse

Rock Creek

Bucks Creek

Injun Jim Cpgr
James Lee

Rock Creek Dam to Injun Jim Cpgr.

SR 70

↑ Read UP the map

Rock Cr. Dam

0 1 2 3 4 5
Miles

to Quincy

© R

MIDDLE FORK - FEATHER RIVER

Steel Bridge to Beckwourth, 5 miles, Class I

SEASON: Spring or after a local heavy rain. BEST FLOWS: 100-400 cfs.
FLOW INFO: 530-832-5161.

ACCESS: Put-in • Steel Bridge on Dyson Lane
5 miles to • A-23 bridge .5 miles west of Beckwourth.

MAPS: AAA — "No. CA Section." DE LORME — p. 71. USFS: "Plumas NF."
530.836.2575.

GAS, FOOD, and LODGING: Portola.
CAMPING: Frenchman Lake, on Frenchman Lake Rd. 8 mi N of Chilcoot, 2 mi. east of
Vinton on SR-70. Lake Davis, 10 mi N of Portola on Lake Davis Road.

BEWARE: Cattle country. Water is brown-colored. Watch for fences and snags.

COMMENTS: Get a close look at the biggest valley in the eastern Sierra as the river
slowly winds its way through. The views are excellent on a clear day, forested Sierra to
the west and dry Nevada hills in the east. The east channel of the W. Fk. of the Feather
River originates near Frenchman Lake. Vinton is at the north end of SR-49—well known
in Sierra gold rush towns.

●●●●●●●●●●●●●●●●

Beckwourth to Portola, 9 miles, Class I & II

ACCESS: Put-in • Beckwourth, A-23 bridge 1 mile west of Beckwourth off of US-70 on
No. Beckwourth-Calpine Road. (NOTE: There are access spots from the old
highway that parallels the river closer to Beckwourth.)
5 miles to • Portola Park, east end of Portola. 1 mile more to Vet. Mem. Hall.
2 miles to • Delleker, behind Lumber yard and cement plant.
3.1 miles to • on A-15 to O'feather Rd., 1 mile dirt road to river.

BEWARE: Cattle country. Fences, trees in the river, and beaver dams.

COMMENTS: A pleasant surprise—there were several water hyacinth "rafts" floating
and in bloom. The river is away from the road, winding through pastures, past pine trees,
over beaver dams, and then near the hill parallel to the old highway. It leaves the road
again closer to Portola and twists, turns, and drops through a rocky area with a few low
Class II rapids. It drops into a pool at the park. It then flows through Portola, including the
sewage treatment plant, on down to Delleker and Mabie. TAKE OUT HERE! Paddled:7-
19-98.

●●●●●●●●●●●●●●●

BEWARE: Maybe (Mabie) to Clio (rhymes with Ohio) is **Class III & IV** and very rocky.
The river is so tame going from Vinton through Portola that it gives the impression of
continuing in a like manner; Wrong!

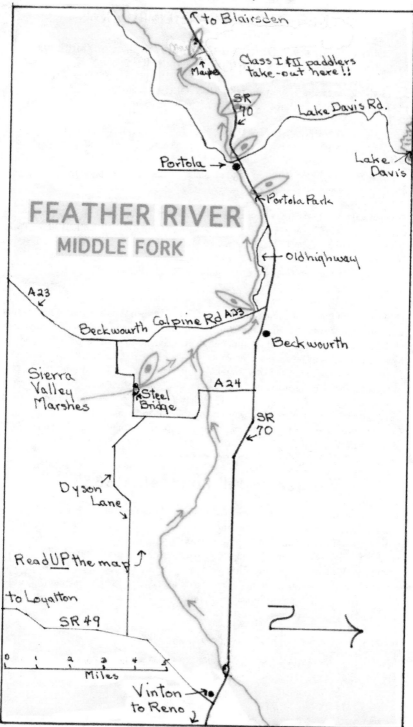

MIDDLE FORK - FEATHER RIVER (con't.)

Clio (rhymes w/ Ohio) to Graeagle/Blairsden/Mohawk, 4,5,6 miles, Class II

SEASON: Spring to early summer (rain). BEST FLOWS: 250-1,000 cfs.
FLOW INFO: Water Resources at Beckwourth: 530.832.5161.

ACCESS: Put-in • Clio & SR-89 at the bridge. Easy access and some parking.
4 miles to • Green bridge on A14 from Graeagle to south end of Blairsden. Easy
    access, parking.
1 mile to • SR-89 bridge near north end of Blairsden. Very limited parking.
1 mile to • Mohawk bridge, CR-A14.

GAS, FOOD, and LODGING: Graeagle and Blairsden.
CAMPING: Lakes Basin NF, 8 mi. S. of Graeagle on Gold Lake Rd. Little Bear RV Park,
1 mi. NW of Blairsden off SR-70 and SR-89 at 102: 530.836.2774.

BEWARE: Air-born golf balls near the golf courses. Snags and trees in the river. "Tubers."

COMMENTS: Late spring rains or heavy summer rains keep this river flowing during the warm weather days. The run from Clio is short but with a variety of fairly easy river challenges to keep paddlers alert, although there are some slow stretches. A rocky shelf, rocks to dodge, and a bit of tricky maneuvering are all a part of the fun. There are several streams that enter the flow, mostly from river left, flowing across the meadow, or cascading down from the east side of the Sierra. Green Bridge is the first access bridge. Take-out on river left below the bridge. The SR-89 bridge is not as easy a take-out; there is a short carry to cars parked along the highway. On to Mohawk bridge there are a few tricky spots. Going from bridge to bridge is a great beginning for river running. Higher water would make for an easier paddle, fewer rocks but bigger waves. Date paddled: 7/98.

•••••••••••••••

Graeagle Mill Pond, el. 4,385'

The pond allows only swimmers and paddlecraft. The water warms, making it ideal for new swimmers, yet with lots of room for distance swimming and paddlecraft. Graeagle is charming—a former company logging town with the remaining company houses still painted red with white trim. Golfing, gold panning, fishing, or mountain biking are all enjoyed in this mountain setting, but especially river running. Take time to visit Plumas-Eureka State Park up the mountain near Johnsville and the museum plus remnants of the recently working gold mine. In nearby Portola, visit the Western Pacific Railroad museum and have a train ride.

RENTALS: Compact kayaks at Graeagle Outpost: 530.863.2414.

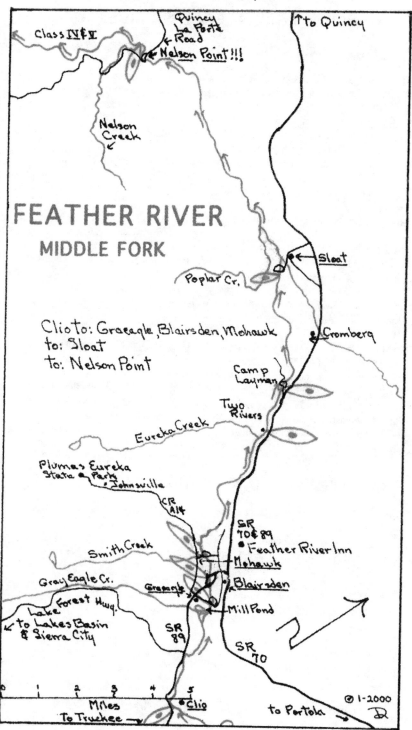

MIDDLE FORK — FEATHER RIVER (con't)

Mohawk to Sloat, 9.5 miles, Class II, II+ (III)

SEASON: Spring & wet summer. BEST FLOWS: 250-1,000 cfs.
FLOW INFO: Water Resources in Beckwourth: 530.832.5161.

ACCESS: Put-in • SR -14, Mohawk - Johnsville Rd. bridge Graeagle.
4 miles to • Two Rivers Camp is off of US-70 & US-89 (now a soccer camp across
the river, foot bridge only) right at the river.
1.5 miles to • Camp Layman Rd. The camp is across the bridge and up the hill.
1.5 miles to • Cromberg.
2.5 miles to • Sloat bridge. Drive into Sloat, follow logging road to the bridge.

MAPS: AAA — "No. CA Section". DE LORME — p. 70. USFS: "Plumas N.F.".

GAS, FOOD, and LODGING: Graeagle and Cromberg.
CAMPING: Jackson Creek near Cromberg. Red Bridge NF Cpgr. near Nelson Point. USFS
Quincy: 530.283.0555.

BEWARE: At lower water there are rock gardens, snags, and trees in the river. At higher
water the rocks are covered but the waves are larger.

COMMENTS: A great run for intermediate kayakers or inflatable kayaks. The turns may
be a bit tight for canoes. The run is fairly easy until after the lodge and golf course on river
left, then there are some rocky areas. Oneof these areas is a rock garden on the left side of
an island—the best route. At Two Rivers, entrance of Jamison Creek on the left, the long
rocky drop before the foot bridge to the camp is very challenging. Another rapid to really
watch for is just above Camp Layman   Bridge (visible) where the river drops about 12'
passing through a fairly large boulder field. Take out on river left at the next bridge at
Sloat. Date last run: 7/98. (Added info. from Dr. Leon Dura & Charles Albright.)

• • • • • • • • • • • • • • • •

Sloat to Nelson Pt. (Eng. Bar run), 8.5 miles, Class II+-III

ACCESS: Put-in • Sloat (see above).
6 miles to • Fells Flat, road from Lee Summit SR-70 & SR-89 between Sloat &
Spring Garden.
2.5 miles to • Nelson Point, where Nelson Creek enters the M. Fk. Feather from
river left. From east Quincy take N.F. 120 via Thompson Valley.

BEWARE: This run is stretching the limits of Class II. In *California Whitewater* it's a
Class III run, by Dr. Leon Dura Class II+ to III- by Charles Albright a Class III.

COMMENTS: Be prepared to scout and portage. About four miles from Sloat the river
splits GO RIGHT and keep going right for the next half mile. Be sure to have the take out
marked. Years ago I did this run in an I -K and loved it.

• • • • • • • • • • • • • • • •

Only Class V paddlers beyond Nelson Point!

MIDDLE FORK
FEATHER RIVER:
(Upper/R-L,Mid. R-L,
lower.)
DOWN A BEAVER DAM
ENROUTE TO PORTOLA
BELOW CLIO
MILL POND FUN
BELOW BLAIRSDEN

UPPER TRUCKEE RIVER

Myers Flat to Lake Tahoe, 10 miles, Class I+ (II)

SEASON: Spring & early summer. BEST FLOWS: 250-500 cfs. EL.: 6,270'

ACCESS: Put in • Elks Club Road. SW of bridge, good parking, short walk.
4.5 miles to • US-89 bridge. Heavy traffic, poor parking.
2 miles to • river left below Venice Dr. East road, parking, awkward take out.
2.5 miles to • (plus 1+ mi. by lake) Tahoe Keys boat ramp from Lake Tahoe. Not
    good if there are big waves in the lake. Parking & RRm.
2.5 miles to • river, plus 1.5 mi. by lake, to beach at So. Lake Tahoe Rec. Area.
    From SR-50 toward the lake on Sacramento Ave. to Lakeview Ave.
    Parking & RRm.
NOTE: Add another 3.5 miles to the run by putting in at the US-50 bridge across the river
W. of SR-89 where SR-89 turns S. to Luthers Pass. This upper part of the river frequently
has log jams that require quick maneuvering and/or portaging.

MAPS: AAA — "Lake Tahoe, etc." & "Bay & Mt. Section." DE LORME — pp. 89 & 90.

GAS, FOOD, and LODGING: South Lake Tahoe.
CAMPING: So. Lake Tahoe Recreation Area: 530.525.7982/583.3074.

BEWARE: Snags and log jams. Icy water if late spring or early summer run. There is an
old dam that can usually be run in the center. At the wooden foot bridge below the airport,
there is a dam to be portaged, or possibly run on river right. Waves on Lake Tahoe.

COMMENTS: The run is picturesque as the river meanders with a moderate flow through
the meadow—complete with flowers and birds, past golf courses and the local airport,
and in view of the surrounding Sierra Nevada with a possible mantel of snow. If so, the
water may be icy, so dress warmly for a cold swim in case of a capsize. If planning to take
out at the marina on Lake Tahoe, be aware of the wind from the lake which can generate
waves. These may be difficult to paddle against. Opt for an alternate take-out.

●●●●●●●●●●●●●●●

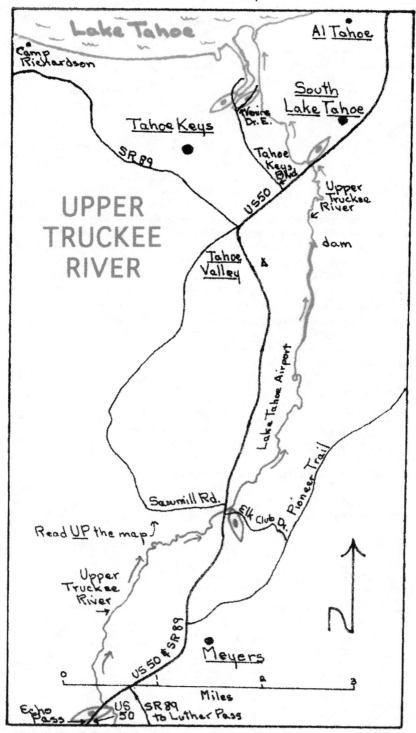

LAKE TAHOE

This Sierra Nevada gem is known and loved worldwide (maybe a little too much) with its crystal clear waters that warm enough on some shores for summer swimming. One time we were at Nevada Beach with 4 foot waves and warm water providing safe body surfing as the waves and wind pushed swimmers to shore. My kids loved it—especially in fresh water. Tahoe has so much to offer! And it is a great paddling lake providing that the wind is gentle and paddlers go around the lake and not across it!

A few years ago I "escaped" to Lake Tahoe to get away from it all. Paddling mile after mile along the shoreline of the spectacular lake brought peace to my soul and refreshed my body. I spent four and a half days paddling the 72 miles of shoreline, three by myself and two with special friends. The weather was very cooperative providing calm weather on all the days, allowing time for enjoying the varied styles of shoreline homes, some very elaborate and some showing elegance of the past interspersed with mountain lodges and campgrounds. The relative shallowness at the north end of the lake shows a rippled bottom in the crystal clear waters deepened along the cliffs before Emerald Bay. A long time wish was fulfilled as I took photos out of each of the four window openings in the roofless rock tea house on Fannette Island, that dot on the map in Emerald Bay.

Always the snow-capped Sierra, the west rim, and the desert-like mountains to the east, show the diversity of the surrounding scenery, each beautiful in its own way. The pine forests along the shore change to the large marshy area at Tahoe Keys and the smoothed boulders in the lake at Secret Harbor. As a child, in the Bay Area we thought Lake Tahoe was bottomless, as the depth had yet to be discovered. In the geology class I took, I learned the lake was caused by diastrophism, meaning the bottom just dropped down. But today we are learning that Lake Tahoe may be "loved" to death, meaning the summer and winter populations in the lake basin may be slowing destroying the clarity of the water and purity of the mountain air.

BEWARE: The wind can create five foot waves very quickly—paddle near shore and/or go to shore when the winds starts to blow. The water is very cold; 39°, so don't take a chance on an impromptu swim far from shore.

INFORMATION: There is an abundance of literature about Lake Tahoe, its statistics, how to get there, where to stay, what to do when there, and where to rent paddlecraft. Coast Guard: 530.583.4433. L. Tahoe Basin Mgnt. Unit: 530.573.2600. N. Lake C. of C.: 530.581.6900. S. Lake C.of C.: 530.541.5255.

BOAT RENTALS: Tahoe Basin F.S: 530.573.2600 also • www.tahoeinfo.com.

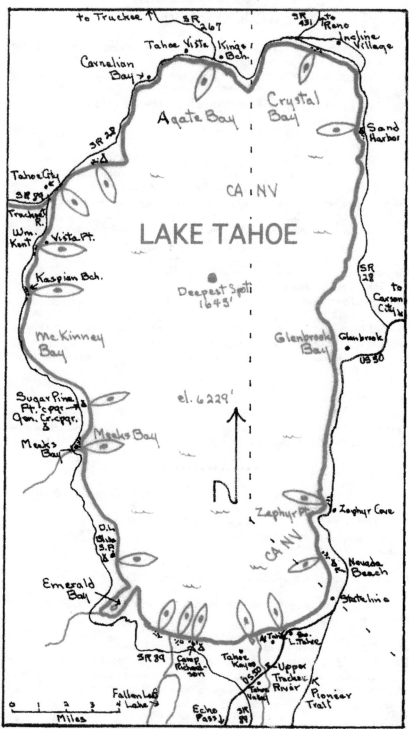

TRUCKEE RIVER

NOTE: Information for the following Truckee River runs was provided by Charles Albright and *Safe River*, from Donner Creek to Mustang.
FLOW INFO: K-Phone • 916.368.8682. Water Master • 775.784.5241.

Tahoe City to River Ranch, 4 miles, Class I+

SEASON: Summer. BEST FLOW: 200 -600 cfs.

ACCESS: Put-in • Wm. B. Layton Park at Tahoe City off US-89 after "Fanny
      Bridge" (so named by the motorist's view of the people ogling the
      enormous trout) turn north into the park. Parking & RRm.
3.75 miles to • river right just before the bend of the Class II rapid that ends in the pool
      at River Ranch.
4 miles to • River Ranch pool. This is the popular commercial inflatable raft and
      kayak rental takeout location, just at the River Ranch Restaurant.

MAPS: AAA — "Lake Tahoe." DE LORME — p. 81.
GAS, FOOD, and LODGING: Tahoe City.
CAMPING: Silver Creek Campground: 530.587.3558.

BEWARE: This is a very popular commercial inflatable rental run when there is enough water. HIGH WATER—take care! There are several bridges across the river which may not have under-bridge "ducking" room at high water for paddlers. Check all of the bridges or ask one of the commercial renters.

COMMENTS: This is Lake Tahoe water, clear and cool. If there is "safety in numbers," this run has it due to the raft rental businesses at Tahoe City. Be wary of paddlers squirting water at other boaters and just having fun. Many summer homes are on river left and busy traffic passes on SR-89 above the river on the right. Solitude? No! The shuttle buses are available for a fee.

•••••••••••••••••

River Ranch to Donner Creek, 9.5 miles, Class II+ & III-

ACCESS: Put-in • R. Ranch, entrance to Alpine Meadows off US-89. Pkg, RRm &fd.
2.5 miles to • Silver Creek Cpgr. off of US-9, Parking & RRm.: 530.587.3558
3 miles to • Goose Meadow Cpgr. off of US-89, Parking & RRm.: 530.587.3558.
3 miles to • Granite Flat Cpgr. off of US-89, Parking & RRm.: 530.587.3558.
1 miles to • Donner Ck. confluence on W. River Street off SR-89, Truckee. Pkg.

BEWARE: Log jams and overhanging trees in this very rocky fast moving route with rock and boulder gardens.

COMMENTS. This is fairly fast moving water that requires quick maneuvering. The first 2 miles below River Ranch to .5 mile below Squaw Valley are tough Class II - III. Better to put in at Silver Creek Cpgr. The flow is a bit easier after this but paddlers still have to be very alert to watch for snags and log jams in the river or across the river. US-89 runs parallel to the river. There are some riverside homes on both sides.

•••••••••••••••••

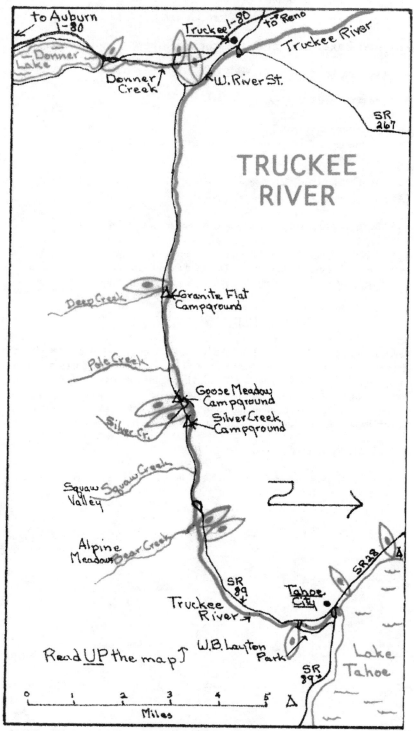

to Auburn I-80

Truckee I-80

to Reno

Truckee River

Donner Lake

Donner Creek

W. River St.

Truckee

SR 267

TRUCKEE RIVER

Granite Flat Campground

Deep Creek

Pole Creek

Goose Meadow Campground

Silver Creek Campground

Silver Cr.

Squaw Creek

Squaw Valley

Alpine Meadows

Bear Creek

SR 89

Truckee River

Tahoe City

SR 28

Read UP the map

W.B. Layton Park

SR 89

Lake Tahoe

0   1   2   3   4   5

Miles

DONNER CREEK

Donner Lake, east end, to Truckee River, 4 miles, Class II

SEASON: Late spring & early summer. BEST FLOW: 300-600 cfs.

FLOW INFO. Donner Memorial SP: 530.582.7894.

ACCESS: Put-in • the east end of Donner Lake.
4 miles to • take-out at the confluence with the Truckee River, W. River St. & SR-89.

GAS, FOOD, and LODGING: Truckee.
CAMPING: Donner Mem. SP: 530.582.7894.

BEWARE: Low water or too high a flow, snags and trees across the creek.

COMMENTS: About a four mile run that has enough water to paddle in late spring and early summer. The creek flows between Deerfield Dr. off of SR-89 south of I-80 and can be viewed in some spots. This could be another approach to running the Truckee River.

• • • • • • • • • • • • • • • •

DONNER LAKE, el. 5,935'

This is somewhat of a small version of Lake Tahoe, as it is much smaller and nestled in the pines and firs of the Sierra. The state park honors the Donner Party and their ordeal encountered in their ill-fated crossing to California during the gold rush. A stop at the visitor center and museum is worthwhile. It is a friendly lake that welcomes paddlers. There are several public access places along the north side and at both ends—some with parks. Explore the 8-mile shoreline for a relaxed day of paddling. It is open to power boats.

INFORMATION: Donner Memorial SP: 530.582.7892.

BOAT RENTALS: Donner Mem. SP: east end of the lake. Truckee Rec. Dept.: west end.

- UPPER TRUCKEE R. LAKE TAHOE:
- BY CANOE
- BY COMPACT KAYAK
- VIEW FROM TEAROOM, NANETTE IS., EMERALD BAY

TRUCKEE RIVER (con't)

NOTE: Much of the following information on the Truckee River from the town of Truckee to Tracy is from the *Safe River*, a waterproof map available at local Truckee and Reno river-oriented stores or by calling Sierra Pacific: 775.834.4827.
FLOW INFO: K-phone: 916.368.8682. Water Master: 775.784.5241. "Lake Tahoe".

Donner Creek - Glenshire Bridge, 8 miles, Class II to III-

SEASON: Spring & summer. BEST FLOW: 300-1,500 cfs.

ACCESS: Put-in • Confluence with Donner Creek at W. River St. & SR-89.
1.5 miles to • SR-267 bridge in Truckee.
4.5 miles to • Glenshire bridge.

BEWARE: Rocky drops and trees. Truckee Falls at mile 4—Class III+ at most flows, Class IV at high flows. This run may be a "stretch" for Class II+ paddlers. The run is very scenic with a lot of rock-dodging needed.

●●●●●●●●●●●●●●●●

Glenshire Bridge to Boca, 5 miles, Class II+

SEASON: Spring to late summer. BEST FLOWS: 250-600 cfs.

ACCESS: Put-in • Glenshire Bridge, east of Truckee on Glenshire Road.
5 miles to • take-out at Old Boca Bridge.

MAPS: AAA — "Bay and Mountain Section." DE LORME — p. 81. *SAFE RIVER map.*

BEWARE: There is a fly fishing club in first 1.5 miles of the run prohibiting fishing in their area. This is the east side of the Sierra and subject to summer storms. Since it is near the desert, this can mean flash floods. Be aware of local weather conditions.

COMMENTS: This is part of the Truckee River that can be seen from the freeway. It is very inviting to paddlers. The run is rocky with some downed trees. Take care. The rocks create bigger hydraulics at higher water and more maneuvering at lower water. Union Valley Creek enters from river right in about 2 miles. A mile and a half later the river flows under the I-80 with Prosser Creek entering from river left very shortly, then another I-80 crossing, and another, making it three I-80 bridges to go under. A mile respite before the Little Truckee enters from river left and the Old Boca Bridge, the take-out.

●●●●●●●●●●●●●●●●

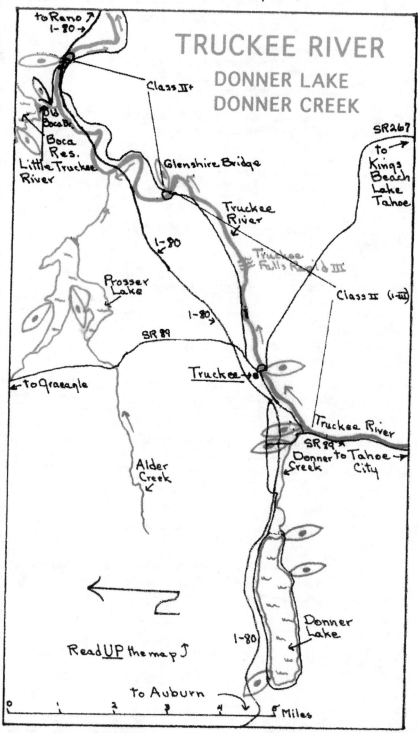

TRUCKEE RIVER
DONNER LAKE
DONNER CREEK

to Reno
I-80

Class II+

SR267
to
Kings
Beach
Lake
Tahoe

Old Boca Br.
Boca Res.
Little Truckee River

Glenshire Bridge

Truckee River

I-80

Truckee Falls Road III

Prosser Lake

Class II (I-III)

I-80

SR 89

to Graeagle

Truckee

Truckee River

SR 89
Donner to Tahoe City
Donner Creek

Alder Creek

Donner Lake

I-80

Read UP the map

To Auburn

0   1   2   3   4   5 Miles

LITTLE TRUCKEE RIVER

Perazzo Meadows, Broken Bridge to Div. Dam, 10 miles, Class I to II

SEASON: Snow melt and/or rains. BEST FLOWS: 150 - 500 cfs.

ACCESS: Put-in • Broken bridge on Henness Pass Rd. at north end of Perazzo Meadows after gorge, below Webber Lake. From SR-89, follow signs to Webber Lake, then go left on the dirt road towards Independence Lake, after crossing the river, take next rt turn on a dirt rd. (Side dirt road in 2 miles goes right to diversion dam. Take out.) The road goes past an abandoned cattle ranch and an active hunting club to a broken bridge over the Little Truckee River.
Take-out • See above.

MAPS: AAA — "Lake Tahoe Region" and "Bay & Mt. Section." DE LORME — p. 81.
SCENERY: Spectacular!

GAS, FOOD, and LODGING: Truckee.
CAMPING: Lower Little Truckee USFS Cpgr. between Stampede Res. & Henness Pass Rd. Tahoe National Forest(530.265.4531) Campgrounds near SR 89, Cold Creek and Cottonwood. Also campgrounds at Stampede & Boca Reservoirs.

BEWARE: Snags. Fences and trees across the river. Scout the diversion dam area for the best take-out BEFORE going paddling.

COMMENTS: This is one of the most beautiful runs I have done. It is fun as well with the crystal clear river flowing through an alpine meadow—minus the cattle, though. The river twists and turns with a moderate to lazy flow and riffles here and there. Just sit, drift, and steer. Enjoy the snow on the mountain peaks above the horseshoe shaped valley and the colorful flowers peaking out of the tall lawn-like carpeting at eye level. Don't go to sleep— the river is "busy" on its way through the meadow into the woods. If there was a way of taking out and hiking up to the Webber Lake Road before the woods, the run would be a Class I. Into the woods the river drops and there are several Class II rapids and more snags.

NOTE: The Little Truckee River, on its way to Stampede Res., runs for about 5 miles parallel to SR-89. It is runnable with sufficient water, although the riverbed is shallow and the river braids, taking several different routes. There are several access points. The river then flows into the Boca Res. and on to the Truckee River above Boca. Prosser Creek Reservoir is named for the creek that fills it. The creek then flows onto the Truckee River about three miles upriver from Boca. All of these reservoirs can be paddled.

●●●●●●●●●●●●●●●

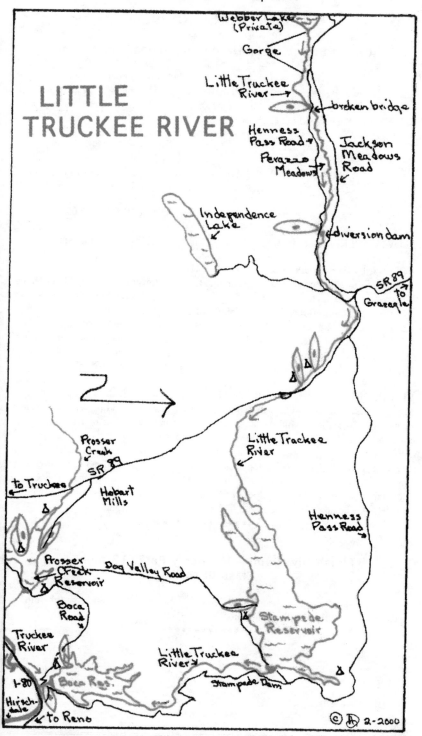

LITTLE TRUCKEE RIVER (con't)

Old Boca Bridge to Floriston, 7.5 miles, Class I to III

NOTE: Paddling 2 miles going past Hirschdale Bridge allows one to go about .5 mile of Class I, followed by a small canyon of Class II - III. Next is a mile of flat Class I and then a long Class III. You can boat to the top of Bronco rapids, but you must do a .5 mile portage along the railroad tracks on river right to Floriston.

• • • • • • • • • • • • • • •

Floriston to Fleish Diversion Dam, 5 miles, Class II+ to III-

SEASON: Spring (or when power plant is down). BEST FLOWS: 400-1,000 cfs.

FLOW INFO: K-phone: 916.368.8682. Water Master: 775.784.5241. "Floriston."

ACCESS: Put-in • Rebuilt diversion dam at Floristan.
1.5 miles to • Farad Power House. The shuttle to Farad Power House from Fleish Diversion Dam; take I-80 east to first Verdi exit, cross I-80 and follow frontage road back to I-80 west entrance. Farad exit is a very tight turn that is poorly marked.
3.5 miles to • Fleish diversion dam, rocky beach before dam on river left. From I-80, Fleish Div. Dam is about 3 miles on I-80, watch for a large turnout on the right. Mark or identify the take-out from the river, as there are no take-outs near the dam. Carry boats to the highway turnout, .25 mile hike.

BEWARE: The Class III rapid is after the Floriston dam site where the water drops quickly through rocks. The other Class III rapid is one mile beyond Farad power house—enter center and stay right to avoid the large rock in the center, or portage on river left. At 2.5 miles past Farad, there is a big hole on a sharp right turn.

COMMENTS: The run is rocky in places, semi-remote, and seldom run due to diversion dams. There is beaver activity, downed trees, and sweepers in some areas. The dam at Floristan was destroyed in 1997 floods and is scheduled to be rebuilt as "Boater Friendly" in 1998-99. The take-out at Fleish has high rock cliffs on river right.

• • • • • • • • • • • • • • •

Fleish Div. Dam — Mayberry Park, 13 miles, Class III to IV

There are about 6 class III-IV rapids in the next 17 miles plus 4 diversion dams before the river slows down flowing through Reno.

• • • • • • • • • • • • • • •

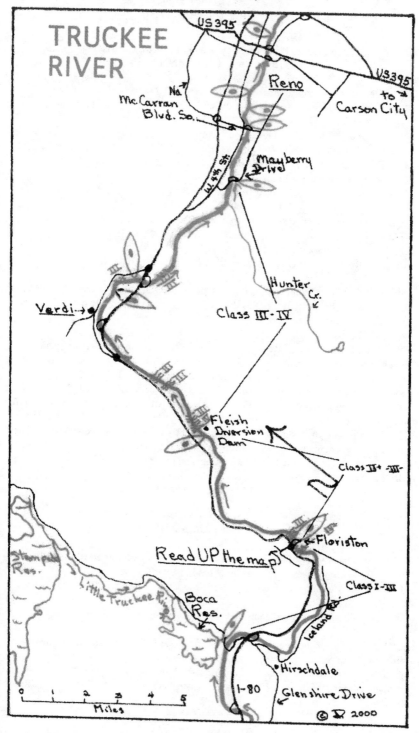

TRUCKEE
RIVER

US 395

Reno

McCarran
Blvd. So.

US 395

to
Carson City

W. 4th St.

Mayberry
Drive

Verdi→

III

III

Class III - IV

Hunter
Cr.

III
III

Fleish
Diversion
Dam

Class II+ -III-

III

←Floriston

Read UP the map

Class I - III

Steampede
Res.

Little Truckee R.

Boca
Res.

Iceland Rd.

I-80

Hirschdale

Glenshire Drive

0   1   2   3   4   5
Miles

© R 2000

LITTLE TRUCKEE RIVER (con't)

(Reno) Mayberry Park to Rock Park, 8.5 miles, Class II- to II+

SEASON: Spring - early summer.BEST FLOWS: 400-2,000 cfs.
FLOW INFO: K-phone: 916.368.8682. Water Master: 775.784.5241. "Floriston."

ACCESS: Put-in • Mayberry Park, about .5 mile south of I-80, take 4th St. exit to Wood-
    land Ave. Parking & RRm.
3 miles to • Crissy Caughlin Park, river right. Parking & RRm.
2 miles to • Booth St. Bridge.
1 mile to • Wingfield Park also Arlington Street Bridge. Parking & RRm.
2 miles to • Fisherman's Park, river left. Parking & RRm.
.5 mile to • Glendale Diversion Dam, portage left.
.5 mile to • Pioneer Diversion Dam, portage left.
.5 mile to • Rock Park, river left. Parking & RRm.
1 mile to: Rock Park, river left Parking & RRm.

BEWARE: Summer "campers" (homeless) along the river banks between Wells Ave. &
Kietzke Lane. There may be dogs as the river goes past backyards. Two diversion dams,
portage on river left.

COMMENTS: The city of Reno is well aware of the Truckee as there are parks along
much of the river, generally on one side. Here's your chance. About a mile down river is
Ambrose Park, watch the abutments. In another mile or so is Chalk Bluff Diversion Dam—
portage on river left. The park was modified in 1998 to be "boater friendly"; it now has a
concrete and rock sloped face. At Wingfield Park and Arlington St. Bridge the river splits,
the left has an almost riverwide dam. The VERY far left has a runnable chute. There is
also a way to go right around the island park but beware of the the diversion ditch. There
are some challenging rapids below Wells Ave. Bridge a mile downriver from Wingfield
Park. Do not attempt to run the rock diversion dam (portage on R best, L OK. At Glendale
Bridge, .5 mile above Rock Pk, is Greg St. dam & bridge, portage on R.

• • • • • • • • • • • • • •

Rock Park to Lower Mustang Ranch Bridge, 10 miles, Class I to II

ACCESS: Put-in • Rock Park on S Rock St. via I-80; also: McCarran Blvd. Bridge, con-
    crete spillway at Larkin Circle (end of Bike Trail in Sparks),
10 miles to • Mustang Ranch bridge at Lockwood, now a state wild horse compound.

BEWARE: There are several dams that should be portaged—scout first.

COMMENTS: This is an easy run without much scenery, with dirty water downstream
from the Reno-Sparks sewage plant, and numerous dams to portage. There is a Class II
rapid below Lockwood. Take-out at the Mustang Ranch second bridge at the parking lot
below the bridge on the right. There is a cable across the river at the first Mustang Ranch
bridge.

• • • • • • • • • • • • • •

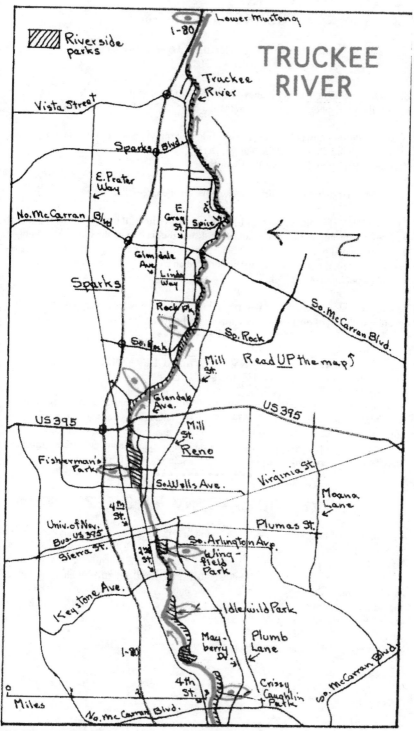

TRUCKEE RIVER (con't)

Mustang Ranch Bridge to Wadsworth,
26 miles, Class I to II

SEASON: Spring or summer high water. BEST FLOWS: 400 - 4,500 cfs.
FLOW INFO: K-phone: 916.368.8682. Water Master: 775.784.5241. "Floriston".

ACCESS: Put-in • Lower Mustang Ranch bridge (see previous write-up), also: Lockwood,
Hafed, Patrick, Clark, Thisbe, Derby.
Take-out • Bridge in downtown Wadsworth.

BEWARE: Private property, dirty water, dams, downed trees, and snags.

COMMENTS: This run is also near I-80, yet remote at times. It is seldom run, has lots of
beaches and meadows and good campsites. It has the feeling of the old west, complete
with cottonwood trees and sagebrush. The dam by the Clark Powerhouse should be portaged on the left, the Derby dam must be portaged on the left, and a dam before Wadsworth
should be portaged on the right.

FLORA & FAUNA: Out in the desert and meadows, there is some very nice scenery on
this run, with lots of ducks and land birds as well as a few land animals.

• • • • • • • • • • • • • •

Wadsworth, NV - Pyramid Lake/Nixon,
12 miles, Class I

We ran this stretch with permission from the Paiute Native Americans as it is in the Pyramid Lake Indian Reservation: 775.574.1000. Class I, snags and trees, with a marshy take-
out near Nixon, before Pyramid Lake. There are 2 major dams to be portaged. The first
dam is about 1 mile below Wadsworth—portage right. The second is Marble Bluff Dam
below Nixon—very dangerous—portage on the left.

• • • • • • • • • • • • • •

PYRAMID LAKE, NV, el. 3,792'

This blue jewel of a lake is worth several hours, if not days, of paddling exploration.
Access is easy and the scenery is good. The access is on the west side and south end of the
lake. The afternoon winds generally blow east! There are interesting tufa formations, caused
by the salty water, at the southeast end and hot springs at the northwest end. Because of
vandalism, the hot springs area is closed to the public. Anaho Island is also closed as it is
the nesting site of thousands of white pelicans, cormorants, gulls, herons, and terns. Another island, shaped like a pyramid, caused John C. Fremont to so name the lake in 1844.

CAMPING INFO: Pyramid L. Paiute Tribe Ranger Sta.: 702.476.1155.

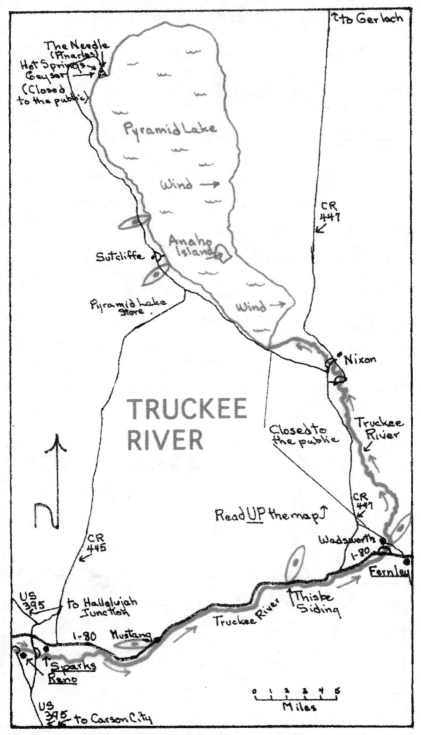

CARSON RIVER — WEST FORK

Blue Lakes Road to SR-89 Hope Valley, 4 miles, Class I

SEASON: May & June. BEST FLOWS: 250 - 400 cfs.
FLOW INFO. & MNG. AGENCY: Toiyabe NF: 702.882.2766

ACCESS: Put-in • Blue Lakes Rd. near SR-89 (Luther Pass) near SR-88 (Carson Pass). Take-out • 1 mile west of SR-88 on SR-89 bridge.

MAPS: AAA — "Bay & Mt. Section." DE LORME — p. 90. Toiyabe NF: "Carson Map."

GAS, FOOD, and LODGING: East to Kirkwood, north to Myers (Lake Tahoe area).

BEWARE: Fences across the river. Short paddling season.

COMMENTS: Another run with the road beside the river for scouting. The distance is long enough, and much of it away from the road, thus making this easy water wilderness trip enjoyable. It is a snow-melt run, so watch the weather and guess the flow.

NOTE: The W. Carson River along the Blue Lakes Road changes from Class I to III as the road goes up the hill. Also after the take-out, the river becomes Class III to Sorenson's Store at the end of Hope Valley. Past Sorenson's, it becomes Class V to below Woodfords.

•••••••••••••••••

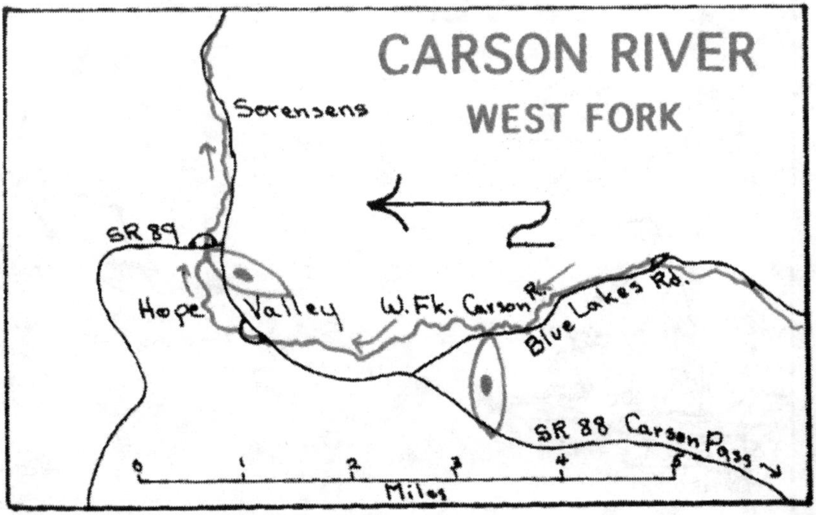

CARSON RIVER
WEST FORK

Sorensens

SR 89

Hope Valley   W. Fk. Carson R.   Blue Lakes Rd.

SR 88 Carson Pass

Miles

- UPPER TRUCKEE R.
- MONO LAKE

- TRUCKEE R., TAHOE C. -
RIVER RANCH, CLASS I+

CARSON RIVER SYSTEM

CARSON RIVER, EAST FORK

Markleeville (Hangman's Bridge) to Div. Dam,
(Wilder. Run), 20 miles, Class II

SEASON: Spring to early summer. BEST FLOWS: 300-700 cfs.
FLOW INFO: Watermaster: 775.784.5241, Gardnerville & K-ph.: 916.368.8682,
"Markleeville."

ACCESS: Put-in • Hangman's Bridge, 1 mile southeast of Markleeville on SR-89.
Take-out • Well marked take-out upriver from the 30 foot drop at the Ruhenstroth Diversion Dam. Parking & RRm.

SHUTTLE: A long way! SR-89 N 7 mi. to SR 88, NE 14 mi. to Minden, S on US-395 14
mi. through Gardnerville to dirt road, right, past the Lohatan Fish Hat., to upstream of the
dam. Used by outfitters.

MAPS: AAA — "Lake Tahoe Region" and "Bay & Mt. Section." DE LORME — p. 90.
Toiyabe NF Carson River Map ($2.50. 702.882.2766).

GAS, FOOD, and LODGING: Markleeville (lodge about 2 miles south).Minden, NV.
CAMPING: Markleeville, 1 mi. NE off SR-89. Forest Service Cpgrs.: 702.882.2766.

BEWARE: Rafts—this is now a commercial raft run. The favorite hot springs campsite
may have a group of happy campers already there when you arrive.

COMMENTS: The flow is good. The rapids are fun and easy to see, but there can always
be surprises. Take care. This has been a favorite run since first "discovered" by river
runners in 1969. It is a great Class II, II+ (the III has become easier) run with plenty of
campsites along the way. With the El Nino 1998 year of heavy and late rains, it was being
run in one day until late July. Dry years means it could be too low to run before Tioga Pass
is open for those who have to cross the Sierra enroute.
NOTE: Warm-up run, read on....

• • • • • • • • • • • • • • • •

Hot Springs Creek, Grover Hot Springs to Markeleeville Campground, 4 mi., Class II to III-

ACCESS: Put-in • Grover Hot Springs State Park, Hot Springs Rd. west of Markleeville.
Bridge at entrance.
Take-out • SR 89 bridge or Markleeville FS campground. Confluence with Carson River
.5 mile downstream of campground.

BEWARE: Fences across the creek, brush, downed trees.

COMMENTS: Much of this run can be scouted from the road to the state park. Look for
snags in the river that might block passage. This is seldom run, but quite scenic and great
on a hot day in early July. Most of the rapids are Class II, but scout when in doubt; there
could be a Class III here and there. Do not put-in above the campground because of a low
pipe across the river and barbed wire.

• • • • • • • • • • • • • • •

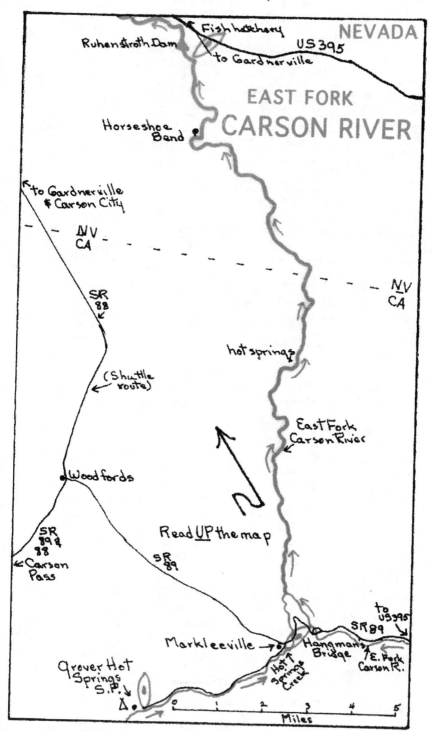

CARSON RIVER (con't)

Ruhenstroth Diversion Dam to Carson City, 29.5 miles, Class I to II

SEASON: Spring & early summer.BEST FLOW: 400 - 2,000 cfs.
FLOW INFO: Water Master: 775.784.5241. K-Phone: 916.368.8682, Markleeville.

ACCESS: Put-in • Below Ruhenstroth Dam, at low-water bridge, off US-395, take dirt road to the right after the Lahontan National Fish Hatchery about 14 miles so. of Gardnerville, NV.
2 miles to • Gardnerville Ranchos bridge.
4 miles to • Gardnerville-Centerville Rd. bridge.
2 miles to • NV-88 bridge.
5.5 miles to • Muller Lane bridge, between NV-206 & US-395.
2 miles to • Genoa Lane bridge between US-395 & NV-206.
6 miles to • US-395 Cradle Baugh bridge, 10 miles south of Carson City.
6 miles to • Mexican Dam(8'+). Take-out 100 yds. upstream for portage. Steep hillside on the left.
2 miles to • Carson Riv. Pk. E. on 5th St. in Carson City 3 m. to Carson River Rd.
2.5 miles to • The Carson River and bridge on to Pinion Road.
2 miles to • Riverview Park, Carson City, E. on 5th St. (NV-513). Pk & RRm.

MAPS: AAA — "Bay & Mountain Section" and "Carson City". DE LORME — p. 90 (partial). Toiyabe NF, Carson Ranger Dist.: 702.882.2766.

GAS, FOOD, and LODGING: Gardnerville and Carson City
CAMPING: Carson City, Comstock Country RV Resort, 5400 S. Carson St.: 702.882.2445.

BEWARE: Diversion dams, Mexican Dam—portage for safety's sake. Fences across the river.

COMMENTS: The river flows through communities and cattle country in the western part of Nevada, including the capitol city. The water reflects the less than prestine conditions of people and animal use. But it is a comforable swimming temperature which is welcome in the desert country for an afternoon cooling swim. Be careful when paddling. Portage around the dams and keep a sharp eye out for any fences across the river. This is mostly private property so be very careful if camping along the river to give river runners a good name. Bury your fire, take out all trash, and leave the site cleaner than you found it.

STORY: Why portage the dams? Story from Charles Albright: "When I first boated this stretch around 1974, I was working in Gardnerville. A fellow worker and friend paddled this run in a canoe and ran a dam above Gardnerville. The canoe capsized and one of the paddlers was recycled in the reversal below the dam for close to thirty minutes as help was very slow to arrive. He survived the ordeal because he was in execellent physical condition." Please portage around the dams!

●●●●●●●●●●●●●●●

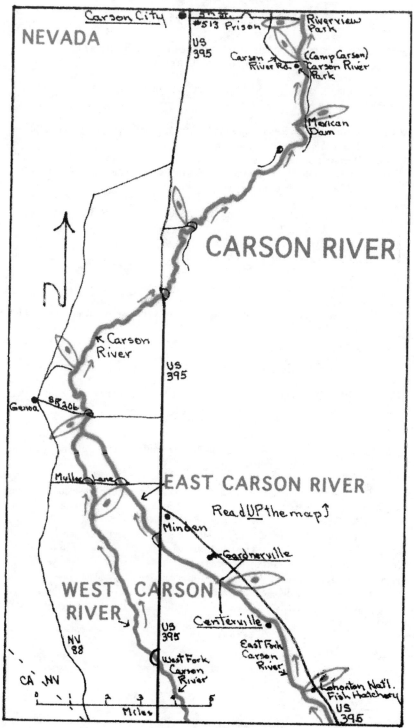

Carson City
5th St.
#513 Prison
US 395
Riverview Park
Carson River Rd.
(Camp Carson) Carson River Park
Mexican Dam

NEVADA

CARSON RIVER

Carson River

US 395

Genoa
SR 206

Muller Lane

EAST CARSON RIVER

Read UP the map ↑

Minden

Gardnerville

WEST CARSON RIVER

Centerville

US 395

NV 88

CA NV

US 395
West Fork Carson River

East Fork Carson River

Lahonton Nat'l. Fish Hatchery
US 395

0 1 2 3 4 5
Miles

CARSON RIVER — MAIN STEM

Carson River Park to Deer Run Bridge, 3.5 miles, Class I

SEASON: Spring & summer BEST FLOWS: 400 - 2,000 cfs
FLOW INFO: Water Master: 775.784.5241.

ACCESS: Put-in • Carson River Park/Lloyd's Low Water Bridge. From Carson City go east on 5th Street to park and river.
Take-out • Deer Run Bridge. Cross river on Carson River Rd. which becomes Pinon Hills Dr. east of the river, go north, turn east on Laurel Rd., go north on S. Deer Run Rd., about 2+ miles to the river.

MAPS: AAA — "Carson City, NV." "Bay & Mt. Section." DE LORME — NV, p. 42.

GAS, FOOD, and LODGING: Carson City, NV.
CAMPING: Dayton State Park, NV: 775.687.5678.

BEWARE: Snags.

COMMENTS: This is a fun, easy run, close to Carson City, that is runnable most of the summer. It is semi-remote, yet close-in.

●●●●●●●●●●●●●●●

Deer Run Bridge to Dayton, 8.5 miles, Class II to III

ACCESS: Put-in • Deer Run Bridge. (See above) (BLM office at Morgan Mill Rd. & Deer Run Rd.)
Take-out • Bridge at Dayton State Park: 775.687.5678. Short carry. Pkg. & RRm.

BEWARE: Brush. Class III rapid into Death Rock, 1+ miles from site of Brunswick and low diversion dam at about 5 miles.

COMMENTS: Another interesting run on the Carson River in sage brush country going through Brunswick Canyon. The Class III drop "Death Rock Rapid," has a large rock in the center that is hard for most novices to avoid. The only other spot that is challenging is a low rock diversion dam that is best run on the far right; the river immediately turns left through some brush and a tree. The tree has always had a lovely color to it—usually yellow—from the wrapped rafts of the cheap variety. This run was used every year for the Carson River raft race usually held in May. Tubes, canoes, kayaks, and rafts used in the race some times end in a disaster on "Death Rock" and at the diversion dam that is about 5 miles down river. There is a dirt road on the north side of the river in the Brunswick Canyon.

●●●●●●●●●●●●●●●

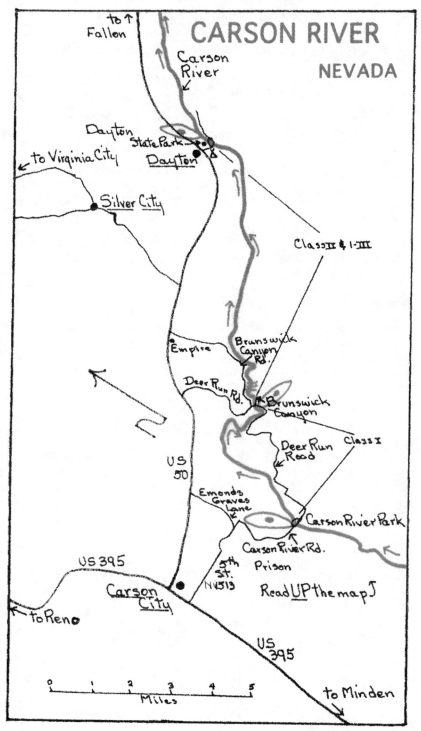

CARSON RIVER

NEVADA

to↑ Fallon

Carson River

to Virginia City

Dayton
State Park
Dayton

Silver City

Class II & I-III

Empire
Brunswick Canyon Rd.

Deer Run Rd.

Brunswick Canyon

Deer Run Road

Class I

US 50

Emonds Graves Lane

Carson River Park

Carson River Rd.

US 395

Prison

Read UP the map ↰

5th St.
NV 513

Carson City

to Reno

US 395

0 1 2 3 4 5
Miles

to Minden

CARSON RIVER (con't)

Dayton to Lahontan Reservoir, 30 miles, Class I+

SEASON: Spring & early summer. BEST FLOWS: 400 - 1,500 cfs.
FLOW INFO: Water Master: 775.784.5241 X 25, "Dayton".

ACCESS: Put-in • Bridge at Dayton State Park. Dayton is 8 miles east of Carson City on
   US-50. Parking & RRm.
23 miles to • Fort Churchill State Park.
1 mile to • Carson River bridge on Alternate US-95.
6 miles to • Lahotan Res., Silver Springs Beach Cpgr. From US-50 E. on Fir Ave. to end.
   Alt. US-95 crosses Fir Ave. W. of Res. Parking & RRm.

MAPS: AAA — "Bay & Mt. Section." DE LORME — NV, p. 43.

GAS, FOOD, and LODGING: Dayton, Virginia City, and Carson City.
CAMPING: Dayton State Park: 775.687.5678. Lake Lahontan: along the shore or at established campgrounds: 775.867.3500.

BEWARE: Diversion dams, shallow water, and winds.

COMMENTS: Paddlers sometimes search for easy water trips of 2 to 3 days. Here is one
on the winding Carson River as it flows through cattle country (yes, dirty water) in desert
flatland with cottonwoods. The river flows past historic Fort Churchill. Any camping
done on the riverbank will be on private property so it is best to cook over a small camp
stove. No open fires. And please, leave the area cleaner than found.

●●●●●●●●●●●●●●●●

LAHONTAN RESERVOIR, el. 4159'

Here the Carson River has slowed, providing flat water for power boating, jet skiing, and
windsurfing on a twisting 11 mile lake. There may be an algae bloom in the summer.
Winds and afternoon thunder storms are not unusual. US-50 and Alt. US-95 are nearby.
Silver Springs is the BIG town in the area and Fallon is the BIG city. Fishing and birding
are also activities at the lake.

INFORMATION: Lahontan State Rec. Center: 775.867.3500.

FACILITIES: Camping is allowed along the shores of the lake although there are also two
established campgrounds and picnic areas. Beaches are used for boat launching although
there are also two boat ramps.

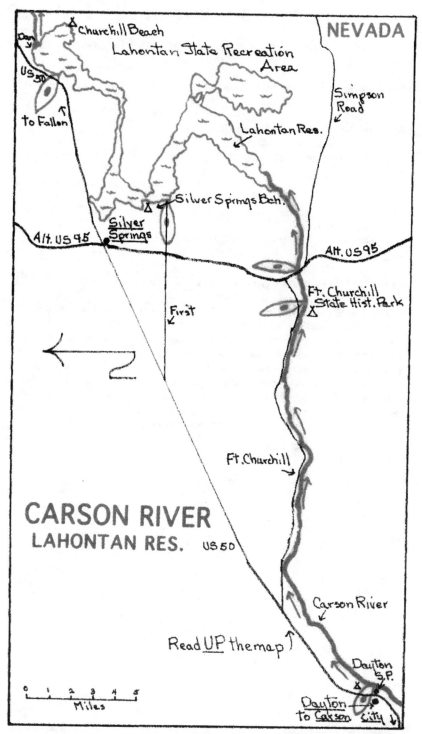

CARSON RIVER (end)

Lahontan Dam to Carson Lake (Sink),
22-29 miles, Class I

SEASON: Spring, summer during heavy runoffs or releases. BEST FLOWS: 400-1,000 cfs. FLOW INFO: Water Master: 775.784.5241.

ACCESS: Put-in • Below the Lahotan Dam.
7 miles to • Carson Diversion Dam.
7 miles to • Bridge on Sheckler Cutoff, 5 miles west of Fallon, US-50.
8 miles to • Bridge on Bafford Lane, 2 miles north of Fallon off US-95.
Or 15 miles on • South Branch to Pasture Rd. off US-95, 9.5 miles south of Fallon.

MAPS: AAA — "Lake Tahoe Region" and "Bay & Mountain Section."

GAS, FOOD, and LODGING: Fallon, NV.
CAMPING: Lahotan State Recreation Area, at the end of Fir Ave. or the dam.

BEWARE: Low flows at the end of the run, diversion dams, and fences.

COMMENTS: Before the Carson River terminates at either the Stillwater Wildlife Management Area or the Carson Lake/Sink, much of the water has been diverted for use elsewhere—primarily agriculture. The Stillwater Marsh receives water from the Truckee River as well as the Carson River, and is a haven for waterfowl. Originally the Carson River entered the Carson sink, an alkaline basin, near Pelican Island and Battleground Point. The alkaline flat extends for miles in every direction, is nearly devoid of vegetation, and is all that is left of a former inland sea that covered the Great Basin at one time. The sink used to share the drainage of the Humboldt, Carson, and Truckee Rivers.

●●●●●●●●●●●●●●●

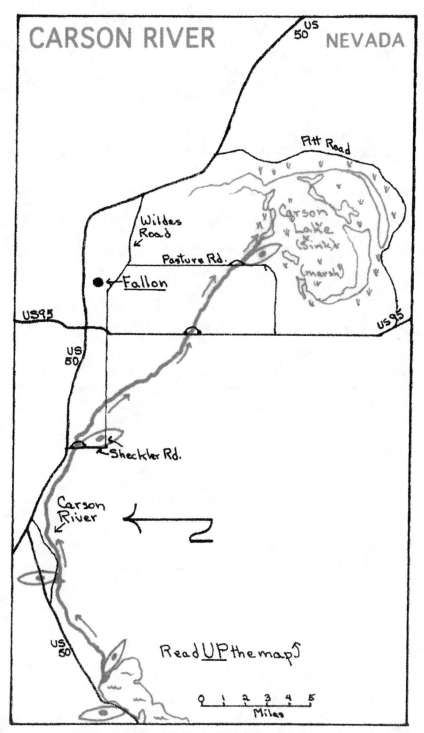

CARSON RIVER

NEVADA

US 50

Pitt Road

Wildes Road

Carson Lake (sink) (marsh)

Pasture Rd.

Fallon

US 95

US 95

US 50

Sheckler Rd.

Carson River

Read UP the map

US 50

0 1 2 3 4 5
Miles

WALKER RIVER SYSTEM

(NOTE: The Walker River in Nevada is not considered navigable, so the land over which the water flows belongs to the property owner, but not the water. A boater can be arrested for being on the land which includes rocks in the river, so be very respectful. ALSO a website for Nevada water flows: www.nv.wr.usgs.gov/rt-cgi/gen_tbl_pg and Water Master:775.784.5241.

W. Walker River, 2 miles above MWTC to Sonora Bridge Campground, 4.5 miles, Class I

SEASON: Spring & early summer. BEST FLOWS: 400 - 1,000 cfs.
FLOW INFO: Water Master: 775-887-7600. Walker River Irrigation Dist.: 775.463.3523.

ACCESS: Put-in • 2 miles upriver from the Marines Mountain Warfare Training Center on SR-108 near US-395.
4.5 miles to • Sonora Bridge parking area where SR-108 crosses the river.

MAPS: AAA — "Lake Tahoe Region" and "Bay & Mt. Section". DE LORME — p. 101.
MANAGING AGENCY: Toiyabe NF Bridgeport Ranger Dist.: 760.932.7070.

GAS, FOOD, and LODGING: Bridgeport.
CAMPING: Sonora Bridge Cpgr. 20 miles SW of Coleville on SR 108: 760.932.7070.

BEWARE: Beyond this Class I run, the river quickly becomes Class III and IV. The portage is a half mile, and the continued Class I portion, only 2 miles. THEN comes a CLASS V run to the small town of Walker. Watch for the Marines going past their area, they may have landed!

COMMENTS: The river flows east through a scenic valley parallel to SR-108. The river has hopefully recovered from the heavy flooding(s). The water is clear, the fishing is excellent, and the feeling is remote.

NOTE The WEST WALKER was one of the "hair" boaters goals, that is until the 1997 New Years day floods after which one kayaker commented "the Walker committed suicide." (See the writeups in *The Best Whitewater in California* by Holbek and Stanley and *California Whitewater* by Cassady and Calhoun.) With this reputation, I drove past to take a look at the "good stuff" only to find miles and miles of Class I and II water—my speed.

●●●●●●●●●●●●●●●

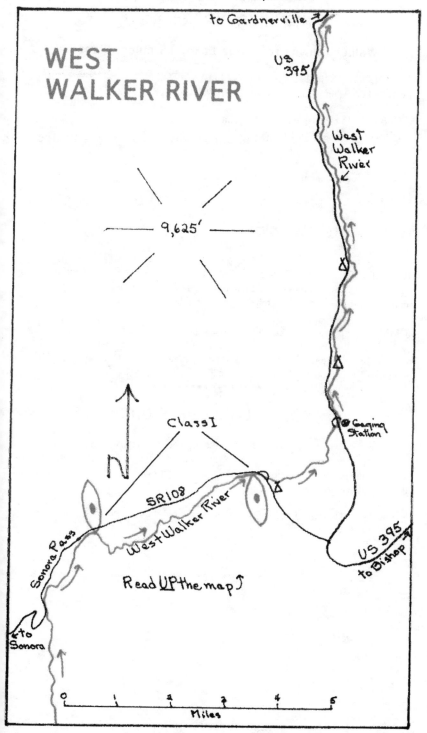

WEST
WALKER RIVER

9,625'

Class I

SR108

West Walker River

Read UP the map ↑

Sonora Pass

← to
Sonora

to Gardnerville →

US 395

West
Walker
River

Gauging
Station

US 395
to Bishop →

0   1   2   3   4   5
Miles

WALKER RIVER (con't.)

Walker (town) to Topaz Lake, 15 miles, Class II+

SEASON: Spring to mid-summer. BEST FLOWS: 400-1,000 cfs.
FLOW INFO: Water Master: 775.887.7600. Walker River Irr. Dist.: 775.463.3523.

ACCESS: Put-in • Eastside Road Bridge in the town of Walker.
3.5 miles to • Larson Lane Bridge.
3 miles to • Cunningham Lane Bridge.
2.5 miles to • Topaz Lane Bridge.
5 miles to • Topaz Lake boat ramp at south end.

MAPS: AAA — "Lake Tahoe." "Bay and Mt. Section." DE LORME — Pp. 91 & 101.

GAS, FOOD, and LODGING: Minden, NV.
CAMPING: Topaz Lake, NV.: 775.266.3343.

BEWARE: After the 1997 floods, the Army Corps of Engineers turned the beginning section into a Class II+ rock-lined ditch until Larson Lane (possibly a better put-in for a run on a free-flowing river). Watch for fences and diversion dams.

COMMENTS: This stretch of river can be very nice as it is seldom run except by locals in tubes and small rafts; however, it was severely affected by the 1997 floods. The flow at the beginning of the run is fairly fast, but slows as it gets nearer the lake. The last part going into Topaz Lake has been channelized.

●●●●●●●●●●●●●●●

TOPAZ LAKE, el. 5,000'

Topaz Lake is a turquoise jewel in the Nevada high desert country just off US-395 as the highway crosses the state line between California and Nevada. Part of the West Walker flows into the reservoir, but most flows past on its way to Walker Lake. It is a power boat lake, so paddlecraft beware. Wind may be a problem.

INFORMATION: Topaz Lake Park, information about the lake, camping, and facilities: 775.266.3343.

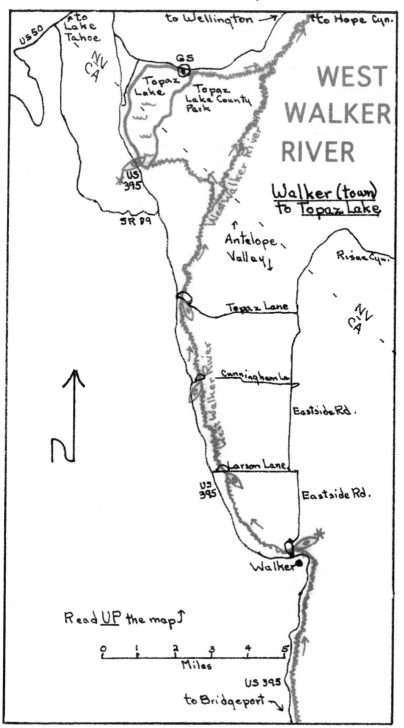

WEST WALKER RIVER

Walker (town) to Topaz Lake

Read UP the map ↑

WALKER RIVER (con't)

Topaz Lake/Hoye Bridge to Wellington, 5 miles, Class I & II

SEASON: Spring and summer dam releases. BEST FLOWS: 400-1,000 cfs.
FLOW INFO: Water Master: 775.784.5241.

ACCESS: Put-in • Below Topaz Lake at Hoye Bridge, US-295 2 mi. N. of Topaz Lake to
      Holbrook Junc., E. 4 mi. on SR 208, right on dirt rd., 3 mi. to Hoye Bridge.
5 miles to • Wellington. Cross river at Hoye Bridge, go on road down river through Hoye
      Canyon to Wellington, turn left to SR-338 bridge.

MAPS: AAA — "Bay & Mt. Section." DE LORME — CA p. 91; NV p. 50.
GAS, FOOD, and LODGING: Wellington, NV.
CAMPING: Topaz Lake: 775.266.3343.

BEWARE: Rattlesnakes and incredible amounts of mosquitoes. Two dams, portage one
on right. "When I ran this run a friend and I were getting eaten alive by mosquitoes 'til we
got on the river. My friend almost stepped on a very large rattlesnake in his haste to escape
the mosquitoes." - Chas. Albright.

COMMENTS:This is a Class I run until Hoye Canyon, then a Class II. Try an upstream
run first. The Hoye Canyon has some big waves and a low dam shortly after entering the
canyon. Run this on the far left. The next dam is in 3.5 miles. Portage it on the right. Class
II after.

•••••••••••••••

Wellington to Wilson Canyon, 17.5 miles, Class I+

ACCESS: Put-in • SR-208 bridge in Wellington.
5 miles to • Day Lane bridge north of Smith.
6.5 miles to • SR-208 bridge east of Smith, top of Wilson Canyon.

MAPS: AAA — "Bay & Mt. Section." DE LORME — CA p. 91; NV p. 50.

GAS, FOOD, and LODGING: Wellington and Yerington, NV.
CAMPING: Topaz Lake: 775.266.3343.

BEWARE: Dirty water, mosquitoes, snags, diversion dams, and cattle country.

COMMENTS: The river slows in the Smith Valley. It is mostly away from the road through
cattle ranches. If camping along the river, please respect the site.

NOTE: Top of Wilson Canyon to SR-208 one mile below canyon is a 3-mile run of Class
II and III dirty water. It is a challenging run over lots of rocks, past downed trees and
brush with one diversion dam. (Thank you Charles Albright.)

•••••••••••••••

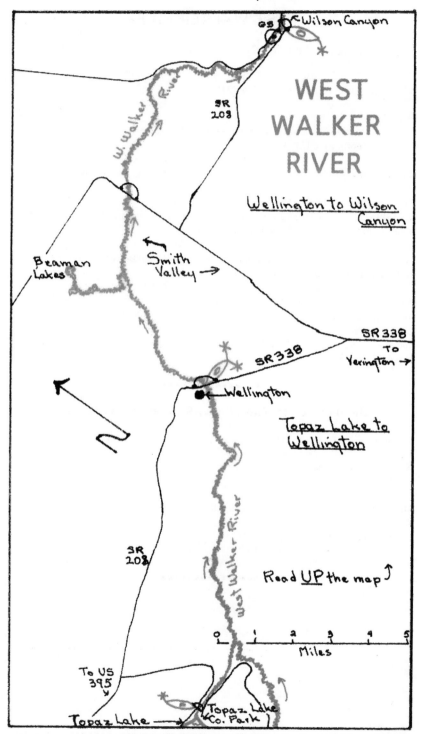

WEST
WALKER
RIVER

Wellington to Wilson
Canyon

GS — Wilson Canyon

SR 208

Beaman
Lakes

Smith
Valley

W. Walker River

SR 338

SR 338

TO
Yerington →

Wellington

Topaz Lake to
Wellington

SR
208

Read UP the map ↑

West Walker River

0   1   2   3   4   5
Miles

To US
395

Topaz Lake →

Topaz Lake
Co. Park

EAST WALKER RIVER

Bridgeport Res. to Devils Gate, 7 miles, Class II & III

SEASON: Spring or dam releases. BEST FLOWS: 400 - 1,000 cfs.
FLOW INFO: Water Master: 775.784.5241.

ACCESS: Put-in • 1.25 miles below Bridgeport Res.
6 miles to • Devils Gate. At the stateline is Devil's Gate on SR-182 (SR-338 in NV), goes
    north from US-395 just east of Bridgeport.

MAPS: AAA — "Bay & Mt. Section." DE LORME — CA p. 101; NV p. 51.

GAS, FOOD, and LODGING: Bridgeport.
CAMPING: Twin Lakes area SW of Bridgeport. Honeymoon Flat FS Cpgr., 8 mi. SW of
Bridgeport on FS-018 Rd.: 1.800.280.CAMP.

BEWARE: Swift water, almost continuous Class II & III rapids, narrow river, brush, mosquitos. Vandalized cars. Class IV rapid to be portaged.

COMMENTS: With Class III paddling skills and equipment, this is a fun run. It is swift
flowing with almost continuous Class II and III rapids for 7 miles. Very scenic. The road
parallel to the river is good for road scouting. With river flows over 400 cfs., the rocks
may be covered. The run is narrow in places and often has brush on both sides for long
distances. There is one Class IV drop below a lake-type area, in about 3 miles. It's the
only flat area to rapids. Portage on river left or right on a dirt road.

•••••••••••••••

Devils Gate to The Elbow, 9 miles, Class I+ to II

ACCESS: Put-in • Devils Gate, SR(CA)-182, 8 miles below Bridgeport Res. dam, very
    near the state line.
9 miles to • The Elbow. On FS-028 Rd. 6 miles past SR-338 where the road meets the
    river. Mostly dirt roads.

BEWARE: No beaches or camping along the river. Private property.

COMMENTS: Nice scenery with dirty water through a high desert meadow with ducks
and deer. There is a nice remote feeling. Class I+ in the first few miles that changes to
Class II.

•••••••••••••••

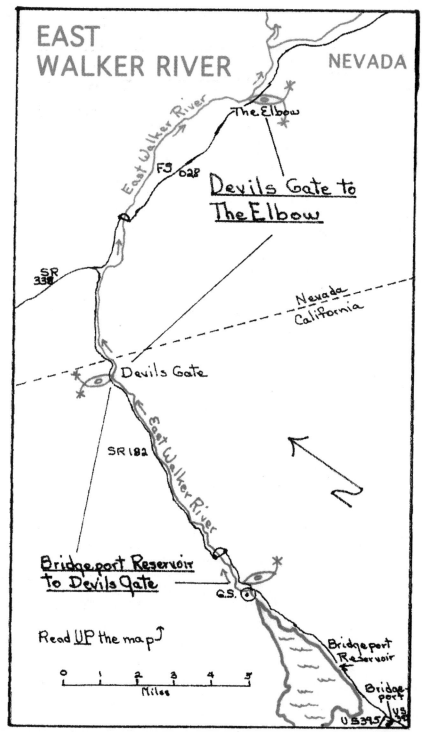

EAST WALKER RIVER

NEVADA

East Walker River

The Elbow

FS 028

Devils Gate to The Elbow

Nevada
California

SR 338

Devils Gate

SR 182

East Walker River

Bridgeport Reservoir to Devils Gate

G.S.

Read UP the map

0 1 2 3 4 5
Miles

Bridgeport
Reservoir

Bridgeport

US 395/

EAST WALKER RIVER (con't)

The Elbow to Pine Grove Rd. Bridge, 13.5 miles, Class II & III

SEASON: Spring & after releases. BEST FLOWS: 400 - 1,000 cfs
FLOW INFO: Water Master: 775.784.5241.

ACCESS: Put-in • The Elbow, on FS-028 Rd. 6 miles past SR-338 where the road meets the river. Mostly dirt roads.
13.5 miles to • Bridge between Aldrich Grade & Pine Grove Roads, 6 miles south of the Flying M Ranch. Dirt roads.

MAPS: AAA — "Bay & Mt. Section." DE LORME — NV, p. 51.
MANAGING AGENCY: Toiyabe N.F., Bridgeport: 760.932.7070.

GAS, FOOD, and LODGING: Bridgeport.

BEWARE: Remote—passes only one ranch. Brush, trees, snags, and fences.

COMMENTS: Class III paddlers only! Boaters should be ready for challenging rapids, the possibility of brush, trees, and fences in rapids. There are big waves at higher water with a moderate flow. Be prepared for the worst. There are sandy beaches, good campsites, but it is private property! Scenic high desert country, but dirty water.

• • • • • • • • • • • • • • •

6 miles south of Flying M Ranch to W. Walker Rd., 35 miles, Class I+

ACCESS: Put-in • Bridge between Aldrich Grade & Pine Grove Roads (Take-out for run above).
35 miles to • the take-out from the put-in, follow the dirt road to E. Walker Rd., east side of the river, turn left, go to SR-208 bridge near confluence with West Walker River.
(NOTE: There are a few other access points along the run.)

GAS, FOOD, and LODGING: Yerington, NV.
CAMPING: Along the river, but it is private property.

BEWARE: Many small diversion dams, mosquitos, dirty water, snags.

COMMENTS: This 35 mile Class I+ run flows slowly through high desert cattle country. There are a few rocks to avoid near the beginning of the run and there may be some shallow places.

• • • • • • • • • • • • • • •

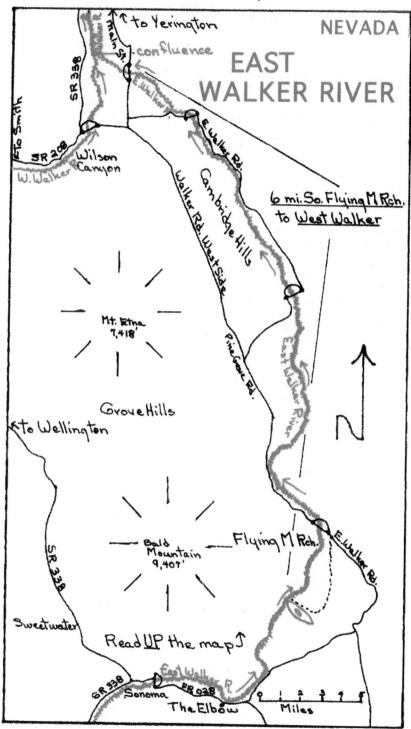

NEVADA

EAST WALKER RIVER

to Yerington

Main St.

confluence

E. Walker Rd.

SR 338

to Smith

SR 208

W. Walker

Wilson Canyon

Walker Rd. West Side

Cambridge Hills

6 mi. So. Flying M Rch.
to West Walker

Mt. Etna
7,418'

Pine Grove Rd.

East Walker River

Grove Hills

to Wellington

N

Bald Mountain
9,407'

Flying M Rch.

E. Walker Rd.

SR 338

Sweetwater

Read UP the map

East Walker R.

SR 338

Sonoma

The Elbow

0 1 2 3 4 5
Miles

WALKER RIVER, NV

SR-208 near confluence to Walker Lake, 61+ miles, Class I

SEASON: Spring & dam releases. BEST FLOWS: 400 - 1,500 cfs.
FLOW INFO: Water Master: 775.784.5241.

ACCESS: Put-in • At bridge, US-95 alternate west of Yerington.
45.5 miles to • Schurz at US-95 bridge.
13 miles to • Walker Lake.
3 miles to • US-95 take-out.

MAPS: AAA — "Bay and Mt. Section" and "Nevada/Utah." DE LORME — NV, pp. 43 and 51.

GAS, FOOD, and LODGING: Yerington and Hawthorne.
CAMPING: Walker Lake: 775.945.2717.

BEWARE: The run is remote (or semi-remote). The run has dams, slow dirty water, can be trashy, is shallow in places, and has no camping in the Mason Valley Wildlife Management Area and the Walker River Indian Reservation. The flows after the Webber Reservoir may be lower, which could make paddling through the delta into Walker Lake difficult. Bring a good supply of drinking water and a filter.

COMMENTS: So many paddlers ask for easy river runs of several days in duration, here's one! This flows through meadows, deserts, wildlife areas, an Indian reservation that ends in a lake. It sounds great. It is especially nice with flowers in bloom in the spring and an abundance of birdlife. Camp sites are fair.

●●●●●●●●●●●●●●

WALKER LAKE, NV, el. 3,976'

Walker Lake is very picturesque, a large blue pool nestled in the desert hills. It is a great picnic and swimming spot. It has easy access on the west side from US-95 with several shade-covered day-use areas. There are also camping sites and easy water access. Walker Lake is a "dead sea" according to Nevada Fish and Game officials. Only 39 inches of water in the lake can be considered life support for fish. Boaters beware of the high winds on this large lake in Nevada. It takes no time at all for large waves to form. Check locally for general wind direction and plan accordingly.

INFORMATION: Walker Lake Recreation District: 775.945.2717.

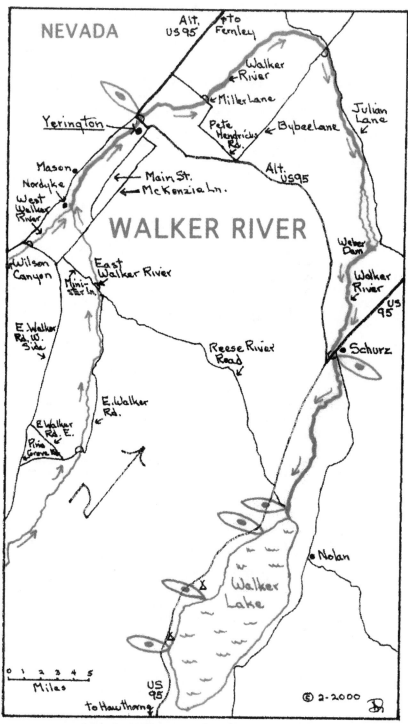

RUSH CREEK, 4.5 miles, Class II

SEASON: Spring run-off. BEST FLOWS: 400 - 1,000 cfs.
FLOW INFO: Water Master: 775.784.5241 x 25

ACCESS: Put-in • US-395 bridge over Rush Creek near SR-258 (June Lakes Loop) 4.5 miles to • bridge over creek on Picnic Grounds Test Station Rd. that goes west from the road to Navy Beach (off SR-120) at Mono Lake.

MAPS: AAA — "Bay & Mountain Section." DE LORME — p. 112.

GAS, FOOD, and LODGING: Lee Vining to the north or June Lakes area to the southwest. Visitor's Center at Lee Vining.
CAMPING: Tioga Pass area or June Lakes area.

BEWARE: Snags.

COMMENTS: This feeder creek to Mono Lake flows through high desert country on its way to fill Mono Lake as much as possible. It passes through several of the June Lakes on its way from the east slope of the Sierra to Mono Lake.

●●●●●●●●●●●●●●●●

MONO LAKE, el. 6,481'

This is a very beautiful lake, steeped in history, both past and recent, and very unique! It is salt water filled with tiny, tiny brine shrimp. It's like paddling in a giant aquarium with sulfur-fuming boils emitting from the lake's bottom and yet with a fresh water inflow to paddle against. It's fabulous, a rare paddling experience. For history, the sea gulls that joined the ferry crossings in the 1930s on San Francisco Bay and were generously fed enroute, flew over the Sierra to nest on the Paoha Island in Mono Lake. The draining of the inflow from Rush Creek and other streams feeding Mono Lake by water-hungry So. California lowered the lake level bridging the islands that allowed predators access to birds eggs and young. Bridges across the bay reduced the number of ferries whose passengers fed the gulls. But times have changed. Mono Lake, with great efforts, is now refilling from the low water levels. This is not a lake for swimming but for admiring the tufa formations and paddling on a very unusual body of water.
INFO: Mono Lake National Forest Visitors Center: 760.647.3044.

PADDLECRAFT RENTALS & TRIPS: Mono L. Com. Visitors Center: 760.647.6331.

JUNE LAKES LOOP

Grant Lake (el. 7,130), Silver Lake, Gull Lake, and June Lake are a chain of lakes to be paddled in this scenic mountain setting. The outlet is Class II Rush Creek (see above). Resorts, campgrounds, water access, and picnic areas are all here.
LOCATION: 7 miles south of Lee Vining and 5 miles south of Tioga Pass, SR-120 on the east side of the Sierra, SR 158, off of US-395.
INFORMATION: June Lakes C.of C.: 760.648.7584.

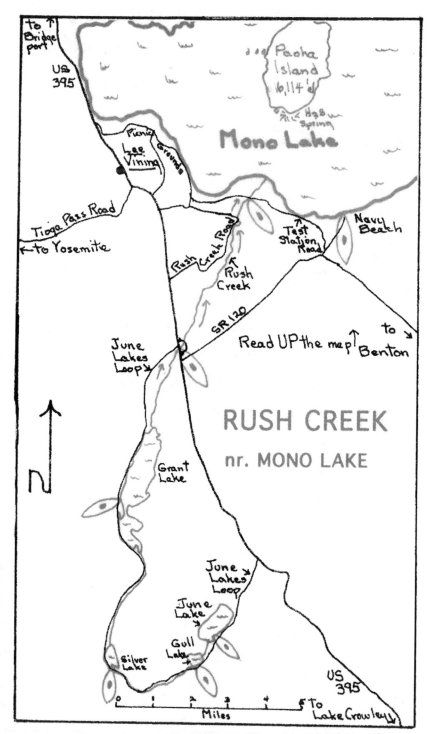

to
Bridge
port

US
395

Paoha
Island
6,114' el

Mono Lake

H₂S
Spring

Picnic
Grounds

Lee
Vining

Tioga Pass Road
← to Yosemite

Rush Creek Road

Navy
Beach

Test
Station
Road

Rush
Creek

SR 120

Read UP the map

to
Benton

June
Lakes
Loop

RUSH CREEK

nr. MONO LAKE

Grant
Lake

N

June
Lakes
Loop

June
Lake

Gull
Lake

Silver
Lake

0   1   2   3   4   5
Miles

To
Lake Crowley

US
395

MAMMOTH CREEK/HOT CREEK

US-395 to Whitmore Tubs Road, 8 miles, Class II

SEASON: Spring & early summer. BEST FLOWS: 250 - 600 cfs.
MANAGING AGENCY: Mammoth Lakes Dist. BLM: 760.934.5500.

ACCESS: Put-in • Below bridge US-395. E. end of Mammoth Lakes.
8 miles to • Take-out near junction of Whitmore Tubs Rd., Sage Hen Rd. & Owens River Rd.

MAPS: AAA — "Bay and Mountain Section." DE LORME — p. 112.

GAS, FOOD, and LODGING: Mammoth Lakes.
CAMPING: New Shady Rest NF Cpgr., Inyo NF: 760.873.2400.

BEWARE: Steaming hot water!

COMMENTS: Paddle this creek going through some of the "hot spots" of the geothermically active east side of the Sierra. But be careful! About a half-mile below the Hot Creek Park there is a weir across the river that can only be run at certain levels.
NOTE: Extend the run by going another 4 miles to the Owens River at the north end of Lake Crowley, taking out at Benton Crossing Road, or paddling on down the few miles to Lake Crowley.

●●●●●●●●●●●●●●●

LAKE CROWLEY, el. 6,720'

The Owens River, after filling 3-by-5-mile Lake Crowley, flows south from Long Valley Dam at the SE end of the lake. Fishing and windsurfing are two popular lake activities, but there's no swimming. Canoeing and kayaking would be best done in the calm of the mornings. At the south end of the lake is a launching ramp and beach. There may be a launching fee. There are numerous campgrounds in the general area, many in Inyo NF: 760.873.2400. Or contact Mammoth Lakes Visitor Bureau: 800.367.6572. The City of LA has jurisdiction: 213.485.4853.

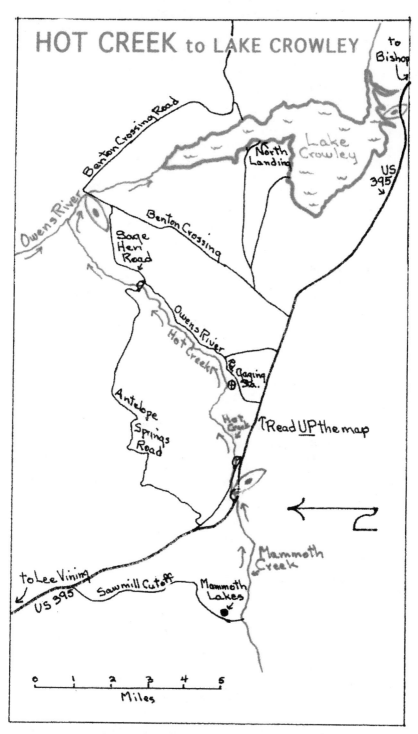

HOT CREEK to LAKE CROWLEY

to Bishop

Benton Crossing Road

Owens River

Lake Crowley

North Landing

US 395

Benton Crossing

Sage Hen Road

Owens River

Hot Creek

Gaging Sta.

Antelope Springs Road

Hot Creek

↑ Read UP the map

Mammoth Creek

to Lee Vining

US 395

Sawmill Cutoff

Mammoth Lakes

0 1 2 3 4 5
Miles

OWENS RIVER

Pleasant Valley Dam Rd. to Five Bridges, 10 miles, Class I

SEASON: All year. BEST FLOWS: 200 - 500 cfs.
FLOW INFO: Dept. of Water & Power, City of Los Angeles: 213.485.4853.

ACCESS: Put-in • Pleasant Valley Dam Road, 5 miles to bridge (campground.) N. of US-395, 5 miles W. of Brockmans Corner and US-6.
10 miles to • Five Bridges area on Chalk Bluff Road near Casa Diablo Road and Jean Blanc Road.
NOTE: The information in the run listed below would be the same for this run. The connecting run is very brushy.

Laws to Big Pine, 30 miles, Class I

ACCESS: Put-in • Bridge on US-6 before Laws, 6 miles NE of Bishop.
12 miles to • Warm Springs Road, 2.5 miles S. of Bishop off US-395, crossing Rawson Canal, 4 miles to Owens River.
3.5 miles to • Collins Rd., 6.5 mi. S. of Bishop off US-395, 3 mi. to river.
14.5 miles to • 1.5 miles on CR-168, east of Big Pine. Parking.

MAPS: AAA — "Bay & Mountain Section." DE LORME — pp. 123 and 124.

GAS, FOOD, and LODGING: Big Pine.
CAMPING: Sage Flat FS Cpgr. 8 mi. SW of Big Pine on Glacier Lodge Rd.: 760.873.2400. Glacier Lodge Cpgr. on Glacier Lodge Rd. 8 miles west of Big Pine.

BEWARE: Paddle craft longer than 12 feet will have to work very hard to make the many sharp turns in the river. A weir 5 miles from the end can be portaged.

COMMENTS: What a fun run for compact kayaks! The views are ever changing as the river twists and turns through the valley. The views range from the few trees along the banks to the dry hills in the east to the snow-capped Sierra, the dominant sight. The 30 miles can be done in a long day with experienced paddlers as the flow is moderate and helpful. The river-wide weir is on a left-hand bend with a spot to portage on the right of the weir. (The weir is only Class II but I was alone so I opted to portage.)

SCENERY: Fabulous!

HISTORY IN THE MAKING: The second time I did this run, a cancellation had me paddling alone. At the trip's end, a little after 5 p.m. on 10/17/89, the woman who took me back to my car said the San Francisco radio station abruptly went off the air reporting "an earthquake or something" in San Francisco. It was the Loma Prieta Earthquake! THE BIG quake of my lifetime and I missed it!

NOTE: Keep paddling 5 mi. to Steward Ln. or 15 mi. to Tinemaha Reservoir.

• • • • • • • • • • • • • • •

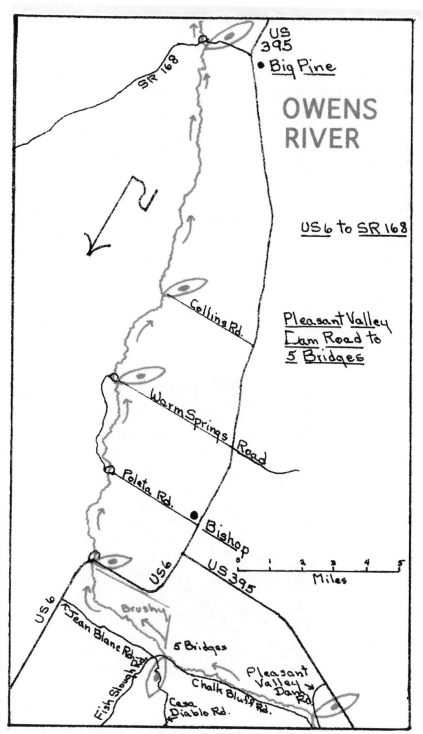

East Slope: Dedicated to Charles Albright

If you haven't met Charles or paddled with him, your west coast paddling book has a chapter missing. My first encounter with him and his paddling brother, Jerry, was with the Redwood Paddling Club, in which they are some of the top paddlers and nice guys. When Charles first moved to Reno he found a few paddlers to go paddling with him on the wealth of fabulous rivers of all classes in the area, but he also became an activist. Now, years later, Reno has pool sessions twice a week in two different olympic-sized pools, one of them thermally heated. Frequent river trips are scheduled, and the Truckee River is now open to paddling all the way through Reno, complete with launching sites. (This took Charles several sessions with the city council.) Some of the blue ribbons awarded in Bay Area Paddling Races end up in Charles's large collection in Reno. He is a Class V kayaker, a sea kayaker, and an open canoeist, as well as an instructor.

When I sent out word that I would not reprint my *Canoeing Waters of California* but planned to rewrite instead, Charles sent me pages and pages of river runs on the East Slope of the Sierra flowing into Nevada's desert lakes. There was a delay between receiving the write-ups and action on my part, so I needed to spend a few hours with Charles in Reno while he updated his original reports.

CHAPTER 10 - SOUTH COAST

CONTENTS

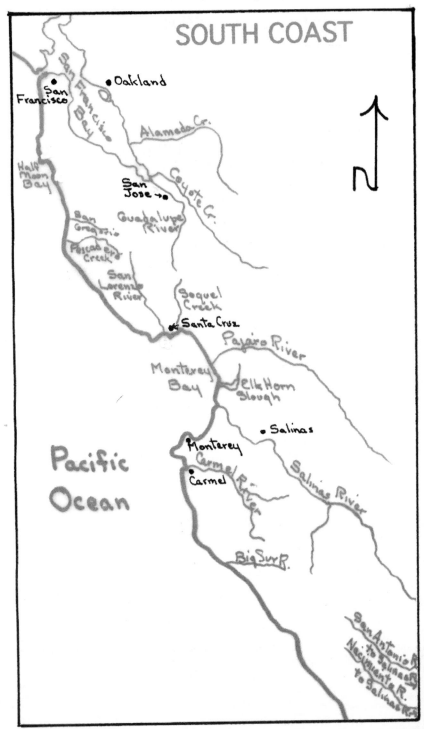

SOUTH COAST

Oakland

San Francisco

San Francisco Bay

Alameda Cr.

Half Moon Bay

Coyote Cr.

San Jose →

Guadalupe River

San Gregorio

Pescadero Creek

San Lorenzo River

Sequel Creek

Santa Cruz

Pajaro River

Monterey Bay

Elk Horn Slough

Salinas

Pacific Ocean

Monterey

Carmel River

Carmel

Salinas River

Big Sur R.

San Antonio R. to Salinas R.
Nacimiento R. to Salinas R.

SOUTH COAST

The coast between San Francisco and Santa Cruz is a lovely area to explore. The area has many nice places to paddle, although some have bird nesting restrictions. There are water birds by the hundreds, many public beaches (some with great surfing), and several parks inland for hiking and being in the redwoods. There are lighthouses to visit, elephant seals to observe during their calving period (by reservation only, Ano Nuevo State Reserve: 800.444.4445), and a very attractive area to drive through.

Santa Cruz Bay, with world-renowned Steamer Lane, is important to kayakers—especially those who surf kayaks. The harbor is interesting with the terminus of the San Lorenzo River and calm water. The whitewater Class III-IV Felton to Santa Cruz run is popular (mentioned in both whitewater books). Monterey Bay is fun for paddlers getting a water view of Monterey Bay Aquarium, Steinbeck's Cannery Row, plus the barking sea lions and an occasional whale.

NATURAL HISTORY: Sea otters, those once almost extinct furry sea mammals, are now a common sighting in Monterey Bay and Elk Horn Slough. (The Russians found a great cash crop to sell their soft luxurious pelts to the Chinese royalty and came close to bringing an end to the species.) The birds at Elk Horn Slough are numerous and change with the seasons. They are well worth a visit, or two, or three.

HISTORY: The Carmel Mission is near the Carmel River and close to the coast. Monterey was an early capital of California and a seaport. Cannery Row, the location of John Steinbeck's novel, is located near the aquarium.

DAM THREAT: Carmel River is a friendly 10-mile run of Class I and II rain-fed water. A very large dam is proposed for the upper part of this river.

Half Moon Bay, 1.5 miles, Class I *KAYAKED IN HARBOR 9/2/07*

SEASON: Sept. & Oct. BEST TIDE: 3'-5'. TIDE LOCATION: Princeton–Half Moon Bay.

ACCESS: Put-in • Many access points along the bay from Pillar Point harbor to the south end, mostly beach launching. The bay is off SR-1 at El Granada, about 10 mi. N. of the town of Half Moon Bay. Parking & RRm.

MAPS: AAA — "Coast & Valley Section." DE LORME — pp. 104 & 114.

GAS, FOOD, and LODGING: Half Moon Bay. Some good and reasonable restaurants. CAMPING: Half Moon Bay State Beach: 650.726.8820.

BEWARE: Winds in the spring and summer. World-class waves off Pillar Point!

COMMENTS: This sheltered bay has a breakwater, which makes it a good spot to practice kayaking and canoeing. There are a marina and good beaches for swimming. The birds are plentiful. Check out Maverick Roadhouse Cafe for the hungry and the maverick waves for the highly skilled. The waves made the news (7/99) showing world-class surfers going down the face of the 30-foot-high waves. At the Pillar Point end is a California Canoe & Kayak store offering sales, classes, and rentals: 650.728.1803.

•••••••••••••••

PESCADERO CREEK

SEASON: Rainy or high tide. BEST TIDE: 4'-6'. TIDE LOCATION: Ano Nuevo.

ACCESS: Put-in • Below bridge on SR-1, NW end. Follow trail to water. the
bridge. Pescadero State Beach. (Water access to the marsh and Butano
Creek is on Pescadero Rd. near SR-1.)

MAPS: AAA — "Coast & Valley Section." DE LORME — p. 114.

GAS, FOOD, and LODGING: Half Moon Bay or Davenport, over 10 miles in either
direction.
CAMPING: Half Moon Bay State Park: 650.726.8820.

BEWARE: Tides, wind, and bird nesting restrictions.

COMMENTS: Birders welcome! This paddle is mostly in the marsh, with a good
variety of wading birds. At higher water it is possible to launch near the bridge in the
quaint town of Pescadero up the creek, but snags could be a great danger. Better to
paddle up and back. Another route is to paddle the southern channel from SR-1, which
is the end of Butano Creek.

NOTE: Bill Tuthill, an active I-K (inflatable kayak) paddler, ran from Portola State
Park to Memorial County Park at high water and reported a scenic Class II run with
several portages around log jams. He mentioned two large redwoods across the waterway and a dam at Memorial Park. "When the creek joins the road, rapids become
more [Class] III-ish." If you have time to run this section, take out at the first bridge
on Pescadero Road."

• • • • • • • • • • • • • • • •

NOTE: There are other streams and lagoons along the coast to be paddled. Give them
a try and let me know. (Ann Dwyer: 707.838.6262)

Butano Creek (pronounced "Butno") flows into the Pescadero area near the
Pescadero Fire House. It is a rain-fed creek with interesting birdlife and maybe too
many snags to paddle around. We tried it one day but found the flow too high in the
trees, so we quickly retreated.

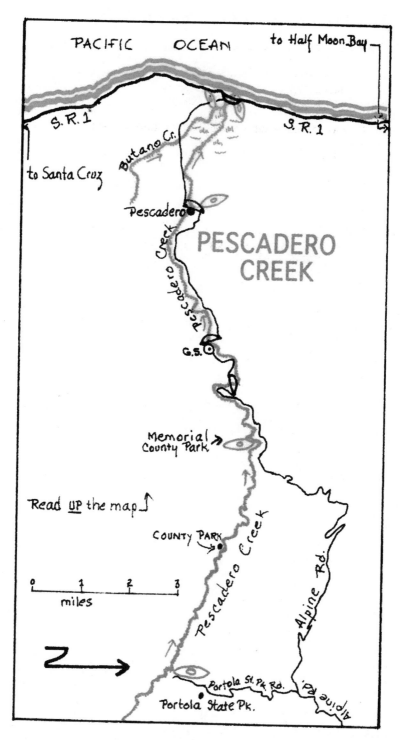

PACIFIC OCEAN

to Half Moon Bay

S.R.1

to Santa Cruz

S.R.1

Butano Cr.

Pescadero

Pescadero Creek

PESCADERO CREEK

G.S.

Memorial County Park

Read UP the map

COUNTY PARK

Pescadero Creek

Alpine Rd.

miles
0   1   2   3

Portola St. Pk. Rd.

Portola State Pk.

Alpine Rd.

SAN LORENZO RIVER — Santa Cruz Mountains

Boulder Creek to Felton, 9 miles, Class II to II+ (III-)

SEASON: Rainy. BEST FLOW: 300 - 400 cfs.

ACCESS: Put-in • Junction Park, Boulder City, 1 block from Central Ave. (SR-9) via Middleton Rd. Excellent river access into a natural pool below the confluence of Boulder Creek and San Lorenzo River. Parking & RRm.

4 miles to • Ben Lomond, below the SR-9 bridge on river left. Short walk up the bank to the road. Very limited parking.

5 miles to • Felton Covered Bridge Park on SR-9 just S. of Felton. Best take-outs are below the covered bridge on river left. Parking & RRm.

MAPS: AAA — "Santa Cruz & Vicinity" & "Coast & Valley Sec." DE LORME — p. 115.

GAS, FOOD, and LODGING: Locally and in Scott Valley.
CAMPING: Big Basin SP, 9 miles NW of Boulder Creek via SR-236: 408.338.8860. Henry Cowell SP, .5 miles south of Felton off SR-9: 408.335.4598.

BEWARE: The San Lorenzo River is an attractive, active, and potentially dangerous river flowing through a narrow redwood canyon. Visibility for scouting may be hampered by willows growing in the river bed. Debris piles, snags, exposed roots, and downed trees are constant hazards. Rocks of all sizes, quick twisting drops, as well as natural and man-made dams and weirs all add up to interest, excitement, and danger. The river can quickly become a raging torrent from the heavy rains. The local authorities can and will "ticket" and levee a fine against someone running the river under dangerous conditions.

COMMENTS: This run has intrigued me for years. I finally ran part of it with three fellow paddlers (2-24-99)—two soloing in whitewater canoes and two in Kopapas. The flow was about 275 cfs after four days of off-and-on rain. The water was clear and the day was beautiful. The many waterfalls added about 25 cfs to the flow. We would have preferred about another 100 cfs. We ran all but one dam, thanks to the WW canoes' better boat-scouting abilities. The pools between the drops were welcome and slow enough for scouting the next rapid. Two dams had boat-breaking concrete works at the downstream base with narrow spaces for boats to go through—a bit tricky, but do-able. The first dam is mentioned in Schwind's book, *West Coast River Touring:* "This concrete bridge is easily recognized since it has a middle pier and wooden posts and fencing along the sides on top. At higher water, these ridges are not easily discernible, but they are boat-breakers." Our plastic canoes and kayaks really helped.

There are many homes built into the steep canyon walls, some with attractive rock work. One was castle-like, complete with a maiden (head) in the turret window. The roads along either side of the river are out of sight, but there are a few bridges (and bridge ramparts), so emergency aid is not too distant.

The easier, Class II run from Ben Lomond to Felton will have to wait for another day. But it is definitely not a "piece of cake." There are a few tricky spots and a 4-foot natural ledge, according to Dick Schwind.

Again, do not run this river when it is rising. Wait for the river to drop, as well as the floatingand lodged debris. Also be in a group of at least four skilled paddlers with rescue training and equipment. The fire crew, headed by Chief Saunders, is one of the few swift-water, rescue-trained crews in the state. He says they have never had to rescue whitewater kayakers.

BEWARE: STOP AT THE FELTON COVERED BRIDGE! Felton to Paradise Park, 6 miles, is Class III-IV. Much of this run is through Henry Cowell Redwoods State Park.

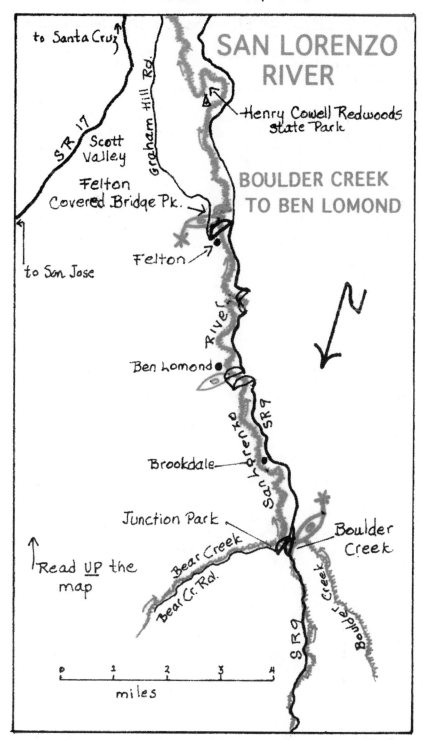

SAN LORENZO
RIVER

to Santa Cruz

Graham Hill Rd.

SR 17

Scott
Valley

Felton
Covered Bridge Pk.

Henry Cowell Redwoods
State Park

BOULDER CREEK
TO BEN LOMOND

to San Jose

Felton

River

N

Ben Lomond

SR 9

Brookdale

San Lorenzo

Junction Park

Boulder
Creek

Read UP the
map

Bear Creek

Bear Cr. Rd.

Boulder Creek

SR 9

0   1   2   3   4
miles

SAN LORENZO RIVER — Santa Cruz Mountains (cont'd.)

NOTE: Public access is lacking and some of the San Lorenzo River is channelized as it flows from Paradise Park through Santa Cruz to the ocean. It is unlawful to paddle up the creek at the mouth below the railroad tracks.

●●●●●●●●●●●●●●

Santa Cruz Small Craft Harbor

ACCESS: Put-in • Boat ramp near Lake Ave. E. From SR-1 exit Soquel Ave. Go SW, then S. on 7th Ave. 1.5 mi. to Eaton St. Turn right, then left on Lake Ave.

COMMENTS: This is a protected and interesting marina to explore. It is about a mile in length with breakwaters as it feeds out into the ocean. Parking.

KAYAK: Rentals, trips, and classes at Kayak Connection, 413 Lake Ave, Santa Cruz: 831.479.1121.

●●●●●●●●●●●●●●

Soquel Creek, 5.5 miles, Class II

SEASON: Rainy. BEST FLOWS: 2.5' - 4'. FLOW INFO: Gage near Soquel H.S.

ACCESS: Put-in • Olive Springs Rd. bridge & Soquel San Jose Rd. 6 mi. N. of SR-1.
7 miles to • River right on Capitola City Beach at Santa Cruz Bay. From SR-1, exit on Bay Ave. Go S., right on Capitola Ave. going S, left on Espanada. Pkng.

MAPS: AAA — "Santa Cruz & Vicinity" & "Monterey Bay Region." DE LORME — p. 115. "South & Central California," p.18.

GAS, FOOD, and LODGING: Capitola and Santa Cruz. Capitola for restaurants. CAMPING: New Brighton State Park, 1+ mile toward Monterey: 408.464.6334.

BEWARE: Snags, downed trees, and upriver winds from the bay.

COMMENTS: This 7 mile run starts in a narrow canyon then flows through agricultural areas, 'neath old bridges, past fields of multi-colored flowers, under the tasting room deck of Bargetto Winery (paddlers welcome), near the well-kept grounds of Shadowbrook Inn, through downtown Capitola, and then into the bay. Because it is rain-fed, the water drops quickly. (Thank you Dennis Lillis.)

●●●●●●●●●●●●●●

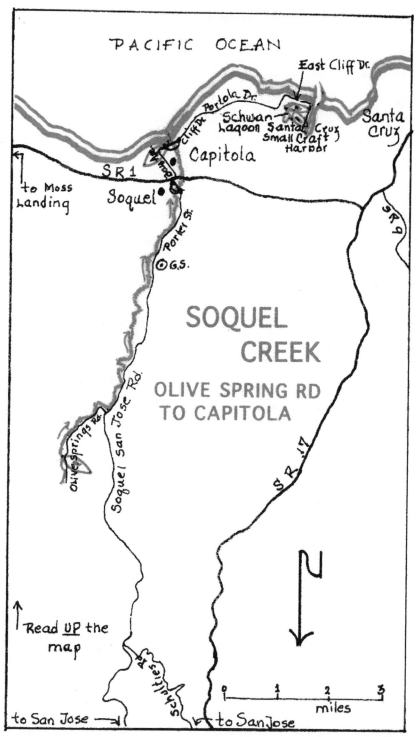

PACIFIC OCEAN

East Cliff Dr.

Portola Dr.

Schwan Lagoon

Santa Cruz Small Craft Harbor

Cliff Dr.

Wharf Rd.

Capitola

Santa Cruz

SR 1

to Moss Landing

Soquel

SR 9

Porter St.

G.S.

SOQUEL CREEK

OLIVE SPRING RD TO CAPITOLA

Olive Springs Rd.

Soquel San Jose Rd.

SR 17

N

Read UP the map

Schulties Rd.

0   1   2   3
miles

to San Jose

to San Jose

ELK HORN SLOUGH

Moss Landing to Kirby Park, 4+ miles, Class 1

SEASON: All year. BEST TIDE: 3' - 6'. TIDE LOCATION: Moss Landing.

ACCESS: Put-in • Moss Landing harbor. On SR-1 south side of Elk Horn Slough. Boat ramp & parking.
4+ miles to • Kirby Park. Turn east on Dolan Rd., south side of the slough, past the Elk Horn Slough National Estuarine Research Reserve, left on Elk Horn Rd., follow signs to Kirby Park. Boat ramp, dock, pkng, and RRm.

MAPS: AAA — "Coast & Valley Section." DE LORME — "So. & Cent. CA," p. 19.

GAS, FOOD, and LODGING: Watsonville.
CAMPING: Sunset Beach SP, 7 miles SW of Watsonville off SR-1: 408.763.7062.

BEWARE: Tides and winds! A fast outgoing tide could cause trouble—unless used as an easy ride back to Moss Landing or with an incoming tide up to Kirby Park.

COMMENTS: One of the most fascinating sloughs in California. It's easy to get to and there are rental craft available, a visitor's center, two opposite-end launching areas, and myriad birds, sea otters, harbor seals, sea lions, and more! Over 375 species of birds have been sighted in the slough, some just passing through.
   There's much more than four miles of paddling water in Elk Horn Slough. Explore the side channels, go around the curve of Rubis Creek (dock and pit toilet), and paddle up past Kirby Park. To the north near SR-1 there's a seal haul-out area. Stay at least 50 feet away if the seals are there. Flowing under SR-1, where the water from the slough is constricted, there could be tricky currents. Stay clear of the pilings.

RENTALS & TRIPS: Kayak Connection, on the north side of Elk Horn Slough and SR-1, has been renting kayaks and leading trips here for many years: 408.724.5692. Check also with Monterey Bay Kayaks: 408.373.5357.

•••••••••••••••••

SALINAS RIVER

Gonzales River Rd. Bridge to Chualar River Rd. Bridge, 9 miles, Class I

SEASON: Rainy BEST FLOW: When there is enough water to float your craft.

ACCESS: Put-in • Gonzales River Rd. bridge. From SR-68, go south on CR-G17.
8 miles to • Chualar River Rd. bridge. On CR-G17.

MAPS: AAA — "Coast & Valley Section." DE LORME — "So. & Cent. CA," p. 19.

GAS, FOOD, and LODGING: Salinas and Monterey.
CAMPING: Marina Dunes RV Park, 3330 Dunes Dr., .25 mi. N. of Marina: 408.384.6914.
Sunset State Beach, 7 mi. SW of Watsonville off SR-1: 408.763.7062.

BEWARE: Wind, sandbars, and low tide.

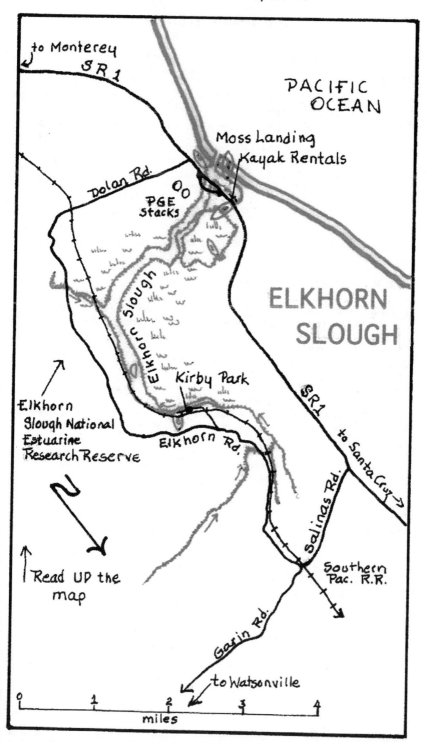

SALINAS RIVER (cont'd.)

COMMENTS: Here the Salinas River flows past farmlands with sandy banks 4 to 6 feet high and no easy exit from the river. The river bottom is coarse, tan-colored sand in a wide flood plain. There are many kinds of birds: great blue heron, kingfishers, coots, and bitterns to name just a few. I did this run many years ago, but it may not be runable now. Cass Schrock, at Monterey Bay Kayaks, reports that there hasn't been enough water even lower down at SR-68 to float a boat.

NOTE: Monterey Bay Kayaks has a short commercial trip from SR-1. Cass reports there is water, with interesting birds, and an attractive section. Private boaters should put-in close to the bridge because next to the road is private property.

●●●●●●●●●●●●●●●●

CARMEL RIVER

Garland Ranch Regional Park to SR-1, Carmel, 11 mi, Class I+ (II-)

SEASON: Rainy BEST FLOW: FLOW INFO: TBA

ACCESS: Put-in • Garland Ranch Regional Park. From SR-1, go SE on Carmel Valley
        Rd. (G-16) 10 miles to park. Riverside launch. Parking and RRm.
11 miles to • SR-1 bridge. Check the take-out before doing the run. Parking.

MAPS: AAA — "Monterey Pen. Cities." DE LORME — "So. & Central CA," pp. 18 &19.

GAS, FOOD, and LODGING: Carmel and Monterey.
CAMPING: Carmel by the River RV Park, 5 mi. SE of Carmel via Carmel Valley Rd:
408.624.9329. Laguna Seca Recreation Area Campground, 6 mi. N. on SR-1 past Monterey to SR-68, Monterey Salinas Hwy., 7 mi. to park and cpgr.

BEWARE: High water and low water. Snags, debris piles in the river, and downed trees. Make sure there is a take-out spot at the end. Up-river winds.

COMMENTS: This is a friendly river but there are a few spots to watch for, especially in the first part where the river drops faster. The flow lessens in the lower valley. There are homes, lodges, and golf courses with bridges for golf carts. Watch for snags. The water is often clear, flowing over a bed of light gray granite pebbles. In one area the flow goes past a vertical rock wall. The river banks were badly eroded during the floods of 1995-96, which also destroyed an SR-1 bridge. Read the plaque.
     Running the Carmel River was the grand finale for the canoe classes I taught several years ago in Monterey. (Kayaked: 4-18-98.)

●●●●●●●●●●●●●●●●

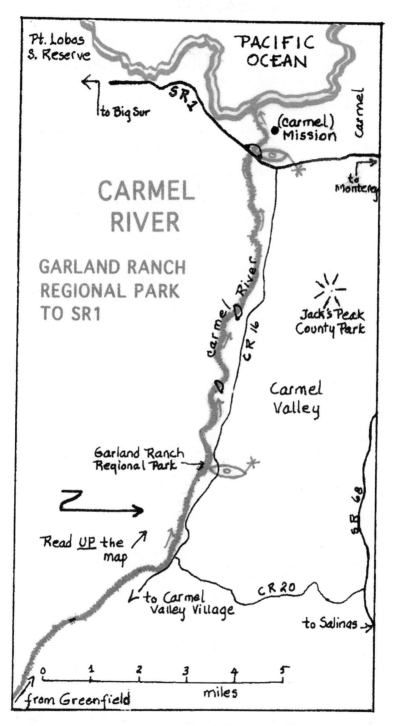

MONTEREY BAY

ACCESS: Put-in • SR-1, via Del Monte Ave. via Pacific St., Lighthouse Ave. parallel to Cannery Row along the waterfront with the Aquarium at the ocean end, continuing on Ocean View Blvd. all lead to bay access either by beach, or boat ramp. The Coast Guard Wharf & ramp.

COMMENTS: Monterey Bay paddling is unique because it is considered open ocean yet it has some protection. The deep channel, popular with SCUBA divers, often encourages whales in the southern migration to come closer to shore than usual. Good for beginning kayakers.

RENTALS: Monterey Bay Kayaks, 693 Del Monte Ave.: 831.373.5357.

LAKES & RESERVOIRS

Loch Lomond, Felton

ACCESS: Put-in • From SR-9 in Felton go SE on Graham Hill Rd. one-half mile. Turn left (N.) on Zayante Rd. In 3 miles, at the V, go left on Lompico Rd. for about 1 mile. Turn left on W. Sequoia Ave. to Loch Lomond Recreation Area. It's a bit tricky to find but well worth it. Boat ramp, RRm.

COMMENTS: This narrow, 3-mile-long reservoir has a spectacular setting nestled in the redwoods and madrones. Paddlers can explore the two arms of the lake. Possible afternoon winds. It is a day-use, seasonal park with picnic areas under the trees on the steep hillsides. No powerboats or swimming: 831.335.7424.

Antonelli Pond, Santa Cruz

ACCESS: Put-in • On Delaware Ave. across from the west end of Natural Bridges S. Beach.

COMMENTS: This is a small pond at the end of Moore Creek.

Schwan Lagoon, Santa Cruz

ACCESS: Put-in • From Cliff Dr. So. of Santa Cruz Sm. Craft Harbor, near Twin Lakes S. Beach.

COMMENTS: This is a good waterway for paddling and birding in the winter and spring, but the summer algae bloom makes it unattractive at that time.

Pinto Lake, Watsonville

ACCESS: Put-in • Going S. on SR-1 turn E SR-152, on Green Vly Rd., follow signs.

COMMENTS: What a surprise to learn that there is a spring-fed lake near Watsonville. The public season is March 1 to Sept. 15. Paddling, fishing, windsurfing, and birding are the primary activities.

Laguna Grande, Seaside

ACCESS: Put-in • On Canyon Del Rey Blvd. via SR 1. Parking, picnic tables & RRm.

COMMENTS: Laguna Grande is a nicely developed park area for a variety of activities. Before it was developed I taught several canoe classes on this lagoon. The attractive park makes it even better and provides a variety of activities.

EGRETS AT ELK HORN SLOUGH

ELK HORN SLOUGH RACES

1972 MERCED RIVER CLEAN-UP, YOSEMITE VALLEY

PHOTO BY REICHARD

Chapter 11– CONSERVATION

Garbage Dumps to Wilderness Preserves

"Just toss it in the river."

"Just toss it in the river." Those used to be common words. Fortunately not any more. Rivers have been regarded as sewers flowing through town. If you wanted to discard something you just threw it in the river. It would be gone soon or definitely with the next flood. Times have changed, rivers are special, to be protected and something to be treated with care. In my early days of paddling in the sixties there were trash piles on the Russian River, a large one at Ft. Seward on the Eel River, and a garbage dump at Colusa on the Sacramento River. The garbage dump was turned into a very attractive park. The project spearheaded by Pat Brown who later became Governor of our state (used this park one of his claims of fame).

Wild and Scenic Rivers Act

The Wild and Scenic Rivers act by the Federal Government changed many attitudes and resulted in the protecting of many rivers in our state and country. River cleanups have become common, many rivers have riverside parks with the river and use of it being the important aspect, not just something to have a park near. River parkways in cities are receiving attention and funding. The American River Parkway in Sacramento being a primary project. (Thirty years ago when I wrote my first guide booklet there were annual articles in the Sacramento Bee about how unsafe the American River was in Sacramento. People were warned to stay away from it. With the parkway the snags in the river, which were the cause of many of the accidents, were removed resulting in a safer waterway with fewer accidents.) With Sacramento's successful lead Fresno now has a river parkway organization encouraging the use and enjoyment of the San Joaquin River, thirty miles upriver from US 99. To make people aware of the San Francisco Bay and to preserve the marshlands, "Save the Bay" has organized guided canoe trips to get people to experience the sloughs from the water. The marshlands are now being preserved throughout the entire bay area. Elk Horn Slough between Watsonville and Moss Landing has become a popular paddling destination. Efforts of bird watchers working for its preservation were successful. Humboldt Bay, Arcata Bay and the sloughs at the mouth of the Eel River have several dedicated wildlife areas. The entire Sonoma Coast is a state park. The continued increase in the awareness of the importance and protection of our waterways is encouraging.

Good news...

Dams are being prevented from being built. The latest a grass roots effort to save the Yuba River. Many river runners involved in that campaign. Recently I paddled the Dos Rios run on the Eel River with *Friends of the Eel River* to help promote the return of some of the Eel waters that have been piped into the Russian River. The Russian River is actively being preserved primarily from gravel miners as is the Garcia River. Often several groups combine efforts to save rivers not just paddlers. If you want to have rivers to run help preserve them and encourage the removal of dams.

CONSERVATION — Chapter 11

Join and participate...

Friends of the River (Primarily statewide)
915 20th St.
Sacramento, CA 95814
916.442.3155
info@friends of the river.org

Sierra Club (National and local)
85 Second street
San Francisco, CA 94105
415.977.5500
(Sierra Club has several chapters in northern California.)

American Rivers
801 Pennsylvania Avenue, SE, Suite 400
Washington, D.C. 20003
202.547.6900

As paddlers, what can we do?

As paddlers what can we do? If a local river or marsh needs protection, cleaning up or reactivating, be a volunteer. It was a grass roots effort that saved the Yuba River from another dam. The measure carried by one vote! The Eel River is probably going to get an additional 15% more water, reduced from the amount generally put into the Russian River system. Gravel mining is being fought on the Garcia River as well as the Russian River. Dams are being removed allowing rivers to return to their natural state and salmon to return"home" to spawn. There has been some interest in a riverwalk along the Guadalupe River in San Jose. There is already a river path along its tributary Los Altos Creek in Campbell. Alameda Creek in Niles Canyon may have some of the dams removed. The reduced salmon population has created a great deal of news in the reporting of the situation and the possible means of increasing the numbers to a former level. Paddlers can join Friends of the River and participate in their annual conference at Fort Mason in March. Join a local paddling club, encourage some of your dues to be spent supporting waterway conservation activities.

On being a considerate paddler...

When paddling know where the protected areas are and double check to determine how near to come. AAA maps are fairly up to date on the preserved sites, or call. Audubon Society knows of many of the protected areas as does the State Dept. of Fish and Game. Paddle slowly by wildlife, don't paddle towards them. Watch, if they become uncomfortable paddle in the other direction. We had one lonely (I guess, it definitely wasn't hungry) water bird follow us on Estero Americano. Sea lions swam under our kayaks at Pier 39. Harbor seals are curious and keep popping their heads out of the water at the mouth of the Russian River. Beware, harbor seals have been known to tip over boats. When paddling in the middle of a school of fish in Bolinas Lagoon we were dive-bombed by hungry terns.

Paddlers have been getting a bad name from going too close to birds and pinipeds. Give them their space, please, so we paddlers can keep a good name.

Camping along the riverbanks. This is one of the fun parts of paddling Class I and II boats, many can take gear for camping trips. As with wilderness camping, leave the campsite as you found it, take out or burn all trash. If having a campfire, keep it small, return the unburned wood to where found, dig a hole, bury the ashes so the area looks as if no one had been there. Many rivers are now so highly used, especially those that are used by commercial outfitters, that it is important to use fire pans for campfires and portable toilets for human waste so nothing is left from your group.

EEL RIVER, DOS RIOS TO ALDERPOINT

PHOTO BY ROGER BOCKRATH

Chapter 12 - Lists

RENTALS

Location	Store	Phone/Internet
San Francisco Bay		
Berkeley	California Adventures	510.642.4006
Castro Valley	Lake Chabot	510.582.2198
Fremont	Lake Elizabeth	510.791.4140
Inverness	Blue Waters Kayaking	415.669.2600
Napa	Mako Marine	888.880.MAKO
Oakland	Lake Merritt	510.444.3807
San Francisco	Outdoors Unlimited (UCSF)	415.476.2078
San Francisco	Lake Merced	415.753.1101
Sausalito	Harbor Dive & Kayak Center	415.331.0383
Sausalito	Sea Trek	415.488.1000
Stinson Beach	Off the Beach	415.868.9445
Stinson Beach	Stinson Beach Health Club & Kayak Rental	415.868.2739
North Coast		
Duncans Mills	Duncans Mills Camping Club	707.865.2024
Duncans Mills	Gold Coast Coffee	707.865.1441
Eureka	Hum-Boat Rentals	707.444.3048
Forestville	Burkes Canoe Rentals	707.887.7662
Gualala	Adventure Rents www.adventurerents.com	888.881.4386
Guerneville	Casini Ranch Family Campground	707.865.2255
Guerneville	Johnson's Beach & Resort	707.869.2022
Guerneville	King's Sport and Tackle	707.869.2156
Healdsburg	Trowbridge Recreation, Inc.	800.640.1386 707.433.7247
Jenner	Lotus Kayak Rentals	707.865.9604
Kelseyville	Blue Heron Kayaks	707.272.0419
Lakeport	Power Boat & Canoe Rentals	707.263.4309
Marshall	Tamal Saka Tom. Bay Sea Kayaking	415.663.1743
Mendocino	Catch-A-Canoe	707.320.2453
Petaluma	North Bay Watersport & RV	800.649.4649
Santa Rosa	California Rivers	707.838.8919
Eureka to Oregon		
Arcata	Humboldt State Univ. Ctr Act	707.826.3357
Willow Creek	StarBrite River Tours www.pcweb.net/laughingheart	530.629.3516
San Joaquin River Area		
Fresno	Herb Bauer Sporting Goods	559.435.8600
Fresno	Camp Pashayan	559.248.8480

East Slope

Donner	Donner Memorial State Park	530.582.7892
Graeagle	Graeagle Outpost	530.863.2414
Kings Beach	Tahoe Paddle and Oar	530.581.3029
Mono Lake	Mono Lake Com. Visitors Center	760.647.6331
Quincy	Bucks Lake	530.283.0555
So. Lake Tahoe	Kayak Tahoe	530.544.2011
Lake Tahoe	Tahoe Basin Forest Service	530.573.2600
Tahoe City	Emerald BayKayak Tours	530.584.2441
	www.tahoeinfo.com	

South Coast

Monterey	Adventures by the Sea	408.372.1807
Monterey	Monterey Bay Kayaks	408.373.KELP
Moss Landing	Kayak Connection	831.479.1121
Santa Cruz	Venture QuestKayaking	408.427.2267
Santa Cruz	Kayak Connection	408.479.1121
Princeton	California Canoe & Kayak -	
	Half Moon Bay Rentals	650.728.1803

CONSERVATIONIST ELIZABETH TERWILLIGER

CLASSES AND GUIDED TRIPS

San Francisco Bay

Los Altos	Kayak and Rolling Lessons	408.779.0710
	kayakdiscovery.com	
Mountain View	Riptides and Rapids	650.961.1240
	www.riptidesandrapids.com	
Oakland	Californai Canoe & Kayak	800.366.9804
San Francisco	Outdoors Unlimited (UCSF)	415.476.2078
San Francisco	Outside Sports	415.864.7205

North Coast

Cloverdale	Kiwi Kayak Classes and Trips	707.894.9629
	www.sonic.net/kkct	
Eureka	Hum-Boats	707.443.5157
Forestville	Mr. Canoe's Paddle Sports	707.887.7416
	www.mrcanoespaddlesports.com	
Inverness	Blue Waters Kayaking	415.669.2600
Olema	Pacific Currents	800.GO.KAYAK
Petaluma	Get Away Adventures	800.499.2453
	www.getawayadventures.com	
Santa Rosa	Wind & Water Sports Center	707.542.7245

Eureka to Oregon

Salmon	Otter Bar Kayak School	503.462.4772
Trinidad	North Coast Adventures	707.677.3124
Willow Creek	StarBrite River Tours	530.629.3516
	www.pcweb.net/laughingheart	
Yreka	Neil's Canoe West	877.50CANOE
	www.snowcrest.net/jrnco/canoewest	

Sacramento Valley

Lotus	Current Adventures Kayak	888.4KA.YAKING
	School and Trips	www.kayaking.com
Nevada City	Wolf Creek Wilderness	530.477.2722
Rancho Cordova	California Canoe & Kayak	800.366.9804
		www.calkayak.com
Sacramento	Adventure Sports	916.971.1800
Sacramento	Sacto. Chap. American Red Cross	916.368.3130

San Joaquin River Area

Fresno	River Parkway Trust	559.248.8480
Modesto	Chris Baltz Kayak School	209.537.9530

East Slope

Lee Vining	Mono Lake Committee	619.647.6595
Mammoth Lakes	Caldera Kayaks	619.935.4942
So. Lake Tahoe	Kayak Tahoe	530.544.2011

South Coast

Monterey	Monterey Bay Kayaks	800.649.KELP
Santa Cruz	ESKAPE! Sea Kayaking	408.427.2297
Santa Cruz	Kayak Connection	408.479.1121

PADDLING CLUBS

San Francisco Bay

Berkeley	POST	510.845.8356
Loma Prieta	SC Loma Prieta Paddlers,RTS	408.996.8335
Mill Valley	California Floaters Society	415.454.1633
	www.cfsonline.org/	
Oakland	POST-Popular Outdoor Sports Trips	510.635.4051
San Francisco	BASK-Bay Area Sea Kayakers	415.457.6094
San Francisco	California Kayak Friends	www.ckf.org/#nextpage
San Francisco	Sierra Club, SF Bay Chapter RTS	925.455.8850
	www.adventuresports.com/club/rts/welcome.htm	
San Jose	Western Sea Kayakers	415.903.9676
San Jose	Western Waters Canoe Club	408.973.1928
	www.westernwaterscanoeclub.org	
San Rafael	Marin Canoe Club	415.883.1852
	www.marincanoeclub.org	

North Coast

Windsor	Sequoia Paddling Club	707.887.7416
	www.sequoiapc.org/~chinglin	
Santa Rosa	Kopapa Kayak Club	707.838.6262

Eureka to Oregon

Arcata	Six Rivers Paddling Club	707.822.4602

Sacramento Valley

Redding	Shasta Paddlers	916.246.2877
	www.snowcrest.net/klewis/index.html	
Belmont	Gold Country Kayakers	605.593.9596
Folsom	River City Paddlers	916.362.2804
Nevada City	Nevada County Paddlers	916.265.3780
	www.ncwebsurfer.com/ncpu	
Sacramento	Sierra Club Mother Lode Chapt.RTS	916.455.1453
Sacramento	Gold Country Paddlers	530.626.0848
Sacramento	River City Paddlers	530.626.0848

San Joaquin River Area

Clovis	California National Canoe Club	559.322.1406

East Slope

Reno, NV	Sierra Nevada Whitewater Club	775.324.5102

South Coast

Santa Cruz	Santa Cruz Kayak Club	408.458.1080

PADDLESPORT STORES

Location	Store	Phone/Internet
San Francisco Bay		
Berkeley	REI	510.527.4140
Berkeley	California Adventures	510.642.4000
Berkeley	AllCraft	510.444.7115
Concord	REI	510.825.9400
Cupertino	REI	408.446.1991
El Sobronte	Pacific River Supply	510.223.3675
Inverness	Blue Waters Kayaking	415.669.2600
Kentfield	Marmot Mountain Works	415.454.8543
Moss Landing	Kayak Connection	831.724.5692
Napa	Mako Marine	888.880.MAKO
Oakland	All Craft	551.444.7115
Oakland	California Canoe & Kayak	510.893.7833
Patagonia	Great Pacific Patagonia	415.771.2050
San Carlos	REI	415.508.2330
San Jose	Western Mountaineering	408.984.7611
Santa Clara	REI	650.508.2330
Sausalito	Harbor Dive & Kayak Ctr	415.331.0983
Sausalito	Sea Trek Ocean Kayaking Ctr.	415.332.8494
		415.488.1000
Saualito	West Marine	415.332.0202
Stinson Beach	Off the Beach	415.868.9445
North Coast		
Fort Bragg	Noyo Pacific	707.961.0559
Gueneville	King's Sport & Tackle	707.869.2156
Petaluma	Clavey Equipment	800.832.4226
		www.clavey.com
Petaluma	North Bay Watersport & RV	800.649.4649
Santa Rosa	Marin Outdoors	707.544.4400
		marinoutdoors.com
Santa Rosa	Sonoma Outfitters	707.528.1920
Santa Rosa	Wind and Water Sports Center	707.542.7245
Ukiah	G.I. Joes	707.468.8834
Eureka to Oregon		
Arcata	Adventure's Edge	707.822.4673
Eureka	North Mountain Supply	800.878.3583
Sacramento Valley		
Chico	North Valley Bicycle	530.343.0636
Citrus Heights	REI	916.965.4343
Lotus	The River Store	530.626.3435
		www.theriverstore.com
Mountain View	Riptides and Rapids	605.961.1240
		www.riptidesandrapids.com
Nevada City	Wolf Creek Wilderness	530.477.2722
Paradise	Kayak Shack Paradise	800.600.2469
Rancho Cordova	California Canoe & Kayak	916.353.1880
Rancho Cordova	Wilderness Sports	
Redding	Camps	
Redding	North County Canoe & Kayak	916.244.1503
Sacramento	Adventure Sports	916.971.1800

San Joaquin River Area

Fresno	Herb Bauer Sporting Goods	559.435.8600
Riverbank	Beyond Limits Adventures	800.234.7238
Riverbank	Stanislaus Kayak Co.	209.869.6060
Sonora	Sierra Nevada Adventure Co.	209.532.5621
Sonora	Sports Connection	209.533.4949

East Slope

Chester	Quiet Mountain Sports	530.258.2338
Reno	Kayaks, etc.	
Reno	P&S Hardware	
Reno	Reno Mountain Sports	702.825.2855
So. Lake Tahoe	Kayak Tahoe	530.544.2011
Tahoe City	Tahoe Whitewater	
Truckee	Truckee Sports Exchange	530.582.4510
Truckee	Mountain Hardware	530.587.4844

South Coast

Monterey	Monterey Bay Kayaks	408.373.KELP
Moss Landing	Kayak Connection	831.479.1121
Santa Cruz	Adventure Sports Unlimited	
Santa Cruz	Kayak Connection	408.479.1121

MAIL ORDER CATALOGS AND WEB SITES

Campmor. 800.CAMPMOR (226.7667.) www.campmor.com. P.O. Box 700-J, Saddle River NJ 07458.

Cascade Outfitters. 800.223.RAFT (7238). www.cascadeoutfitters.com.

Clavey River Equipment. 800.832.4226 or 707.766.8070. www.clavey.com. P.O. Box 180 Petaluma, CA 94953.

Northwest Ourdoor Center. 800.683.0637. www.nwoc.com. 2100 Westlake Ave North, Seattle, WA 98109.

NRS — Northwest River Supplies, Inc. 800.635.5202. www.nrsweb.com.

Rivers and Mountains. 800.243.5522. riversandmountains@compuserve.com. 862 San Antonio Rd., Palo Alto, CA 94303

Sierra Trading Post & Sierra Outdoors. 800.713.4534. www.sierratradingpost.com. 5025 Campstool Rd. Cheyenne, WY 82007.

Splash Gear. 800.WYO.WEAR. www.wyomingwear.com. 604 E. 45 St., Boise, ID 83714.

Wyoming River Raiders. 800.247.6068. P.O. Box 50490, Casper, WY 82605.

MAGAZINES

Canoe and Kayak. www.canoekayak.com; P.O. Box 420235, Palm Coast, FL 32142.

Paddler. www.aca-paddler.org/paddler; 7432 Alban Station Blvd., Suite B-232, Springfield, VA 22150.

River: Journal of Paddlesport & River Adventure. 877.582.5440. www.rivermag.com.

Sea Kayaker. www.seakayakermag.com; 7001 Seaview Ave. NW, Suite 135, Seattle, WA 98117.

REFERENCES

The American River: A Recreationsl Guide Book. PARC, Audurn, CA: 1989.

Boating Trails for California Rivers. State of California Dept. of Parks and Rec., Sacramento, CA: May 1978.

California Water Atlas State of California.. State of California. Sacramento, CA: 1979

Canoeing. The American National Red Cross. Doubleday & Company, Inc, Garden City, NY: 1977.

Cassady, Jim, & Fryar Calhoun. *California Whitewater.* North Fork Press, Berkeley, CA: 1995.

Coale, John. *Canoeing the California Highlands: A quiet water guide to paddler's paradise.* Changing Sky, Cedar Ridge, CA: 1998.

Dewey, O.L. *Drawbridge, California: A Hand-Me-Down History.* San Francisco Bay Wildlfe Society, San Francisco: 1989.

Dirkson, D.J. & R.A. Reeves. *Recreation Lakes of California.* Recreation SalesPublishing, Burbank, CA: 1990.

Fisher, C & J. Morlan. *Birds of San FRancisco and the Bay Area.* Lone Pine, Redmond, WA: 1996.

Gaines, David. *Mono Lake Guidebook.* Mono Lake Com./Kutsavi Books, Lee Vining, CA: 1981.

Garepis, Demece. *Sea Kayaking Northern California.* McGraw-Hill, San Francisco: 1999.

Gleason, Duncan. *The Islands and Ports of California.* Devin-Adair Co, New York: 1958.

Holbek, Lars, & Chuck Stanley. *Best Whitewater in California.* Watershed Books, Coloma, CA: 1998.

Martin, Charles. *Sierra Whitewater.* Fiddleneck Press, Sunnyvale, CA: 1974.

Meloche, Ernie. *Quiet Waters: A Cartop Paddler's Guide to the Lakes & Bays of Northwestern California..* Advanced Miller Printing, Eureka, CA: 1988.

Parsons, Mary Elizabeth. *Wildflowers of California.* Dover Publications, New York, NY: 1966.

Peterson, Roger Tory. *A Field Guide to Western Birds.* Houghton Mifflin Co., Boston: 1990.

Pough, Richard H. *Audobon Water Bird Guide.* Doubleday & Co., Garden City, NY: 1951.

Quinn, J.W. & J. M. Quinn. *Handbook to the Klamath River Canyon.* Educational Adventures, Inc. Redmond, OR: 1983.

Reisner, Marc. *Cadillac Desert.* Penguin Books, New York, NY: 1986.

Schwind, Dick. *West Coast River Touring: Rogue River Canyon and South.* Touchstone Press, Beaverton, OR: 1974.

Silberstein, Mark & Eileen Campbell. *Elkhorn Slough.* Monterey Bay Aquarium, Monterey, CA: 1989.

Summary: California Recreational Trails Plan. State of California Dept. of Parks & Rec., Sacramento, CA: May 1978.

Stienstra, Tom. *California Boating and Water Sports.* Foghorn Press, San Francisco, CA: 1996.

Stindt Fred A. & Guy Dunscomb. *The Northwestern Pacific Railroad.* Fred A. Stindt, Redwood City, CA: 1964.

Stindt, Fred A. *Trains of the Russian River.* Fred A. Stindt, Redwood City, CA: 1974.

Tejada-Flores, Lito. *Wildwater: The Sierra Club Guide to Kayaking and Whitewater Boating.* Sierra Club Books, San Francisco: 1978.

Trinity River Recreation Access. US Dept. of the Interior by Cal Dept. of Water Res., North District. CA: 1979.

Van der Ven, William. *Up the Lake with a Paddle: Volume I.* Fine Edge Productions, Bishop, CA: 1998.

Watts, Tom. *California Tree Finder.* Nature Study Guide, Berkeley, CA: 1963.

WATERWAYS BY DIFFICULTY
Class I Runs

River	Put-in	Miles	Season	Page

Chapter 3 — San Francisco Bay

River	Put-in	Miles	Season	Page
Napa R.	Trancas Street	10.5	All Year	SFB-28
Petaluma R	Petaluma	14	All Year	SFB-32
San Antonio Cr.	Mira Monte Marina	7	Tidal	SFB-34
Novato Cr.	Black Point Marina	7.5	Tidal	SFB-34
Corte Madera Cr.	Greenbrae	4+	Tidal	SFB-38

Chapter 4 — North Coast

River	Put-in	Miles	Season	Page
Russian R.	Guerneville	15	All Year	NC-26
Navarro R.	Dimmick SRA	8	Spring	NC-36
Albion R.	SR-1 (Albion)	7	All Year	NC-38
Big River	Mendocino	8	All Year	NC-38
Noyo R.	Noyo Harbor	4	All Year	NC-40
Eel River	S. Fk. Confluence	44	All Year	NC-58

Chapter 5 — Eureka to Oregon

River	Put-in	Miles	Season	Page
Redwood Cr.	Tall Trees	8	Spring	EO-8

Chapter 6 — Sacramento Valley

River	Put-in	Miles	Season	Page
Hat Creek	Hat Cr. Pwrhs. Rd	5	All Year	SV-8

Chapter 7 — The Delta

All of the Delta is class I. All Year and Tidal

Chapter 8 — San Joaquin River Area

River	Put-in	Miles	Season	Page
Tuolumne R.	La Grange	23	Winter	SJ-8
Tuolumne R.	Waterford	30	Spring	SJ-10
Tuolumne R.	Shiloh Fishing Ac.	20	Rainy	SJ-12
Merced R.	Yosemite Valley	4+	Spring	SJ-14

Chapter 9 — East Slope

River	Put-in	Miles	Season	Page
N.Fk. FeatherRiv.	Quincy	4+	Spring	ES-6
M. Fk. Feather R.	Vinton	15	Spring	ES-10
W Fk. Carson R.	Blue Lakes Rd.	4	May/June	ES-34
Carson River	Carson River Park	3+	Spring/Summer	ES-40
Carson River	Lahonton Dam	29	Spring	ES-44
W. Walker River	MWTC	4+	Spring	ES-46
Walker River	SR-208	61+	Spring	ES-56
Owens River	Pleasant Vly. D.	40	All Year	ES-62

Chapter 10 — South Coast

River	Put-in	Miles	Season	Page
Half Moon Bay	Half Moon Bay		Sept. -Oct.	SC-2
Pescadero Cr.	SR-1		Tidal	SC-4
Elk Horn Sl.	Moss Landing	4+	Tidal	SC-10
Salinas River	Gonzales Riv. Rd.	9	Rainy	SC-10

Class I+ Runs
Chapter 4 — North Coast

Russian River	Talmage	14+	Summer	NC-20
Russian Rive	Cloverdale	32	Summer	NC-22
Russian River	Healdsburg	16	Summer	NC-24
Austin Creek	Ft. Ross Road	7+	Spring	NC-28
Gualala River	House Creek	27	Spring	NC-30
Garcia River	Voorhees Park	18	Spring	NC-32
Navarro River	Hendy Woods SP	12	Spring	NC-36
Mattole River	Honeydew	22	Rainy	NC-42
Eel River	Alderpoint	30	Spring	NC-52
Eel River S. Fork	Garberville	37	Spring	NC-56

Chapter 5 — Eureka to Oregon

Mad River	Blue Lakes	11	All Year	EO-6
Klamath River	Weitchpec	46	All Year	EO-24

Chapter 6 — Sacramento Valley

Fall River	Glenburn	Varies	All Year	SV-6
Tule River	Glenburn	Varies	All Year	SV-6
Sacramento River	Redding	78+	All Year	SV-12
Sacramento River	Woodson Br.	74+	All Year	SV-16
Sacramento River	Colusa	86	All Year	SV-20
Feather River	Marysville	64	All Year	SV-28
Yuba River	SR-20 Bridge	14	All Year	SV-32
Bear River	Marysville	14	Spring	SV-34
Cache Creek	Rumsey	9	Spring-Summer	SV-52

Chapter 7 — The Delta

Mokelumne River	Woodbridge Pk.	12	All Year	TD-18

Chapter 8 — San Joaquin River Area

Stanislaus River	Knights Ferry	37	All Year	SJ-4
Merced River	McConnell SRA	19	All Year	SJ-20
San Joaquin R.	Lost Lake	20	All Year	SJ-22

Chapter 9 — East Slope

Truckee River	Tahoe City	4	Summer	ES-20
Carson River	Dayton	30	Spring	ES-42
Walker River	Wellington	17+	Spring	ES-50
East Walker Riv.	Devil's Gate	9	Spring	ES-52
East Walker Riv.	Flying M Ranch	35	Spring	ES-54

Chapter 10 — South Coast

Carmel River	Garland Ranch Pk.	11	Rainy	SC-12

Class II Runs

Chapter 3 — San Francisco Bay

Guadalupe River	San Jose	13	Spring	SFB-16

Chapter 4 — North Coast

Russian River	Coyote Dam	4+	Spring	NC-18
Noyo River	Northspur	14 (22)	Spring	NC-40

Chapter 5 — Eureka to Oregon

Klamath River	Seattle Creek	17	Summer	EO-18
Trinity River	Steel Bridge Rd.	27	Spring	EO-26
Trinity River	Hawkins Bar	15+	Spring-Fall	EO-30
Trinity River	So. Fk. of Trinity	9	Spring	EO-32
Smith River	Hiouchi	9	Spring	EO-38

Chapter 6 — Sacramento Valley

Pit River	SR-139	21+	Spring	SV-4
Stony Creek	Stony Gorge Res.	7+	Rainy	SV-26
American River	Greenwood Br.	7	Summer	SV-38
American River	Sacramento	22	All Year	SV-42
Cache Creek	Long Valley	9	Spring-Summer	SV-48

Chapter 8 — San Joaquin River Area

Merced River	Snelling	12	Spring/Fall	SJ-18

Chapter 9 — East Slope

Feather River N.	Chester	5	Spring	ES-4
Feather River N.	Poe Dam	1	Spring	ES-8
M. Fork Feather	Beckwourth	9	Spring	ES-10
M. Fork Feather	Clio	6	Spring	ES-12
Upper Truckee	Myers Flat	10	Spring	ES-16
Donner Creek	Donner Lake	4	Spring	ES-22
Little Truckee	Perazzo Meadows	10	Spring	ES-26
Truckee River	Reno	10	Spring	ES-30
Truckee River	Mustang Ranch	26	Spring	ES-32
Carson River E.	Markleeville	20	Spring	ES-36
Carson River E.	Ruhenstroth Dm	29+	Spring	ES-38
Walker River	Topaz Lake	5	Spring-Summer	ES-50
Rush Creek	US-395 Bridge	4+	Spring	ES-58
Hot Creek	US-395	8	Spring	ES-60

Chapter 10 — South Coast

Soquel Creek	Olive Springs Rd.	5+	Rainy	SC-8

Class II+ Runs (some with IIIs)

Chapter 4 — North Coast

Russian River	Old Hopland	17	Summer	NC-18
Russian River	Squaw Rock	11	Summer	NC-18
Rancheria Creek	Fish Rock Rd.	10	Rainy	NC-34
Rancheria Creek	Mtn. View Rd.	12	Rainy	NC-34
Eel River	Hearst	17	Spring	NC-46
Eel River	Outlet Creek	6+	Spring	NC-46
Eel River	Dos Rios	49	Late Spring	NC-48
Eel River	Big Bend	25	Rainy	NC-54
Mattole River	Ettersburg	17	Rainy	NC-42
Van Duzen River	Ltl. Golden Gate	23	Rainy	NC-60

Chapter 5 — Eureka to Oregon

Klamath River	Oregon Border	6+	Summer	EO-10
Klamath River	Iron Gate Dam	17+	Summer	EO-12
Klamath River	Tree of Hvn. Cp.	22+	Summer	EO-14
Klamath River	Brown Bear Accs.	24	Summer	EO-16
Klamath River	Dillon Creek	12+	Summer	EO-20
Klamath River	Orleans Bridge	15	Summer	EO-22
Trinity River	Big Flat	18	Spring-Fall	EO-28
Trinity River	Willow Creek	26	All Year	EO-34
Smith River	Panther Flat	7+	Spring	EO-36

Chapter 6 — Sacramento Valley

Pit River	Pit R. Pwrhs. #1	3	Spring	SV-8
Butte Creek	Steel Bridge	6	Rainy	SV-24
Stony Creek	Stonyford	7	Rainy	SV-26
Bear River	Ben Taylor Rd.	3+	Spring	SV-34
N Fk.American R.	Yankee Jim's Rd.	8	Spring	SV-36
S. Fk.American R.	Chile Bar	11	All year	SV-40
Cache Creek	SR-20	22	Spring-Summer	SV-50

Chapter 7 — The Delta

Putah Creek	Monticello Dam	5	Spring-Summer	TD-6
Mokelumne River	Electra Powerhs.	4+	All Year	TD-14

Chapter 8 — San Joaquin River Area

Merced River	Millers Gulch	6	Spring	SJ-16

Chapter 9 — East Slope

N Fk. Feather R.	Greenville "Y"	10+	Spring-Summer	ES-6
N Fk. Feather R.	Oakland Camp	10	Spring-Summer	ES-6
N Fk. Feather R.	Virgilia	10+	Spring-Summer	ES-6
Feather River N.	Rock Cr. Dam	4	Spring	ES-8
N Fk.Feather R.	Bucks Cr. Pwrhs.	2+	Spring	ES-8
M Fk. Feather R.	Sloat	8+	Spring	ES-14
Truckee River	River Ranch	9+	Summer	ES-20
Truckee River	Donner Creek	13	Spring-Summer	ES-24
Truckee River	Old Boca Bridge	14	Spring	ES-28
Truckee River	Reno	8+	Spring	ES-30
E Fk. Carson R.	Markleeville	4	Spring	ES-36
Carson River	Deer Run Bridge	8+	Spring-Summer	ES-40
Walker River	Walker	15	Spring-Summer	ES-48
E. Walker River	Bridgeport	7	Spring	ES-52
E. Walker River	The Elbow	13+	Spring	ES-54

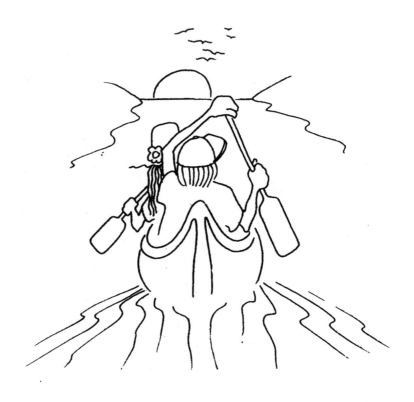